THE PHILOSOPHY OF RAILWAYS:
THE TRANSCONTINENTAL RAILWAY IDEA
IN BRITISH NORTH AMERICA

A.A. DEN OTTER

The Philosophy of Railways: The Transcontinental Railway Idea in British North America

UNIVERSITY OF TORONTO PRESS
Toronto Buffalo London

ISBN 0-8020-4161-2

Printed on acid-free paper

Canadian Cataloguing in Publication Data

Den Otter, A.A. (Andy Albert), 1941–
The philosophy of railways : the transcontinental
railway idea in British North America

Includes bibliographical references and index.
ISBN 0-8020-4161-2

1. Canadian Pacific Railway Company – History.
2. Railroads – Canada – History.   I. Title.

HE2810.C2D46 1997   385'.0971   C97-930105-X

University of Toronto Press acknowledges the financial assistance to its
publishing program of the Canada Council and the Ontario Arts Council.

This book has been published with the help of a grant from the
Humanities and Social Sciences Federation of Canada, using funds provided by
the Social Sciences and Humanities Research Council of Canada.

To Harry Kiefte

Contents

Acknowledgments

In gestation for over a decade, this book has taken a completely different direction than initially intended. As a result, the primary sources cited represent but a small portion of the archival material consulted over the research period and I am grateful to the many archivists whose collections do not appear in the notes but who nevertheless supplied important material that helped me formulate my themes. Staff at the provincial archives of British Columbia, Alberta, and Saskatchewan were extremely helpful, as were their colleagues at the Glenbow-Alberta Archives, the J.J. Hill Library, Harvard's Baker Library, the municipal archives of Amsterdam, and the corporate archives of Barings in London. I am hopeful that the data they provided will appear in subsequent publications.

For this volume, I owe a large debt to personnel at the National Archives in Ottawa as well as the provincial archives of Manitoba, New Brunswick, Newfoundland, Nova Scotia, and Ontario. The archivists at the New Brunswick Museum, at the University of New Brunswick, and at the Historical Society of Pennsylvania also were extremely helpful and made my visits to their institutions not only profitable but pleasurable.

The archival work would not have been possible without assistance from the Social Sciences and Humanities Research Council and Memorial University of Newfoundland's Vice-President's research grants. I am extremely grateful for the financial assistance these two programs provided.

The grants also enabled me to hire student assistants to help in the laborious task of reading the large collections of microfilmed newspapers that form an invaluable source for this manuscript. Debra Andrews, David Bradley, Christina Burr, Sean Cadigan, and Godwin Nwokeji helped me sift through the enormous back files of mid-nineteenth-century newspapers. Special thanks, however, must go to Nikki Cox, who patiently double-checked the end notes, and to Vince Power, whose research and analysis are very much a part of chapters 4 and 7.

Many colleagues took valuable time to read portions of the manuscript and to share with me their insights. Since several chapters of this book were first presented as conference papers, I acknowledge the perceptive remarks of commentators Tom Traves, Dave Sutherland, and Pat Roy. Participants at seminars at the University of Calgary and Lethbridge were generous with their insights, in particular, Henry Klassen, David Bercuson, and William Baker. So too were Harry Van Dijk and Hugh Cook at Redeemer College. Other colleagues consented to read what was intended as a scholarly paper but formed instead the basis of the last chapter. David Breen, John Eagle, David Hall, and Gerald Friesen made valuable suggestions and encouraged publication.

Although their anonymity prevents me from properly thanking them, the reviewers who read my applications for SSHRCC grants, submissions to scholarly journals, and drafts of this manuscript fulfilled an important role. They helped me avoid serious pitfalls and cul-de-sacs. Special thanks go to the two readers for the University of Toronto Press and the Aid to Scholarly Publications Programme. Their suggestions removed ambiguities, fuzzy generalizations, and careless errors.

Two colleagues at Memorial University were enormously helpful in the preparation of this manuscript. Joe Cherwinski read most of the work, while Stuart Pierson reviewed the entire manuscript once and some difficult passages twice. They, as well as John St James, copy-editor at the University of Toronto Press, contributed immeasurably to the readability of this book.

In some ways, the manuscript became a family project. Michael and Lori-Kim den Otter and Curtis Rumbolt read microfilm and bits of early drafts, while my niece, Michelle den Otter, conveniently domiciled in Ottawa, searched out some last-minute sources. Lori-Kim helped proof pages. By doing this work, they not only saved me considerable time, but offered interesting viewpoints and important encouragement.

It goes without saying that I received great support and assistance from Dini den Otter, my wife and good friend. Not only did she read several drafts and endure numerous lectures on the philosophy of railways, but she assumed many of my household tasks, thereby giving me more time at the word processor, or in libraries or archives.

Of course, only I am responsible for the final product and any errors of omission or commission that remain.

Lastly, this book is dedicated to my friend, colleague, and neighbour

Harry Kiefte, who died this January. An eminent physicist, internationally renowned for pioneer work in laser light scattering spectroscopy, Harry was keenly interested in philosophy and history. He was more confident of my work than I, and his constant encouragement can never be repaid.

Abbreviations

AO	Archives of Ontario
CHR	*Canadian Historical Review*
CJE	*Canadian Journal of Economics*
CJEPS	*Canadian Journal of Economics and Political Science*
CPR	Canadian Pacific Railway
DCB	*Dictionary of Canadian Biography* (Toronto 1966–)
HBC/PAM	Hudson's Bay Company Archives/Public Archives of Manitoba
HSP	Historical Society of Pennsylvania
JCS	*Journal of Canadian Studies*
NAC	National Archives of Canada
NAC/HBC	Hudson's Bay Company Archives at NAC
NBM	New Brunswick Museum
PANS	Public Archives of Nova Scotia
UNBA	University of New Brunswick Archives

PHILOSOPHERS OF RAILWAYS, ATLANTIC CANADA

Joseph Howe, 1871

Charles Tupper, 1868

Leonard Tilley, 1879

PHILOSOPHERS OF RAILWAYS, CANADA AND GREAT BRITAIN

Francis Hincks, 1869

Edward Watkin

Alexander Mackenzie, 1878

A major obstacle in the way of the Grand Trunk Railway was the St Lawrence River, finally crossed in 1859 with the three-kilometre-long Victoria Bridge at Montréal.

The need to minimize rail-bed grades often required the removal of enormous amounts of overburden. Pictured above is a great clay cut near Trois-Pistoles on the Intercolonial Railway.

Cutting thirty-metre embankments near Higgins Brook, Nova Scotia, on the Intercolonial Railway

Despite human efforts and technology, a snowstorm could still stop a locomotive, as illustrated in this 1869 photograph.

Regardless of the weather, well-heeled passengers could travel and dine in sumptuous comfort.

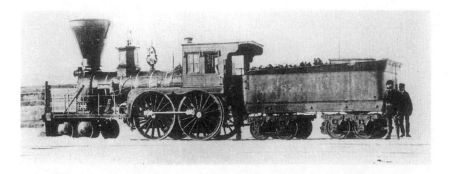

One of the first locomotives on the St Lawrence and Atlantic Railway

Probably the first locomotive purchased by the European and North American
Railway

Engine No. 209, 'Trevithnick,' built for the Grand Trunk in 1859

To meet Canadian conditions, engines quickly grew in size and power, as evidenced by this Grand Trunk locomotive, likely built in the late 1860s.

Sophisticated erecting shops such as this Grand Trunk facility at Point Charles (1860) were needed to service, and later to build, locomotives.

Stations reflected the growing importance of railways in the provincial life. Pictured here is Toronto's Grand Trunk station in 1857.

Montréal's Bonaventure Station in 1870

Shortly after Confederation, Halifax station (in 1868) was still a relatively crude and utilitarian assembly of buildings.

THE PHILOSOPHY OF RAILWAYS

1

Technological Nationalism:
The Backdrop

It was the same world then as now – the same,
Except for little differences of speed ...
Men spoke of acres then and miles and masses,
Velocity and steam, cables that moored
Not ships but continents, world granaries,
The east-west cousinship, a nation's rise,
Hail of identity, a world expanding,
If not the universe: the feel of it
Was in the air – 'Union required the Line.'

E.J. Pratt[1]

Thus E.J. Pratt, the Newfoundland-born poet, introduced his epic, 'Towards the Last Spike,' thereby adding his voice to the mythology that envelops the Canadian Pacific Railway, the backbone of the Canadian nation. In a similar vein, singer Gordon Lightfoot's haunting 'Canadian Railroad Trilogy' reinforced the popular concept of the CPR as an integral part of Canada's identity. Meanwhile, across the country, newscasters, editors, and commentators regularly invoke the nation-building mantra and vigilantly protest the smallest change in the company's logo or denounce any branch-line abandonment as a betrayal of the railway's national mandate.

Historians too have contributed to the CPR legacy, the titles of their work clearly revealing their viewpoint. Two of the earliest works – *The Romance of the Canadian Pacific Railway* by R.G. MacBeth and *Steel of Empire: The Romantic History of the Canadian Pacific* by John M. Gibbon

– openly revered the incredible achievement of driving a railway through the seemingly impassable wilderness; they elevated this accomplishment to an exalted act of nation building.[2]

The first major academic historian to present a scholarly analysis of the Canadian Pacific Railway as the builder of a national economy was Harold Innis. His doctoral dissertation, subsequently published as *A History of the Canadian Pacific Railway*, is a straightforward account of contracts, passenger traffic, freight rates, and profits cast in the mould of traditional historiography. Yet interspersed among the tables and charts are some startlingly sweeping conclusions. At one point Innis noted that 'the fulfilment of the contract in the completion of the main line of the [CPR] was a significant landmark in the spread of civilization throughout Canada ... With this addition to technological equipment, the civilization of [the North-West] changed in its character, and its extent, and became more closely a part of a civilization narrowly described as Canadian, and typically, western. These changes are recorded to some extent in the history of the Canadian Pacific Railroad and the history of Canada.'[3]

With scattered hints about centralization and domination, *The Canadian Pacific Railway* contained the seeds of Innis's subsequent thought on communication techniques and their impact on societies. Railway technology, in contrast to canoe transport, he reasoned, represented the triumph of human ingenuity over physical obstacles; the CPR was 'the result of the direction of energy to the conquest of geographic barriers.'[4] Thus, his dissertation presaged a lasting interest in the conditions that facilitated the spread of western civilization over the North American continent; it became the foundation upon which Innis built his staple thesis and communication theories.

In subsequent works, Innis developed his staple trade theories, concepts in which transportation technology played a dominant part. While his observation that fur, lumber, and wheat had to be transported from the continent's interior to distant markets was not particularly startling, his contention that transportation techniques actually affected the Canadian identity was both profound and innovative. His classic *The Fur Trade in Canada* noted that the birch-bark canoe enabled London-based merchants to use an indigenous, muscle-powered transportation technology on the north-western waterways to draw Rupert's Land into their commercial empire and to superimpose upon the vast territories and its native people a British character. According to Innis, Canada was not an artificial political creation but a natural geographical entity, its unity based on the Shield, its rivers, and the fur trade. 'The present Dominion,' he concluded, 'emerged not in spite of geography but because of it.'⁵ In other words, a transportation system prepared the groundwork for the political division of North America, separated Canada from the United States, and laid the foundation for confederation and the modern transcontinental nation. Moreover, it welded the northern community firmly into the British empire. By 'organizing the transport of supplies and furs over increasingly greater distances,' Innis argued, 'the waterways of the beaver area were of primary importance and occupied a vital position in the economic development of northern North America.'⁶

In several essays specifically devoted to transportation, Innis summarized many of his conclusions. Transportation technology, in his view, was a fundamental determinant in Canada's political and economic development. In sweeping terms, he noted that 'the necessity of checking competition from the United States, and of overcoming the seasonal handicaps of the St Lawrence and the handicaps incidental to the Precambrian formation and the Rocky Mountains' determined the need for the 1841 Act of Union, the St Lawrence canals, the Grand Trunk Railway, Confederation, the Intercolonial Railway, the National Policy, the CPR, and subsequent transcontinental railways.⁷ North America's geography and its political divisions specified the most efficient transportation techniques available and the current technology in turn defined the continent's political divisions.

Harold Innis's broad postulation that the CPR, like water transportation before it, bound together a new nation was given specific treatment in an overlooked dissertation by Leonard Bertram Irwin entitled *Pacific Railways and Nationalism in the Canadian-American Northwest, 1845–1873*.⁸ In a detailed study of various northern transcontinental railway schemes, Irwin concluded that the promoters of the Northern Pacific Railroad attempted to control the railways of British North America as well as of the northern United States. Composed mainly of annexationists, the Northern Pacific alerted Canadians to the dangers of manifest destiny, and, as a defensive consolidation, they founded a confederation. According to Irwin, therefore, the Canadian union was not a spontaneous movement of people who wanted unity but a reaction to a perceived encroachment from the south; nor was the planned Pacific railway an economic enterprise but a response to an apprehension that the Americans would take over the north-western plains. In other words, British North Americans believed that centralized government and easy communication were the means to protect themselves from United States annexationists.

The struggle for control of North America is an equally dominant theme in D.G. Creighton's *The Commercial Empire of the St Lawrence.*[9] In this monumental work, Creighton portrayed the St Lawrence River as a broad artery leading from the heart of the North American continent to the sea. In his comprehensive theme, Creighton suggested that the great river formed the foundation of the Canadian economy and that the struggle to improve traffic on it informed most political debates in the provinces; it explained political unrest and reform, including the Rebellions of 1837 and the unification of the Canadas. Even if the emphasis on geography appeared to make his theme virtually identical to that of his mentor, Creighton softened Innis's harsh economic determinism by enlivening the actors who developed the river system and formulated political economy. If *The Commercial Empire of the St Lawrence* appeared to end in failure, the river symbol nevertheless constituted the inspiration for a transcontinental nation, a motif that Creighton developed fully in his classic biography of John A. Macdonald. In two volumes, Creighton added a human personality to Innis's comprehensive, impersonal generalizations, placing Macdonald at centre stage in the dramas of Confederation, the National Policy, and the CPR. Creighton also instilled a heroic anti-American passion into his character as his Macdonald articulated a dream of a Canadian nation as an antidote to the relentless expansion of the American empire across the continent. The completion of the CPR was the last step in the realization of that difficult process. 'The prime purpose of Canada was to achieve a separate political existence on the North American continent. The prime function of the Canadian Pacific Railway was to assist in this effort – to help in the building of the national economy and the national society which alone would make this ambition possible of achievement. Like Canada itself, the railway would find its most powerful rivals, its most dangerous enemies, in the continent of North America ... American railways were its natural enemies.'[10]

The intertwining themes of nation building and anti-Americanism were reaffirmed in John Lorne McDougall's *Canadian Pacific*, a company-sponsored history. The primary reason for the construction of the Canadian Pacific, McDougall boldly asserted, was the political necessity to connect British Columbia with the rest of country. It was, he declared, the 'answer to a basic national problem' – how to create an independent North American nation in competition with the United States. By casting the CPR's mission in terms of national survival, it is little wonder that McDougall applauded state subsidies to the venture even though it was 'in economic terms ... a desperately premature enterprise.'[11] Similarly, by adopting the CPR nation-building theme, McDougall also presupposed a conjunction of interests between the CPR syndicate and the Canadian government. 'Both wanted to see a railway built to the Pacific to tie the country together,' McDougall wrote. 'There was a very real patriotism here. Until it was built, Canada was vulnerable and Canadians could not hold up their heads in pride. They always knew that to reach British Columbia they had to go by way of the Union Pacific–Central Pacific route to San Francisco.'[12]

The nation-building strain, so clearly asserted in McDougall's brief history, was supported subsequently by W. Kaye Lamb's more substantial monograph.[13] In his survey of events leading up to the construction of the CPR, Lamb described how the all-Canadian vision for the Pacific railway triumphed over the more practical, piecemeal approach that intended to tie the railway scheme into the American system. Answering the supposed accusation that Prime Minister Sir John A. Macdonald adopted the Pacific railway to ensure his personal political survival, Lamb conceded that the old chieftain was aware of the political ramifications of the Pacific railway, but he insisted that partisanship was not the prime minister's basic consideration. Indeed, Lamb countered that Macdonald was one of very few who realized the significance of Canadian sovereignty over half a continent. 'To strengthen that control, as yet extremely tenuous west of Ontario, a railway was essential,' Lamb asserted. 'It would bring British Columbia into the new union, would throw an unmistakable mark of ownership across the West, and would provide the means of settling and fully possessing it. And in view of the annexationist sentiment in the United States, delay would be perilous.'[14]

Lamb's starkly stated thesis was overshadowed by the publication of Pierre Berton's munificently promoted two-volume epic, *The Great Railway*.[15] With his penchant for human-interest stories, his flair for dramatization and abundant humour, Berton created in *The National Dream* and *The Last Spike* a compelling, suspenseful tale of heroic giants pitted against the harsh and nearly impregnable North American landscape. Although Canada's rugged terrain presented the most dangerous obstacle for Berton's champions, they also fought myopic opponents of the grand transcontinental vision as well as greedy American railway men backed by villainous politicians fired by a sense of America's manifest destiny. The first volume's concluding paragraph aptly summarized the romantic struggle.

The future would not be easy ... The granite shield of Canada had to be cracked open to let the railway through. The mountain barrier must be breasted and broken. There would be grief aplenty in the years to come – frustration, pain, hard decisions and, as always, bitter opposition.

But the great adventure was launched. Tomorrow would take care of itself, as it always did. At last the dream was about to become a reality. The triumph lay just a few short years ahead.[16]

Backed by impeccable research, an eye for fascinating detail, and an imaginative writing style, Berton clearly fixed the great Canadian Pacific Railway saga in the public mind, further popularizing the chronicle in paperback and abbreviated editions as well as a hugely successful television serial. *The Great Railway* secured the CPR a prominent place in Canadian mythology.

By the early 1980s, therefore, when the corporation commemorated various centennial occasions, its legendary stature appeared unassailable. Bill McKee and Georgeen Klassen celebrated the *Trail of Iron* with a Glenbow Museum exhibit and a lavishly illustrated coffee-table book that concluded with the classic formulation of the accepted doctrine that the CPR was 'one of the major instruments of national policy, designed to ensure the survival of the young Dominion of Canada ... It forged the dream of a transcontinental British North America into a reality by physically joining the distant sections together with steel.'[17] Meanwhile, a volume of essays tellingly entitled *The CPR West: The Iron Road and the Making of a Nation*, collectively acclaimed the positive contribution of the railway to the settlement and development of the North-West.[18] Similarly, John Eagle's carefully balanced, detailed study of the role of the CPR in western Canada at the turn of the century polished the lustre of the nation-building saga.[19] Thus, each work in its own way reinforced the tenet that the CPR's primary mission was the creation of a nation-state and implicitly bolstered the notion that the earning of profits was but an incidental objective.

Even Robert Chodos's acerbic *The CPR: A Century of Corporate Welfare* upheld the nation-building theme.[20] Although he denounced the principle of state aid to private enterprise because it reduces the element of risk, Chodos still argued that 'the idea of Canada as a nation made little sense without the great North West, and Canada's hold over the North West was extremely tenuous without a railway. That there would be a country, and what kind of country it would be, was only decided on November 7, 1885 [at the last spike ceremony].'[21] Chodos explained that without the completion of the CPR, north-south ties with the United States would have prevailed, the North-West would not have been settled, and central Canada (or the East as Chodos calls it) would not have been industrialized. To be sure, the author ridiculed the concept of public-spirited capitalists and altruistic politicians working together primarily for the national welfare of

Canada; he observed that many of the Fathers of Confederation had financial interests in railways; and he suggested that for most of them personal profit motives remained dominant. Moreover, he noted that Canada's relatively small but powerful business élite retained its excessively strong grip on the nation's economy, and he censured the Canadian government for continuing to grant the CPR – a wealthy multinational conglomerate – unjustified subsidies and powers. On the one hand, then, Chodos criticized the commercial aspect of the CPR myth; but, on the other hand, he reaffirmed the traditional nation-building historiography.

The only serious challenge to the nation-building myth has come from Maurice Charland.[22] In a perceptive article, Charland affirmed the ability of railway technology to draw together disparate sections of the country, but argued that the creation of such a technological nationalism produced a defective national identity. The CPR, the author acknowledged, was an ideal candidate for a survival mythology because of its easily romanticized struggle against nature, political opponents, and financial adversity. Canadians savoured technology's powerful icons, its mighty locomotives, soaring bridges, and piercing tunnels; they gladly ascribed to it the capacity to create a nation; and they willingly permitted the state to marshal the myth to legitimize its purpose and its policies. In other words, according to the rhetoric of the technological nationalists, the CPR was more than a mode of transportation; it was a rationale for survival; its legend epitomized Canada's endurance despite overwhelming geographical, economic, and political odds. Implicitly, therefore, the union of British North America and its subsequent expansion from ocean unto ocean owed more to technology than to the Fathers of Confederation, more to conquest over nature than to political will.

Having described the rise of technological nationalism, Charland perceptively observed that its teaching is insidious because it 'ties a Canadian identity, not to its people, but to their mediation through technology.'[23] Technological nationalism offers a bankrupt vision without substance or commonality for the nation except communication itself. More ominously, if communication is the primary cause of its nationhood, Canada is vulnerable to domination by the more powerful cultural industries of the United States, which deploy the same communication techniques to assert their own self-serving messages on the Canadian people. While this insight applies most directly to radio and television technologies, it was also true for the railway industry. Even while the CPR's bonds of steel were securing the plains and British Columbia to central Canada, the railway's managers were building branch lines to the United States. Similarly, American railways crossed the border at several locations, so that by the start of the twentieth century the railway systems of the two countries were fully integrated.[24]

Technology's role in the amalgamation of North American culture and its economies was similarly deplored by George Grant in his *Lament for a Nation*, a gloomy requiem that presaged his brilliant *Technology and Empire*.[25] In these works, Grant described the basic contradiction in Canada's self-perception. While the country's leadership professed a basic conservative loyalty to ancestral British traditions, it enthusiastically embraced the basic tenets of American liberalism, particularly the belief that technology could liberate mankind from the frustrating bonds of nature and human frailty. Practised most ardently in North America, Grant noted, the liberal faith asserted that technology promotes human excellence and power. The highest good, according to this view, was progress through technological advancement. But, Grant warned, technology also erodes all particularisms and individualities; it homogenizes and universalizes cultures; it is imperialistic and dominating. By adopting technological 'progress' therefore, Canadians accepted a common faith with their southern neighbours, the 'belief in progress through technique.'[26] Consequently, Canada fell prey to technology's consolidating powers and was absorbed by the stronger and more aggressive American economic and cultural empire. Although George Grant did not refer to the Canadian Pacific Railway, he would have concurred that a railway technology, whose primary purpose was to forge a distinct northern nation, became by its very nature an integrating continentalist force. Ironically, therefore, according to Grant, the universalizing and homogenizing attributes of technology fused Canada into the American empire. Thus, his lament for the demise of an independent nation.

Not only did technology unleash continentalist forces, it also contributed to alienation among the various regions in Canada. Harold Innis concluded his history of the Canadian Pacific with a moralistic critique of Ontario's covetous and selfish use of the CPR to exploit the resources and people of western Canada. As he explained subsequently in *Empire and Communications* and *The Bias of Communications*, communication technologies are not marginal forces but constitute the basic determinants of economic change; they also exert strong influences on cultural institutions and mould social identities.[27] Innis would describe railway technology as a space-biased medium, a significant designation because space-biased media encourage centralization, territorial expansion, nationalism, state authority, bureaucracy, and secularism; they aid the development of metropolitan centres and monopolies and erode the sense of time and permanence. Used by the Canadian state as a centralizing force, the railway simultaneously strengthened the economic and political controls wielded by central Canada while it eroded the economic and political power of the peripheral Maritimes and North-West. Soon these regions perceived the railway as an instrument of imperialistic domination, forcing their local economies to operate for the benefit of the central provinces. Alienation became a defining feature of regional identities. 'The national dream,' Maurice Charland concluded sombrely, 'offers only the dark sun of alienation.'[28]

In addition to continental integration and local resentment, technological nationalism, which ascribes nation-building powers to a physical object, 'commodified' Canada's cultural identity, making it liable to obsolescence. If one assumes that the CPR was in fact a major force in the creation and maintenance of an independent northern nation, then any change in its corporate mission that supposedly deviates from that nationalist objective – such as the elimination of transcontinental passenger service – erodes the nation's foundations. Unfortunately, as Charland warned, modern 'space-binding' technologies constantly change with current fads, presenting themselves in 'constantly mutating forms'; they, therefore, offer no stability to national self-understanding.[29]

Despite this fatal flaw, technological nationalism continues to play a dominant role in Canada's national identity. Today the CBC has assumed the same exalted culture-building status as the CPR, which, for better or worse, still possesses an important place in the national mythology. To better understand the origins of the latter's nation-building status, a study of some aspects of the origins and growth of the philosophy of railways, which conceived the idea of the transcontinental, is appropriate. Apart from H.A. Innis, no CPR historian has examined the ideological background of the railway, the contemporary understandings of nationalism, or the evolving notion of a transcontinental union. In fact, most authors begin the CPR story with the Pacific Scandal. Pierre Berton, for example, scorned earlier transcontinental schemes as frivolously premature and idealistic. Consequently, he and others describe only the nationalist rhetoric that immediately preceded the construction of the CPR in the early 1880s, and they hold a relatively simplistic interpretation of the complex and influential events that preceded the 1879 contract with the Canadian Pacific syndicate.

The following study will add depth and breadth to current CPR historiography, not by retelling the oft-repeated story of the railway's construction, but by examining the evolution of the powerful philosophy of railways that motivated mid-nineteenth-century British North Americans to construct a number of massive railways that eventually linked Halifax with the Pacific coast. A detailed examination of several distinct but related topics will amplify the general themes that coursed through British America's philosophy of railways. It will help explain how the transcontinental railway came to play such a powerful symbolic role in the evolution of the Canadian identity. By placing Canada's obsession with railways in its ideological context, the purpose of railways in the confederation of British North America and the new nation's expansion to the Pacific coast will emerge not primarily as a defence against American aggression but as a complex and ambiguous process that included metropolitan economic objectives, a civilizing mission, and political-economic theories of growth and development.

An analysis of the ideology behind the transcontinental railway will uncover many contradictions. Although British North Americans inherited the philosophy of railways from Europe, they adapted it to their own purpose, that is, to help in establishing themselves on the continent. Even though heavily dependent on Great Britain for financial and technical support, the colonists used steam technology, in the context of the railway doctrine, to build a sense of solidarity and confidence in their own abilities. Representing a remarkable consensus, the drive for railways embodied a sense of divine purpose, a mission to conquer the surrounding wilderness, that made the colonists, rather unexpectedly, less British and more American. Although contemporary as well as modern mythology spoke of preserving the north-western continent from encroachment by the United States, railway technology by its very nature fostered cross-border communication, trade and commerce, and the exchange of ideas. At the same time, the liberalism that spawned the railway credo, and that idealized individualism and freedom, demanded state intervention and centralization for the implementation of its vision. Moreover, while commentators, then and now, asserted that railways formed the backbone of the new nation, the reliance on technological nationalism accentuated regional disparities and alienation. In sum, the following chapters will demonstrate that in the British North American colonies the philosophy of railways, with all its subtleties, ambiguities, and complexities, profoundly affected each society even before contractors drove the CPR's first spike.

After charting, in the remainder of this chapter, the intellectual currents that helped to form the philosophy of railways, chapter 2 will use the Guarantee Act of 1849 to explain how the transfer of the profound belief in science and technology, as the panacea for colonial development, created a remarkable political consensus that prompted Canadians to build more railways per capita than any other country in the world. Despite their enthusiasm, however, Canadians were relatively cool about a transcontinental railway, particularly its Halifax-Québec section. Absorbed with tapping the growing market of the midwestern United States, Canadians at mid-century preferred to support links to the American Atlantic seaboard rather than to Saint John or Halifax.

In contrast to Canadian indifference about an intercolonial railway, Maritimers were enthusiastic. Chapter 3 will demonstrate that in the early 1850s Nova Scotia's Joseph Howe developed a rationale for that project and the eventual union of British North America. For a decade and a half, Nova Scotians debated these issues but, discouraged by intercolonial jealousies and regional rivalries, they turned inward and constructed only a minor local railway. Meanwhile, successive provincial governments continued to nurture a common rhetoric of economic progress through railway technology. Thus, at the 1864 Charlottetown and Québec conferences, Nova Scotia's delegates were well informed and active participants in the creation of the Dominion. Eager to realize their vision of an intercolonial railway, they willingly subsumed their province's limited autonomy in order to participate in founding a large nation-state.

Since historians see the CPR as a central Canadian project and because they view it as a post-confederation saga, virtually all dismiss the influence of the Grand Trunk Railway on the idea of a transcontinental railway. Few take seriously the company's attempt, under the leadership of Edward Watkin, to undertake a Pacific railway. John L. McDougall, for example, in his history of the CPR, treated the pre-confederation period lightly and argued that the Grand Trunk was not interested in the Pacific railway because it believed an all-Canadian road was not viable. 'The Grand Trunk's economic interest cut squarely across the national interest of Canada,' he noted, as it was designed to carry traffic from the midwestern United States to Portland, Maine, and had designated Chicago as its logical terminus.[30] In other words, it did not share Canadian ambitions. In actual fact, however, the Grand Trunk's business mission was very much in tune with contemporary economic and political objectives, and the railway played a crucial role in shaping nationalist rhetoric in pre-confederation Canada. Moreover, as described in chapter 4, the company's first decade clearly illustrates how its directors, though assisted by imperial officials, failed to implement their plans largely because Canadian politicians and businessmen had a different, independent agenda.

Chapter 5 will demonstrate that the philosophy of railways played a defining role in New Brunswick's drive to confederation. Focusing on the powerful commercial élite of Saint John, the chapter will show that New Brunswickers shared British North America's expansionist doctrines and that the city's pro-confederation leaders sought to achieve metropolitan stature by building railway links to Canada as well as to the United States. Although they quarrelled about priorities in their construction program, New Brunswickers agreed on the importance of railways in their economic-development strategies. Moreover, once all the railway objectives were met, confederation enjoyed significant support in the province.

New Brunswick's attitude towards railways and confederation demonstrated that British North America's philosophy of railways saw no inherent contradiction between railway links with the United States and the task of building a new northern nation. In contrast, most CPR historians view the Pacific railway as an antidote to annexation to the United States. They couch their interpretation of the Pacific Scandal, for example, in terms of a struggle between Canadian and American forces. W. Kaye Lamb, for one, strongly believed that John A. Macdonald was from the beginning a committed Canadian nationalist who never deviated from the principal concept of no American ties whatsoever. 'But these after all were details,' he writes. 'Macdonald and Cartier, utterly convinced that a transcontinental railway was essential to Canada's survival and future, had succeeded in committing the country to its construction.'[31] In keeping with this assumption, Lamb and others interpreted the Pacific Scandal in such a way that Macdonald emerges as a pure-hearted Canadian nationalist, firmly committed to an all-Canadian CPR, without any American controls.

If one assumes, however, that Prime Minister Macdonald, like his New Brunswick peers, saw no inherent dangers in large-scale American investment in the Pacific railway, then the scandal emerges as a bungled clash between political and business objectives. Chapter 6 will demonstrate that Macdonald was clearly aware of American involvement in the first Pacific railway scheme and actively encouraged this participation. His own political interference in a business association caused him to fall prey to an opposition that was not nationalistic but purely partisan in its motivation. By the end of 1872, political, commercial, and regional jealousies had exposed a seamy flaw in technological nationalism and temporarily discredited the philosophy of railways.

Driven into opposition, the Liberal-Conservatives began to formulate an economic nationalist position. Chapter 7 will survey the concept of technological nationalism as it emerged in the National Policy and the Canadian Pacific contract. It will demonstrate that both the Liberal and Conservative parties supported the settlement of western Canada, the construction of the Pacific railway, and the establishment of a transcontinental economy. The Liberals, with strong agrarian, individualist roots, were willing to permit a transcontinental railway to follow its economically determined international route. The Conservatives, meanwhile, devised a protectionist tariff, in part to ensure that the railway ran entirely across Canadian soil. They introduced the concept of technological nationalism into the philosophy of railways.

In conclusion, chapter 8 will make some preliminary observations about the impact of technological nationalism on the new nation. While many of the observations are conjectural, the chapter will show that by facilitating the rapid interchange of people and ideas, the transcontinental railway played a crucial role in the cultural integration and unification of the young Dominion. At the same time, however, the CPR, and government policies designed to support it, were instrumental in creating deep-seated feelings of alienation in the country's peripheral regions and assisted in strengthening their ties with the United States. Thus, in contradictory fashion, it appeared that the CPR aided the task of creating a homogeneous Canadian culture and a transcontinental economy while, at the same time, it facilitated the rise of deep-seated animosities against a dominating metropolitan relationship. Railway technology, which recognizes no national boundaries, moreover, contributed to Canada's gradual absorption into an emerging North American culture.

An understanding of British America's transcontinental railway idea must begin with a survey of the revolutionary convergence of concepts and the dramatic transformation of institutions in the late-eighteenth and early-nineteenth century. This intersection of ideas and upheavals, which comprised the liberalization of political and social establishments, the scientific and industrial revolutions, and the abandonment of mercantilism, created an ideology that in turn optimistically placed its trust in technology as the engine of economic and moral growth.[32] In this liberal, progressive milieu, the dark and powerful, steam-puffing locomotive assumed a central place.

The optimistic trust in technology as the engine of economic progress germinated in the warm soil of liberalism, an ideology born in the Renaissance and refined by two centuries of political, economic, and social thinkers. Matured in Europe's scientific and industrial revolutions, liberalism eroded the old mercantilistic empire, replacing it with looser and informal bonds better suited to Britain's modern technological society. By redefining concepts of empire, liberalism established a new relationship between the imperial metropolis and its colonial hinterland; it justified the transformation of political institutions in British North America, giving colonists sufficient independence to create a favourable climate for the massive investments needed to build the continent's extensive railway system. Liberalism also created the ethos of progress and economic expansion, which excused the enormous debts that colonial governments accumulated in order to construct their railways. Liberalism, in short, created the philosophy of railways.

The heart of the new creed of liberalism was the belief in the freedom of rational man, the concept that every person was an autonomous individual, independent from anyone else. In the area of politics, for example, this meant that governments had to be curbed, preferably by a constitution; that they could be replaced, violently if necessary, if they frustrated the ambitions of the majority. Concerning religion, liberals argued that the church should only play a subservient role in society and must not interfere in political or economic affairs. In science, the liberal creed supposed that man could free himself from nature's bonds by using its principles to create powerful technologies. These intoxicating ideas, which sought to liberate men from the restraints of natural forces, political tyrants, or religious teachings, affected European thought deeply and opened the way for radically new cultures.[33]

Accompanying the liberalization of social and political institutions came a revolution in science and technology that promised to liberate mankind from nature and conflict.[34] The implicit belief that science and technology could, more powerfully than ever before, establish humans as lords over nature arose out of a gradual evaluation of the environment as a boundless resource to be used for economic ends. The Renaissance and Reformation, which placed mankind at the centre of God's creation, taught that nature must serve humanity and, conversely, that man's vocation was to subdue the earth in the service of the Maker. Subsequently, seventeenth-century scientists propounded a deistic view of nature that envisioned the universe as an orderly, dynamic, and predictable process, created by God and allowed to run the course He had ordered according to great unchangeable laws. By uncovering these ordinances, humans could exploit and supposedly control creation.[35] Although various strands of thought countered that nature contained divine attributes, inherent beauty, and intrinsic value, the mechanistic stream prevailed and, by emphasizing the autonomy of the individual rather than the absolute goodness and power of God, it presumably freed humanity from natural as well as supernatural forces. Western Europeans, especially, celebrated their new freedom and, glad in the sense of liberation, they acquired a feeling of mastery over creation.[36] In a practical sense, that belief translated into the suggestion that nations could attain economic and social growth by encouraging their citizens to acquire land, to convert wilderness into productive fields, that is, to conquer nature.

A powerful corollary to liberalism's doctrines of science was the new economic principles taught by Adam Smith, professor of moral philosophy at the University of Glasgow. Smith's *Wealth of Nations*, published in 1776, shook the mercantilistic foundations of the British empire and provided the rationale for colonial governments, like those in British North America, to define their own fiscal and economic-development objectives.

Crucial to Smith's economic theory was the deistic view of nature and society, a creed that rejected the biblical concept of the hierarchical ranking of nature, managed by a provident God. Instead, Adam Smith accepted the deist's mechanistic universe and claimed that social and economic relations were mechanical and controllable. He assumed that autonomous individuals lived within a mechanistic society set in an orderly, predictable natural environment. The market place was the centre of economic life, a machine that ran according to laws that could be identified and explained. In Smith's market place, all persons acted according to their self-interest, but competition, like an invisible hand, blended all selfishness into one harmonious whole; it regulated the machinery of the market. Although the economy experienced the uncertainties of undulating business cycles, gyrating between booms and depressions, it grew consistently, regularly, and inevitably to a better, more prosperous world. Thus, Smith's economics represented the culmination of eighteenth-century belief in the inevitable triumph of rationality, natural law, and freedom over faith, randomness, and regulation.[37]

Not surprisingly, Smith's *Wealth of Nations* protested against government interference with the natural 'liberty' of the commercial system. Believing that governments were spendthrifty, irresponsible, and unproductive, Smith recommended that they allow the machinery of the market to seek its own level of production, wages, and prices, and inevitably propel the world to progress.[38] Taking this message to its full conclusion, Smith challenged the traditional, time-tested doctrine of mercantilism, the creed that had built the great European empires. 'If any of the provinces of the British empire cannot be made to contribute towards the support of the whole empire,' he concluded his work, 'it is surely time that Great Britain should free herself from the expence of defending those provinces in time of war, and of supporting any part of their civil or military establishments in time of peace.'[39] Britain must destroy all barriers to trade, such as preferential tariffs for colonies and navigation laws, because they hindered trade with countries outside the empire.

Smith's radical views slowly seeped into the political consciousness of British leaders, and gradually their perception of empire began to change. As the trauma of the American revolution receded and the New World matured and moved away from European control, the legal structure of mercantilism began to lose its relevance. Although the Napoleonic Wars prevented an immediate overhaul, a steady growth in mining, metallurgy, manufacturing, commerce, and finance called for greater flexibility in imperial and foreign trade. Clearly leading its Continental rivals, Britain's new economy demanded a greater variety of easily accessible resources and preferred relatively open and competitive world markets.[40] For Britain at least, the need for formal imperial structures had passed.

Yet another important eighteenth-century development assisted Britain's conversion to free ..de. If liberalism provided the theory that autonomous man could control the forces of nature, the industrial revolution, fuelled by brilliant scientific discoveries, demonstrated that he could actually do it. The deistic view of creation, which was stronger in the United Kingdom than on the Continent, permitted greater experimentation with nature, while its relatively fluid society permitted easy interchange of ideas. Since Protestantism taught that private gain and business success were worthy and natural ambitions, the basic liberty appeared to be the freedom to make a profit.[41] The resultant mood, which encouraged the energetic pursuit of material prosperity through hard work, held that the primary avenue to national happiness was technological and economic expansion. Industrialization, once started, snowballed, and, by the middle of the nineteenth century, Britain was the world's leading manufacturer, able to compete around the globe.[42]

The advanced stage of Britain's industrialization and technology created a feeling of superiority among many of its leaders. Pointing to the vast empire, protected by a powerful navy, the incredible advances in medicine, transportation, and manufacturing, the nation's leaders agreed that the convergence of science and technology had produced the means by which humanity was progressively improving its environment. Even though critics accusingly pointed to polluted and filthy slums, widespread abject poverty, and the exploitation of adult and child labour, while they denounced defects in political and social institutions, none condemned technology itself. Social reformers proposed only the amelioration of working and living conditions. Consequently, the view that machines had bettered the life of mankind prevailed and generated an attitude of supremacy and uniqueness. The British believed that they had created this industrial and scientific revolution and that therefore their nation was more civilized than any other. As measures of this superior civilization, they noted its material culture as well as its common law and political institutions. As James Mill explained in his *History of British India*, there was no better 'index of the degree in which the benefits of civilization are anywhere enjoyed than in the state of the tools and machinery.'[43] Industrialization and technology – like the doctrines of laissez-faire economics, capitalist enterprise, and human liberty – were considered among the essential prerequisites for development and civilization.

This aura of distinctiveness and arrogance had a major impact on the attitude towards colonies. While the economic value of the empire decreased in importance, the belief that Britain must share its superior civilization increased. Though never as a comprehensive or official policy, British bureaucrats, businessmen, and politicians adopted as a mission the need to civilize the empire. In other words, they began to regard the colonies in a radically different way. Even though economic motives always remained important, the new imperialism was more than mere colonization but involved a radical new way of looking at the world. The civilizing mission was a moral rather than an economic statement.[44]

The feelings of superiority and uniqueness, based as they were on technological and scientific accomplishments, accentuated the attitude that humanity could conquer nature and freely exploit its seemingly limitless resources. Distinct from and above nature, men could master previously untapped resources and reshape their environment to suit their needs and desires. The view that providence had created an abundance of resources for the use of mankind to improve the quality of life was not new, but Britons felt it more strongly than ever before and it became a vital source of Victorian optimism.[45] Thomas Carlyle, the early Victorian essayist, criticized the adverse effects of industrialization on the lives of workers, but he shared with his Victorian contemporaries the love of the machine as the 'predominant symbol of the age's harnessing of nature.'[46] Despite his ambivalence, Carlyle boasted, 'We remove mountains, and make seas our smooth highway; nothing can resist us. We war with rude Nature; and, by our resistless engines, come off always victorious, and loaded with spoils.'[47]

Thus twinned, the tenets of mastery of nature and abundant resources gave Britain's businessmen the mandate to expand into undeveloped regions, especially if occupied by less advanced peoples, and to exploit nature's riches. Of course the basic need for raw materials to feed insatiable mills remained prominent, but the search for resources became imperative when bolstered by the moral obligation to civilize the wilderness. Sir Roderick Murchison, the director of the British Geological Survey, dispatched scientists to all sections of the globe, including British North America, in search of minerals, precious stones, and scientific samples.[48] Carlyle angrily denounced poverty in England when there was 'a world where Canadian Forests stand unfelled, boundless Plains and Prairies unbroken with the plough ... green desert spaces never yet made white with corn; and to the overcrowded little western nook of Europe, our Terrestrial Planet, nine-tenths of it yet vacant or tenanted by nomades, is still crying, Come and till me, come and reap me!'[49] Thus the civilizing mission mixed destiny and duty, 'humanitarian sentiment, cultural arrogance, and self-serving rationalization,' as well as commercial and financial greed into a powerful expansionist creed.[50]

The central feature of the new industrial imperialism, and its civilizing mandate, was the transportation revolution. As historian Rick Szostak has convincingly argued, a modern transportation system, which could move bulky goods at low cost or high-value items at high speeds, was a necessary factor in Britain's industrial revolution.[51] An extensive canal and turnpike system, he posited, permitted British businessmen to extend their markets and increase production, and allowed regions to specialize in certain products and processes. With better access to large quantities of raw materials, the country could change from domestic to factory production. Meanwhile, wheeled transport helped to convert the method of distribution from individual peddlars to faster and more reliable wholesale establishments. In sum, Szostak maintained, Britain's efficient land-based transportation network created opportunities for industrial expansion. It also accelerated the rate of technological innovation, and, by lowering the cost of food, it stimulated urbanization. Lastly, he noted, an efficient system of transportation facilitated increased information flows and created an integrated, unified economy.

Although older forms of transport – including roads, rivers, and canals – had carried the initial stages of Britain's industrialization, the most revolutionary technique was the railway. Not fully developed until the 1830 opening of the Liverpool & Manchester Railway, rail transportation introduced the greatest change in the tempo of land transport ever. Substituting machine for muscle power, it was capable of moving large numbers of people and high volumes of goods at unprecedented speeds. With extraordinary rapidity of movement, raucous noise, lights, and smoke, producing pollution and urban blight, the railway shocked society to its core. As it thrust like a cannonball unimpeded through the landscape, towns, and cities, it uprooted a nation.[52] Although those living near the tracks may have cursed the soot and noise, Britain's commercial and political élite found in the railway all the symbols of their nation's pre-eminence – speed, power, size, and control. They actively expressed their admiration and their great expectations of profit in two periods of incredible construction frenzy. In the first era, 1837 to 1840, the country laid 2400 kilometres of track; by the end of the second frantic phase, 1845 to 1847, it built another 7200 km; in total, a quarter of current trackage. When the boom collapsed, the nation possessed the outlines of an entirely new transportation system and in the process had created the modern business enterprise.[53]

Although the bubble burst and shattered some fortunes, British investors did not lose faith in the seductive power of the new technology because the railway, more than any other machine, embodied the material advances of the industrial revolution. According to Lewis Mumford, the railway was the 'most characteristic and the most efficient form of technics.'[54] Dependent upon highly sophisticated engineering principles, technical skills, and knowledge of metallurgy, the railway's tracks, bridges, rock cuts, and tunnels reshaped the landscape. Little wonder that the *Edinburgh Review* called the locomotive the 'great wonder-worker of the age.'[55] Expanding rapidly through the countryside, the railway first overwhelmed and then captured the imagination of poets, novelists, and social commentators. Its powerful speed, its scheduled regularity, its precision and discipline reminded people that man had mastered time and space. The locomotive represented the epitome of experimentation, innovation, and technological progress. Although novelist Charles Dickens complained about the negative ethical implications of the machine, he adulated the steam train, 'Breasting the wind and light, the shower and sunshine, away, and still away, it rolls and roars, fierce and rapid, smooth and certain, and great works and massive bridges, crossing up above, fall like a beam of shadow an inch broad upon the eye, and then are lost,' he marvelled, yet wistfully remembered the passing of the pastoral countryside. 'Away, and still away, onward and onward ever: glimpses of cottage homes, of houses, mansions, rich estates, of husbandry and handicraft, of people, of old roads and paths that look deserted, small, and insignificant as they are left behind.'[56] The railway, in every sense, defined industrial Britain.

The Victorian love for railways quickly infected North Americans because steam technology appeared perfectly in tune with the New World character. Here the joyful celebration of man's dominion over nature gradually pushed aside the placid vision of the environment as a peaceful undisturbed wilderness. Instead, an imperialist mission of agricultural and commercial exploitation degenerated into an arrogant assertion that the human race was destined for unlimited lordship and freedom.[57] Equipped with increasingly sophisticated tools, immigrant Europeans believed that finally they were able to control nature and develop a completely free society. While the machine allowed man to transform command into mastery, a new view of history taught that society was moving inevitably towards a fuller unfolding of freedom.[58] The wide-open spaces of North America amplified these ideals into a powerful creed, and the optimistic pioneer, armed with technology, activated this vision of man as lord over nature and vigorously assaulted the environment. Assured in the belief that technology liberated them from the bonds of nature, the newcomers felt keenly that the highest good was to spread civilization over the continent.[59]

In a dramatic oration, American senator Daniel Webster reconciled the triumph of the possessive over the pastoral view of nature. After the standard ode to progress and brotherhood, Webster cleverly expressed his annoyance at the locomotive's raucous invasion of a peaceful landscape, appearing to denounce the cut-and-slash techniques that destroy the pristine character of nature. Then, abruptly, he changed his tone, leaving his audience without doubt that his complaints must not be taken seriously. It was foolish, he avowed, to deplore these adverse side-effects, because those 'who live along the line of road must already [have begun] to feel its beneficial effects.'[60] While the pastoral scene is beautiful, it is trivial and effete, and those who are disturbed by the piercing whistle of the iron horse are effeminate and squeamish. Webster rejoiced in the changes brought about by the machine and implied there is a cosmic harmonious spirit that, according to a divine plan, is uniting man, the nation, and the machine into a progressive historical force.[61]

As Leo Marx has demonstrated so effectively in *The Machine in the Garden*, even the many American artists who idealized the pastoral view of nature often included the machine in their garden images.[62] This happened primarily because Americans abhorred wilderness. They believed that for nature to be truly nature, to have its potential fully realized, it must be altered, tamed, exploited, and civilized. Since technology enabled mankind to accomplish this mission more effectively than ever before, most Americans welcomed the machine into the garden. And, of all the machines that could help Americans build a garden in the wilderness, the locomotive seemed the most effective, especially because it appeared just at the moment when Americans were preparing to enter the vast interior plains.[63]

No machine captured the American imagination like the locomotive. By the 1830s the iron horse had become an obsession, and in the next thirty years the United States laid nearly 50,000 kilometres, of track. Considered the indispensable pivot of the transportation revolution, the locomotive quickened the nation's pace of industrialization. It embodied the age. For here was an instrument of power and speed, noise and fire, iron and smoke, confined to a predetermined path. 'We believe that the steam engine, upon land, is to be one of the most valuable agents of the present age, because it is swifter than the greyhound, and powerful as a thousand horses,' the *Merchant's Magazine* enthused, 'because it has no passions and no motives; because it is guided by its directors; because it runs and never tires; because it may be applied to so many uses, and expanded to any strength.'[64] Elsewhere, periodicals and the press regaled the public with stories of railway projects, accidents, and profits; songs, speeches, and magazine articles tirelessly adulated the machine's ability to unceasingly drive the progress of mankind. By harnessing the power of steam, they said, mankind for the first time could realize its dream of abundance as well as its hopes of peace, equality, freedom, and happiness. Yet the dark simplicity of the locomotive's force hardly required the poet. Its message of progress was powerfully direct. To the pioneer, faced with colonizing the expansive plains, the meaning of the railway was dramatically obvious. Seen in an uncultivated, wild countryside, the train's physical attributes clearly stated that the present moment was superior to the past. In the cliché of the era, the railway obliterated time and space.[65]

To many Americans, then, the railway seemed the ideal technology to accomplish two vital aspects of the national dream, the occupation of the soil and internal unity. On the one hand, the railway promised to provide easy access to the land and to permit its cultivation. 'By transforming presently poor and uncultivated earth, the railroad would guarantee the country's agrarian basis and fulfil America's promise as Eden.'[66] Mobility would bring prosperity. On the other hand, the railway supposedly fostered unity and community; it promised a 'moral, intellectual, class, and most of all political intimacy that many Americans feared could not be achieved through any other means.'[67] Thus, current literature and promotional pamphlets employed an ingenious array of metaphors, usually linked to nature, to demonstrate hopes and fears for the future of the fragile nation. Deeply concerned about sectional conflict, writers created images of fluidity, expansion, and movement to symbolize the railway's civilizing mission, while counterpointing these with conceptions of constriction, binding together, and holding immobile. Similarly, metaphors of youth, power, and speed denoted both the need to tie together the states and to spread their culture outward.[68] As Henry Varnum Poor, editor of the *American Railroad Journal*, put it, the railway was civilization. 'To us ... it is essential,' he claimed; 'it constitutes a part of our nature, is a condition of our being what we are.'[69]

The exuberant faith in railway technology and its ability to dismantle historical and cultural barriers was epitomized in September 1851 at the Boston Jubilee celebrating the completion of a railway link between Boston and Montréal. The Bostonians invited their fellow Americans and Canadians to gather in commemoration of the completion of the rail connection between their city and the Canadas, and to celebrate 'the peaceful and beneficent triumphs of science and skill.'[70] The president of the United States, Millard Fillmore, accepted the invitation, as did the governor-general of Canada, Lord Elgin, and the premier of Nova Scotia, Joseph Howe. The mayors of Québec, Montréal, and Toronto, accompanied by many of their councillors, came and so did several leading legislators, congressmen, and senators. Noisy parades, races, excursions, lunches, and speeches crowded the days, while formal balls, banquets, and flowery orations filled the evenings. Threaded through the frantic activities was a common theme, the unity of two peoples. The scores of colourful banners, fancy arches, and brightly decorated storefronts that adorned the city proclaimed the noble sentiments of harmony and cooperation. 'Boston and the Canadas, United by Bonds of Iron' blazoned one side of a giant street-spanning banner; 'Union Is Strength' trumpeted the other side. While most speakers alluded to the revolution that split the two countries, they all promised their audiences that the railway would reunite them in peaceful concord. President Fillmore assured Canadians, 'I am not ... in favor of annexation, in a certain sense of the term, (for I think we have already territory enough)'; nevertheless, he was 'entirely in favor of all the means by which States and Countries can be bound together by ties of mutual interest and reciprocal commercial advantage.'[71]

Francis Hincks, soon to be premier of Canada, emphasized the economic aspect of the Boston to Montréal railway. As a liberal, he emphasized the need for free trade between Canada and the United States and he explained the specific nature of the new relationship. 'We want to furnish you with raw products ... of our agriculturalists. We wish you to give us, in exchange, your domestic manufactures, as well as teas, sugars, fruits, and other commodities obtained by you from other countries in exchange for your manufactures.'[72]

Canada's governor-general, Lord Elgin, more muted in his applause of Boston's achievement than President Fillmore, pointed to the social implications of the railway connection. Always the careful diplomat, Lord Elgin confessed that he 'wanted to show by my presence here, that I appreciate and value the moral and social, as well as the economical effects of these increased facilities of intercourse ... your lines are made for the transport of men and women, as well as for the carriage of bales of goods and barrels of flour.'[73] Elgin's perceptive speech strongly implied that the recently completed railway technology was to be an integrating force, welding together diverse regions.

Boston's mayor, John Bigelow, was more explicit in his observations. He noted that the 'iron pathways, the result of scientific labor and skill unequalled by ancient times ... unite in friendly relations the inhabitants of widely separated regions – minister to their mutual wants – diffuse abroad the means of knowledge – "and scatter plenty through a smiling land."'[74] Like many of the remarks, the mayor's speech echoed North America's remarkably ebullient confidence in the ability of science and technology to bring economic and social progress. Significantly, his remarks also noted the homogenizing influence of railway technology.

The buoyant optimism, which flowed freely amid the bubbly champagne, imported wines, and gourmet food at the Boston celebrations, represented not only a confident faith in technology but also an assurance that God wisely intended its development and blessed it. One anonymous speaker, obviously carried away with the high emotions and generous libations, soared to lofty heights to describe God's role in the expansion of railways across the continent and their universalizing effect upon society.

But Providence had another and a higher use for those iron tracks and flying trains. After the mercantile heart had devised and secured them, God took them for his purposes, without paying any tax for the privilege, he uses them to quicken the activity of men; to send energy and vitality where before was silence and barrenness; to multiply cities and villages, studded with churches, dotted with schools, and filled with happy homes and budding souls; to increase wealth which shall partially be devoted to his service and kingdom, and all along their banks to make the wilderness blossom as the rose. Without any vote of permission from legislatures and officials, even while the cars are loaded with profitable freight and paying passengers, and the groaning engines are earning the necessary interest, Providence sends, without charge, its cargoes of good sentiment and brotherly feeling; disburses the culture of the city to the simplicity of the hamlet, and brings back the strength and virtue of the village and mountain to the wasting faculties of the metropolis; and fastens to every steam-shuttle that flies back and forth and hither and thither, an invisible thread of fraternal influence, which, entwining sea-shore and hill-country, mart and grain-field, forge and factory, wharf and mine, slowly prepares society to realize, one day, the Saviour's prayer, 'that they all may be one.'[75]

The pious references to a divine purpose in the construction of railways, although hyperbolic, were neither glib nor insincere. They denoted a definitive feature of British North America's philosophy of railways. At mid-century, people keenly felt the overwhelming presence of God in their personal lives and community affairs. Nowhere was this more true than in British North America, where citizens were deeply religious and churchly. The Christian religion, especially its fervent evangelical wing, profoundly affected the formation of colonial cultures. Since it enjoyed strong support within many Anglican and Presbyterian churches, and obviously among Methodists and Baptists, evangelicalism set the religious tone for colonial Protestantism. Acutely aware of a continuously active, provident God working in their lives, and sharply sensitive to human sin, evangelicals shared an intense concern for the spiritual health of themselves and the community. Emphasizing personal repentance and conversion, faith and discipline, piety and devotion, they tended to be ascetic and serious, striving to be industrious, honest, sincere, and sober. Moreover, driven by a Puritan sense of purpose and mission, they eagerly assumed the task of creating God's kingdom on earth.[76]

Although evangelicalism had roots in the United States, British North Americans fostered a stronger attachment to British and European traditions. Church governance and clergy ensured that colonial congregations remained close to Britain and its intellectual and theological developments, giving their faith a different tenor than that in the United States. In general, British North American clergy were likely to be educated and not anti-intellectual. To be sure, they believed that knowledge must serve a useful purpose, that is, it must fulfil God's design. Thus, they established colleges and universities to teach the liberal arts, emphasizing science rather than the classics. Still, convinced that history had a strong evolutionary purpose, colonial evangelicals also emphasized their British heritage. Although eager to exploit the enormous resources of the continent, they were less likely than their American counterparts to view the destiny of British America as a great social experiment. More cognizant of the interplay of North Atlantic cultures, they appreciated the blending of old traditions in a new environment.[77]

Since British Americans clearly saw the hand of God in nature, they were very interested in science. Like many Victorians, they viewed science as the revelation of God's plans and activities in nature. Deeply appreciative of the complex web of life and the interrelationship of all organisms, they marvelled at His creation and admired science for discovering His marvellous design. They also believed that God had made man His steward on earth and that He had placed him above and beyond nature. All of creation, they thought, was arranged for the advantage of mankind: geological history was a preparation for its benefit; coal deposits were a result of divine foresight; while the flow of the Gulf stream was established to moderate the climate of western Europe. Concomitantly, the Bible enjoined man to use and subdue nature and its creatures, to convert the wilderness to a fit abode, and to enjoy dominion from sea to sea.[78]

Awed by the miracle of divine creation, British Americans had, by the middle of the nineteenth century, a manifest intellectual interest in nature. The colonists adopted Francis Bacon's emphasis on gathering facts through observation and experiment and Isaac Newton's focus on the mechanical universe. While they strongly identified nature with rationality, they also possessed a growing awareness of the world as an organism in the process of historical change. Facing an enormous, unknown continent, they made natural history especially a popular pursuit. Academics, assisted by doctors, pharmacists, clergy, and even some businessmen and lawyers, eagerly assumed the task of exploring new and exciting physical phenomena. Convinced they could make a unique contribution to global knowledge, they mapped and catalogued, gathered specimens and displayed artefacts, published papers and sponsored public lectures. Beginning with the Canadian Institute in Toronto in 1849, each province established similar organizations devoted to the study of natural history. Along with chairs at universities and colleges, they dedicated themselves to the perpetuation and extension of the British tradition of popular science. As in Victorian England, natural history became a respectable activity, associated with wealth, religion, and self-improvement.[79]

On the other hand, a strong dose of utilitarianism infused British American science. Epitomized most clearly in the founding of the Geological Survey in 1842 at Montréal, the perceived utility of inventory science grew because of the need to locate good soils and valuable mineral deposits, to cope with the climate, and to find commercial uses for plants and nature. Science, colonists believed, could provide the means to dominate their physical surroundings, to exploit the resources of the new land. Moreover, utilitarian science gave purpose and meaning to the task of settling the continent. Thus science, aided by technology, provided the ideological framework for civilizing the continent.[80]

For most citizens, however, technology was of greater import than science. Overwhelmingly rural, most British Americans struggled for survival in an unfamiliar and seemingly hostile environment. The densely dark forests were to them a harsh, unyielding wilderness only partially tamed by back-breaking toil. Wanting to build a home and create verdant fields, they, their wives, and children saw only the rocks, the stumps, and the barrens. Fighting extremes of weather, hordes of insects, and choking weeds, they sought stability in the midst of an unpredictable and ruthless landscape.[81] Unschooled in the scientific method, the settler did understand technology; it appeared to offer some equilibrium in an unpredictable and brutal world. In particular, the mighty steam locomotive, scheduled to the minute, provided a measure of security in an uncertain environment. Not only did it open an access to the wilderness and facilitate the export of surplus produce, its haunting whistle in the dead of night was the lonely pioneer's audible link with the urban world. It clearly signalled the ability to survive in the wilderness, a fundamental trait of the emerging Canadian identity.[82]

The optimistic, pragmatic faith in science and technology, the evangelical fervour that accompanied it, and the opportunity to civilize a large empty continent not surprisingly produced an innate belief in progress. Felt more strongly in nineteenth-century North America than anywhere else, the progress attitude sensed that history embodied an advance to a better – materially and morally – world.[83] History was purposeful and its utopian destiny, while distant, was palpable. Partly the grace of God and partly the product of human endeavour, progress possessed a strong religious overtone and reflected a deep belief in the efficacy of science as well as the frontier ideal of equality and the opportunity to conquer a vast wilderness. Writing on New Year's Day, 1885, the Halifax *Morning Herald* recalled Canada's great history and, sensing a fullness of time, challenged its readers to the task of conquering the continent. 'Here are the boundless stretches of virgin soil crying for the plough and the hoe. Here are the interminable forests waiting for him who is mighty to lift up "axes against our trees." Here are inexhaustible mineral treasures beneath our feet. Here is wealth unknown, swarming in our bays, and teeming in our seas. Here – best of all – is a free government, by the people for the people.' Thus, the resounding summons to tame the seemingly empty environment, translated into the idea of progress, was a prime motivation in the transcontinental railway idea. As a consensus, progress was respectable. 'Politicians of all persuasion could agree that progress, like virtue, was a good thing and ought to be encouraged.'[84] Virtually all speeches from the throne, no matter what party was in power, enumerated the progress the province or country had experienced and was bound to make. Equally prominent in the speeches was a reminder of the crucial role that railways were expected to play in achieving that progress.

Thus railway technology assumed an important place in North America's pioneer society. In both the United States and in British America, it became a powerful symbol of man's ability unitedly to challenge the constraints of his environment. By the early 1850s, railway promoters in New England and British North America were building a consolidated railway network that disregarded the diplomatically drawn international boundary. While they planned each railway for a particular economic purpose, the system as a whole was more than a mode of transportation. It became a method of blending diverse and competing social and national ideals. Even if politicians, orators, and editors did not consciously comprehend the homogenizing and universalizing power of railroad technology, they assumed that its integrative drive would promote human excellence and understanding. Their Canadian, as well as American, listeners applauded this liberal ideal.

As the Boston Jubilee had demonstrated, British North America's philosophy of railways closely followed that of the United States. As Britain gradually loosened the formal ties of empire, the colonists cast about for a new identity and political economy. To be sure, the British connection remained exceedingly strong as British North Americans, and later Canadians, found inspiration in a common political and historical heritage and also depended upon large infusions of British capital to build their railways, factories, and mines. At the same time, however, British North Americans were anxious to develop stronger ties with the newly emerging empire to the south. Envious of the vigorous United States economy and its rapidly expanding railway system, British North Americans eagerly sought to increase trade and commerce, and to borrow its engineering and railway expertise. They never intended any of their railways to isolate them from the United States. On the contrary, they designed most railway projects to enhance commercial relations with the southern neighbour. In sum, British North America's philosophy of railways recognized no inherent contradiction between British and American technological ideals, but mixed both into its own vision of economic and social progress and a transcontinental nation. It gladly echoed the confident assertion of the aptly named *The Harbinger* that 'the age that is to witness a rail road between the Atlantic and Pacific, as a grand material type of the unity of nations, will also behold a social organization, productive of moral and spiritual results, whose sublime and beneficent character will eclipse even the glory of those colossal achievements which send messengers of fire over the mountain tops, and connect ocean with ocean by iron and granite bands.'[85]

By choosing technology as a consolidating force, Canadians could not avoid its integrating and universalizing character. On the one hand, technology's unifying role was evident in the growing influence of the state in the social and economic affairs of the provinces and in the intertwining functions of business and government. On the other hand, the railway's homogenizing feature was present in the confederation process and the attempt to establish a northern transcontinental economy. But, the consolidation process did not stop at the southern border; the railway also facilitated the gradual encroachment of the rising American empire into Canadian affairs. While pre-confederation's transcontinental railway rhetoric envisioned a united British North America as an counteragent to American encroachment, its businessmen, more concerned with immediate profits, constructed railways to the United States and enmeshed the young nation into several networks of domination. Neither the Grand Trunk nor the Canadian Pacific railways created a nation by isolating British North America from the cultural influence of the United States.

Although Canadians employed the discourse of technological nationalism to overcome regional jealousies and to establish a sense of unity and national identity, this popular means of communication failed to produce a common Canadian culture. Discontent in both the Atlantic and western regions of the nation attest to the fact that railways were not unanimously accepted symbols of national unity. For some, railway technology posed a threat; it represented an dangerous vehicle for creating a national identity because it favoured centres of power and promoted the suppression of marginal communities.

While journalists, politicians, and commentators blithely refer to the CPR myth, the recent history of branch and main-line abandonment, diversification into unrelated enterprises and multinational objectives, and participation in VIA Rail have eroded its nation-building symbolism. The CPR's decision to display an American flag as part of its logo merely acknowledged its international character. Although lamenting the new reality, Canadians have become aware that technological nationalism creates a false sense of identity, based not on the ideas and feelings of a people but founded on a disposable commodity. Unfortunately, as the erosion of railway transportation across the nation clearly illustrates, any technology can become obsolete and thus cannot provide a lasting sense of community.

Neither does technology, which is expansive and integrative, recognize international boundaries; it is, therefore, an unsuitable vehicle for creating a distinct national identity. Communication technologies, which improve intercourse regardless of political boundaries, especially offer no defence against the power and seduction of a culturally dominant and technologically more experienced nation like the United States. Surely, the existence of the Canadian Radio-television and Telecommunications Commission is vivid proof that still today communication technology is unable to isolate a country from its neighbours.

British North Americans did find common purpose in the philosophy of railways. Sharing a broad ideological movement, which had its origins in Europe and blossomed in the United States, British North Americans developed a unifying railway doctrine that echoed through all the colonies and bridged provincial particularisms.[86] This ideology, based on liberal views of science, economics, and politics, elevated railway technology to an exalted stature. It was to be not only a panacea for the colonies' economic stagnation but also an avenue to social and moral growth and progress. Infused with an evangelical fervour, and coloured by its commercial, industrial, and technological bias the railway ideology was mainly a bourgeois, city movement. The middle classes, who dominated the provinces' political institutions, enunciated and implemented the philosophy of railways. They accepted the great consensus that viewed the locomotive as the great civilizer. While they disagreed on specific economic and commercial objectives, they all agreed that it was the most efficacious instrument for taming the expansive wilderness outside the settled communities. Thus, the Canadian Pacific Railway arose out of an international urban consensus on the place of technology in society. It emerged from a railway rhetoric that was also present in Great Britain and the United States. Although subject to regional and national considerations, political ambitions, and metropolitan goals, the primary objective of the philosophy of railways was the civilization of the North American wilderness.

2

The Guarantee Act:
Signpost for an Era

Whereas at the present day, the means of rapid and easy communication by Railway, between the chief centres of population and trade in any country and the more remote parts thereof, are become not merely advantageous, but essential to its advancement and prosperity ...

Preamble to the Guarantee Act[1]

The proposal of any new law or regulation of commerce which comes from this order [merchants, industrialists, and financiers], ought always to be listened to with great precaution, and ought never to be adopted till after having been long and carefully examined, not only with the most scrupulous, but with the most suspicious attention. It comes from an order of men, whose interest is never exactly the same with that of the publick, who have generally an interest to deceive and even to oppress the publick, and who accordingly have, upon many occasions, both deceived and oppressed it.

Adam Smith[2]

Early in the spring of 1849, the Legislative Assembly of the United Canadas passed the Guarantee Act by which the province secured for investors a return of 6 per cent interest per year on the bonds of any railway at least 120 kilometres long and half completed. Even though the act promised virtually unlimited financial support for most qualified railway ventures, all political factions supported the resolutions and the legislature approved the measure sixty-two to four.[3] This extraordinary consensus, obtained in one of the most rancorous sessions in Canadian parliamentary history, represented a political understanding that dominated mid-nineteenth-century Canada; it symbolized a general faith in railway technology as the panacea for Canada's economic and social ills; it epitomized a remarkable agreement on the liberal principle of economic progress achieved through technological advancement. The Guarantee Act of 1849, a unique harmonious moment in a divisive session, signalled the convergence of several streams of thought in Western civilization and indicated the direction of the colony's future. The act created the climate for a railway-construction frenzy, a land-based transportation revolution that helped Canada cope with the loosening transatlantic ties of an old imperialism and facilitated the colony's integration into a new continental economy. The Guarantee Act, which stimulated railway construction as the avenue to economic growth, was the signpost for the consolidating and centralizing forces of railway technology.

The 1849 session of the Canadian legislature was the arena for conflicting ideas and events. It sat uneasily in an extremely turbulent period in Canadian history. Most obviously, the session witnessed a bitter debate between Conservative and Reform factions, a clash of political values that ultimately degenerated into a fierce riot and the burning of the legislative building. Less conspicuously, the consuming blaze aptly symbolized the revolutionary force sweeping across the continent, a liberal philosophy that was radically attacking current traditional perceptions of colonial society, its culture, and its economy. Yet, even while the rioters violently protested their apparent loss of political power, they had only days earlier gladly accepted one of the foundational tenets of the new doctrine, the need to utilize the most modern technologies to achieve economic progress. If the 1849 session reflected the deep divisions in Canadian society – clashes between new democratic ideas and traditional hierarchical values, between regions, classes, and languages, and between continentalist forces and transatlantic ties – it also revealed a strong common denominator. Despite their profound differences, Canadian politicians were firmly united in their unshakable belief that the new technology of steam railways would be able to lift the colony out of its perceived backward, stagnating economy and transform it into an advanced, dynamic society. The doctrine that technology could generate economic and even social progress was a powerfully coherent force; it counteracted the centrifugal forces threatening to split the province asunder.

The optimistic trust in technology as the engine of economic progress, so popular in Great Britain and the United States, was articulated in a remarkable pamphlet written in 1849 by Thomas C. Keefer, a well-known engineer. Entitled the *Philosophy of Railroads*, Keefer's work exalted the technology of steam and iron as an indispensable agent of economic development and civilization.[4] According to Keefer, railways brought more than economic progress; they fostered social integration and stimulated intellectual and moral growth. Canada must find the money to build railways, Keefer exhorted his readers, otherwise the province would not survive in a modern world. Writing with elegant grace and sardonic wit, Keefer captured the ethos of a generation; his *Philosophy* was a best-seller, serving as the source for all railway promotions in British America and some in New England.

To illustrate his theme, Keefer employed a clever literary device. He described a stagnant agricultural community, Sleepy Hollow, that, without any means of transporting its produce to markets, subsisted on barter and lacked job opportunities for its youth. Sleepy Hollow had reached the limits of development, its 'venerable church yard [was] slowly filling up with tombstones.'[5] In contrast, Keefer also pictured an unnamed village that accepted railway technology and consequently sent surplus products to distant markets, enjoyed rising land values, and created jobs and a future for its children. More important, Keefer enthused, 'the moral influence of the iron civilizer upon the old inhabitants ... [brought] a rapid "change over the spirit of their dreams."'[6] While the tranquil pre-industrial veneer of Sleepy Hollow belied a spirit of self-indulgence, ignorance, and prejudice, the excitement of progress in the railway town produced ambition, knowledge, and tolerance: while the blacksmith wanted his son to become a maker of locomotives, the tailor discussed sophisticated ideas.

Naming one village and not the other allowed Keefer's readers to disassociate themselves from Sleepy Hollow and mentally attach the name of their town to the progressive community. The technique also permitted Keefer to reject the romantic pastoral ideal.[7] Pristine nature, he felt, was wild and undeveloped; it must be civilized and tamed. Arguing that the locomotive ranked second only to the printing press as a revolutionary invention, he believed that the railway freed man from the limits of muscles, wind, tides, and weather. Able to haul thousands of tons of goods for hundreds of miles unhampered by disease or fatigue, it reduced time and distance, disregarded rain or snow. Not limited to river valleys, the railway traversed mountains and plains and spread numerous branch lines everywhere to reach every wharf, every warehouse in every village and every city. It was this ability of the steam train to conquer the constraints of the natural environment that created in Keefer's writings a giddy sense of freedom, a boundless optimism that envisioned not only inevitable economic progress but also an eventual improvement in human relations. 'The civilizing tendence of the locomotive,' Keefer noted, had ended poverty, indifference, religious intolerance, and bigotry. Requiring intensive cooperation to build, shrinking distances between communities, the railway 'impels [people] to a more intimate union with their fellow men.'[8] For Keefer, then, the philosophy of railways was more than economics; it was a recognition that the logical consequences of technology were social, economic, and moral.

Keefer translated his exuberant philosophy into concrete action. If Canadians wanted to prosper, they had to adopt the new transportation technology. During the winter season the Canadian economy was stagnant, he stressed; its businessmen languished. Montréal alone lost enough commerce to aggressive American merchants to pay for 80 kilometres of railways. Specifically, Keefer observed that with the St Lawrence system held captive by winter weather, Montréalers had to build a railway eastward to an ice-free Atlantic port and westward to Toronto. Even if they built only 80 kilometres they could supply the city daily with fresh food and dairy products. Possessing the resources and manpower to build railways, Canada could not afford to remain behind. 'To stand still is to retreat,' Keefer lectured his readers.[9] They had to have faith in the pinnacle of transportation technology; they had to take the initiative to secure their future. To worry that a railway to Canada West could not compete with the province's new canal system was folly because only a train could haul perishable foods quickly, only a locomotive could operate throughout the winter. But more to the point, Keefer asked, if a merchant in Canada West could travel to New York within twenty hours and have his merchandise shipped weekly, why should he continue to rely on sleepy ice-bound Montréal, necessitating huge spring and fall inventories?

Time and time again, Keefer reminded Montréal businessmen that the railway had revolutionized business techniques and that they must adapt to the new economic environment or perish. Inverting their protests that technology was too expensive for a colonial economy, he demanded action. 'We cannot any longer *afford* to do without Railroads. Their want is an actual tax upon the industry and labour of the country.'[10] Canadians must emulate the example set by their American neighbours, Keefer concluded; they must learn to cooperate, to associate together, to get rid of the 'mistaken love of sole proprietorship.' They must work 'as *a people*, through our Government,' to construct a railway network that would expand their primitive, provincial society into an integrated, flourishing nation. 'Every year of delay but increases our inequality, and will prolong the time and aggravate the labour of what, through our inertness, has already become a sufficiently arduous rivalry: but when once the barriers of indifference, prejudice and ignorance are broken down – no physical or financial obstacle can withstand the determined perseverance of intelligent, self-controlled industry.'[11] Most important, and fundamental to his philosophy, Keefer argued that Canadians had to realize that railways generated traffic and increased economic activity. 'The essence of a Railway system,' Keefer emphasized, 'is *to increase its own traffic.*'[12]

Keefer's eloquent treatise must be regarded as a model of promotional literature. While it was not unusual at the time for North American railway promoters to engage an engineer to make a superficial survey of a railway route and praise the resources of the countryside with overwhelming statistics, few attained the ardent eloquence of Keefer. Most engineers gladly provided optimistic assessments of a project's expected costs and glibly predicted its ultimate success, but Keefer – hired by a group of Montréal businessmen to promote their plans for a railway west of Montréal – surpassed them all. Born in 1821, the son of an Upper Canadian miller, he was trained as a practical engineer, acquiring in the process an evangelical zeal for technology. He was an excellent propagandist. In readable style, backed by quiet authority, he engaged his readers, persuading them that technology was not a monster but an avenue to the material advancement and moral perfection of man.[13]

Keefer's philosophy of railways was no isolated voice of unrealistic optimism but mirrored the views of many colonials. Although less focused than Keefer, local newspapers continuously published editorials that espoused railways as prerequisites for economic prosperity. The Montréal *Gazette*, for example, argued that railways would make Canada 'rich in revenue, teeming with population, a source of envy to her neighbors.'[14] Like Keefer, the newspaper claimed that railways were more valuable than canals because they could conquer winter conditions and provide year-round transportation. Linking its aggressive railway program to a protective tariff policy, the *Gazette* constructed a new and comprehensive economic-development platform.

It is railways, not canals in junction with sound tariff structures that will ensure that Western produce passes through Montreal and on to New England ports. Railways are ice free year round and can provide access to ice free year round ports.

Canals have cost too much already without yielding anything of profit to Montreal.

Let our present Canals go on and properly enlarge the channels of trade as you may ... but give us in Canada free and ready access to the best markets, at all seasons, and no winter barriers to trade.

All this, and nothing less, the necessities and the spirit of the age demand; by no other means possible than Railroads.[15]

Other editors carried the *Gazette*'s Montréal-centred argument further, claiming that all businessmen benefited from railways because they would stimulate manufacturing, increase trade, encourage immigration, and escalate property values. The Toronto *Globe* even went so far as to argue that, because railways had a beneficial 'magical effect' on local economies, they need not be profitable themselves. 'Our belief is, that were the property-holders of Toronto to *give* the whole sum necessary for building the [rail]road, they would have it returned in the increased value of their property. And it is not only property-holders – mechanics and tradesmen of every grade are directly interested in the matter. The trade of the city would be much increased, and the price of many necessaries of life greatly reduced. There can be no question that whether the road pays or does not pay, every business man in Toronto would be much benefitted by it.'[16]

Québec's *Morning Chronicle*, perhaps the most enthusiastic proponent of railways, advanced beyond economics and suggested that railways had moral value. 'It seems to us that the more canals, railroads and bridges there are the better. We care little about where they may head to; the U.S. railroads create trade and benefit beyond a doubt every part even of this province, while carrying off the outpourings of its industry. Of that there can be no question. That which we need still is railroads, canals, steamboats, telegraphs so that by travelling our people may gain intelligence and be excited to industry.'[17]

Like Keefer, the *Chronicle* also appealed to a unity of spirit that railways would engender among people and nations. Railways as 'the life lines of a country' are not only 'the means by which goods can be exchanged over large distances,' the *Chronicle*'s editor suggested, but also a way by which 'men can enter into extended relationships with each other.'[18] Losing himself in the enthusiasm of his own rhetoric, the editor appreciatively cited Major Carmichael Smyth, a leading proponent of a transcontinental railway: 'The time is probably not so far distant when a great railroad will be "the means of binding all the nations of the earth into one family, with mutual interests and with mutual desire of promoting the prosperity of their neighbours, in order that they may advance their own, and forming thereby the most powerful antagonistic principle to war that the earth has ever known."'[19]

The *Chronicle*, like many Canadian newspapers, echoed Keefer's *Philosophy of Railroads*, and thus reflected the complex mosaic of mid-nineteenth-century ideas. While the press differed passionately on specific political issues, they concurred on several fundamental liberal doctrines. They implicitly endorsed the deistic view of nature and its mechanical universe. They accepted the liberal faith in the supreme ability of science and technology to liberate mankind from the bonds of nature and establish mastery over it. They presumed that nations could use technology to conquer creation, to convert the wilderness into productive fields, and to attain unlimited economic and social growth. Although most decried the end of the colony's comfortable preferential position under mercantilism, they applauded Adam Smith's liberal economics and his prescriptions for the unrestricted pursuit of material growth. Like their counterparts in Great Britain and the United States, they encouraged a vigorous urban bourgeois ethic.[20] They agreed that the business élite should dominate politics and set the economic agenda. While the editors differed on specific approaches and energetically debated practical issues such as public spending and tariffs, they conceded the basic presupposition that the state must create a climate for dynamic growth. Even those who were politically conservative endorsed the liberal dogma that businessmen must be free to make a profit; in fact, the accumulation of wealth was not only legitimate but imperative.

As Keefer's *Philosophy of Railroads* so aptly demonstrated, the technology of railways and its attendant ideologies of liberal economics and science captured the imagination of British North Americans; it also subtly eroded the conservative tradition that characterized their society. Born in the Thomistic hierarchical structure of authoritarian New France, conservatism was firmly embedded in the Canadian mentality when refugees from the American Revolution fled northward and asserted British North America's loyalty to the empire. Although the Loyalists believed in the principle of representative institutions, they shared with conservative-minded immigrants and the French hierarchy the predominant belief that political power must reside with an élite, those who are educated or hold property, or as they put it, the respectable element in society. In sum, they emphasized the value of language, custom, religion, law, and community as the cement of society.[21]

Even though British North Americans supposedly rejected the social and political doctrines of liberalism, they gladly adopted its economic and technological slogans. On the one hand, many colonists maintained a strong faith in British institutions; they strove to copy its hierarchical, aristocratic society, complete with an established church; and they consciously affirmed their transatlantic ties and minimized their continental setting. On the other hand, while they consistently maintained that the aristocratic ideals of the British Empire were the antidote to the ravages of American republicanism, they antithetically adopted the view that social controls could only be preserved within a dynamic colonial economy. Among the Lower and Upper Canadian élites were many urban businessmen who enthusiastically embraced the liberal tenets of economic progress and in doing so came to admire the economic vigour of the United States.[22] As Jane Errington has so aptly demonstrated, the Upper Canadian establishment, which embraced a vibrant range of opinion, never rejected all intercourse with the southern neighbour because it realized that Canada shared with the United States a common geographic and economic destiny.[23] They supported bold schemes for improvements in transportation, for example, plans that would lead them into American markets.

For the Canadas to maintain a competitive edge in overseas markets they needed low-cost transportation.[24] The provinces possessed rudimentary trails and roads, but passenger travel was extremely hazardous, particularly in rainy weather. Meanwhile, contemporary vehicles were unable to haul the colonies' principal exports – timber and grain. Both of these commodities were bulky and heavy in relation to their value and had to be carried over extraordinarily long distances. Consequently, the St Lawrence River had become the main highway of commerce, but in the early 1820s the river system was threatened by the construction of the Erie Canal, which linked Lake Erie by way of the Mohawk and Hudson rivers to New York.[25]

The Erie Canal diminished the natural advantages of the St Lawrence River because the port of New York was superior to Montréal's. Possessing a large, ice-free harbour, only kilometres from the open ocean, New York became the most desirable gateway to the American continent. By contrast, Montréal was hundreds of foggy, icy miles from the Atlantic, a handicap reflected in higher insurance rates and pilotage charges. Nevertheless, Canadians firmly believed that they could outmanoeuvre the Americans because the Erie Canal, built only for barge traffic, was less efficient than the ship canals of the St Lawrence; they realized that the Erie required more trans-shipments, charged higher tolls, and experienced longer delays; therefore, they believed that if they could lower shipping costs on their river, Montréal could compete with New York and other Atlantic seaports.[26]

Challenged to beat American technical ingenuity, the colonial and imperial governments committed large amounts of public funds for costly improvements to the St Lawrence River, a policy forcefully encouraged by optimistic businessmen. Launched as relatively modest projects, the Welland, Lachine, and Rideau canals became expensive transportation works that did not succeed in establishing the St Lawrence as the primary waterway into the continent's interior. Unless Canada committed still more funds to refurbishing navigation on the river, it might lose all western commerce to the United States.

Meanwhile, the 1837 rebellions of small minorities against the conservative élites in Upper and Lower Canada incidentally sparked a whole new approach to the colonies' transportation problems. Lacking numbers, strong wills, and good organization, the insurrections were quickly quashed by imperial authorities, but the British government was sufficiently concerned to send Lord Durham, an uncompromising liberal aristocrat, to investigate the causes of dissatisfaction and recommend solutions. Although hastily written, Durham's report provides an important insight into the spirit of the nineteenth century; it embodied the concepts of economic and political liberalism, its firm faith in progress through science and technology. Significantly, the liberal underpinnings of the report presaged Keefer's *Philosophy of Railroads* and foreshadowed the rationale of the Guarantee Act of 1849.

The testy son of a wealthy coal-mine owner, Lord Durham represented the easy move of the old landed aristocracy into the new industrial economy.[27] Educated in the Whig tradition, Durham believed that the power of the Crown must be limited. Hence he became an active supporter of various parliamentary reform movements, earning the nickname Radical Jack. As a utilitarian, he held a very practical view of society, which clashed with some aspects of British North America's conservative politics but meshed well with its materialism.[28] His firm belief that economic prosperity and growth were crucial prerequisites for political progress provided a common touchstone for most factions in the central colonies.

Durham's report, published early in 1839, exposed his belief in economic progress based on industrialization. Repeatedly contrasting the backward character of British North America with the progress evident in the United States, Lord Durham emphasized the commercial and industrial activities of the latter, particularly its bustling transportation network consisting of a mature mix of canals, roads, and railways. In British North America, he snorted with ill-concealed disdain, 'all [with few exceptions] seems waste and desolate. There is but one railroad in all British America, and that, running between the St Lawrence and Lake Champlain, is only 15 miles long.'[29]

Equally evident in the report is Durham's innate prejudice against America's francophones. With his undiluted admiration for industrialization, Durham belittled what he thought were a rural, unprogressive people, without a history or literature, still living in a pre-industrial society.[30] His attitude also represented an arrogant confidence in the superiority and divine mission of the English people. Durham believed that North America's natural resources and channels of communication were 'the rightful patrimony of the English people, the ample appanage which God and Nature have set aside in the New World for those whose lot has assigned them but insufficient portions in the Old.'[31] By controlling the Lower Canadian legislature, however, French-speaking members hampered the economic activities of the progressive Anglo-Saxon business community. Consequently, Durham recommended the absorption of French culture into British society. Lower Canada must be given 'the national character ... of the British Empire; ... that of the great race which must, in the lapse of no long period of time, be predominant over the whole North American Continent.'[32] Thus, allowing his imperialist feelings full reign, Lord Durham advised the disenfranchisement of the French Canadians through the unification of the two Canadian colonies. If they were provided with representation by population, he prophesied, a vigorous immigration policy would result eventually in the political supremacy of English-speaking Canadians.

Durham also recommended that Britain grant the colonies a measure of self-government through the instrument of responsible or cabinet government. He did not suggest that the colonies should control fully all their economic affairs, especially not the regulation of foreign trade, but only their local, provincial concerns. Nevertheless, clearly echoing the sentiments of Adam Smith, he submitted that limited but free institutions would strengthen imperial links; they would 'continue to bind to the British Empire the ample territories of its North American Provinces.'[33]

Consolidation was a central theme in Lord Durham's report. Apart from a desire to integrate French Canada, he wanted to make the St Lawrence River a continuous highway, under one central government, penetrating deeply into the heart of the American continent.[34] He also, however, suggested the unification of all of British North America. A continental federation, he argued, 'would form a great and powerful people, possessing the means of securing good and responsible government for itself, and which, under the protection of the British Empire, might in some measure counterbalance the preponderant and increasing influence of the United States on the American Continent.'[35] In sum, Durham envisioned a British-held northern American free-trade market, a thriving commercial system to serve as the economic foundation for a prosperous, self-governing nation, able to support itself and thus no longer a drain on imperial resources.

To make the union of British North America viable, Durham recommended the construction of a railway between Halifax and Québec, which 'would, in fact, produce relations between these Provinces, that would render a general union absolutely necessary.'[36] Noting that previous surveys pronounced the scheme feasible, Durham concluded that 'the formation of a railroad from Halifax to Quebec would entirely alter some of the distinguishing characteristics of the Canadas. Instead of being shut out from all direct intercourse with England during half the year, they would possess a far more certain and speedy communication throughout the winter than they now possess in summer.'[37] An intercolonial railway would reduce the journey from Ireland to Québec to ten to twelve days 'and Halifax would be the great port by which a large portion of the trade, and all the conveyance of passengers to the whole of British North America, would be carried on.' A railway, of common interest to all colonies as well as the imperial government, made good sense, Durham concluded, for if the St Lawrence River provided a rationale for uniting the Canadas, then 'the artificial work which would, in fact, supersede the lower part of the St Lawrence, as the outlet of a great part of the Canadian trade, and would make Halifax, in a great measure, an outport to Quebec, would surely in the same way render it advisable that the incorporation should be extended to Provinces through which such a road would pass.'[38]

In the report's appendix B, Charles Buller, Durham's secretary, gave economic legitimacy to Durham's seemingly visionary intercolonial railway scheme. Borrowing freely from Edward Gibbon Wakefield's theories on colonial emigration, Buller argued that the proceeds from the sale of Crown lands could be used as a subsidy to private enterprise for constructing canals, roads, and railways.[39]

Durham's prophetic comments on an intercolonial railway previewed a half-century of debate in British North America. Touting an intercolonial as an iron bond linking the colonies, as a channel for trade and commerce into the heart of the continent, Durham advanced ideas that recurred in countless editorials, books, pamphlets, and speeches. His prediction that the Halifax–Québec railway would become a vital stage in the St Lawrence seaway to the Great Lakes and the American Midwest became an equally popular topic in subsequent discussions. Significantly, like many British North Americans, Lord Durham believed that the northern provinces were distinctly British and should remain so. He proposed an intercolonial railway as a means to create a robust nation and thus maintain strong imperial bonds. Ironically, he also articulated the curious mixture of envy and fear, the undisguised admiration for America's progressive and prosperous economy, and the candid apprehension about that nation's increasingly dominant position on the continent. Subsequently, Canadians would unambiguously seek to tap into their neighbour's wealth by constructing efficient north–south transportation systems while advocating separate political cultures. That seemingly contradictory position was based on the optimistic assertion of economic progress through industrialization and efficient transportation, a principle so eloquently enunciated in Durham's report. Thus, hidden in his case are all the essential components of the philosophy of railways.

For the time being, however, Canadians rejected Durham's transportation schemes as visionary. With the union of the Canadas in 1841, they launched another canal-building program instead. The combined credit of two provinces, bolstered by an imperial guaranteed loan, established the broad financial base essential for costly undertakings. In 1843, the province completed the three Cornwall canals, which totalled 19 kilometres and comprised six locks, at a cost of nearly $2 million. The nine locks of the 18-km Beauharnois Canal, completed in 1845, cost $1.3 million. Three years later, six more locks were completed near Williamsburg. Meanwhile, the government deepened both the Welland and Lachine canals to nearly three metres.[40] Thus, more than twenty years after the Americans completed the Erie Canal, Canadians finished a seaway that allowed unhampered passage of relatively large steamers from Montréal to Sault Ste Marie.

Recognizing an opportunity, Canadians had demonstrated that they were willing to vote public funds for transportation projects. On the surface, they had every reason to assume that if they took advantage of the mighty St Lawrence, their economic future was assured. Typical of the rhetoric of technological expansion, however, the completion of one project exposed the need for another undertaking elsewhere, which in turn necessitated improvements still further along the system. Meanwhile, politicians rationalized that the greater the outlay, the heavier the traffic a canal could accommodate, and the bigger the income available for still larger public works. By this circular reasoning, the St Lawrence canals emerged as expensive but important models for future colonial policies. Navigation improvements on the river had become an accepted public expenditure because the construction of canals supposedly was essential to the economic and political survival of a united Canada.[41] Technological nationalism was making its appearance.

The remarkable growth of the Canadian economy in the early 1840s appeared to vindicate the confidence in canal technology. The construction of the canals themselves created employment and stimulated industrial development; the projects also inspired confidence in the Canadian economy that encouraged further investment. Meanwhile, the frantic railway boom in Great Britain produced an insatiable demand for railway ties, sharply stimulating Canada's timber industry. Lumber sales to Britain, which constituted two-thirds of Canadian exports, rose to 7.3 million metres in 1845. Similarly, by 1843, the Canada Corn Act gave colonial wheat and flour a substantial preference on the British market. The flow of grain and flour via the St Lawrence mushroomed from 1.2 million bushels in 1843 to 3.3 million in 1846.[42] While the impact of imperial preferences upon Canadian commerce may have been less important than bumper crops and increased immigration, colonial merchants were pleased. They believed that preferential tariffs, combined with superior canal technology, enabled them to beat the Americans in Britain. In anticipation of increased business, they significantly expanded their flour-milling and grain-handling facilities.[43]

Colonial merchants should have known that the Canada Corn Law was only a tack in the course that British Prime Minister Robert Peel had set towards free trade and the elimination of the preferential structure. Pressure from British industrial interests, who wanted cheap food for their labourers, slowly moved Peel's Tory government towards free trade. Relentlessly, liberal thinkers preached the economic gospel of free trade and denounced preferential tariffs and the cost of defending the colonies. The final blow, which destroyed the old imperial structure, was the terrible Irish potato famine, which called for massive importations of cheap grain. In the spring of 1846, the Peel government, backed by the Whig-Liberal opposition, repealed the Corn Laws, symbols of the old imperialism. That summer, John Russell's free-trade Whigs captured the government and enthusiastically set out to dismantle the last remnants of mercantilism. The new colonial secretary, Earl Grey, an ardent free-trade liberal, launched a vigorous campaign to reform the political and economic structures of the colonies.[44]

Coincidentally, the United States government passed a series of drawback laws that exempted from customs duties all Canadian imports and exports passing through American channels. This policy had a profound effect upon the St Lawrence system because Upper Canadians preferred to import items like tea and sugar, or export wheat, by way of New York, already the cheapest route. The drawback laws, combined with the end of preferential treatment on the British market, seriously threatened the almost completed St Lawrence canal system. Still, Montréal shippers were confident that the canals, which could accommodate screw steamers, were superior to the Erie system, which was limited to horse-drawn barges. The Montréal *Gazette* trumpeted: 'when the internal communications of this Colony are completed and the trade in Western produce put on a regular footing, the artificial superiority [of New York] will rapidly disappear.'[45] Shrewd Montréal merchants, however, began to discuss the construction of a railway to the Atlantic seaboard, while the provincial government prudently lowered import duties on American grain.[46]

The repeal of the Corn Laws and the institution of the drawback acts forced Canadians to reassess their economic policies. Perhaps they might have accepted the new order more peacefully had the Western world economy not collapsed in the late 1840s and exposed the province's vulnerability to global conditions. In the first instance, the tragic Irish potato famine sparked an unparalleled flood of immigrants to Canada. In 1847, more than 90,000 destitute, starving, and often sickly Irish refugees descended on the colony. Canada, faced with feeding and treating them, rigidly restricted immigration the following year, but the Irish problem was a severe drain on the provincial treasury. Coincident with Irish immigration came the collapse of the British railway boom, deflating the demand for railway ties and seriously damaging Canada's lumber industry, already suffering from serious over-cutting.[47] In the summer of 1848, as an economic depression settled on the Western world and Europe flared in revolution, Canadians, too, were restless. That winter, with the warehouses of Montréal full of wheat and flour, with ships frozen at their wharves, the price of grain began to tumble. Many merchants, millers, and shippers, with heavy investments in the forwarding process, were in deep distress. Bankruptcies were common and unemployment massive. The coffers of church and state emptied as Montréal experienced unprecedented cries for charity.

Thus opened 1849. Beaten by economic depression, alienated by British free-trade policies, and outwitted by American technological progress, Montréal's businessmen faced a bleak future. Moreover, at that very moment they faced the loss of political power. Contrary to expectations, the disenfranchisement of the *Canadien* proposed by Lord Durham had not occurred. In fact, English-speaking, reform-minded politicians had been able to forge an alliance with French Canadians and force the principle of responsible government upon the Legislative Assembly. Taking advantage of the governorship of Lord Elgin, who as son-in-law of Lord Durham shared his belief that responsible government was necessary to keep the colonies in the empire, French Canada attained political power. The midwinter election of 1847–8 produced an overwhelming Reform victory in both Canada East and West, permitting the formation of a politically liberal reform alliance under the dual leadership of Louis-Hippolyte La Fontaine and Robert Baldwin.[48] The test of the coalition's power came early in 1849 when the government proposed a bill to compensate Lower Canadians for losses suffered in the rebellion of 1837, including some of the leaders in that uprising. In the late afternoon of 25 April 1849, the resilient Lord Elgin, personally opposed to the measure but constitutionally bound to uphold it, signed the Rebellion Losses Bill into law. That evening, angry Tories burned the parliament buildings.

Obviously, the rampaging Tories saw the Rebellion Losses Act as proof of French domination, but the legislation had greater import to them than impending political impotence.[49] While the principle of responsible government was reprehensible to politically conservative colonists, its implementation hardly advanced Canada to the contemporary level of constitutional development in Britain. Rather, to conservative minds, responsible government represented the dissolution of the empire. They could not believe that self-governing colonies could remain loyal to British objectives.[50] Yet, even this apprehension, grounded in fundamental ideology, would not have led them to a violent act that contradicted the very essence of conservative doctrine – loyalty to constituted authority. To be sure, the rebellious Tories resented the victory of liberalism in imperial politics, but that concern was insufficient for an act of disobedience to the representative of the Crown. Thus they cheered lustily when a Tory politician rescued Queen Victoria's portrait from the blazing parliament building. The real fear that drove Montréal's staid establishment to riot was the full impact of Smith's economic principles on their ledger books. His liberal economics appeared to threaten their very existence; free trade and responsible government brought the realization that Canadians had to fend for themselves on the world market. The collective temper of the Montréal business community, disproportionately represented in the Tory party, snapped. The Rebellion Losses Act, the symbol of their political emasculation, was the last straw. Feeling abandoned by Britain and vulnerable to world competition, they rioted.

Behind the revolt of the Montréal Tories also lay the fear that new forms of transportation were eroding traditional paths of commerce. The spread of railways in North America rendered Canada's expensive canal system obsolete just as it became fully operational. The Tory merchants struck out in fear and anger at the powers that seemed to be destroying their existence but their panic-stricken rearguard action was doomed to fail because it resisted the momentum of history. The ideology of liberalism, which introduced responsible government and free trade to British America, was too strong to be reversed; by opposing overwhelming revolutionary changes, the Montréal Tories momentarily lost the initiative.

The rapid introduction of a new order and the loss of Montréal's transportation advantage impelled the bewildered Tories to re-examine their commercial policies. Their initial reaction, sparked by feelings of betrayal and the apparent loss of imperial unity, was anger. They discussed union with the United States and in the fall of 1849 issued the Annexation Manifesto. This remarkable document, signed by many prominent businessmen, sharply rebuked Britain for abandoning her colony and expressed a strong desire to join America's economic empire with its expanding markets, abundant capital, Atlantic ports, and protective tariffs.[51] Although the change in loyalties appeared dramatic, it was easily made. Businessmen were more committed to the mercantilistic position of the city than to empires of culture or sentiment. The manifesto revealed that some Montréalers were ready to sacrifice the fledgling economic nationalism of the Canadas on the altar of continentalism. Economic efficiency, they argued, demanded that obsolete policies be dismantled in favour of new means to wealth; business sense required Montréal's absorption into the financial and transportation systems of the United States.

Montréal's annexationist outburst impelled the Tories of Canada West to form the British American League, which sought to define Canada's place in the new economic order with retrenchment in government spending, a protective tariff for home industry, and a union of British North America.[52] Like the Annexation Manifesto, the British American League found little support in the colonies, and the union idea dissipated once annexationism faded from public view. The positive notes struck at its meetings were lost in a cacophony of negative causes espoused by the myriad of political factions it represented.[53] Nevertheless, the league had made public a rudimentary policy, which rejected Canada's exclusive reliance on the export of its natural resources.[54]

The league's call for a protective tariff to stimulate the growth of factories received inspiration from similar movements in the United States and Europe, where the manufacturing wealth of Britain had kindled an industrial consciousness.[55] In 1791, Alexander Hamilton, the American secretary-treasurer, had endeavoured to strengthen the power of the young nation with a vigorous industrialization policy that included temporary high tariffs to foster infant industries.[56] By the late 1820s, the United States had adopted high tariffs as a strategy to encourage manufacturing, as a step towards material prosperity, economic self-sufficiency, and national strength.[57] Meanwhile in Europe, Friedrich List sought to help Germany counter the overwhelming superiority of British manufacturing through commercial union of all the German states, free importation of agricultural products and raw materials, a protective tariff for domestic industries, and a national system of railways.[58] List's ideas were echoed, during the 1830s, by Louis Kossuth in his drive for a Hungarian national economy. Factories, tariffs, and railways appeared to be replacing law, spirit, and culture as the building blocks of nationhood, a trend eagerly accepted in the Canadas.

In the 1820s the writings of John Rae, the province's most original economic thinker, launched the protectionist movement in Canada. Rae argued that technological progress was essential to a nation's economic welfare. The state should grant subsidies for inventions, technical schools, and transportation; it should establish protective tariffs to encourage manufacturing and stimulate economic growth.[59] A select committee of the Upper Canadian legislature echoed Rae's teachings, but without self-government such statements were mere rhetoric.[60] With the union of the Canadas, however, protectionist feelings became more pronounced. Increasingly apprehensive about the rising industrial power of the United States and the free-trade movement in Great Britain, Canada increased its tariffs, an act that was disallowed by the imperial government because the measure was hostile to British manufacturers. A year later, in 1846, Canada's response to the repeal of the British Corn Laws was a retaliatory tariff: it decreased the tariff on American goods but raised it on British products, bringing both to the same level.[61]

Industrialization, fostered by high tariffs, was not the direction the imperial government wanted Canada to take. Late in 1846, the colonial secretary, Lord Grey, penned a detailed memorandum in which he argued in typically liberal, laissez-faire fashion that industry had to emerge naturally, without state assistance. Industrialization and commerce, he warned, could only be stimulated by low rather than high tariffs. On a more positive note, Grey outlined a broad economic strategy for British North America. The colonial secretary, who wanted the colonies to be economically self-sufficient, suggested the unification of the colonies in one large common market, linked by an intercolonial railway.[62] 'I am convinced,' he wrote Lord Elgin, 'that there is nothing more important to their interest & also to ours' than to have a union of the colonies.[63] In the end, Grey approved the tariff and subsequent increases only because, in his opinion, they were more expressly designed for revenue rather than for protection.[64]

When the Reform party came to power, it raised the tariff, but primarily to increase government revenues. As disciples of English liberalism, supported by agrarian French Canada, they were theoretically free traders. In practice, however, their position was confused. Robert Baldwin Sullivan, the provincial secretary in the La Fontaine–Baldwin ministry, was a vocal advocate of industrialism and protection. In a passionate lecture to the Mechanics' Institute of Hamilton he likened Canadians to plantation slaves toiling for their British masters. Canada was a poor, 'semi-barbarous' province because she had no manufacturing sector to create real wealth. 'Unless you have in your country the classes of men in whose hands money will accumulate, the nature of whose occupation makes them natural reservoirs, and conductors of money, as the motive power of enterprise, you must, as a country, be, and continue helpless, dependent, and inferior.'[65] Sullivan's strident economic nationalism, founded on industrialization, was at odds with the classic free-trade thought of Canada's inspector-general, Francis Hincks. 'You cannot protect any class of labourers,' Hincks argued, 'except at the expense of the great body of consumers; and the error into which persons reasoning on this point are apt to fall, is that of considering themselves only in the light of producers, instead of consumers, which all persons are.'[66] Because it sheltered such diverse views, the Reform ministry was neither protectionist nor purely free trade. In a way, the debate within the party mirrored the furious discussion in the province at large, a controversy that attempted to define Canada's place in the new economic order.

Tariff protection, colonial union, and annexation gradually disappeared as politically unacceptable schemes. Protectionism and unification were premature concepts, legitimate choices for the future, while annexation was but a symptom of a distressed era, a blip on the provincial consciousness.[67] The quick rejection of the Annexation Manifesto and the flirtation with protection demonstrated that Canadians desired a destiny independent from the United States. But that was not a decisive resolution. Powerful forces were seeking closer economic ties with the southern neighbour. Particularly strong among Upper Canadian grain merchants was the reciprocity movement, which proposed free trade between British North America and the United States on several designated unprocessed natural products. In 1849, William Hamilton Merritt, a prominent Welland grain dealer, successfully guided a motion favouring reciprocity through the legislature. Although a similar measure failed in the United States Congress, Merritt travelled to New York as a government member but found little support.[68] Reciprocity with the United States was another premature alternative.

Throughout turbulent 1849, then, Canadians debated their economic future. The old imperial order, in which British North America enjoyed preferential treatment, was consumed in the flames of the Parliament Building, forcing Canadians to adjust to an open, competitive world market. While still uncertain about their position within the new empire and ambiguous about their relations with the United States, they refused to accept a pure, comprehensive free-trade policy. Instead, the various ideas – protection, unification, and even reciprocity – separately proposed and vigorously debated, gradually moved the colonists towards an integrated political economy that rejected doctrinaire liberal economics as an effective method of combatting British industrial power.

Pre-eminent in the Canadian approach to economic development was transportation. All options – unification, industrialization, or reciprocity – hinged on finding an efficient means of shipping goods over immense distances. Canadian merchants, facing incredible geographical and climatic obstacles, naturally devoted much of their energy to establishing efficient transportation techniques. Not surprisingly, the steam railway, which seemingly defied geographic and climatic barriers, became the central feature of the restructuring of the Canadian economy. The railway assumed such great importance because for five months of the year, the St Lawrence river lay frozen, its thick ice mass trapping ships, and preventing travel except by sled. The winter season relentlessly regulated business, affecting it more dramatically than economic cycles. For decades, merchants closed their offices during winter while millers shut their plants. Without the use of the river, Canada hibernated.

In 1849, ice threatened the empire of the St Lawrence more ominously than ever before. While Montréal languished, bustling railways were carrying goods to Boston and New York in defiance of snow and ice. Frustrated Montréal merchants, yearning to compete with their Atlantic rivals for the lucrative western trade, determined to build a railway to an Atlantic seaport. They had two options: the first, a route entirely through British territory from Québec to Halifax, the other, a line by way of the United States from Montréal to Portland, Maine. While both concepts merited serious consideration and competed for government support, the routes they proposed reflected and affected the debate on the place of Canada in the American continent and in the British empire. That debate also influenced the wording of the Guarantee Act.

The Halifax-Québec railway concept was not new, having surfaced first in the late 1820s. It was revived periodically in subsequent years, but never moved beyond preliminary surveys, partly because of the simmering dispute over the Maine–New Brunswick border. The Webster-Ashburton

Treaty of 1842, which settled the controversy, thrust Maine far northward, forcing any planned intercolonial to make a tortuously long detour.[69] In 1846, the three mainland British North American legislatures petitioned the British government to order a survey, at colonial expense, to determine a feasible route from Halifax to the St Lawrence River, and two years later Major W. Robinson, a British engineer, recommended a 1000-km railway skirting the northern shore of New Brunswick. While he emphasized the necessity of this road for the defence of the colonies, most of his report was a detailed justification of the economic feasibility of the northern route, noting especially the agricultural potential of New Brunswick as a haven for immigrants. He also believed that an intercolonial railway would enable the St Lawrence system to compete successfully with Boston and New York for western traffic. 'Ultimately,' Robinson concluded, 'if not at once, the line will in a commercial point of view be a very productive one.'[70] Moreover, he added, it promised to be the first step towards the union of British North America.

Colonial Secretary Earl Grey received Robinson's report with mixed feelings. On the one hand, an intercolonial railway was central to his plans for restructuring and integrating the British North American economy so it could be weaned from imperial support. He proposed to recruit about 24,000 destitute Irishmen and to train them as soldiers and railway labourers. When not on military duty, the men would work on the intercolonial railway and be paid in cash and land. 'I am more & more persuaded that it is not wise to attempt in the first instance to settle Emigrants on Land,' he lectured Lord Elgin, for 'the right course is to provide them the means of maintaining themselves by Labor by opening roads ... until they can purchase land for themselves from their savings.'[71] Military discipline was also essential to success. 'The wild Irish of the Western Counties are so utterly ignorant of all useful labor at present that they are not easy to provide for when they first arrive in the Colonies,' he added, 'but they are peculiarly teachable & capable of being disciplined, and under good officers wd soon become excellent laborers, & while employed upon the railway wd learn what wd be of great use to them afterwards as settlers.'[72] Grey also suggested that the emigrants be settled on prepared land and housed in small villages along the railway. His approach would, he thought, significantly lower construction costs, alleviate the problem of overpopulation in Ireland, add to garrison strength in the colony, and ease the imperial defence burden. Lastly, railway construction would increase land values in the colonies, stimulate resource development, and encourage further investment. According to Earl Grey, then, an intercolonial railway was the panacea for the transportation, immigration, defence, and economic problems of the colonies.[73]

Since the colonial governments stood to benefit directly from the project, Grey believed that they should be prepared to make substantial contributions. While all the necessary funds could be raised in the United Kingdom through the sale of bonds, the provinces should be willing to guarantee and pay the interest on these bonds by means of a duty on British North American timber landed in Great Britain. He also suggested that a committee sell all ungranted Crown lands in the colonies and use the proceeds for railway construction and emigration promotion. Despite his demand that the colonies should bear the brunt of construction costs, he did not believe that cabinet would approve the scheme.[74]

Various circumstances dictated Grey's parsimony. The Board of Railway Commissioners for Great Britain rejected the Halifax-Québec railway on the grounds that it was not economically viable and could only be justified on the basis of emigration and defence. With the economic depression eroding government revenues, the tight-fisted Whig-Liberals in the House of Commons refused to approve expenditures designed to benefit only the colonial economies. Lastly, the burning of the legislative buildings and the Annexation Manifesto completely eroded investor confidence in the venture.[75]

Britain's reluctance to support the intercolonial even in principle disappointed Lord Elgin. 'As a merely commercial speculation it [an intercolonial railway] has very little to recommend it,' he pleaded and suggested that even with the immigration program it would be too expensive for colonial treasuries.[76] 'With respect to the employment of Immigrants on Public Works,' he suggested to Earl Grey, 'you must allow me to observe that money is indispensable to all schemes of this nature and in the present condition of the market this commodity is not procurable on colonial Securities.'[77] With characteristic realism, Elgin solicited imperial financial assistance in order to make this non-commercial venture attractive to investors. He protested that it was unfair to expect the provinces to make firm commitments without reciprocal assurances of imperial support.[78] Steadfast in his conviction that only prosperity would keep the colonies in the empire, Elgin's pragmatic views reflected the important place that railway technology had assumed in contemporary economic thought:

So confident am I that the mere undertaking of the work in question will tend to raise the Colonists from the despondency into which recent changes in the Commercial Policy of the Empire have plunged them – to unite the Provinces to one another and to the Mother Country – to inspire them with that consciousness of their own strength and of the value of the connexion with Great Britain – which is their best security against aggression, – that I would not hesitate to recommend that an immediate and considerable reduction should take place in the Force stationed in Canada in the event of the execution of the Quebec and Halifax Railway being determined on.[79]

Imperial authorities thus advocated an intercolonial railway as an instrument to unite British North America and wean it from imperial financial and military support. The railway was to be an integral component of the political economy of a new northern nation, helping to make it distinctly different from its southern neighbour; yet, while the projected intercolonial was to be a defining element of the new nation, it was clearly an imperial project, an efficient instrument for spreading British civilization and economic influence across the entire continent. Elgin's colleague, Sir John Harvey, lieutenant-governor of Nova Scotia, boldly prophesied that the intercolonial was to become the most important link 'in the great line of communication which may be destined at no remote period to connect the Atlantic with the Pacific.'[80] A British author added that Britain should renew the attempt to reach the Far East by way of the northern Atlantic route. 'We shall yet place an iron belt from the Atlantic to the Pacific, a railroad from Halifax to Nootka Sound, and thus reach China in a pleasure voyage.'[81] Thus, according to some, an intercolonial was but the first stage in a railway that would replicate the old fur trade across the rugged Canadian Shield, vast prairies, and majestic Rockies to the Pacific Ocean. It would also provide the empire with the long-sought North-West Passage to the Orient.[82]

By 1849, therefore, a transcontinental railway was but a vision shared by ardent imperialists, an imperial project designed to uphold the power and wealth of a grand empire. Few of Canada's citizens shared the dream and only a handful of its political and business élite talked seriously about such an enormous venture. Subsequently, whenever British North America's politicians met to plan the eastern portion of a transcontinental they squabbled and quarrelled endlessly about details. They could not reach an agreement until 1867, when the intercolonial became part of the confederation accord. Still, the newly formed Dominion government required more than a decade of bitter debates and fierce opposition before commencing a concerted effort to construct the Pacific railway.

Without imperial assistance for railway construction, Canadians refused to consider Halifax their primary Atlantic port. They turned to more practical plans to gain competitive access to ice-free harbours. One such scheme proposed to connect Montréal to Portland, Maine, via the Eastern Townships. This concept had gained prominence in 1845, when John A. Poor, a Bangor lawyer, popularized the idea amidst growing concerns about the advent of free trade.[83] Canada East's business community recognized the value of the projected railway. In a clearly argued public letter, Alexander T. Galt, the commissioner of the British American Land Company, a London-based firm holding extensive properties in the Eastern Townships, reasoned that transportation costs from the Great Lakes to Montréal were less than to New York or Boston; consequently, a rail connection to Portland would enable the merchants of Montréal to expand beyond the confines of Canada and compete with American ports for the rich and growing markets south of the Great Lakes. Galt challenged his readers to consider 'that the same causes which render New York or Boston the seaports for Canada West, equally entitle Montréal or Québec to compete with them for the trade of the vast territory of the United States, around or near the Great Lakes.'[84] This region, which already had a population 'of five million, and [was] increasing with unexampled rapidity,' would dwarf the existing provincial market and bring untold wealth to British and Canadian investors. Galt's panoramic vision placed the commercial welfare of Montréal in a continental perspective; he set it squarely within the broad context of North American trading patterns. His message received broad support among the realistic businessmen strategically ensconced in the legislature. That a railway to Portland must traverse American soil was of little concern to them. They knew the direct Montréal-Portland route was commercially viable; the circuitous Québec-Halifax line was not.

Alexander Galt, a Scottish-born businessman, shrewdly recognized the impact the Portland railway would have on the value of his company's lands and assumed a leading role in implementing Poor's railway scheme. He persuaded several of his Montréal friends to form the St Lawrence and Atlantic Railway Company to build a line from Montréal to Vermont to meet with the Atlantic and St Lawrence coming from Portland. Although the list of incorporators was an impressive cross-section of wealthy Montréalers, they were too timid to finance such a long-term, unprecedented venture themselves, and they dispatched Galt to London in the summer of 1845 to seek financial support among his business associates. Reaching London at the height of the railway mania, Galt quickly gathered sufficient backing only to lose it within the year when the boom collapsed. Most of his backers wanted to withdraw as well, but Galt, unabashed, persuaded a few directors to sign a commitment to begin construction in the spring of

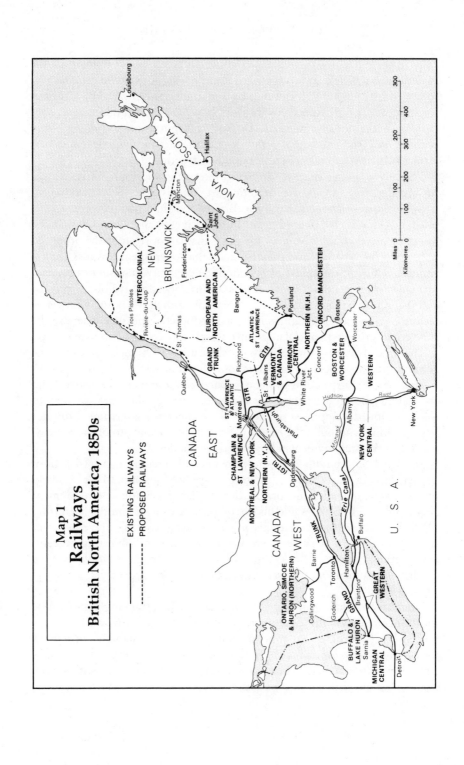

Map 1
Railways
British North America, 1850s

——— EXISTING RAILWAYS
- - - - PROPOSED RAILWAYS

1846. This audacious move, which coincided with the enactment of the American drawback laws, was narrowly approved by the board, and was followed by a highly successful campaign among the citizens of Montréal for support. The provincial government, however, proved reluctant to contribute to the advancement of the new transportation technology, and without government backing the St Lawrence and Atlantic could not attract sufficient capital to permit rapid construction.[85]

The severe winter of 1848–9 revived interest in the Portland railway as Montréal's exit to an ice-free Atlantic port. Shortly after the annual freeze-up, grain prices dropped sharply in Britain and the value of wheat stockpiled in the city fell accordingly. Irate businessmen calculated that the losses incurred could have paid for the Canadian portion of the proposed railway to the Atlantic, and they prodded the government to subsidize the venture. Thus, in the midst of economic uncertainty and political unrest, provincial politicians set aside partisan considerations, regional interests, and theoretical debates. United by a common faith in the positive power of technology and an impending crisis, they adopted a measure whereby the state could provide financial assistance for railway construction.

The task of writing the subsidy legislation fell to Francis Hincks, Canada's inspector-general. Hincks favoured public assistance to railways because large construction projects created employment. He insisted that the St Lawrence and Atlantic, for example, was a public work essential to the economic development of the province. Since the government did not have the money to build the road by itself, he was willing to provide financial aid to privately owned and operated companies.[86]

Steeped from childhood in the principles of liberalism, the Irish-born Francis Hincks was ideally suited to prepare the legislation. Like so many of his contemporaries, he pragmatically placed economic development above political reform. While his liberal principles won him the friendship of William Lyon Mackenzie, his practical business sense prevented him from following the fiery Scot into the 1837 rebellion. Preferring peaceful constitutional reform, Hincks argued that armed resistance would damage English investment in the province and seriously impede its economic progress.[87]

Practical economics continued to dictate Hincks's thinking. As editor of the reform journal the *Examiner*, he stridently and provocatively supported Lord Durham's attempt to create a politically stable environment for economic development. This willingness to compromise political principles for economic benefits clouded his prominent role in the struggle for responsible government and he lost the full trust of the reformers, especially when, as Governor Bagot's inspector-general, he overrode his free-trade principles and raised the tariff in order to increase revenues. But in 1844 he regained Baldwin's friendship by resigning his cabinet post on a patronage issue. Shrewdly reasoning that an alliance between French and English Canadian reformers would result in a reform majority in the house, Hincks also helped engineer the coalition of Louis-Hippolyte La Fontaine and Robert Baldwin, a partnership that brought them political power in 1848.[88]

In the spring of 1848, when Hincks was forty-one years old, Lord Elgin named him inspector-general in the La Fontaine–Baldwin administration. At the height of his physical and mental abilities, Hincks was the outstanding thinker on the province's financial and economic issues. When he assumed office, Canada faced a serious financial crisis. The economic depression had sharply reduced trade and tariff revenues, making it difficult for the province to meet its financial obligations. Nevertheless, Hincks passionately argued that the best way to reduce the era's political discord was to stimulate the economy with the construction of public works.[89] Because he deemed them essential to Canada's economic development, he claimed that railways, like canals, should be considered public works, deserving state support. Unfortunately, the province's depleted treasury made it difficult to devise a feasible economic policy. Moreover, British investors were not interested in Canadian securities, partly because they were rarely offered for sale but also because investors feared that the colonies would soon leave the empire and might repudiate foreign debts.[90]

In December 1848, Francis Hincks wrote a lengthy memorandum for the Colonial Office outlining how the province could support the construction of railways without adding to its public debt. 'The great disadvantage under which Canada labours,' he explained, 'arises from the want of capital required to construct those Public Works which have become almost indispensable as auxiliaries to the canals on securing the Western trade.'[91] Unlike Americans, Canadians did not invest their money in industries but in land development schemes, which yielded virtually no surplus capital for transportation development. Therefore, Hincks continued, the government had been forced to pay for the St Lawrence canals, a system rendered idle by the imperial government's free-trade policy. Under these conditions, Canada could neither borrow on the English money market nor take on further debts on transportation works.

Nevertheless, railways were essential to the economic development of the province. The plans for a branch line from Québec to Sherbrooke to link with the proposed Halifax-Québec railway was 'almost indispensable.'

A Montréal-Portland railway was needed, Hincks wrote, to 'open an extensive market for Western produce all of which will pay toll on the canals.' Improvements to the Québec harbour were also necessary, as were the plans for a canal from the St Lawrence to Lake Champlain and a railway to the Ottawa valley. In Upper Canada, the most notable project was the Great Western Railway, intended to connect the New York Central in the east with the Michigan Central in the west.[92] The proposed incorporation of a Toronto-Huron railway would also benefit the province as a whole and thus deserved provincial support. With 'reasonable encouragement,' Hincks believed all these projects could be completed.

To help finance Canada's ambitious plans, Hincks echoed Earl Grey's suggestion that immigrants help construct transportation projects. He proposed that the imperial government subsidize emigration to Canada. Assisted emigration would benefit the mother country, he argued, because it would relieve her of surplus population and increase her market for manufactured goods. Hincks cleverly pointed out that for various reasons British emigrants preferred the United States, where they bought domestically produced goods protected by high tariffs. Settlers diverted to Canada, however, would raise agricultural products for the British market in exchange for her manufactured commodities. Moreover, Hincks argued, while working on Canadian public works, labourers could earn enough money to buy land. 'It appears clear therefore that the furtherance of an extensive scheme of colonization may safely be combined with the profitable investment of capital.' He believed that subsidized emigration and railway construction were inextricably intertwined. Although railways were still, in Hincks's mind, only a necessary prelude to settlement, the hint that large-scale immigration was crucial to the success of railways was becoming apparent.

Another theme in Hincks's memo was the vital role that Canada's vast lands could play in railway construction. In the first place, Crown lands provided the security for the bonds, debentures, and imperial guarantees needed to construct a rail network. Paying the large numbers of workers with land would significantly reduce the cost of labour. Moreover, railway construction would provide opportunities for immigrants to earn enough money to buy land. And lastly, as a beneficial side-effect, railways would increase land values, attracting more immigrants and earning more money for the provincial government. In this circular fashion, Hincks skilfully wove his railway, immigration, and land schemes into a coherent development policy. It was an argument a succession of Canadian governments would reiterate to justify their railway plans.

Several months after composing his memorandum, Hincks introduced the Guarantee bill into the legislature. Whereas in his 1848 memorandum he had suggested that the province pay half of construction costs, by 1849, after he had travelled to London to arrange a substantial loan, the draft legislation was more restrictive. Undoubtedly influenced by the province's London bankers, the legislation only secured the interest on railway bonds. Specifically, the bill guaranteed an interest of 6 per cent on the bonds of any railway at least 120 kilometres long and half completed.[93] In defence of his measure, Hincks argued that railways were 'necessary to the prosperity and advancement of the Province.'[94] In thinly populated countries, he continued, governments had to assist private railway companies to finance their lines.

Hincks was preaching to the converted, however, and the assembly, which included several directors of the St Lawrence and Atlantic as well as other railways, passed the legislation with virtually no opposition. The bill appealed even to members of Canada's conservative élite, which contained a strong contingent of urban entrepreneurs. These businessmen willingly accepted the economic-progress platform of the Reformers, a program that eventually translated into a steadfast confidence in railway technology as the panacea for Canada's economic, political, and diplomatic problems. While they continued to disagree fundamentally about their political agendas, moderates in the conservative and reform camps merely quarrelled about the details of the government's economic-development plans.

Given the broad agreement on economic issues, for instance, it is not surprising that Hincks's Guarantee bill received strong support from Sir Allan Napier MacNab, an inveterate Tory politician and Hamilton businessman. Intensely ambitious, MacNab was a lawyer by profession, a wealthy land speculator, founder of the Gore Bank of Hamilton, and owner of a steamship business. Family background, law career, and political ambitions tied MacNab to the provincial establishment, but his Tory stands were often more the result of pragmatic considerations than partisan concerns. As a result, his political positions were not easily predicted. Although a deep emotional attachment to the British empire dominated all his political actions, he eagerly encouraged American investment in Canadian enterprises and American immigration to his properties.[95] Throughout MacNab's erratic political career, one strand remains consistent, however – an ideological belief in economic progress as the best means to preserve his ideal society. All his political postures betrayed the complex mixture of flexible Tory attitudes streaked with liberal tendencies and commercial ambitions. Although a vehement defender of privilege and social class, MacNab unwittingly but relentlessly promoted the technology that destroyed his beloved old pre-industrial society.

Among his many business interests, MacNab was also president of the Great Western Railway. Incorporated in 1845, the Great Western was designed primarily to provide a shortcut between New York and Michigan by way of the Niagara River, Hamilton, and Windsor. Initially its promoters failed to find sufficient capital for the venture, and thus MacNab eagerly awaited passage of the Guarantee bill.[96] While he would strongly object to Canadian assistance to an intercolonial railway because it offered no advantages to Upper Canada, he eagerly supported state subsidies to less ambitious plans, particularly if they assisted his own enterprise.

MacNab's position, in sum, was at best paradoxical. Although a committed imperialist, he clearly recognized that his Great Western Railway was merely a thoroughfare between the eastern and midwestern United States. Even though he was fiercely conservative, he must have recognized the social and political changes the introduction of modern transportation technologies would bring to the province. To be sure, the fabulous profits from railway bonds and land speculation must have stilled the fear of social and political change; in any case, economic objectives transcended political, social, sectarian, and even ethnic differences, and MacNab found common cause with many moderate reformers. His undaunted faith in economic progress and the powers of technology permitted a sympathetic understanding of the economic objectives of moderate Reformers. Confessing that his politics 'were all railroads,' MacNab 'resolved to support any party that would carry on the railways of the country. He did this because nothing could conduce more to the prosperity of Canada than the construction of railroads.'[97]

Personal profit obviously affected Sir Allan MacNab's views; nevertheless, his belief in economic progress, encapsulated in his motto, softened his arch-Toryism, and after 1849 he helped Hincks bridge the gap between moderate Conservatives and moderate Reformers. His opinions also represented the connection between the pre-industrial colonial economy and the age of steam and industry. After succeeding Hincks in 1854, his administration completed several broad social reforms that prepared the province for the age of industry. In sum, Sir Allan represented a set of beliefs which ensured that in the early 1850s British North American politics were railways.

True to his dictum, Sir Allan MacNab enthusiastically supported the Guarantee bill. As the chairman of the assembly's influential Standing Committee on Railways and Telegraph Lines, he was the first to reply to

Hincks's introductory remarks. He believed that all the railways likely to enjoy the benefits of provincial loan guarantees would be successful and repay their investment. Wisely, he declined to mention his own interest in the Great Western but instead argued that the St Lawrence and Atlantic 'would have the effect of drawing a great deal of commerce down our public improvements on the river St Lawrence, and materially benefit our shipping interests on the upper Lakes, and indeed all parts of the Province.'[98] More to the point, MacNab implored his colleagues to shun political biases and approve the government's resolutions. 'This was not a political matter,' he pleaded; 'every man who desired to see his country prosper and improve, must support it. In matters of this kind there could be no difference of opinion.'

Sir Allan MacNab's ringing call for an all-faction endorsement of the Guarantee bill received warm support from French Canadian members of the legislature. Typical was their leader, Louis-Hippolyte La Fontaine, who represented a new attitude in Lower Canada. Although conservative in his cultural objectives, La Fontaine had abandoned the old Toryism and dreams of independence, the fur trade, and seigneurialism in favour of a new conservatism willing to work within the British system and the emerging industrial economy. Instead of fighting responsible government and the end of mercantilism as a threat to French culture, La Fontaine adopted a belief in moderation, in working within the nascent federal institutions. Rather than adulate nationalism as an end in itself, La Fontaine preferred to use it subtly and pragmatically to gain concessions and political power. With his open attitude towards English politicians, he constructed a powerful alliance that included the Gallican clergy – the dominant francophone political power – as well as English politicians.

As with many of his English and French compatriots, La Fontaine's moderate conservatism allowed him to be progressive in commercial matters; he embraced a commitment to economic progress and individualism, believing that urbanization and industrialization would bring wealth and employment opportunities. But he also recognized that Lower Canada required extensive reforms in education, legal institutions, and landholding to prepare it for the age of steam. And he also instinctively understood the young francophone Montréalers who were challenging the anglophone and Tory merchant and banking élite; La Fontaine knew that the growing French bourgeoisie wanted to profit from the growth in shipping, the emergence of industries and urbanization, as well as their changed political status. His support of the Guarantee bill encapsulated the rising ambitions of the new French leadership.[99]

Although La Fontaine feared the republicanism of the United States, he summed up the debate on the Guarantee bill by applauding a rail connection to the Atlantic through Maine. 'Now the question was,' he challenged the assembly, 'whether Canada should push forward and try to put herself in communication with the civilization and prosperity of our neighbour – in communication with the ocean, or whether Canada should remain locked up during six months in the ice.'[100] With his endorsement of the Guarantee bill, La Fontaine revealed that his staunch French conservatism sheltered a strong liberal faith in the ability of technology to overcome the obstacles of the natural environment and thus generate a prosperity based on unhampered commerce between the provinces and countries of the North American continent.

The Guarantee Act of 1849 became a significant milestone in Canada's history, articulating a new era in its social and economic development, facilitating the railway age and its centralizing forces. On the surface, the act represented the tacit understanding among moderates, who formed the majority in the colonial legislature, that economic development, energized by vigorous transportation development, was the best way to cope with Britain's attempts to dismantle the formal structures of the empire. Specifically, the legislature followed the lead of several New England states by asserting that railways were 'not merely advantageous' private investments but public concerns, 'essential to [the] advancement and prosperity' of the province.[101] Consequently, the legislature approved state assistance to private railway enterprises and, in doing so, launched one of Canada's most frenetic railway-construction programs ever, a policy so costly that it nearly bankrupted the province.

The Guarantee Act also clearly symbolized how the turbulent late 1840s were changing imperial relationships. While few would question the value of political and emotional ties to Great Britain and the authority of the Crown, loosening economic ties and trading relationships were being accepted. Meanwhile, the giant growing market of the western United States and its ice-free ports were becoming increasingly attractive as did the ice-free eastern American ports. The commercial ambitions of Canadians, unlike those of imperialist dreamers, did not extend into or beyond the Canadian Shield. Nor did they hold much stock in either British North American union or the intercolonial railway. Upper Canadians were most interested in an economical access to the port of New York, while Montréal and Québec shippers were most concerned with capturing the trade of the American Midwest. That objective too required a direct, economically efficient rail route to the Atlantic.

Not surprisingly, Francis Hincks questioned the commercial value of the intercolonial. It must be regarded 'as a great national work,' he explained, and 'not in the light of a mercantile speculation.'[102] Although he acknowledged the importance of the scheme, he did not think it essential to Canada's economic development and, therefore, he denied that it deserved financial support from the Canadian government. Although the Guarantee Act included a clause on the Halifax-Québec railway, it did not extend the guarantees to this clearly perceived imperial project. The legislation merely provided a modest £20,000 annual subsidy and a 16-km belt of land on both sides of the right-of-way.[103] Since the Canadian segment of an intercolonial would be relatively small, the land subsidy was negligible. 'Every person here knew it to be nothing at all,' Hincks asserted, 'since the waste lands were worth nothing.'[104] The assistance to the Halifax-Québec was to be relatively modest and clearly defined. By contrast, the support for private railway ventures was open-ended and theoretically unlimited. The longer the railway, the larger the provincial obligation.

The St Lawrence and Atlantic Railway was among the first companies to benefit from the Guarantee Act. Conceived in the new free-trade canon, it was designed to provide a fairly direct, competitive route from Montréal to the Atlantic. In any case, the Guarantee Act encouraged the City of Montréal, the Sulpician Seminary, and the British American Land Company to invest in the St Lawrence and Atlantic. Although the financial difficulties of the railway did not end, the company eventually completed enough of the road to qualify for the government guarantee. By 1853, when both the American and Canadian portions of the railway were finished, Montréal possessed the access to the Atlantic it always wanted. By supporting the St Lawrence and Atlantic, Montréal had chosen to ally itself with Portland, which was a relatively small city and thus unlikely to dominate the relationship.[105] In the future, however, Portland's minor status would prove a serious handicap, necessitating further railway expansion.

The Guarantee Act also breathed life into the Toronto, Simcoe and Lake Huron Union Railroad Company, which had been incorporated early in 1849 with the intention of opening the fertile and timber-rich territory north of Toronto. But the line, subsequently known as the Northern Railway, was also designed as a portage between Toronto on Lake Ontario and a proposed port on Lake Huron, providing a gateway to the rich grain and flour sources of the upper lakes and Chicago. The Guarantee Act revived the project after an initial attempt to finance construction with the proceeds of a raffle foundered on the moral shoals of nineteenth-century Toronto. Built at a cost of $32,500 per kilometre, the road reached Lake

Simcoe in 1853 and the new port of Collingwood on Lake Huron two years later.[106]

Lastly, the Guarantee Act assisted the financing of the Great Western. The interest guarantees provided under the act and subsequent direct municipal investments enabled the Great Western to tap into American money markets, especially American railroads such as the Michigan Central. Construction, commenced in 1851 largely by American firms at an exorbitant $40,600 per kilometre, was virtually complete by 1855. The company's suspension bridge at Niagara Falls (a contemporary engineering triumph) and its ferries at Detroit made the Great Western a link between the New York Central and the Michigan Central, and part of a railway system that spanned half a continent and gave Canada West economical access to the New York and Boston harbours.[107]

By 1849, then, the Guarantee Act's dry legalistic language had translated Canada's philosophy of railways into life. A product of the newfound faith in railway technology, the act implicitly enunciated what was rapidly becoming an accepted truth for economic-development rhetoric. Railways 'have become necessary to the age,' Major Robinson asserted, 'and that country which has them not must fall behind in the onward march of improvement and in the development of its resources.'[108] Canadians agreed with Robinson and through the Guarantee Act committed themselves to a costly transportation technology.

The Guarantee Act was Canada's response to the arrival of a new transportation technology, an advance colonists sensed would radically transform their economic institutions. While imperial officials were planning to loosen the costly formal political ties of empire in favour of more lucrative informal business bonds, Canadians were exploring continental relationships. The citizens of Canada East and Canada West, Tories and Reformers, francophones and anglophones examined the crumbling British connection and realized that in the approaching era of free trade and responsible government they needed new transportation initiatives. While imperial administrators envisioned British North American unity by railways, merchants from Canada East and Canada West intended to use the principles of free trade and the efficiency of railway technology to challenge traditional imperial trade connections and establish independent North American economic structures. They used the Guarantee Act as a means of building a modern mode of transportation. That technology defied traditional political boundaries; it permitted Canadian businessmen to eschew imperialist objectives, including an intercolonial railway. Canadians would seek their destiny in closer economic ties with their American neighbours.

3

Nova Scotia:
Railways and the New Economy

I am neither a prophet, nor a son of a prophet, yet I will venture to predict that in five years we shall make the journey hence to Quebec and Montreal and home through Portland and St. John, by rail; and I believe that many in this room will live to hear the whistle of the steam-engine in the passes of the Rocky Mountains and to make the journey from Halifax to the Pacific in five or six days.

Joseph Howe[1]

The mere expenditure of money on unprofitable undertakings, is of no benefit to a country – it is only changing productive labor for that which is useless, and is consequently thrown away.

A. Lawson[2]

Beginning in the late 1840s, Nova Scotians commenced a decades-long debate on the profound changes in their economic environment. The industrialization of the North Atlantic world, the growth of the United States economy, imperial free trade, and especially the transportation revolution forced many Nova Scotians to examine their political economy. Predictably, as they debated their future, a spectrum of positions emerged but opinions coalesced around two relatively opposite courses of action. While many favoured radical changes in policies, including adoption of new steam technologies, a continentalist orientation, and the federation of British North America, others preferred traditional approaches, appreciating the established techniques of sail and wind, the retention of an Atlantic outlook, and the independence of their province. Significantly, however,

Nova Scotia's leaders engaged each other in debate so that whatever way the province chose to meet the new economy, its citizens were fully cognizant of the issues and had exercised some measure of control over their destiny.[3]

The philosophy of railways featured prominently in the debate. As first articulated in the late 1840s by Joseph Howe, a Reform leader, the railway promoters favoured the construction of a railway to Québec and eventually westward to the Pacific. Although the concept was continentalist, initially it was set firmly in a British imperialist mould. The envisioned transcontinental nation would be an integral part of the British empire and would embody an agricultural purpose, the civilization of the wilderness. Perhaps because Halifax was to be the entrepôt for the federated British territory, and because it had no overland links to the United States, Nova Scotia was the most insistent advocate of an intercolonial railway and incidentally of confederation. Internal regional rivalries, competition with Saint John, a recalcitrant Canada, and an impotent Colonial Office, however, thwarted the plans for a Halifax-Québec railway; consequently, Nova Scotia, biding its time, became the first province in British America to build a local railway completely as a public work, a clear testimony to its commitment to the philosophy of railways. Moreover, Charles Tupper, the Conservative leader, subsequently adopted Howe's railway doctrine and actively pursued the intercolonial and its ancillary unification movement. Moreover, he added an industrial purpose, a feature compatible to current Canadian thinking.

Nova Scotians began to discuss an economic-development policy almost immediately after they won responsible government in 1848. The debate was profoundly affected by the province's landscape. With its population scattered through countless coves and bays along a rugged coastline as well as in many river valleys, the province lacked cohesion; its physiography accentuated particularisms and produced small-scale, internally competitive enterprises.[4] Although it possessed the largest coal deposits on the eastern seaboard, by 1849 Nova Scotia still had no major industries outside of shipbuilding. For more than twenty years, the British-based General Mining Association, which enjoyed a total monopoly of the resource, had produced coal only for export. The collieries' impressive smokestacks, steam-operated hoists and ventilators, and busy railway were no harbingers for impending industrialization. With no significant local market, the mines operated seasonally, forcing workers to seek supplemental employment.[5] Similarly, the province's small and scattered shipyards provided an important cash income but did not spur industrial development. As in mining, the yards purchased most supplies abroad.[6] The lumber industry too, dispersed among small wood lots, did little to create secondary processing. In fact, since most of the prime locations were depleted, by the late 1840s the industry was in decline. Meanwhile, isolation permitted local merchants to dominate the fishery. Paying for catches with over-priced supplies, the truck system produced a subsistence economy with frequent, long-term indebtedness. With little alternative employment or few opportunities to leave, fishermen accepted the exploitation because it assured them the necessities of life. But their reduced, cashless earning powers, as well as the conservative attitude of the fish-merchants, resulted in economic stagnation and rampant poverty.[7] Lastly, the province's farmers were equally isolated, most tilling the marginal soil for a meagre income that often had to be supplemented with fishing, lumbering, or mining. Although a few possessed large tracts of land and sold surplus production on local and foreign markets, the vast majority managed only a subsistence life, while a large minority lived in poverty.[8] Nova Scotia's farmers were seldom able to supply the local market with sufficient food, and the province imported considerable quantities every year. In sum, a disparate society with a scattered economy shaped the debate on Nova Scotia's future.[9]

Isolation cast Nova Scotia society into a loose collection of religiously, ethnically, and politically divided people with different needs and diverse interests. Most of its citizens lived in small and isolated communities where the arm of the state and law seldom reached. Except at election time, when patronage rather than political ideology prevailed, they were scarcely involved in debating long-term economic policies or political directions. Life was hard and daily survival their primary occupation. At the same time, the folk in the fishing outports and on the isolated farms resented increased intrusion of the state in society. Nova Scotians, as historical geographer Graeme Wynn has observed, were deeply 'suspicious of centralized government, opposed to taxation, and attached to local custom.'[10] Those regional, parochial feelings, instinctively expressed, became a powerful force that strenuously resisted the seemingly idealistic and expensive solutions offered by urban and often remote politicians to the countryside's economic problems.

Despite the province's particularisms, by the mid-1800s its élites were becoming conscious of common characteristics and a growing provincial awareness. According to the province's intellectual historian, D.C. Harvey, as early as 1812 Nova Scotians were articulating rudimentary traces of a distinct identity. Certainly by 1837, when Thomas Chandler Haliburton published *The Clockmaker*,[11] his apt depiction of the half-Yankee and half-

English Bluenose as a superior being signalled that Nova Scotians were cognizant that their young culture, embracing a variegated blend of American, English, Scottish, Irish, and even German experiences, was exhibiting a distinct personality. With growing self-confidence, they founded newspapers, published pamphlets, built schools and universities, and led the way in British North America for representative political institutions and responsible government. By 1849, Nova Scotia's intellectual, political, legal, and business leaders were hopeful, ambitious, and self-confident. Even if far from unanimous on political programs, they all wanted to catalogue the extent of their rational and economic resources and to utilize them in the development of their province. These were, according to Harvey, Nova Scotia's 'spacious days.'[12]

By mid-century, then, after the province had achieved responsible government, its leaders commenced a lively debate about its future in the new free-trade economy. Absolutely central to that discussion was Nova Scotia's relationship to Britain. For if one thing united all colonists it was their common ancestral roots in the island nation. Politicians and newspaper editors repeatedly referred to the British origins of the province's legal and political institutions. They sang praises to Britain's rich political tradition, its industrial ascendency, and its imperial achievements. With their heritage firmly set across the Atlantic, Nova Scotia's orators adulated British history and its political culture and constantly referred to them as real and symbolic touchstones. Not surprisingly, Nova Scotians also adopted the Victorian confidence in progress, in the possibilities for improvement through increased productivity, through perseverance, and through systematic effort; and they also wanted to emulate the mother country's modern, Western capitalist society with its calculating, disciplined, and industrious ethos.

In addition to imperial loyalty, two closely interwoven motifs were rising to challenge the province's particularisms – the philosophy of railways and Maritime or British North American union. Closely linked to the assertion that railway technology was the inevitable path to economic and social advancement was the belief that British North Americans could best adapt to the new international industrial economy by pooling their resources into a large, prosperous free-trade zone. The backbone of such a union, some argued, would be an intercolonial railway that some day would be extended to the Pacific.

The Nova Scotian who most clearly articulated the unification and railway options was Joseph Howe, an ardent imperialist, conservative reformer, insatiable activist, and nervous gadfly.[13] Born in Halifax in

December 1804, Howe inherited an almost mystical veneration of the British empire from his Loyalist father, John Howe. A self-educated voracious reader and avid traveller, Howe projected a contradictory public image. On the one hand, his strong moral and physical courage was anchored in a deep personal knowledge and understanding of biblical principles; on the other hand, his unrelenting ambition and restless quest for fame, power, and influence was driven by an unsettled personal insecurity. Unable to tolerate the ordinary and humdrum, he searched ceaselessly for new worlds to conquer. Only at home did he find stability in a life-long marriage to Catherine MacNab, a union fused by intense tragedies involving the loss of five of the couple's ten children.

In December 1827, after brief flirtations with other newspapers, Howe took over the *Novascotian* and quickly fashioned it into the province's most influential journal, a leading contributor to Nova Scotia's intellectual awakening and its developing liberal political economy. Seeking to elevate the character of the province and teach it liberal economic principles, Howe unabashedly used the paper as an instrument for his own and his readers' education. He freely shared his perceptive observations on the works of Adam Smith and other economic liberals; he informed his readers about affairs in Europe, Britain, and North America; and, in every issue he exuded a confident belief in material progress and the possibility of infinite economic expansion. The editorials and numerous extracts from other papers and periodicals developed the concept of a direct connection between investment and progress, between active entrepreneurs and public prosperity.

Although often perceived as a political reformer, Howe was in fact relatively conservative, beginning his political career as a moderate Tory, ever mindful of the prerogatives of Crown and empire. Furthermore, his growing interest in political reform was always tempered by his mythical veneration of British institutions that he believed preserved liberty by correctly dividing power among various classes. Howe favoured the middle class, however, and its perceived virtues of hard work and thrift. Nova Scotia, he felt, could only achieve prosperity if its entrepreneurs were aggressive and hardworking. Thus, he eventually turned to reform in order to emasculate Nova Scotia's merchant and military élite whose garrison mentality and defeatist attitudes, he believed, obstructed the economic development of the province. He wanted to reorganize government so that it could create a favourable climate for investment and economic development.

Howe's robust advocacy of economic growth cut through all his contradictions. While he supported the principle of responsible government, in practice he refused to press his case too strongly if that threatened funds for roads and bridges. On the other hand, like Francis Hincks in Canada, he willingly participated in any administration no matter what its attitude on reform if cooperation could realize economic benefits. Although he feared partisan politics because its selfish, rigid factionalism restricted freedom of action, he worked hard to elect Reform majorities to the assembly because he believed that political reform was necessary to rehabilitate Nova Scotia's lagging economy. Skilfully mixing a message of entrepreneurial and political harmony under responsible government and laissez-faire capitalism, Howe promised to usher in a new age of material prosperity through steady, piecemeal political reforms.

A gifted speaker and determined reformer, Howe became a successful politician. He was first elected for the county of Halifax in the general election of 1836 shortly after winning notoriety by successfully defending himself in a libel suit. He joined the executive council in 1840 and a year later became speaker; in 1842 he was appointed collector of excise at Halifax. By the 1848 election, Howe's position on responsible government had crystallized and he fought hard for a solid Reform victory, making Nova Scotia the first British North American colony to achieve responsible government. Although J.B. Uniacke became the nominal head of the Reform government, Joseph Howe, as provincial secretary, was in fact the first minister and for the next six years he toiled to adapt provincial institutions to responsible government and the new economy.[14]

Once in power, the energetic Howe focused his attention on realizing the economic and fiscal implications of responsible government. The new political reality, which was in large measure a product of the demise of mercantilism, empowered colonial governments, he believed, to shape their own tariff policies as long as they did not discriminate against British trade. Perhaps more important, responsible government permitted British North Americans to raise funds for large projects by issuing debentures backed by their own general revenues and provincial credit. In other words, responsible government gave provincial administrations the political power to shape their own fiscal policies and economic-development strategies.[15]

Joseph Howe clearly recognized the new powers and he produced a comprehensive economic-development plan that called for a North American free-trade market facilitated by modern communication and transportation technologies. Explaining his plan to George Moffatt, the president of the British American League, Howe argued that British North America could not survive as long as it remained a cluster of fragmented and isolated colonies; the new industrial, free-trade order required large nation-states with dynamic economies; consequently, the prerequisite for significant economic progress in British North America was a union of the small, unproductive provinces into a large economically efficient nation. 'We desire free trade among all the Provinces, under our national flag, with one coin, one measure, one tariff, one Post Office. We feel that the courts, the press, the educational institutions of North America, would be elevated by union; that intercommunication by railroads, telegraphs and steamboats would be promoted; and that, if such a combination of interests were achieved wisely and with proper guards, the foundations of a great nation, in friendly connection with the mother country, would be laid on an indestructible basis.'[16] Thus, in several sweeping sentences, Howe summarized a complex of future political initiatives. Simply put, Howe wanted Nova Scotia to be part of the new economic order, an initiative that required efficient transportation links and close economic ties among the British North American colonies.

Eager to translate his ideas into reality, Joseph Howe moved quickly to implement his ideas. In the first instance, he called for closer commercial ties with the United States, preferably a reciprocal free-trade agreement on natural products. To woo the Americans, he offered them access to Nova Scotia's fisheries and ports. At an intercolonial conference, held in Halifax in September 1849, Howe and Canada's Louis-Hippolyte La Fontaine drafted a memorial asking the British government to negotiate such a reciprocal trade agreement with the United States. Meanwhile, the provincial delegates agreed in principle that colonial legislatures should remove all fiscal barriers to intercolonial trade.[17]

As a second policy, Howe vigorously pushed for a telegraph connection with Boston. As one of five government commissioners, he supervised the construction of a telegraph line to the New Brunswick border. On the one hand, the spirited prosecution of telegraph construction indicated Howe's intention of bringing Nova Scotia into the era of modern communications; on the other hand, the technique of using government commissioners signalled his desire to avoid monopolistic profiteering by keeping control in the hands of the government. Completed by the end of 1849, the telegraph linked Nova Scotia by way of New Brunswick to Portland, from where messages were carried by train to Boston.[18]

The third, and perhaps the most important item in Howe's agenda was the introduction of railway technology to Nova Scotia. As early as 1834, Howe had revealed his keen interest in a railway as a vehicle for economic growth by suggesting that the government should help Halifax build a railway to Windsor. 'If the thirty miles of bad land, lying between Halifax harbour and the Ardoise hills, were annihilated to-morrow,' he asked, 'would not Halifax command the whole trade of the Basin of Minas and be so identified with the interests and advancement of the midland counties as to grow into a place of immense wealth and importance within a very few years?'[19] Such a railway, he argued later, would raise the province to a higher level 'from the little peddling muddy pool of politics ... to some thing more ennobling, exalting and inspiring.'[20]

Apart from its local value, Howe also viewed the Halifax–Windsor railway as the first stage of a much larger scheme – an intercolonial line to the St Lawrence River. Advocated at various times, the Halifax-Québec railway was always popular in Nova Scotia. Only a few years earlier a meeting in Cumberland had proposed a railway from Halifax via Saint John to Québec and asked the provincial assembly to pledge the public credit to 'this National Railroad.'[21] Although Howe cautioned that anyone investing 'his money in it, with the expectation of profit, would be mad,' he supported the Halifax-Québec scheme 'because it will form a great back bone through these colonies – it will be a great Roman highway – a military road to bind these provinces to each other, and to the mother country.'[22]

On 25 March 1850, when Howe moved a non-partisan private resolution in the legislature to provide £330,000 for the construction of the Halifax-Windsor railway, he broadly surveyed the progress of railways in Europe and the United States, concluding that '[t]hese and many others, penetrating the wide extent of the Union, connecting not only the larger cities, but the most remote villages and hamlets, are of modern date, and have already given an astonishing impulse to national industry, developing new resources and creating trade in the most unproductive regions.'[23] Moving the spotlight to Nova Scotia, Howe continued that the Minas Basin had developed as far as it could without a railway; to take advantage of free trade, it required speedy and efficient transit for people and produce. Even if it did not earn a profit immediately, the railway would increase commerce, population, and revenue; it would bring prosperity to the region. 'Let this railway be built,' he concluded, 'and Windsor will become a city and Halifax will double in size and population before five years have passed away.'[24]

In Howe's grand scheme, the Windsor railway would serve not only as a segment in the proposed intercolonial railway, it would also become a link to the United States. He enthusiastically accepted a proposal by John A. Poor, the aggressive Portland lawyer and tireless promoter of north-eastern railways, for the European and North American Railway, an international scheme envisioning a railway eastward from Bangor, Maine, through

New Brunswick and Nova Scotia, to Cape Breton Island. With no one questioning the source of capital for this ambitious plan, a public meeting on 24 August 1850 in Halifax's Temperance Hall eagerly endorsed the concept and forwarded a confident resolution to Lieutenant-Governor Sir John Harvey: 'The completion of the great work contemplated by the resolution will not only elevate this Province to the most conspicuous and important position on the western continent, by rendering it the direct channel of communication between our parent country and the United States on the most enlarged and magnificent scale; but the rich though now unproductive resources of our Province, both mineral and agricultural, will become developed and be made available to the public good, its commercial interests rapidly advanced, and its revenue materially aided and increased.'[25]

With equal enthusiasm, Sir John Harvey and his council supported the Halifax resolution, believing it was 'suited to the age in which we live. The cost of constructing Railroads is light compared with the cost of doing without them. Nova Scotia ... owes it to the civilized world to make her portion of "The European and North American Railroad" which must become the shortest Highway between the great families of the Anglo Saxon Race.'[26]

By 1850, then, Joseph Howe had worked out a comprehensive economic-development plan, and like an itinerant evangelist he travelled extensively in Britain and North America hoping to sway imperial and colonial officials to his cause. While his basic message was relatively plain and straightforward, it contained complex strands of thoughts, old as well as novel ideas. Like Canada's Thomas Keefer, he built his ebullient development message on the fundamentals of liberal economics and technological progress, but unlike Keefer, Howe's themes contained an emerging rhetoric of technological nationalism, which extended westward beyond the Canadas to the Pacific Coast. His ringing calls for national transcontinental institutions, however, never eschewed vigorous imperialist ideals. Howe's agenda encompassed more than elementary economic aims; for him, British North American's ultimate mission was to spread British civilization across the northern continent.

In its most elemental form, Howe's gospel centred on the economic development of Halifax. Consciously founded by the British government as a bulwark against the French in America, the garrison town was the political centre of the colony. Its English and American citizens, mainly government officials and military officers, formed a strong sense of partnership between empire and colony and exhibited an enthusiasm for intellectual activity, the arts, and higher education.[27] By the mid-1800s, a new class, comprising several hundred merchants, had asserted itself and worked in accord with the older establishment to create a close-knit community, which relished their common roots, intermarried, and immersed themselves deeply in local politics. In the legislature, the merchant-politicians sought to create a secure environment for their businesses and when necessary eagerly lobbied for change and reform. Acutely interested in developmental politics, the merchants articulated a focused metropolitan perspective. Their primary objective was to create the largest possible hinterland in which to operate their trade. They – and colleagues in other major ports – welcomed the free-trade era because it permitted them to trade outside the imperial confines; they expected to increase their commerce with the United States, Europe, South America, and the British West Indies.[28]

Imbued with a trader mentality, Howe's advocacy of Halifax became an obsession and he worked hard to divert its Atlantic orientation to a continental mission. If only the port could be connected by rail to the St Lawrence River and to the growing railway network of the United States, he pleaded, the city could become the pre-eminent Atlantic harbour for an enormous and expanding market. Time and again Howe optimistically asserted that once the railways were completed no other Atlantic port could compete for transatlantic passenger traffic because a London–New York journey via Halifax would save as much as fifty-six hours over an all-sea route.[29]

When his Halifax-oriented policy encountered hostile criticism from the province's peripheries, Howe expanded his case to embrace the entire province. He argued that all of Nova Scotia needed to break away from its resource economy, its coal-mining monopoly and its exploitive fishery; it must establish new commercial links and develop new industries. To accomplish this end, all regions must support an energetic railway-construction program. Once completed, railways to Canada and the United States, Howe maintained, 'would give an impetus to the social and material prosperity of Nova Scotia, which her people anticipate, in confident reliance upon their own resources and on the bounties of Providence.'[30] In other words, Howe urged the back lands to realize that although Halifax, as the terminal of the railways, appeared to benefit most from the proposed railway, it would, in reality, spin off growth and prosperity to the entire provincial economy.

Howe also assured his listeners that Nova Scotia could easily afford to undertake the work. As the province's population grew, its railway debt would diminish. 'I never see a bride going to church with orange blossoms in her bonnet or a young couple strolling to Kissing Bridge of a summer evening, but I involuntarily exclaim, Heaven bless them,' he joked, 'there go the materials to make the railroads. So long, then, as love is made in Nova Scotia, and love makes children, we shall have fifty or sixty thousand added to our population every five or six years.'[31]

Not content with a narrow Halifax focus, Howe's railway rationalization also included the economic and political union of British North America. Howe concluded that 'this Railway will, we trust, before many years, be extended across this continent, securing to the mother country upon British soil, and under the protection of the national flag and of the queen's own subjects, easy and rapid communication, not only with the rising communities upon the Pacific, but with the rich and populous provinces and nations which lie beyond.'[32] The transcontinental would enable the colonies to unify 'into one prosperous community, animate them with new hopes and aspirations,' and transform them from mere colonies into 'a great and prosperous nation.'[33] Clearly and unequivocally, Howe summoned British North Americans to add to their traditional transatlantic commercial activities a new continental orientation:

All classes in the Provinces look forward to the establishment of those great lines of intercolonial and continental communication, which are not only to bind us together and secure to the British Provinces great commercial advantages, but which would with cheap steamboats reduce the Atlantic to a British Channel and continue the Strand in a few years to Lake Huron, and ultimately, perhaps, even in our time (so rapidly does the world advance), to the Pacific Ocean ... [Canada's] interest in these great works cannot be exaggerated ... They would bring her productions to the seaboard at all seasons of the year, connect her by lines of communication with all the other Provinces and with the mother country; preparing the way for a great industrial if not political union, of which the citadel of Quebec would ultimately form the centre.[34]

According to Joseph Howe, the railway would be a precursor to political union. Everywhere he spoke he consistently argued that the railway must be built before political union was attempted. Whether that union was to be federal or legislative in nature was of less importance to Howe than that an intercolonial railway must precede unification.

Once he had included all of British North America in his railway rhetoric, Howe freely borrowed Earl Grey's immigration and public-works ideas and integrated them into his railway proposal. Howe intimated that

the progress of British North America was inhibited in part by the restrictive policies of the United Kingdom. Even though it had large numbers of
poverty-stricken citizens, Great Britain had done little for its northern colonies, he chided. Why did Britain not ship its poor to British North America, he questioned, where they could be turned into useful workers rather
than burdensome charges? Echoing Earl Grey's own thoughts, Howe
painted a grim picture of privation and destitution among children in
England. This grinding poverty, he submitted, was the prime cause of
crime, a blight that could be ended through productive work in the colonies. Britain should subsidize a clean and inexpensive transatlantic steamboat line, assist in a vigorous program of colonial public works, and help
British North Americans furnish prepared lands for settlers. Such an
assisted emigration program would not only alleviate a British problem,
but would help the colonies overcome their disadvantages and compete
with and overtake the United States.

Implicit in Howe's call for a mass migration of urban poor to British
North America was a pastoral myth. In contrast to the poverty, pollution,
and crime of Britain's industrial cities, the vast North American continent
offered an unredeemed wilderness that the righteous toil of healthy farmers
could turn into a prosperous, clean, and moral garden. Although he never
explicitly articulated his presuppositions, Howe appeared to have adopted
a Thomas Jefferson–like appreciation of agriculture. He certainly shared
Jefferson's romantic belief that farming was truly productive, virtuous, and
democratic. He seldom spoke about industrialization and his vision for a
transcontinental nation was for an agricultural sanctuary, a haven for good,
plain-living folk.[35] Moreover, deeply imbedded in Howe's ideology was
the Puritan thought that the settlement task carried a religious imperative,
that an undeveloped wilderness was evil, that to make it good, people must
cultivate it. Thus, the clearing of the forest was not only a sign of progress,
it was an act of redemption.[36] Civilizing the wilderness was a religious mission.

For Joseph Howe, therefore, settling the valleys of Nova Scotia and the
great plains of North America was a sacred calling. He castigated Nova
Scotians for occupying but a minuscule portion of the vast continent. Nova
Scotians, he cajoled, must seize the opportunity that railway technology
provided to move beyond the fringes of the vast continent and develop its
expansive interior:

Will you then put your hands unitedly, with order, intelligence and energy, to this
great work? Refuse, and you are recreants to every principle which lies at the base

of your country's prosperity and advancement; refuse, and the Deity's handwriting upon land and sea is to you unintelligible language; refuse, and Nova Scotia, instead of occupying the foreground as she now does, should have been thrown back, at least behind the Rocky Mountains. God has planted your country in the front of this boundless region; see that you comprehend its destiny and resources – see that you discharge with energy and elevation of soul the duties which devolve upon you in virtue of your position.[37]

Lest they missed the point, Howe linked the intercolonial railway and western settlement directly to the will of God. 'I believe this to be God's work, and I believe that He will prosper it,' he confidently asserted. 'I believe that a wise and beneficent Providence never intended that millions of square miles of fertile territory behind and around us should lie waste and unoccupied, while millions of our fellow-creatures rot in almshouses and poorhouses over the sea or perish for lack of food. I regard these railroads after all but as means for the accomplishment of elevated and beneficent ends.'[38] Thus, years before Canadians turned their eyes to the rich resources of the interior plains, a Nova Scotian was projecting powerful images of a mighty transcontinental nation bound together by a new transportation technology.[39] Howe's speeches testified to a deep faith in the ability of railway technology to unite British North America, to facilitate the settlement of western Canada, and to create a mighty and prosperous agricultural and trading nation. Mixing generous doses of liberal economics and capitalist greed with dashes of romanticism, patriotism, and Protestant Christianity, Howe cooked a potent manifest-destiny brew for his fellow colonists.

Howe's strident missionary cry also contained a profound belief in the integrity of the British Empire. In all his speeches, Howe summoned the spirit of imperialism. His idealistic vision of a new transcontinental nation was always nestled within his dream of a consolidated British Empire. The metropolitan centre that should inspire the new nation and set its cultural tone was not Halifax or Québec but London. 'Until the time arrives when North America shall rise into a nation, nothing can be more honourable than our connection with the parent state,' Howe cautioned. '[w]e must have a metropolis, an imperial centre somewhere, and I do not hesitate to acknowledge that I prefer London, with her magnificent proportions, to Washington, with her "magnificent distances."'[40]

Thus, Howe's vision of the transcontinental railway and its connection with the colonies never implied a separation from the mother country. 'To reproduce England on the other side of the Atlantic,' he told an audience in

Southampton, 'to make the children, in institutions, feelings and civilization, as much like the parent as possible, has been the labour of my past life; and now I wish to encourage the parent to promote her own interests by caring for the welfare and strengthening the hands of her children, to show to the people of England that across the Atlantic they possess Provinces of inestimable value.'[41]

Speaking to a Halifax audience, Howe sketched the outlines of a new northern transcontinental nation. British financial support was offered, he said, 'for the purpose of enabling [British North America] to complete in an incredibly short space of time and with security and ease great internal improvements which their advanced condition renders so desirable, which will bind them together into one prosperous community, animate them with new hopes and aspirations, and ultimately elevate them from the colonial condition to that of a great and prosperous nation, in perpetual amity and friendship with those glorious islands to which we trace our origin and to which through this great boon so much of our material prosperity will in all time to come be traced.'[42] Britain's agreement to guarantee the railway loans was to Howe a sure sign that she wanted British North Americans to go ahead 'in the formation of national character and national institutions ... to bind these disjointed Provinces together by iron roads; to give them the homogeneous character, fixedness of purpose, and elevation of sentiment, which they so much require.'[43]

Paradoxically, even while insisting that railway technology would stop British North America's drift towards the United States and thus reinforce imperial ties, Howe was promoting a railway link to the United States. Although he never clearly articulated his attitude towards the republic, his ardent imperialism implied a disdain for its political institutions. Yet, he sought closer commercial ties with the United States as well as an international railway. Obviously, he did not assume that closer trade relations and transportation links might lead to cultural integration. Like his Canadian counterparts, Howe appeared to be concerned mainly about British North America's inability to compete with the United States for trade and immigrants, only slightly concerned about political intrusion, and hardly anxious about cultural domination.

Nevertheless, Howe cleverly exploited the fear of American influence in the colonial economies. Unless Britain provided financial assistance, he pointed out, the European and North American Railroad would fall entirely into the hands of American financiers; and surely imperial authorities would agree 'it to be ... equally sound provincial and sound national policy that that portion of what must become a great highway of nations ...

should be kept under British control.'[44] Unless the imperial government assisted the province's railway project, Howe warned Earl Grey, the Americans would gain control over a very important communication link and the loyalty of Nova Scotians would be strained.

In an angry lament, Howe complained that Nova Scotia, positioned between Great Britain and the United States, was penalized for belonging to neither. As a colony, she could not participate in imperial councils; but, because she was British, she could not enter the large protected American market.[45] If Britain wished to maintain the loyalty of its colonies, Howe warned, it must be prepared to assist them financially. Only vigorous domestic economies could keep them British.

Superficially, Howe's concentric arguments, which led him from Halifax, through Nova Scotia and a united British North America, to a strong British Empire, appeared to be concerned only with economic development. Significantly, however, he also spoke of social and political progress. The merit of the railway, he told a Québec crowd, 'can only be measured by the value I set upon our connection with the mother country and upon our material and social elevation as a people.'[46] The railway, as a precursor to political union, would 'elevate [the British North Americas] to a higher status than any of them separately can ever occupy. I believe that railroads will be of very great use to these Provinces; but I believe, also, that it is necessary, nay, almost indispensable, to produce a social and political organization of the people, to raise these Provinces to a higher position than they can ever singly attain.'[47]

Thus, Howe asserted in typical liberal fashion that the technology of railways would bring a spiritual unity to North America; it would end the rivalries and jealousies between them. It would also furnish young people with a sense of purpose by giving them a country with a clearly defined policy. The railway would change the whole tone of the North American mind, he asserted; it would create pride in country and the empire. 'Among all ranks and classes the Railroads seemed to be regarded as indispensable agencies by which *North Americans* would be drawn into a common brotherhood,' Howe declared, 'inspired with higher hopes – and ultimately elevated, by some form of political association, to that position, which, when these great works have prepared the way for union, our half of this Continent may fairly claim in the estimation of the world.'[48]

Howe's frequent references to British North America's civilizing mission fitted perfectly into contemporary thought. Many nineteenth-century observers believed that the railway, more than any other machine, embodied the triumph of reason, science, and technology over ignorance, superstition, and the vagaries of nature. The locomotive required the most advanced knowledge of metallurgy and tools; it hauled enormous loads and numerous passengers over tracks that negated the contours of landscape, bridged rivers, and maintained regular schedules and speed in the face of adverse weather and seasons. To the nineteenth-century European mind, railway technology had mastered nature; it gave humans the means to expand and develop regions occupied by less-advanced people. When applied to the vast North American interior, the adulation of the railway reached its zenith. As historian Michael Adas has observed, when railways were introduced into North America, 'many European observers fixed upon them as the key symbol of the superiority, material as well as moral, that Western societies had attained over all others.'[49]

Despite the exuberantly optimistic rhetoric, Joseph Howe's railway plans were premature. In the first place, in March 1850 the imperial government agreed to guarantee only the interest on the bonds of an intercolonial railway, the Halifax-Québec, and not the European and North American. Although Earl Grey had no objection to the construction of railways to the United States, he expressly limited the guarantee to the intercolonial scheme because it was the only project with a clear imperial rationale.[50] The Halifax-Québec project fitted imperial objectives, he claimed, because 'its construction tended to draw closer the bonds uniting the North American provinces with each other, and with the mother country.'[51] By contrast, the European and North American had a purely commercial aim designed to benefit only the colonial economies.

Without an imperial guarantee for the European and North American, the intercolonial foundered on the shoals of provincial disagreements. New Brunswick refused to participate in the Halifax-Québec railway unless it passed through Saint John. Nova Scotia, motivated by the commercial rivalry between Halifax and Saint John, refused to pay for its substantial share of construction costs in New Brunswick if Saint John rather than Halifax was to become the intercolonial's real ocean terminal.[52] Meanwhile Canada's premier, Francis Hincks, saw no great value in either the intercolonial or the European and North American. Committed to a railway between Montréal and Portland, Maine, and a trunk line to southern Ontario, Hincks baldly stated, 'It is well known that the line between Québec and Halifax is not a favorite one with the people of Canada.'[53]

Colonial parochialism, an obsession with immediate profits, economic realities, and narrowly defined goals defeated the first attempt at intercolonial cooperation on railway construction and, by implication, colonial unity. In the early 1850s, British North Americans were not ready to forego sectional interests for a vaguely defined idealistic common good.

Even if they did not say so publicly, all participants agreed that the bottom line on the intercolonial railway was commercial utility. Since such a railway could not be expected to earn sufficient profits to pay the interest on its capital debt, provincial governments feared falling into a vicious cycle of ever-increasing liabilities that would deplete the funds needed to attract the settlers required to create traffic for the railway and revenues for the province. Meanwhile, politicians preferred to place the blame for their failure to reach agreement on the petty attitudes of their colleagues. As New Brunswick's Edward Chandler petulantly put it, 'The construction of a great trunk line of railway to the chief centres of commerce in Canada and New Brunswick, and the union of the great provinces of British America, in close commercial and friendly relations, are not sufficient inducements for Nova Scotia to co-operate with her sister colonies.'[54] Although Joseph Howe preferred to blame the Colonial Office and fellow colonial leaders, he had learned that he and his peers shared a basic belief that economic and social progress could be achieved through technological expansion. In little more than a decade that theme was to overpower sectional interests.

The failure of the intercolonial negotiations impelled Nova Scotia to return to its domestic agenda and construct a number of local railways as public works. Admitting that there were many areas in which the state must not intervene, Joseph Howe argued that railway construction was the proper preserve of governments. He feared unfettered private control over communications and claimed that people and goods should be permitted to move about freely on government-constructed highways, unchecked by tolls and gateways. The state, he reasoned, could build the railway sooner and more rapidly because it could borrow money more cheaply and because it did not expect immediate returns on this investment.[55] 'Sir,' he exclaimed, 'there is greater unity of action, greater power for good, in a Government than in a private company ... [T]he wasteful reckless expenditure, the utter disregard of everything which might ensure success, which characterized the operations [of the Shubenacadie canal, for example], would have been avoided and that splendid failure would never have taken place.'[56] Lastly, he concluded, if the state constructed railways, then private enterprise could invest capital in other segments of the economy.

Although Nova Scotia's attempt to stimulate economic development through publicly constructed railways arose from the same optimistic belief in the powers of technology that motivated Canada's railway policy, the Atlantic province pursued a more prudent approach than its western counterpart. Nova Scotia's railway program was more measured than Canada's primarily because it did not enjoy a political consensus on its railway philosophy. The Atlantic province, with its scattered and fragmented economies and its predominating ocean orientation, had a press that sharply criticized the value of railway construction, an opposition reflected in the legislative assembly. Without a strong and united commitment to railways, the province was unable to make extravagant concessions to private enterprise and, receiving no serious offers, assumed the responsibility of constructing the lines on its own resources.

Although judicious, Nova Scotia's course was radical. In 1854, Joseph Howe introduced a set of private resolutions in the assembly that asked the cabinet to name a six-member railway commission to oversee the construction of the Nova Scotia Railway. To be built by the government, the railway was to consist of a short main line from the outskirts of Halifax, supporting two branches, one to Windsor and the other to Truro. Significantly, Howe's proposals limited government spending on the railway to £200,000 per year.[57]

Howe's motion aroused considerable opposition, most of which centred on the assumption that the province could not afford expensive railway technology. J.W. Johnston, the member from Annapolis, led the attack by accusing the government of proposing 'that we should engage in the construction of a Railway without setting forth where that Railway is to run; without providing for its completion or showing how anything like a sum adequate for its construction is to be obtained.'[58] Johnston, an agent for William Jackson, the powerful British construction magnate, chagrined that the government was intent on constructing the railway itself, argued that the timing was inopportune and that private enterprise would build the project as soon as it became economically profitable. He also suggested that Howe's scheme would drain public funds away from other necessities such as roads and education.[59]

Other members opposed the railway mainly because they feared the province could not afford the plan and that the state was not the appropriate agent for its construction. Some critics accused the government of attempting an experiment that would lead to wasteful and widespread corruption. Others felt that the state should be concerned only with protecting the liberties of the people. Still others worried that the province could not afford the technology, that its debt would increase yearly, and that eventually it would fall hostage to international bankers. One member believed that Nova Scotia's geography and climate was unsuited for railway technology, while another argued that the railway would not generate any commerce not already accessible by water. Lastly, the opposition charged the scheme was unjust because it planned massive spending on a

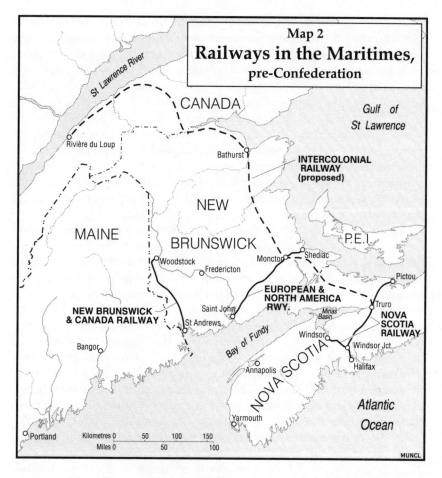

Map 2
Railways in the Maritimes,
pre-Confederation

project of benefit to only a small section of the province. There was a strong sense of outrage that this was merely a Halifax strategy to compete against Saint John. In concluding the debate, one member suggested that the Nova Scotia Railway was a prime example of Toryism: it not only increased the power of government but it taxed one people for the benefit of another.

Not unexpectedly, Joseph Howe dismissed all objections, assuring his critics that the government was not about to spend beyond its means. Frequent surveys of the route had established a relatively accurate estimate of construction costs, he assured the house; in his view, moreover, the province was prosperous and could afford the project. He urged the opposition to consider that the full exploitation of the province's resources demanded that it escape from its total reliance on water transport, which was slow and often hampered by ice. It must also understand that the most advantageous place to commence the construction of the province's railway network was near Halifax, the central point of the province. Lastly, he advised the opposition to study the affairs of Canada's Grand Trunk Railway if they wanted to see corruption and extravagance. In sum, Howe also pleaded with the assembly to understand that the railway meant more than economic prosperity, that it would lead to better interchange of ideas and greater understanding among Nova Scotians.

Surprisingly, Howe's defence was relatively cool and free of its usual exaggerated rhetoric. In fact, the most ardent defender was the speaker of the assembly. Echoing Howe's hyperboles, the speaker intoned, 'Sir, to trifle longer with the people of this Country, to remain supine, inactive and indifferent to these great modern improvements while the busy, bustling, progressive world beyond our borders is moving onward with vast strides, would be to declare our own imbecility or acknowledge that we are not awake to the incalculable advantages resulting from the construction of Railways in our Country.'[60]

In 1854, therefore, because many Nova Scotia politicians refused to support government expenditures on a railway that appeared to profit only certain privileged areas of the province, Howe's resolutions passed by a slim majority of only three votes. As in past divisions, some Liberals from the western counties joined the Tories to oppose railway legislation. These persistent pockets of opposition kept Nova Scotia's railway program comparatively modest.[61]

The strong resistance to public finance expressed in the legislature was based in part on local feelings, the strongest reaction coming from western Nova Scotia and enunciated most clearly by Angus Gidney and A. Lawson, successive editors of the Yarmouth *Herald*. Publishing their paper in one of the most prosperous ports outside of Halifax, Gidney and Lawson focused on the Atlantic and the region's prosperous shipping industry.[62] Although both editors repeatedly admitted that they appreciated the value of railways for economic development, they feared that blind boosterism and irrational rhetoric would create an unfair burden for future generations. Pointing to the disastrous results of Great Britain's railway mania, Angus Gidney coolly and rationally deflated the impractical expectations of railway promoters. He continuously punctured Howe's overblown assumptions: he doubted that Nova Scotians could raise sufficient capital to build the works; he questioned whether Halifax would become the great

North Atlantic terminal of the intercolonial, suggesting that Saint John might be a more likely candidate; and he suspected that Nova Scotia's population density was insufficient to support a railway, particularly when it already possessed efficient coastal transportation. 'The conviction is deeply imbedded in our mind,' Gidney wrote, 'that if the Executive persist in the course already indicated, there is nothing before us but fiscal embarrassment – if not bankruptcy and ruin.'[63]

Convinced that the proposed railway would become an unprofitable burden, the Yarmouth *Herald* railed against any attempt to build it as a public work. 'We fully agree with Mr. Howe that the highways of the country should be under the care and control of the Government,' Gidney opined, 'but no highways should be opened by the Government, which the necessities of the people do not imperatively call for, and which cannot be opened without incurring an enormous amount of debt.'[64] His successor, A. Lawson, agreed and argued that public spending on 'unprofitable undertakings' was 'of no benefit to a country – it is only changing productive labor for that which is useless, and is consequently thrown away.'[65] Suspecting that the proposed railways were designed solely for the benefit of Halifax, the *Herald* reasoned that funds budgeted for railways should be spent on more essential services such as roads and education, which it believed were more effective avenues to economic growth.

The Yarmouth *Herald* was not the only newspaper to resist the public-enterprise policy. Opposing indiscriminate public works, the *British Colonist* argued: 'We have always advocated the construction of railways in Nova Scotia upon the only plan sanctioned by free countries, as Great Britain and the United States, and every day's experience but adds to the conviction that the less any Government has to do in their construction the better for the people and the country through which they pass. Even Canada ... is no exception to this rule, for politicians of the Howe-Hincks school *will* use them as the means to corruption and self-aggrandisement, until the people awakened by a watchful and vigilant press, indignantly cast them off.'[66]

Faced with strong opposition, which limited its ability to attract private investors, Nova Scotia's government adopted an unprecedented policy of constructing a local railway as a public work. This strategy did not arise out of a clear ideological consensus on state intervention but out of practical considerations, fuzzy concepts, and foreign models. Governments in Britain, Continental Europe, and the United States were moving into social and economic spheres in order to alleviate the negative side-effects of the industrial revolution and to orchestrate economic-development policies.[67] At the same time, with no private contractors willing to build the railway on the government's terms, the province was eager to accept the easy credit that large British banking firms offered on the security of its tax base. Moreover, the expectation that the impending reciprocity treaty with the United States would increase trade and government revenues lessened concerns about repaying the public debt. In any case, obsessed with the notion of economic progress through technological advancement, the Liberal administration joined its North American counterparts and mixed a small but discernable dose of economic interventionism into its laissez-faire policies.

Although parochial, sectional, and ideological concerns severely curbed Joseph Howe's idealism, his appeal to the stronger integrative forces associated with railway technology prevailed, even if narrowly. On the one hand, Howe's charisma and the euphoria of political reform under responsible government injected an exuberant development optimism into many legislators; on the other hand, potent political, social, and economic forces concentrated and compelled the province to adopt a coherent railway-development policy. Perhaps most important, Howe's policy prevailed because it did not threaten the province's traditional economy. Pressed by young and aggressive merchants in Halifax and by upstart industrialists in coal-mining counties, driven by the liberal ideology of economic and social progress through technology, Howe's administration opened a new sphere of investment. Meanwhile, Nova Scotia's old commercial élite continued to develop the province's marine-based economy and built a disproportionately large sailing fleet.[68] While the pubescent activist state provoked the ire of some merchants, the electorate generally supported the new approach because it appeared to preserve a traditional maritime way of life while promising a new and bright future in agriculture, mining, and continental trade.[69]

The railway promoters, therefore, prevailed. Shortly after the 1854 railway debate, Joseph Howe resigned his seat in the legislature and took charge of the railway commission. Under his meticulous supervision, work continued for the next four years and was completed late in 1858.[70]

The construction of the Nova Scotia Railway signalled the end of the province's relatively conservative fiscal policies. It required the province to increase its revenues. Aware that tariff hikes were politically unpopular, particularly among the mercantile community, the province retained its low tariffs; instead, its politicians turned to more palatable solutions like borrowing from British or provincial savings banks or by issuing treasury notes. Most popular, however, was the sale of provincial bonds. In June

1855, for example, Nova Scotia asked London's Baring Brothers to sell £150,000 of 6¼ per cent bonds at par, redeemable after twenty years.[71] The first of several issues, totalling £800,000, the bonds represented a dramatic change in fiscal policy, and over the next few years, while public-works expenditures rose from 38.6 per cent of annual government spending to 53 per cent, revenues from tariffs fell from 80.3 per cent to 68 per cent of total income. In other words, in the period of public enterprise, which in Nova Scotia lasted from 1854 to 1860, the provincial government restructured its capital accounts completely to pay for its railway policy. Backed by popular support, it permitted its debt load to rise significantly in order to make Nova Scotia competitive in a new global economic order.[72]

Although Nova Scotia adopted a more prudent approach to public finance than Canada, it nevertheless found that it was irrevocably committed to an activist policy. In 1857, when the Conservatives came to power, they had little choice but to follow the broad outlines of their opponents' railway and public finance policies; the newly appointed receiver-general, James McNab, instructed the British bankers: 'As the season now admits of it, it is the desire of the Government to proceed as rapidly as possible with the public works and therefore trust you will lose no favourable opportunity of disposing of the Bonds that the necessary funds may be provided.'[73] Meanwhile the attorney-general, worried that the province might have difficulty repaying its debts, nevertheless stated that the administration would 'be prepared to carry on the Railway in the most prudential and economical manner.'[74]

Equally typical was the attitude of Charles Tupper, the new provincial secretary and member from Cumberland County. Born in Amherst, Nova Scotia, in July 1821, Charles Tupper received his education in the colony. A very intelligent student, Tupper prepared himself for medical studies and in 1840 moved to Edinburgh to complete his education. Three years later, he returned to Amherst and established a medical practice. Keenly interested in Conservative politics, Tupper captured Joseph Howe's Cumberland County seat in 1855. Although relegated to the opposition, Tupper managed to establish himself as a forceful, articulate speaker, revealing his deep conservative heritage, which appreciated an orderly, stable society but also included a tolerance for race and creed as well as rapid economic development through railway construction.[75] Even though he never missed an opportunity to criticize Howe's railway policy, Tupper told his fellow legislators in 1856, 'That we are to have [Railways] is no longer a question. The policy of having Railroads, and Railroads by Government, is now settled.'[76] He participated in the Conservative government's study of the railway commission on the grounds that more information was needed on this 'public work, built from the revenues and on the credit of the province' because its operation would influence 'not only ... the section of country through which it immediately passes, but ... the whole province.'[77]

Born in a preacher's family, the young Tupper was deeply religious, and his ardent evangelicalism, tempered by a gradually acquired pragmatic and utilitarian approach, made him a passionate reformer within the Conservative party. Aggressive and brash, he preferred quick and dramatic action to carefully devised schemes; when he deemed it necessary, he seldom hesitated to use executive powers to overcome delaying tactics. Although his oratory was less flamboyant and relied less on wit and hyperbole than Joseph Howe's, it hinged more on force of argument and careful reasoning laced with generous measures of sarcasm and condescension. His upbringing in Nova Scotia's coal region and his education in Scotland likely contributed to his strong affinity for industrialization, and once in office he endeavoured to prepare Nova Scotia for the new age. Despite deep-grained opposition, Tupper resolved to reform and centralize Nova Scotia's educational system, for example, and displayed in that cause his determination for and dedication to reform and modernization.[78]

Soon the most influential Conservative proponent of railway construction in Nova Scotia, Charles Tupper was instrumental in persuading his Tory colleagues to accept public ownership and extension of railways. He also gave the province's railway policy an industrial twist. As the representative of a coal-mining county, Tupper moved beyond Howe's conception of Nova Scotia as entrepôt for a transcontinental nation and predicted that the railway would form the basis of a diversified industrial economy. An intercolonial railway linked to a union of British North America, he suggested, would make Nova Scotia the future industrial heartland of a united Canada.[79] Though cast in a different form, Charles Tupper's vision adopted the essence of the policies so ardently espoused by his chief political rival – Joseph Howe.

The Conservatives, more optimistic than the Liberals, argued for even greater investments in railways, at least until the inevitable returns would come. This upbeat attitude was instrumental in their 1863 election victory and, true to form, Charles Tupper negotiated further bond issues with the Barings, partly to upgrade the Windsor line to acceptable standards but also to start an extension to Pictou.[80] Clearly aware that the cost of construction would increase the province's debt and possibly exhaust Nova Scotia's financial reserves, Tupper was still anxious to construct railways. His expansionary politics were also motivated initially by the colonies' failure in 1863 to agree on a Halifax-Québec railway and subsequently by his ingenious scheme to increase the province's debt before confederation in 1867.[81] But his unreserved support for the Pictou extension was primarily a clear indication that he wanted year-round railway transportation for his county's coal.[82] As a representative from a coal-mining community, Tupper was concerned with industrial development and understood the integral role that railways played in the growth of manufacturing.

The concern for industrial development also made Charles Tupper and his supporters eager proponents of the union of British North America. The juxtaposition of their railway and unification policies became apparent in the mid-1860s, when the Nova Scotia legislature conducted several lengthy and intense debates on both issues. The debates demonstrate clearly how the twin themes of railway expansion and confederation both pivoted on the economic-progress argument.

In 1864, Attorney-General J.W. Johnston introduced the Pictou railway resolutions in the legislature. He reminded his colleagues that even though the Conservatives had traditionally opposed government-constructed railways, they were forced to continue the policy. Johnston argued that the Pictou line should be built because it would increase Nova Scotia's trade generally and provide an expanded market for Pictou coal specifically. He urged his colleagues to forgo sectional interests and stand behind the government, as this project would benefit the entire province and would not diminish public-works expenditures elsewhere. Moreover, he reminded his listeners, the venture would form part of the long-awaited intercolonial railway, a project dear to the government because it would facilitate the union of British North America. 'I do not desire for one moment to conceal my conviction of the great importance of railroad communication between the three Provinces of Canada, New Brunswick, and Nova Scotia. I look at the question in a broad light; I consider it in its national aspect. The aspiration of my heart has always been for the union of these provinces. I believe that it is the duty of every man in Nova Scotia who desires to raise his own position as well as that of his country, to do his utmost to bring that union about. I look upon the Intercolonial Railway independent of its commercial advantages.'[83]

In defending his government's railway policy, Charles Tupper also played the unity theme, calling for the opposition to eschew sectional interests and to consider that one day the railway would be extended to all parts of the province. Following the logic of many practical-minded railway promoters, who became visionaries because they knew that immature railways must grow to survive, Tupper exhorted his audience to remember that while the Nova Scotia Railway was still not earning money, its revenues and traffic were growing; it only needed an extension to make it more productive.

Later in the 1864 session, Tupper introduced a resolution calling for union of the Maritime colonies, defending it primarily in terms of economic necessity. Echoing Adam Smith, he essentially suggested that larger economic units were more efficient and prosperous than smaller ones. 'With this country united in common bonds, associated together by a common interest, thus rendered more important in every requisite particular, we shall attract to our shores such an amount of capital, population and skill as will speedily advance this country to the influential position which it is evident God and nature intended that she should occupy.'[84]

In the next year, Tupper elaborated on this theme. Reiterating the economies-of-scale argument, Tupper asserted that, left to its own resources, Nova Scotia would remain insignificant; if the proposed confederation plan were implemented, however, Nova Scotia would become part of a great nation. Geography, he declared, has made the province the gateway to the continent and nature gave it the resources to fit easily into the economic framework of the new nation. 'If Nature has intended anything in the construction of this country,' Tupper argued, 'it has been that we should become a great manufacturing people.'[85] He noticed that Nova Scotia was blessed with the same minerals and resources that made Britain prosperous. Thus, 'under proper arrangements this Province might become a great hive of industry – the great manufactory of British North America, if not for a much larger country.' For Tupper the provision in the confederation agreement for the construction of an intercolonial railway fitted perfectly into his grand program. The railway would be of enormous advantage to Nova Scotia because it promised to end the flow of emigrants from the province and stimulate immigration. Although Tupper touched on other issues, particularly defence, the main thrust of his argument was that union would spur economic growth.

In 1866, while defending the government's confederation policy, Tupper refuted most of the anti-confederation arguments. He also countered the opposition's suggestion that the intercolonial railway should be built before unification. Construction of the railway required the combined resources of the provinces, he claimed, emphasizing that all previous attempts had failed because there had been no common policy and no mutual aims. To illustrate the intimate connection between the intercolonial and confederation, Tupper quoted Joseph Howe extensively and restated the argument that economic progress required that both be implemented.[86]

Several opposition members also articulated the relationship among railways, industrialization, continental integration, and confederation. A.G. Archibald, formerly a supporter of Joseph Howe and still leader of the Liberals in the assembly, supported the Pictou extension primarily because it would enhance Nova Scotia's internal commerce as well as its trade with other British North American colonies. At the same time, he obliquely referred to the moral rationale for railway construction. He espoused building an intercolonial because he had 'always looked at it as the precursor of that union which has so long been the hope of every intelligent man who wishes to see the arena of politics in these Provinces enlarged and ennobled.'[87]

In both the 1864 and 1865 sessions, Archibald advocated British North American union because it would elevate politics and lead to economic progress. In the latter debate, he again stressed the importance of the intercolonial railway, which he felt was the most significant concession Nova Scotia gained at the Québec conference. 'With Nova Scotia, the great forefront of the continent, behind us, with Halifax, the great entrepôt of the markets of the far West – with steamers running – not fortnightly – but daily to Europe – with the mail communication not only of our own colonies but of the United States passing over our soil – with all the commercial and material prosperity that such a state of things would produce,' Archibald rhapsodized, 'who can estimate the position we would occupy in a few years time should this Union be accomplished?'[88] Lastly, he observed that just as unity had been the greatest contributor to the prosperity of the United States, federation would be good for British North America. Although Archibald broke with the government's local railway policy in 1866, he continued to support the intercolonial railway scheme and the confederation initiative.

While most pro-railway members emphasized economics, at least one member returned to the civilizing theme. Caleb Rand Bill, a farmer from Kings North, reached beyond economics to the social-progress refrain. 'We want intercourse with Pictou, we want exchange of sentiment with that county,' he urged. 'Pictou is a rising place and we want facilities to communicate both materially and mentally with her. We want to be in a position to receive lessons of wisdom from her, and impart instruction in return ... [Once railways are constructed] then we will have accomplished a work that will bind the interests of the Province together with the ties of friendly intercourse and beneficial associations.'[89]

Ironically, the former chief advocate of an intercolonial railway and British North American union was not present in the legislature. After he suffered an electoral defeat in 1863, Joseph Howe accepted an imperial posting. Ship-bound, he was unable to accompany Tupper to Charlotte-town in September 1864. Attendance at the confederation conferences and their sumptuous banquets and glittering balls might have helped him accept the accord, but its flaws were deep and numerous. Although Howe never rejected the principle of British North American federation and the inter-colonial railway, he exposed serious defects in the Québec agreement. He criticized some of the constitutional arrangements, thinking the federation too loose in some aspects and too firm in others. He noticed a diminution of power for Nova Scotia and argued that Maritime union should precede general federation in order to give the region greater legislative control. Moreover, the order of procedure was all wrong. 'My feelings have always leaned towards a union of the provinces by Railroads first, social and com-mercial intercourse afterwards, and then when we were prepared for it by a natural development of our system on the model we admire at Home.'[90] Perhaps most important, Howe repeatedly emphasized the point that Nova Scotians should have been consulted on such a crucial issue by means of a general election.

These arguments, however eloquent, Howe could express only outside the legislature. In fact, he had little impact on the confederation debate. As his biographer, Murray Beck, observed, Nova Scotians had already made up their minds. 'His part in the emergence of anti-Confederate sentiment was in fact a modest one and the oft-repeated statement that he roused his countrymen against the Québec scheme is based largely on myth.'[91]

Nevertheless, Howe's arguments echoed in the legislative assembly. In countering the optimistic assumptions of the advocates of unification, crit-ics concentrated on the constitutional details of the agreement and the lack of consultation. The adversaries also dismissed the argument that union and consolidated defence would lessen the threat from the United States. Nova Scotia's defence cost would likely increase, the critics rebutted, because Britain would no longer automatically spring to her defence. In fact, one legislator suggested, the province already was a member of a strong union, namely the British Empire. The opposition also criticized the constitutional arrangements, noting that representation by population was a disadvantage to Nova Scotia; that the province was underrepresented in the Senate; and that there would be continual conflicts between the provin-cial and federal governments. Perhaps the most important opposition argu-ment was the suggestion that confederation would weaken imperial ties.

Not surprisingly, the foes of federation also opposed the government's railway policy. Many Liberals were disillusioned that the railway project they had launched was not bringing the expected benefits. Their hope that railway-generated economic growth would ease the payment of the public debt was dashed as the earnings of the Nova Scotia Railway were unexpectedly small and quickly absorbed into general revenues. In fact, in 1861 the province learned the painful lesson that interest payments remained constant even when tariff revenues declined. By that year, interest on the provincial debt was consuming 18 per cent of all government revenues. 'In practice,' as Rosemarie Langhout, a historian of public administration, has observed, 'once railroad construction began, and financing was arranged to cover its costs, there could be no return to the limited state of earlier years because of the fixed carrying cost of debt.'[92] More and more Liberals moved to oppose the Conservatives' development policies, including the greatest expansionary scheme of all – confederation.

One of the chief critics of the government's confederation policy was William Annand, Reformer and publisher of Halifax's *Morning Chronicle*. Although he still favoured an intercolonial railway constructed by the imperial government, he criticized the Pictou extension as too expensive for the province's treasury. But his primary target of attack was confederation. Belittling the economic arguments for union, Annand believed that Nova Scotia could increase its trade with Canada without resorting to federation. In fact, he believed that because Canada was more advanced industrially than Nova Scotia, trade might be largely eastward. Annand believed that the intercolonial railway had to be completed, to be followed first by increased trade and subsequently by political union. Citing the collapse of previous railway negotiations, Annand accused the Canadians of being untrustworthy. 'One reason why I have a strong feeling against this Union with Canada is, because I have no faith in Canadian statesmen.' In an emotional charge, he exclaimed,

When I feel that the institutions of our country are to be swept away, and that the control of our resources is to be handed over to a people with whom we have no sympathy, am I not right in asking this House to pause? What chance would there be, in such an event, of our being able to push forward those public improvements that are now being carried on? All our *surplus* revenue, as I have said, will go to Ottawa; and I ask gentlemen who look forward to the time when railway communication will extend from Pictou to Antigonish, to Guysboro, aye, even through the Island of Cape Breton, and again westward to Annapolis and Digby and Yarmouth, what chance will there be of having their anticipations realized?[93]

Annand believed the intercolonial had little economic value. 'That railway thus bringing us into connection with Canada, however valuable it may be in time of war, as affording a passage for troops, I never regarded as of much importance in relation to trade, because while communication is open with Portland, there will be little or no traffic across the Intercolonial line.'[94] Having exposed the intercolonial's Achilles heel, Annand went on to observe that it was not necessary for Nova Scotia's existence. 'We live by the sea,' he concluded, 'and have free access to other countries.'[95]

The opposition thus dismissed even the economic arguments for confederation. In an uncannily prescient argument, Isaac LeVesconte, a merchant representing Richmond County, warned Nova Scotia would lose financially even if predictions of increased manufacturing and a bustling seaport might be true. All the real benefits will go to Ottawa, he asserted, rather than to the provincial government because of its political minority position.[96]

Acting in his usual role, Yarmouth's Thomas Killam, shipbuilder and owner, summed up the opposition's deepest concern in the 1865 debate: 'Nova Scotia wants the whole world for a market – she wants free communication with the great producing country, the United States, which furnishes us with luxuries and necessaries which we have not got. We want our carrying trade, upon which we so largely depend to be unrestricted in its extent. All this is necessary to our prosperity: but adopt this Confederation scheme, and we will hedge ourselves in as it were, and shut ourselves out from the markets that are now open to us.'[97]

Killam's powerful speech delineated the sharp division that by the mid-1860s polarized Nova Scotia. Whereas the proponents of confederation relied mainly on economic arguments to support their position, contending that increased continental trade and commerce, facilitated by an intercolonial railway, would create a strong vital nation, its opponents believed that the province's continued strength was the vast Atlantic, its fisheries, boat yards, and international trade. Sceptical of the Québec scheme, the anti-confederates believed that the power to develop the economy would slip to the central government and that the province would become an insignificant unit on the periphery of a weak state. The confederates, confident that Nova Scotia would retain control over the development of its resources, argued that the province would prosper in a transcontinental union, that united they could compete successfully against the emerging industrial giant, the United States. As Alexander McFarlane observed, 'It is essential for these provinces to make such arrangements as will make them independent, as far as possible, of the States, and give them a market where they will not be met by hostile restrictions.'[98] In sum, Tupper and his followers articulated a continental and industrial vision, which was in harmony with the orientation of the Canadas but sharply at odds with the ocean-based, commercial alignment of most of Nova Scotia's Reformers.

The confederation debates, therefore, precipitated two distinct visions of Nova Scotia's future,[99] a conflict that was mirrored in the province's railway debate. Although the Liberals had initiated the railway policy, by the mid-1860s they were opposed to it, while the Conservatives, who had criticized the scheme in the early 1850s, had made it their own and gave it an industrial twist. While most Reformers resisted more government spending on economic development, the Conservatives were convinced that further efforts were needed to bring the railway program to its successful conclusion; they constructed the Pictou extension and in the process significantly raised Nova Scotia's per capita debt.[100]

Although successive Nova Scotia governments had advocated a vigorous railway-construction policy as the catalyst for the economic development of their province, they were unable to fully achieve their ambitious plans. One the one hand, few local businessmen were willing or able to invest significant amounts of capital in railways; on the other hand, a pivotal number of community leaders were loath to give provincial administrators a free hand to implement their policies. When they agreed to the terms of confederation, therefore, Nova Scotians had not followed the advice of Joseph Howe – the completion of an intercolonial railway – before they committed themselves to economic and political union. It can be argued that as a consequence Halifax was not afforded adequate opportunity to exploit its advantageous position as the Atlantic terminal on a transcontinental railway, to foster its regional hinterland, and to develop its industrial specializations before it was fused into the national political economy and was relegated to peripheral status.[101] In other words, Nova Scotians did not enter the union on equal terms.

Nevertheless, Nova Scotians developed a comprehensive railway and centralization policy. The debate in Nova Scotia's legislature, which commenced in the late 1840s, was therefore an important rehearsal for the confederation discussions. Through the years, various administrations had viewed the railway as the precursor and facilitator of commercial, social, and ultimately political integration. Immediately after winning responsible government, Nova Scotia struggled against considerable opposition to realize a consolidated railway and unification package. While the promoters of these initiatives changed during the next decade and a half, the basic objectives remained the same. From 1849 on, Nova Scotians articulated the same philosophy of railway rhetoric so common in the rest of North America and Europe, a discourse that elevated a means of transportation to mythical stature. The technology of railways would, so they believed, facilitate commercial and social intercourse and lead to economic advancement and moral improvement. And, in order to introduce this expensive new technology into their underdeveloped province, they willingly accepted a stronger and more activist government. In fact, by the mid-1860s, they were amenable to subsuming their self-governing province into a large nation-state dominated by a strong, centralized government. In other words, Nova Scotians were anything but unwilling and uninformed parties in the confederation negotiations. Nor were they merely cogs in an impersonal technological process: a legislative majority actively sought technological progress and saw unification as a means of obtaining it; they debated the issue intelligently and knowledgeably and in the discouraging realization that they no longer enjoyed the support of their electorate.

4

The Grand Trunk Railway:
The New Imperialism

If these forefathers of ours could rise from their graves this day they would be inclined to see in our hospitals, in our railroads, in the achievements of our physical science, confirmation of that old superstition of theirs, proofs of the kingdom of God, realizations of the gifts which Christ received for men, vaster than any of which they had dreamed.

The spinning-jenny and the railroad, Cunard's liners and the electric telegraph, are to me, if not to you, signs that we are, on some points at least, in harmony with the universe; that there is a mighty spirit working among us, who cannot be your anarchic and destroying Devil, and therefore may be the Ordering and Creating God.

Charles Kingsley (1851)[1]

During the 1850s, British investors financed the construction of a 2200-km railway across Canada at the cost of £12 million.[2] Considered at the time to be the longest international railway in the world, the Grand Trunk Railway of Canada appears to be an example of British imperialist expansion. Prominent London bankers, like Sir Thomas Baring and George Glyn, invested heavily in the project, while the large British railway construction firm of Peto, Brassey, Jackson & Betts built much of the railway. In addition, the British investors, who held the vast majority of the company's shares and bonds, assumed virtual control over the firm's daily management. By all appearances, then, the Grand Trunk was an imperial design in a colonial setting.

Viewed from a colonial perspective, however, the project takes on a much different character. The massive transfer of railway technology to

Canada emerges not simply as imperialist domination but rather as a complex interaction between Colonial Office bureaucrats, Lombard Street financiers, and British North American promoters and politicians. The railway-construction program instilled in Canadians a measure of self-confidence. It made them more assertive and nationalistic. While Canadians actively sought British financing to bring railway technology to North America, they adapted it to their harsh environment; they used it to loosen the ties with Great Britain, to launch a process of state centralization and regularization, and to implement the first stages in the creation of a transcontinental nation. Assisted by railway technology, Canadians began to revolutionize North American trade and commerce, looking increasingly to the rapidly expanding market of the United States, and gradually abandoning their total reliance on staple exports to Great Britain. Yet, they shared with the British imperialists a fundamental ambition – the conquest of the vast continental wilderness; like the imperialists, they came to believe that the locomotive would assist them in their dominion over nature. It was this mutual faith in steam technology, the philosophy of railways, that had a greater impact upon the fiscal, political, and national evolution of Canada than Britain's expansive, commercial imperialism.

The Grand Trunk Railway was conceived within the context of the new free-trade imperialism, the recognition that mercantilism was no longer needed to maintain Britain's commanding lead as the world's largest industrial producer. Free-trade imperialism, instead, concentrated its attention on trade and commerce; it sought to ensure a constant supply of inexpensive raw materials and foodstuff to feed the insatiable appetites of its workers and their machines. Moreover, if it could encourage its colonies and other countries to concentrate their energies on producing these wares, it could at worst slow, and at best halt, their own industrialization. In any case, the empire, with its enormous variety of resources, was to be a secure fountain of supplies as well as a stable market.[3]

Despite its free-trade doctrines, then, Britain continued to expand its influence across the globe. Throughout the last half of the nineteenth century, it used a constantly changing mix of formal and informal methods to advance its political and economic status. If necessary, it employed political and military means to retain or acquire territories, but if possible it preferred informal techniques – trade and commerce, investments and technology, immigration, education, and Christian missions – to integrate new regions into its expanding economy.[4] In short, the British people did whatever was required to maintain global economic supremacy.

Among the various means of extending empire, the transfer of railway technology was central. Along with steamships and telegraphs, the railway made rapid and efficient communications, and mass transfers of people and goods, possible and economically feasible. As well as conveying the other modes of empire enlargement, railways were also the principal generators of informal empires. In eastern Europe, Asia, Africa, and America, European powers employed railway imperialism to thwart rivals, maintain control, and expand their spheres of influence.[5] The transportation revolution, which rail technology produced, carried enormous territorial implications. 'The locomotive clearly had a unique propensity for integrating and annexing territory,' Ronald Robinson has recently argued, 'for monopolizing its resources, and for preempting the future of great stretches of country.'[6]

British America was not exempt from the integrating powers of steam transportation. Beginning in the late 1840s, the Colonial Office initiated or actively supported several schemes for an intercolonial railway in the colonies and at various times offered or approved guaranteed loans to implement the plans. The most obvious purpose of its strategy was to preserve the delicate balance of British interests in North America. In the first place, imperial officials sought to protect the extensive investments that British bankers, financiers, and even manufacturers had made in the United States, particularly in the South.[7] Second, in order to reduce the risk to their global economic hegemony, the diplomats endeavoured to prevent Americans from gaining territorial control over the entire continent.[8] Lastly, they tried to maintain the allegiance of British North America with a moderate, tactful approach. Ever mindful of the lesson of the American Revolution, the Colonial Office rarely imposed its policies on reluctant colonies; it much preferred subtle pressure and cautious diplomacy.

Behind Britain's strategy lay the philosophy of railways. Enchanted by the vision of conquering the North American continent through technology, the Colonial Office strongly supported a Halifax-Québec railway as the first stage in a transcontinental railway. But, in keeping with the new imperialism, the cabinet agreed only to share but not assume the entire cost of constructing the project. In other words, it believed that colonists must shoulder the primary financial responsibility for the scheme. Meanwhile, it permitted colonial leaders to play an important and active part in setting the economic agenda for their provinces; it did not interfere when colonial governments committed virtually all their resources to building local railways that suited their own purposes and at times contradicted imperial objectives.[9]

From its inception, the Grand Trunk Railway of Canada was part of a visionary ocean-to-ocean scheme. The railway emerged from the unsuccessful round of negotiations that Joseph Howe had launched late in 1851. A conference of colonial officials and railway contractors in Toronto in January 1852 had developed the outlines of a giant railway from Halifax through Québec, Montréal, and Toronto to Detroit, a branch line through Saint John to Bangor, Maine, and eventually a main line from the Canadas to the Pacific coast.[10] Portentously, metropolitan rivalry between Halifax and Saint John and a decided lack of interest among Canadians prevented immediate implementation of any of the grandiose plans. In sum, colonial governments were unwilling to make substantial investments in this massive railway project if they did not recognize instant benefits for their taxpayers.

Faced with a collapsed accord and an indifferent constituency at home, Canada's chief negotiator, Francis Hincks, abandoned the Maritimers and concluded an arrangement for the construction of a railway from Montréal to Hamilton. The large British railway construction firm of Peto, Brassey, Jackson & Betts agreed to build the railway, while Baring Brothers and Glyn, Mills and Company, the powerful London banking firms and the province's financial agents, undertook to arrange the capitalization. British interests, then, were to build a large segment and finance most of the proposed trunk railway.[11]

Lacking domestic capital, the Canadian government prepared several strategies to attract British investors. In 1851, the Main Trunk Line of Railway Act augmented the Guarantee Act of 1849 by securing the principal as well as the interest of Canadian railway debentures.[12] As in 1849, the province's financial agents warned the government that such open-ended, unlimited guarantees exposed the province to unscrupulous contractors who might artificially raise costs, propose unrealistic projects, and build competing lines. Ostensibly, the bankers expressed reluctance to interfere in the province's fiscal affairs; nevertheless, they bluntly warned Francis Hincks that they would not extend the province's credit unless it restricted the guarantee legislation to trunk lines.[13] Since the stipulation did not threaten the Grand Trunk project, and having no alternative sources of capital, Hincks accepted the condition and also assured the Barings that he would award them and Glyn, Mills the Grand Trunk portfolio.[14] But the Hincks government ignored the bankers' warning and expanded state support of railway construction in 1852 by establishing the Consolidated Municipal Loan Fund, which permitted municipalities to borrow money to subsidize transportation improvements.[15]

If the actions of the Canadas caused the London bankers considerable worry, subsequent events probably produced sleepless nights. Anxious to

grab a substantial part of lucrative construction contracts, colonial entrepreneurs and politicians, led by Alexander Galt, president of the St
Lawrence and Atlantic Railway and member of the legislative assembly,
forced Hincks to incorporate some completed as well as projected railways
into his plans. As a result, the Montréal-Hamilton scheme burgeoned into
an international railway system with its eastern terminal in Portland,
Maine, and its western in Sarnia. Concluded early in 1853, the deal entailed
a very costly buyout of the St Lawrence and Atlantic, an overly expensive
lease of the Atlantic and St Lawrence, as well as profitable construction
contracts for Galt and associates for the lines west of Toronto. Galt's irre-
pressible demands that local businessmen win a sizeable share of the lavish
spending expanded the project's length from 530 to 2200 kilometres and its
cost from £3 million to £12 million. All this was based on an exceedingly
optimistic estimate of earnings backed by a favourable assessment of Canada's economy and a blatant disregard for potential competition.[16]

Despite the ballooning expansion in plans, Baring Brothers, Glyn, Mills
and Company, and Peto, Brassey, Jackson & Betts retained their interest in
the Grand Trunk Railway. In fact, even though they were the province's
bankers, Thomas Baring and George Glyn invested directly in the project
by subscribing for one-twelfth of the capital and accepted, albeit reluctantly, positions on the London board of directors. Consequently, the
financial health of two prominent London banks and a major construction
firm, with close and interlocking interests, was irrevocably tied to the welfare of the Grand Trunk.[17]

Within years, however, it was evident that the railway was not to be a
profitable venture. Many factors contributed to its sluggish growth. The
acquisition of the Montréal-Portland railway, for one, came at an excessively high cost and became a burdensome drain on the company's
resources. Meanwhile heavy start-up costs placed the company at a severe
disadvantage. Its engineers often chose uneconomical routes encumbered
with steep gradients and sharp curves; and many local contractors over-
charged the company. Moreover, the political decision to build on the
broad rather than standard gauge common in the United States meant that
the Grand Trunk faced heavy trans-shipment costs whenever it accepted
American traffic. To make matters worse, the economic downturn, especially the crash of 1857, eroded traffic and dissipated railway investments.

Good and efficient management might have alleviated some of these
problems, but the company's board of directors, based in London, misun-
derstood the Canadian context of the railway's competition; it naively
applied British experience to North American circumstances. The London

board of directors, for example, did not appreciate that, unlike British railways, Canadian roads could not better river or canal freight rates because most freight was comparatively bulky and had to be moved over long distances to remote markets through thinly populated districts. Consequently, failing to recognize that west of Montréal the Grand Trunk competed headlong with one of the finest waterways in the world, they bypassed major port cities like Kingston and even designed a poor access to Montréal. West of Toronto, the Grand Trunk competed with the Great Western Railway, which, as a connector between several American railways, complemented the north-eastern railway system. The Grand Trunk, on the other hand, unrealistically attempted to vie directly with American railways for long-distance through traffic. In sum, the Grand Trunk's promoters, with little direct knowledge of North America, believed the propaganda of colonial promoters and their brochures and dangerously underestimated the power of their competitors.[18]

The railway's financial troubles, which became chronic, appeared quickly. By 1855, virtually bankrupt, its shares discounted at 50 per cent, the company appealed to the colonial government for interest guarantees on a new £900,000, 6 per cent bond issue.[19] Subsequently, the firm returned on several occasions for still more government assistance, but each infusion of new capital failed to boost the value of its securities.

The Grand Trunk's predicament was worsened by its entanglement in sectional politics, a direct result of having to accept government assistance. The decision to abandon the Halifax-Québec railway, for instance, turned the line east of Montréal into an unprofitable local road. When company officials asked for permission to postpone construction of that section, the government refused.[20] Members of the legislature representing Canada East, who felt their region was being marginalized in railway development, made it clear they would only support further Grand Trunk guarantees if the eastern section was completed. A.A. Dorion, who usually opposed railway aid, stated it candidly. 'Even if the section from Quebec to Trois-Pistoles were likely to be as unprofitable as has been represented, yet justice to the inhabitants of this part of the country requires that it should be completed,' he asserted, for 'the burden of the interest will be felt by the whole population from one end of the Province to the other, and therefore every portion of the community should derive from it as much benefit as possible.'[21] Consequently, in 1856, the government required the corporation to use part of an aid package to proceed with the St Thomas line eastward for at least 120 kilometres. That demand sparked sharp criticism from Canada West, which did not need the Grand Trunk to reach the Atlantic.

The Toronto *Globe* lambasted the government that 'compelling the Grand Trunk Company to build this unproductive road [from St Thomas to Rivière-du-Loup] is one of the worst points of the Government scheme.'[22] Company officials noted that the eastern section was 'sadly unremunerative,' and complained that the government should not require them to spend any more money on construction nor compel the company to operate east of Richmond in winter without an operating subsidy. The company's Canadian directors noted that inadequate traffic and heavy operating costs east of Montréal severely drained company revenues.[23] They had little choice, however; with Canada West adamantly opposed to financial assistance, the company could not afford also to alienate Canada East. Sectional politics, therefore, forced the Grand Trunk to carry out its obligations and operate the eastern line all year.

Burdened with operating the costly line east of Québec, the Grand Trunk pressed for the construction of an intercolonial railway as part of a national undertaking. The Canadian directors argued that the Richmond–Rivière-du-Loup section must be viewed as 'a National rather than a private undertaking,' and urged the provincial government to make this section part of the proposed intercolonial.[24] Meanwhile George C. Glyn merely noted, 'I hope the Eastern line to the other provinces will be sanctioned,'[25] thus making the eastern section profitable and the sale of Grand Trunk bonds much easier.

The company's motivation for building an intercolonial railway was astutely recognized by the *Canadian News*, a tireless and not unbiased booster of colonial securities. In a particularly observant and hard-headed editorial, it noted that everyone with investments in British North America had a vital interest in an intercolonial railway because without it the Grand Trunk remained 'shut out from the main source relied upon for the through traffic by the failure of the Imperial Government fulfilling their pledge with respect to the line to Halifax and St John.'[26] Faced with competition from American railways, imperial postal subsidies to New York and Boston, and a much larger volume of British immigrants to the United States than to the colonies, the paper argued that the Grand Trunk must develop long-haul through traffic. The paper also observed that the colonies had gone as far as they could in assisting the construction of rail lines and could only increase their revenues 'by making those works remunerative.' Clearly, then, those with investments in British North America had a stake in urging the British government to subsidize the intercolonial project.

Even the cautious London *Times* supported an imperial subsidy for the intercolonial project. It laconically observed that 'upwards of £20,000,000 of British capital invested in Canadian railways is in great jeopardy, owing to the want of access to and from the Atlantic through British territory.'[27] Imperial assistance was justified because 'the Grand Trunk Railway was constructed on the distinct assurance [from the imperial and provincial governments] that the line would be continued through New Brunswick and Nova Scotia' to the Atlantic.

The importance of an intercolonial railway to the survival of the Grand Trunk and the significance of the railway program to the colonial economy became dramatically evident in a political debate that raged in the Canadian legislature in the late 1850s. With an economic depression seriously eroding government revenues, just as Canada's major railways and several municipalities were near bankruptcy, the government faced a worrisome budget deficit, exacerbated by the full weight of the railway debenture guarantees. The economic crisis was complicated politically by chronic constitutional clashes between English- and French-speaking, Upper and Lower Canadians, a stalemate that virtually crippled the legislature. In an attempt to end the interminable debates and free the chamber to address the province's economic woes, Alexander Galt, the member for Sherbrooke, asked the legislators to repeal the union of the two Canadas, to rejoin them under federal principles, to invite the Maritimes to enter the rejuvenated constitution, and, lastly, to expand the new nation westward to the Pacific.[28] Taken one-by-one, none of Galt's proposals was uniquely his own. The total package was. And casting the government's economic-development focus to the British North American West was a novel twist to an emerging economic nationalism in Canada. Clearly asserting that the rich natural resources of the territories promised limitless opportunities for new investments and economic growth, Galt pleaded with his colleagues to stop quibbling over trivialities. 'Half a continent is ours if we do not keep on quarrelling about petty matters [cultural concerns] and lose sight of what interests us more [economic development],' he implored.[29] If Canadians really wanted to prosper, they had to adopt a 'firm national policy,' a comprehensive plan that would transform several insignificant provinces into one mighty economic power spanning the continent. As part of this 'national policy,' Galt also proposed higher tariffs in order to restore 'vitality' to certain 'languishing' branches of Canadian manufacturing.

Political union, western expansion, and a transcontinental railway were premature concepts in 1858, but a year later, as minister of finance, Galt introduced a protective tariff that he believed would stimulate Canadian industries by shielding them from foreign competitors, including British manufacturers. In his 1859 budget, Galt called for a strong central government with sufficient powers and revenues to create an independent and integrated British North America. The speech clearly signalled that Canada considered responsible government to mean considerable independence in fiscal policy as well as political programs.

Although his choices were limited, Galt deliberately increased the tariff on manufactured goods but did so in an unusual and highly effective way.[30] In keeping with the spirit of the Reciprocity Treaty then in effect, Galt placed most raw materials on the duty-free roster, divided semi-processed merchandise between the free and 10 per cent categories, and charged fully finished products a standard 20 per cent levy. In this very systematic way, Galt allowed industrialists to import raw stock freely and partly processed items at greatly reduced rates. In other words, he provided effective tariff protection both to partly and fully processed manufactured goods and in the process wrote 'a tariff schedule that would set the stage for the development of a broadly based industrial structure in the Province of Canada.'[31]

Galt's tariff also kept in mind the expensive transportation network the province had just completed. In order to remain competitive, Galt argued, Canada had built 'the most rapid and complete means of communication which modern science has placed at our command.'[32] Its enormous cost was fully justified, he suggested, as the works had drawn millions in foreign investment into the Canadian economy and had resulted in the reduction of freight rates. More efficient transportation benefited Canadian industrialists and farmers alike because it provided them with cheaper tools and other input items while it gave them better returns on their productions. Galt even attempted to assuage irate British manufacturers by declaring that decreased freight costs ameliorated the increased tariffs somewhat. More to the point, however, he acknowledged that 'unless Canada could combine with her unrivalled inland navigation, a railroad system connected therewith, and mutually sustaining each other, the whole of her large outlay must for ever remain unproductive.'[33] To survive as a relatively independent economy, it had been necessary for Canada to adopt the most modern transportation technology available; once committed to that strategy, the government had to protect its investment by continuing commitments. The increase in tariffs, Galt emphasized time and again, was required not for the ordinary needs of the civil government but to finance a philosophy of railways that envisioned Canada's escape from British commercial domination and the ability to meet competition from American trading systems.[34]

Concomitant with the need for an efficient transportation network was the requirement of sufficient traffic to support it. In Galt's opinion, the lack of freight was the major reason for the financial difficulties of Canada's railways. To remedy the problem, he made what was perhaps the most significant alteration in Canada's tariff structure. He changed it entirely from specific to *ad valorem* duties. As he explained it, specific duties placed the tax on items – a box of tea, a barrel of flour, a keg of nails – rather than on their value or quality. In *ad valorem* duties the levy was calculated on the value of the product at the place where a Canadian merchant bought it. Using sugar as an example, Galt observed that Canada's refiners bought virtually all their stock in New York. Under the new *ad valorem* rates, customs officials would calculate the Cuba–New York freight charges into the amount of duties payable. Not so if Canadian refiners bought their sugar in Cuba and shipped it directly by water to Montréal.[35] In other words, Galt wanted to use the tariff to wrest Canadian trade away from American seaports back to the St Lawrence River and the Grand Trunk Railway, a policy directly aimed at United States importers. More subtly, the new technique, Galt was quick to reassure British manufacturers, gave them a slight benefit over American competitors because the heavy transatlantic transport costs would not be reflected in the duties on their products if Canadians shipped them directly via Montréal.

Despite these assurances, Galt's 1859 budget explicitly provided a measure of protection for Canadian manufacturers and St Lawrence merchants. As he put it in his budget speech: 'I hold it most important that we should have a national policy as regards trade and commerce.'[36] The Canadian government was set on shielding its costly transportation systems and forcing as much traffic as possible through Canadian channels even if this policy was contrary to imperial designs.

Not unexpectedly, Galt's tariff revisions aroused considerable opposition, particularly from George Brown, member of the legislature and editor of the Toronto *Globe*. As a Liberal, Brown instinctively disliked protectionism in any form, preferring to see industry rise on its own without government intervention. In the assembly he charged that the tariff threatened the Reciprocity Treaty and placed an excessive tax burden on consumers, particularly the farmers of Canada West. He also hammered home one of his favourite themes – the reduction of government expenditures as the solution for the government's financial difficulties.[37] But protectionism was only one stumbling block. Toronto itself was becoming industrialized, and the city and surrounding urban centres were cultivating a strong protectionist lobby, a phenomenon not entirely lost on a politician and businessman like George Brown.[38] The *bête noir* was sectionalism. The *Globe* came directly to the point. The *ad valorem* duties would 'force the current of western trade into a new channel for the benefit of an insignificant class.'[39] Lest anyone miss the identity of the 'insignificant class,' the paper fumed that Galt aimed 'to secure to Montréal importers in a single year the command of Western markets; inflicting injury upon every merchant of Toronto, Hamilton, and London.' While George Brown, the *Globe*, and the Toronto Board of Trade did not attack Galt's basic premises – economic expansion, unity of the St Lawrence, the improvement of the transportation system – they decried the specific techniques he employed to achieve them.[40] They had uncovered one of the most serious flaws in Galt's 'national policy' – a sectional bias that favoured Montréal over Toronto.[41]

The debate, following the Galt budget, reflected contemporary attitudes. Canadians at mid-century agreed that territorial expansion and further railway construction were the keys to the province's future prosperity and the creation of a nation.[42] Moreover, they also concurred that to some extent the state was to be an agent in economic planning and direction. While Reformers often challenged the details of this strategy, the Liberal-Conservative party was no longer reticent and its 1859 tariff was a manifestation of its stand. The party put Canada firmly on the protectionist path and commenced the move towards a British North American *Zollverein*, an intercolonial railway, and western annexation. With the philosophy of railways as its foundation, tariffs, factories, and rails had replaced heritage, language, and patriotism as national building blocks.

Neither Galt's nationalistic fiscal policy nor the completion of the main line from Portland to Sarnia in November 1859 eased the Grand Trunk's financial difficulties. Less than a year later, it was in deep financial trouble and suspended interest payments on its ordinary bonds. By the end of the year, the company required more than £2.5 million in government assistance to meet interest payments in London and Canada and to undertake improvements, including the purchase of rolling stock. A special committee, which had assessed the predicament, argued that the corporation had a right to further subsidies because it had been required to build lines that no investor would have undertaken merely on business grounds.[43] The company's position remained precarious, however, and in the last half of 1861 it did not earn enough to pay interest on its first preference bonds. Moreover, it could not sell a second preference bond issue at a 21½ per cent discount. Should the Grand Trunk collapse, Baring and Glyn and most other London bankers would be seriously compromised as would the credit of the Canadian government and colonial banks. Little wonder that the *Times* predicted catastrophe should the business fail. 'No single event in the history of finance,' the paper intoned, 'has ever caused such wide-spread anxiety as now prevails regarding this undertaking.'[44]

Faced with virtual bankruptcy, in July 1861 the Grand Trunk directors appointed Edward Watkin, an experienced railway manager, as their special representative to Canada. Born in 1819, the son of a wealthy Manchester cotton merchant, Watkin grew up in the dawning age of railways and telegraphs and intuitively adopted its ideology of material progress and supremacy over nature. Driven by a forceful, persistent entrepreneurial zeal, he applied his exceptional managerial talent to several British railways, including the Trent Valley, the London and North Western, and the Manchester, Sheffield and Lincolnshire. Aside from his considerable practical experience, Watkin also moved easily among London's political and financial élite and knew the colonial secretary, the Duke of Newcastle, personally. Watkin also had some familiarity with America, having toured the United States and Canada in 1851. In deference to his extensive experience, the board gave Watkin 'the fullest powers of action in respect to investigation into the affairs, organization & management of the Company.'[45] In November 1862, it named him company president, succeeding Sir Thomas Baring.

The first and most practical of Watkin's remedial measures was a thorough financial reorganization of the company, a plan he introduced to the shareholders at a special meeting in London on 9 August 1862. His scheme was designed to give the company a five-year breathing space so that it could ease its massive debts and improve its profitability. In a comprehensive action plan, the shareholders approved new borrowing, a reduction on rents and leases, and a decrease in interest rates paid on its first and second preference bonds. The meeting also declared that arrears in bond interest, dividend payments, and various rents were to be capitalized into bonds or stocks and it required current creditors to accept half their payments in cash and half in bonds. The proposed changes, approved by the Canadian government in the Grand Trunk Re-organization Act later that year, resulted in a significant net reduction of total annual rental and interest charges.[46]

Meanwhile, Watkin restructured the company's management, eliminating many wasteful practices. He transferred more and more of the financial accountability and management control to the British directors. He hired C.J. Brydges, an aggressive, independent manager, away from the Great Western Railway and named him the Grand Trunk's superintendent.[47] Although Brydges's intimate connections with Canada's leading politicians and questionable financial practices often raised pointed questions in the press, in the provincial legislature, and at shareholders' meetings, he helped Watkin reform the company's local management and operating practices. They purchased heavier rolling stock, for example, and switched to a better type of iron rail; they gained a good access to Montréal's harbour; and they improved connections with the ports of New York and Boston.[48]

Besides management reforms, Watkin sought to alleviate the high cost of competition with the Great Western and the Buffalo and Lake Huron railways, both of which served as portage roads across southern Ontario. Although the three railways had negotiated covert operating and rate agreements as early as 1853,[49] in January 1862 Watkin completed the negotiations for a formal merger of the firms. In justifying the scheme to government, he argued that it would enable the combined railways to compete more successfully with water transport as well as American railways. Watkin also cited reduced working expenses, more efficient operations, and less need for future capitalization. Lastly, he asserted, an amalgamation would enhance the credit of Canada and of the railways and improve freight and passenger service.[50] Despite the elaborate rationalization, the Canadian government refused to sanction an obvious monopoly; nevertheless, the Grand Trunk continued to explore cooperative arrangements with the Great Western and did eventually complete a merger with the Buffalo company, thus gaining crucial access to American railways along the Niagara River.[51]

Besides implementing practical and effective management reforms, Edward Watkin also developed a set of ambitious and idealistic expansion plans. These schemes were a product not so much of Watkin's practical railway experience as of his immersion in the technological culture of the mid-nineteenth century. An unshakable faith in the ability of railways to free man from the obstacles of landscape and climate permeated his practical business sense. Like many of his contemporaries, Watkin's functional managerial expertise was infected by an excessive optimism in railway technology; he believed that the new transportation technique was the panacea for lagging, stagnant economies and that it could create unprecedented national wealth and prosperity. At the same time, however, he also understood that the Grand Trunk did not collect sufficient revenues to support its staggering debt because it had failed to meet its primary mandate, that is, to carry long-haul freight from the midwestern United States and Canada West to the Atlantic seaboard. 'This line, both as regards its length, the character of its works, and its alliances with third parties, is both too extensive, and too expensive, for the Canada of today,' he explained to Baring and added that if 'left, as it is, dependent mainly upon the development of population and industry on its own line, and upon the increase in traffic of ... [Canada] west, it cannot be expected for years to come to emancipate itself thoroughly from the load of obligations connected with it.'[52]

The Grand Trunk's fiscal problems, Watkin claimed, could not be solved merely by practising greater economies; they demanded bold, expansionist measures. Although savings effected through careful management would certainly improve the company's financial situation, he believed that ultimately success could come only by developing an entirely new and possibly monopolistic market. He proposed that the Grand Trunk expand westward to the Pacific through British territory, that it open the expansive northwestern prairies to settlement, and that it stimulate trade on the Pacific rim. That the ailing railway would triple its size appeared of little concern to Watkin. His mind, infused with an exhilarating confidence in the limitless possibilities of railway technology, was captivated by a grandiose scheme.

Try for one moment to realize China opened to British commerce: Japan also opened: the new gold fields in our own territory on the extreme west, and California, also within our reach: India, our Australian Colonies – all our eastern Empire, in fact, material and moral, and dependent (as at present it too much is) upon an overland communication, through a foreign state.

Try to realize, again, assuming physical obstacles overcome, a main through Railway, of which the first thousand miles belong to the Grand Trunk Company, from the shores of the Atlantic to those of the Pacific, made just within – as regards the northwestern and unexplored district – the corn-growing latitude. The result to this Empire would be beyond calculation; it would be something, in fact, to distinguish the age itself; and the doing of it would make the fortune of the Grand Trunk.[53]

Keenly aware that the nearly bankrupt Grand Trunk Railway could not raise the capital for such a massive project, Watkin expected colonial and imperial governments to assist in the construction of the transcontinental railway. He also required them to support a large-scale immigration scheme to populate the North-West.

To elevate his proposal beyond a mere business rescue scheme, Edward Watkin resurrected the transcontinental railway rhetoric. Echoing the schemes of Lord Durham, Earl Grey, and Lord Elgin, Watkin assumed that the unification of British North America was desirable and he argued that the railway would be essential for the economic development of the newly formed nation. Any investment in a Pacific railway, he maintained, no matter how large, was small in comparison to the anticipated economic benefit because 'such a route must become the great highway to and from Europe; and whatever nation possesses that highway, must wield of necessity the commercial sceptre of the world.'[54]

In making his proposal, Watkin took advantage of changing popular perceptions of British America's north-western interior. Worried about escalating land costs, unprofitable railways, and high unemployment, politicians and businessmen began to look to these vast territories for new investment opportunities, markets, and jobs. In 1857, Lorin Blodgett, an American climatologist, had published a massive work suggesting that the North-West was suitable for agriculture because average temperatures and precipitation were more favourable than previously believed. Blodgett's work coincided with an increased curiosity about the western territories and its vast untilled soil resources.[55] The Toronto *Globe*, for example, edited by the fiery, expansionist George Brown, launched a barrage of articles and editorials extolling the fertility of the North-West.[56] The need for more accurate knowledge prompted the Canadian and British governments to send scientific expeditions to Rupert's Land. The Canadian party, associated with naturalist H.Y. Hind, and the British group, led by Captain John Palliser, identified a fertile belt along the Saskatchewan River and a large arid region to the south.[57] Their qualitative distinction, soon associated with good and bad lands, made a lasting impression on the public mind and set the stage for future colonization, administration, and transportation policies. The prairies had taken on new economic value, a utility that could be realized only through exploitation, by adapting the environment to agricultural needs. In 1858, the Canadian legislature linked western annexation with a Halifax-Québec and a Pacific railway, wrapping it all in imperialist rhetoric.

That in our view of the speedy opening up of the Territories now occupied by the Hudson's Bay Company, and the development and settlement of the vast regions between Canada and the Pacific Ocean, it is essential to the interests of the Empire at large, that a highway extending from the Atlantic Ocean Westward, should exist, which would at once place the whole British possessions in America within the ready access and easy protection of Great Britain, whilst, by the facilities for internal communication thus afforded, the prosperity of those great Dependencies would be promoted, their strength consolidated and added to the strength of the Empire, and their permanent Union with the Mother Country secured.[58]

With these words ringing in the background, for the next decade Canadian governments struggled to gain political and economic control over the North-West.[59]

Edward Watkin neatly dovetailed his expansionist ambitions for the Grand Trunk with Canada's western objectives. Citing H.Y. Hind, Watkin observed that while the American plains were arid and barren, justly earning the sobriquet of the Great American Desert, the British North American plains were rimmed on the north by a wide fertile belt eminently suitable for settlement. Annexed to the federated colonies, the North-West was Canada's vital connection to the Pacific. Thus, he concluded, a unified British North America, linked from the Atlantic to the Pacific by a transcontinental railway, would not only provide a great land route between Europe and Asia, it could also open a vast new territory.[60]

To this exhilarating nation-building theme, Edward Watkin – who was in every sense a British citizen – added a potent imperialist sentiment. The projected land route, he believed, must of necessity remain in imperial hands, not just for narrow economic or patriotic reasons but because the British had a duty to share their liberal and progressive civilization with the world. Like many of his contemporaries, Watkin elevated the political institutions and technological culture of the British Isles to dizzying heights. He assumed that this treasure must be shared with the world.[61] Watkin was convinced that it was the God-given duty of all citizens of the British empire to use the most advanced available communication technologies, like the transatlantic telegraph cable, to extend their enlightened, progressive industrial culture across the globe. But the most important tool in this civilizing mission was the railway. The proposed transcontinental rail line, then, was in his view more than a means of extricating the Grand Trunk from its financial difficulties; it was an evangelical mission that would transmit British culture across the continent.

Watkin's vibrant, idealistic ideology of technological progress, which shaped his practical business observations, unwittingly articulated the new imperial dream – the spread of British civilization worldwide. While restrictive legislation and preferential treatment, backed by naval power, had served as the traditional methods of controlling settled colonies, by the middle of the nineteenth century the security and order provided by constitutional and legal provisions had taken their place. The new informal empire was to be bound by the ties of free trade, commerce, and economic improvement. At the same time, Victorians wanted to spread abroad the muscular Christianity and education that they believed had made Britain powerful, wealthy, and enlightened. And, as all these new techniques of empire-building depended upon communications, they looked to technology, especially the railway, as the primary bond of empire. Not only did it smash natural obstacles, but the locomotive also broke the barriers of distance, of region, and even of class. The British Victorian age clearly recognized the universalizing power of the steam engine; the railway was to be the greatest missionary of all.[62]

With such imperialist rhetoric preached from the pulpit, expounded in the press, and proclaimed in countless pamphlets and novels, little wonder that Watkin's pragmatic business ethic was infused with an urgent altruistic sense of mission, the growth of empires. 'I struggled for the union of the Canadian Provinces,' he later recalled, 'in order that they might be retained under the sway of the best form of government.'[63] He reaffirmed that the proposed new transcontinental federation would be 'a great British nation, planted, for ever, under the Crown, and extending from the Atlantic to the Pacific.'[64] That union would bring the 'great outspread of solid prosperity and of rational liberty, of the diffusion of our civilization, and of the extension of our moral empire.' That new nation, he asserted, must never stand-still but must always move forward. 'The measure of its accomplishment must, century by century, rise higher and higher in the competition of nations.'[65]

Even if Watkin's lofty rhetoric cloaked the desperate financial position of the Grand Trunk, it nevertheless represented a genuine belief in the efficacy of technology and its ability to launch a nation onto the path of economic progress. That article of faith was not merely a powerful rationalization for incessant appeals for public assistance to private enterprise, it also inspired the entrepreneurial mind to accept expansion and growth as primary business principles. And when tied to a romantic vision of taming the North American wilderness, it impelled businessmen, like Edward Watkin, Sir Thomas Baring, and George Carr Glyn, to take extraordinary financial risks.

Thus, even the most utilitarian investors were infected by the spirit of romance and adventure invoked by Watkin's call for a transcontinental railway and the settlement of the mysterious North-West. The *Railway Times* applauded Watkin's expansionist plans because they were in 'unison with the temper and necessities of the times.'[66] At last, the paper enthused, these vast territories, with their enormous resources, were to be 'called upon to contribute their quota to English wealth in a manner, and to an extent, totally distinct from that to which this country has hitherto been accustomed.' Finally, the journal sighed with evident relief, aggressive entrepreneurs were ready to undertake the task for which the territories were created. 'It must yield its fruits and resources to the chief of all dominion – Civilized Man.' Was it not the duty of British businessmen – able to establish orderly development – to take up the charge? 'Standing as it were on the Grand Trunk railway at Kingston, and looking west to the copper region of Lake Superior, we begin to comprehend the extent of miles which spread beyond, and we settle down in a solemn conviction that it is indeed only by well-ordered steps that the mighty work of subduing the wilderness is to be accomplished.'

By the early 1860s, then, the London business community had accepted a revised perception of the North-West. The positive reports of the scientific expeditions had eroded the long-held belief that the vast northern expanse of the American continent was a barren and frozen wilderness, suitable only for the fur trade. The new view still saw a wilderness, but it was no longer hostile and barren but fertile and welcoming; and with the assistance of steam and telegraph technology it could be tamed and made serviceable to imperial purposes.[67]

Consequently, Watkin's stirring appeals to Britain's civilizing mission in North America struck a responsive chord among many imperial officials and politicians as well as British investors. Equally beguiled by the apparent omnipotence of railway technology, Colonial Office authorities readily embraced the intercolonial project as the eastern segment of a transcontinental railway. The Duke of Newcastle, who served as colonial secretary from 1859 to 1864, was an enthusiastic proponent of an intercolonial railway as the precursor to an economically strong and politically mature united British North America.[68] Newcastle saw the Halifax-Québec railway as a powerful antidote to the strident manifest destiny of the United States. He worried about the pro–United States feelings he detected in British America, particularly in New Brunswick and Nova Scotia.[69] While he accepted traditional arguments that the intercolonial was essential to the defence of British North America, especially in winter, he articulated a more sophisticated understanding of the impact of railway technology on society. Newcastle argued that the strongest case for the intercolonial could be made on political grounds. For the colonies to be weaned from their dependence on Great Britain, yet remain separate from the United States, they must be united. But unification was not possible unless communication between the provinces was improved. 'Canada cannot for ever – perhaps not for long – remain a British Colony. Upon this Railroad in my opinion depends in great measure her future destiny. Without it she cannot separate from England as an independent state. She must become a portion of that powerful Republic ... on her southern frontier ... [W]ith the Railroad made and the union with the Lower Provinces effected, she would

become to us a strong & self-reliant Colony so long as her present relationship with the Mother country continues, and when she separates she could
be a powerful and independent Ally.'[70] Newcastle, therefore, acknowledged the importance of the railway project, 'not only to the British American Colonies, but also to the mother country.' He viewed it as 'the
preliminary necessity' for the unification of British North America and 'an
iron-road, onwards to the Pacific.' In other words, Newcastle believed that
'the union of all the provinces and territories into "one great British America," was the necessary, the logical, result of completing the Intercolonial
Railway and laying broad foundations for the completion, as a condition of
such union, of a railway to the Pacific.'[71]

Thus bolstered by the enthusiastic support of some of London's most
influential financiers and politicians, Watkin's vision for an imperialist-
inspired British American transcontinental union seemed assured. He
believed quite sincerely that his duty was not only to solve the Grand
Trunk's precarious financial situation but also to be Newcastle's unofficial
and unpaid agent. The grand task before him, so he recalled later, included
more than the resuscitation of a dying corporation; he wanted to be 'somewhat useful in aiding those measures of physical union contemplated when
the Grand Trunk Railway was projected, and which must precede any confederation of interests such as ... the creation of the "Dominion of Canada."'[72] The blending of state and private interests, mutually resting on an
unshaken faith in a destined progress driven by technology, was complete.

To win support for the transcontinental scheme, Edward Watkin and the
Grand Trunk Railway Company launched an extremely active, carefully
prepared public-relations campaign. They organized several petitions to
Parliament signed by most of the influential businessmen in the City of
London, including directors of the Bank of England, the Bank of British
North America, the Canada Company, the British American Land Company, the Trust and Loan Company, the Hudson's Bay Company, as well
as Baring and Glyn. They also garnered petitions from Belfast, Manchester,
Bristol, Glasgow, Sheffield, and a dozen or so other centres. They led several delegations, representing all major interests in British North America,
to meetings with the Duke of Newcastle and other cabinet members and
they organized a number of public meetings that were extensively reported
in the London press.[73]

In February 1862 Edward Watkin was one of the founders of the British
North American Association, an informal alliance of businessmen with
North American interests. Although relatively short-lived and quiescent,
the association represented the common interests of a significant number of

influential businessmen in an intercolonial railway. An informal executive committee of the British North American Association transmitted most of the memorials on the railway to the British government. Though it declared itself ready to form a company to build the railway, it was never more than a community of interested people. Its significance was not in measurable achievements but rather in its relative size. Simply, the association represented an influential group of businessmen that gave the Halifax-Québec railway a certain sense of urgency.[74] By all appearances, railway imperialism, embodied in an Atlantic to Pacific railway initiative, was set to make a major expansion on the northern part of the American continent.

It was not to be, however, as Canadians had different priorities and preferred their own agenda. The Clear Grit Toronto *Globe*, for one, vigorously articulated Canadian opposition to the eastern portion of the transcontinental railway:

Nothing is offered which the English public think of any moment whatever. And no wonder, because we who are much more nearly concerned think quite as little of the scheme as they do. We shall never make a penny by it. Politically it might come in time to be of importance, commercially it is not worth a farthing. We in Upper Canada look westward for communication, not eastward; we have plenty avenues to the ocean, we have none to the ocean-like prairies of the North West ... The only Canadians who care a straw for the road are the few hermits in the wilderness which lies between Trois Pistoles and the New Brunswick line, and the members of the Cabinet, who desire to keep Mr. Watkins [sic], the Grand Trunk agent, amused and occupied during his sojourn in this country.[75]

Meanwhile, francophones in Canada East profoundly expressed the reservation that the delegates were reversing the real relationship between railways and nation-building. 'Ce n'est pas avec les chemins de fer que l'on crée un pays, c'est avec un pays déjà fait, c'est-a-dire, déjà peuplé, qu'on fait les chemins de fer,' *Le Pays* believed. 'Que l'on veuille bien remarquer que le chemin d'Halifax, d'ici à 25 ans au moins, ne peut être qu'une ligne militaire plutôt qu'une ligne commerciale. Le principal objet de cette ligne, c'est la défense des colonies, conséquemment le maintien de la suprématie anglaise.'[76] This perceptive comment, which implied that the state was more than railways, displayed a lively understanding of the complex cultural implications of massive technological projects and was also a clear warning that any Canadian administration had to proceed cautiously.

In fact, the lack of strong public support and the presence of pockets of outright opposition everywhere in British North America ultimately led to the failure of the negotiations. For more than a year, colonial negotiators braved the stormy Atlantic as they engaged in a seemingly endless round of interviews on both sides of the ocean, a perpetual cycle of meetings, social engagements, memoranda, and counter-arguments. And everywhere they went, Edward Watkin, the skilful conciliator, smoothed the way. If the colonist felt neglected by London society, Watkin arranged invitations to social events; if the negotiations appeared stalled, he organized new interviews; and, if imperial politicians balked, he initiated more petitions. He too crossed the Atlantic frequently, keeping a close watch on the Canadian and British legislatures, advising ministers on railway matters, and lobbying parliamentarians on both sides of the Atlantic.[77]

The obstacles that Watkin faced were formidable. In the first place, the imperial administration insisted that the intercolonial route be well away from the United States boundary, a condition that guaranteed a row between Nova Scotia and New Brunswick. Second, the British government refused to grant outright subsidies and demanded that colonial governments accept the principle of loan guarantees, a stipulation that substantially increased their contributions to the project. But, third, the Canadian government was reluctant to assume a sizeable increase in its debt to pay for a railway whose future benefits were not appreciated by most voters. In the end, late in 1862, Canada backed out of the latest agreement, ostensibly because Britain insisted on an unacceptable sinking fund. In fact, its weak government could not overcome widespread opposition to an expensive project that promised so few economic returns; it could not even muster political support for the project in Canada East. As *Le Pays* commented, 'Considérant sans doute que le point le plus fondamental du programme du ministère McDonald-Sicotte [sic] était la nécessité immédiate de réduire les dépenses publiques au niveau des recettes, et de faire disparaître les déficits avant de créer de nouvelles dettes, M. Dorion a jugé qu'une nouvelle addition à la dette publique rendrait peut-être impossible, au moins dans un temps assez prochain, le rétablissement de l'équilibre de notre budget.'[78]

Once again, the Québec paper had perceptively exposed a major problem. By the early 1860s, the Canadas were just emerging from one of the most serious financial crises in their history. Facing the near bankruptcy of several railways, a major bank, and several municipalities, the government had very few choices and virtually no funds for expansionist schemes. Before it could seriously consider transcontinental ideals, it had to face practical reality and put its finances in order. A succession of finance ministers began the difficult process of dismantling the haphazard methods of collecting, keeping, and spending money and instituting a formal system of budgets, accounts, and audits. These recovery measures, which also included a refunding of the provincial debt and a dramatic increase in tariffs, were devised to make Canada's free-spending businessmen-politicians fully accountable to the legislature and to decrease the colony's dependence on foreign bankers.[79]

Since the primary cause of Canada's fiscal plight was state support to private railways, the province also had to devise a new relationship with the Grand Trunk Railway, a task eased somewhat by the fall of the George-Etienne Cartier and John A. Macdonald government early in 1862. The defeated Liberal-Conservative government had been relatively favourable to the imperial agenda and, although reluctant to bail out the Grand Trunk, it had pushed the Re-organization Act through the 1862 session despite extreme and vocal opposition. Cartier and Macdonald had also proposed to end a lengthy Grand Trunk grievance by establishing an impartial board of arbitration to satisfy the company's demands for a more remunerative rate for government freight and mail. But the government did not have the political support to meet the conditions the imperial government set as the price for guaranteed loans for an intercolonial railway – lower tariffs and increased defence spending.

In May 1862, the Cartier-Macdonald government lost a crucial vote on a militia bill, and a new government came to office.[80] The new administration, headed by John Sanfield Macdonald and Louis Sicotte, was supported by Reformers and radicals, all of whom had severely criticized the corruption and venality of the railway boom, particularly the Grand Trunk Railway. J.S. Macdonald immediately scuttled the proposal for arbitration on mail subsidies and would have stopped the Grand Trunk Re-organization Act if such action would not have threatened to bankrupt the railway, with all the attendant and unthinkable financial consequences such a huge bankruptcy would bring with it.[81] With the centre of its support in Toronto and Canada West, the Macdonald-Sicotte government was initially lukewarm towards the intercolonial railway because it did not believe that an invasion from the United States was imminent or that a blockade on American railways to the Atlantic was likely. Moreover, once it fully comprehended the cost of the project, the government slowly began to extricate itself from any serious commitments. By the end of 1863, a re-formed ministry, led by J.S. Macdonald and A.A. Dorion, formally announced its inability to accept any imperial guarantees for an intercolonial railway. Meanwhile, it continued the comprehensive fiscal reforms commenced in the late 1850s by Alexander Galt. The new measures included a balanced budget achieved through decreased expenditures, increased taxation and user fees, the transfer of some expenses to local accounts, all offset somewhat by a decrease in import duties. These reforms were necessary, J.S. Macdonald argued, in order to strengthen the government's financial circumstances and bolster its bargaining position with London bankers and imperial officials. Like previous administrations, the Macdonald-Dorion government wanted to disengage itself from the tangled web of London bankers, Grand Trunk investors, and Colonial Office bureaucrats, all of whom were pushing unwanted agendas on the province. Thus, at the very time that imperial officials and Grand Trunk backers were pressing Canada to take dramatic expansionist steps, the provincial government was increasingly preoccupied with local programs.[82]

In an attempt to force Canadians to adopt an imperial perspective and to gain the support of Canada West for an intercolonial railway, Edward Watkin and the Duke of Newcastle tied the project to western annexation, an extremely popular prospect in the region. For nearly a decade, the Toronto *Globe* had advocated an aggressive western expansion policy in order to build a productive hinterland for Toronto, to revitalize the region's stagnating economy, and to solve the province's political stalemate. As a relentless critic of the Grand Trunk and alleged corruption associated with it, the *Globe* was unlikely to consent to any railway project that involved the British company but it might be persuaded if its favourite project, western annexation, were advanced.[83]

Newcastle's tactic appeared to work. In 1862, at an intercolonial conference at Québec, delegates resolved to extend the Halifax-Québec railway to the Pacific. Even if the resolution was little more than a sop to the people of Canada West, from this point on the Pacific railway was irrevocably attached to the intercolonial.

Despite the resolution, made after several days of enthusiastic meetings topped with convivial meals and copious amounts of wine and liquor, the Canadian government was not prepared to move quickly. As John S. Macdonald observed, 'To tell you the truth, the scheme of the In[ter] Col[onial] Road is anything but palatable throughout Canada, except in the District of Quebec & to the Eastward, and unless we can manage to galvanize it a little by assurances from the Colonial office of a move towards its Western extension, I do *not think we can float it in the Assembly.*'[84] Realizing, however, that an intercolonial railway would be very expensive as well as a political liability in Canada West, the executive council resolved that 'the realization of the hopes entertained in relation to the opening of the North West is essential to render the construction of the Intercolonial acceptable to the Province.'[85]

Meanwhile, the imperial government, which thought the intercolonial more important than western annexation, was not beyond a little blackmail to push its point. Newcastle made it clear that imperial assistance for transferring the western interior from the Hudson's Bay Company to Canada hinged on Canadian acceptance of an intercolonial railway. 'You may assure your Ministers if you like,' Newcastle warned Canada's Governor Lord Monck, 'that the degree of liberality with which Canada will be treated in the district in dispute between the Colony and the Hudson's Bay Company will depend on the manner in which they fulfil or repudiate their engagements in the East – if they break faith with the Lower Provinces and oppose all Imperial measures for their own party objects, I shall insist upon extreme rights belonging to England and the new Company in the West.'[86]

The Duke of Newcastle's reference to 'the new Company in the West' was the International Financial Society, a group of wealthy London investors that, inspired by Edward Watkin, had purchased the Hudson's Bay Company.[87] In the belief that the International Financial Society would commence the settlement of the western interior, Watkin worked hard throughout 1863 to maintain momentum for his plans. Besides continuously lobbying colonial and imperial administrations on behalf of the intercolonial railway, he founded the Atlantic and Pacific Telegraph and Transit Company as a precursor to a transcontinental railway. Typically, the new company, established in April 1863, had an exaggerated perception of its own importance. 'It is impossible,' its prospectus claimed, 'not to perceive that the establishment of direct Telegraphic Communication across the North American Continent, and entirely through British Territory, may exercise, sooner or later, a powerful influence on the Postal arrangements and commerce of British settlements in China and Japan and the Colonies of Australia and New Zealand.'[88]

Meanwhile Newcastle's heavy-handed interference in colonial affairs was foundering on the shoals of government parsimony. By the beginning of 1863, it was clear to the colonial secretary that 'unless this miserable creature [Sicotte] and his colleagues are turned out of office on the first day of the Session,' the intercolonial railway scheme was finished. 'And in that case,' he added, 'I shall be unwilling to play into their hands, by giving them the N.W. Transit scheme.'[89] In May, he turned down Watkin's request for imperial support for his telegraph and road project. Among the several objections cited, he stated explicitly that there would be no assistance for the project 'unless there were good reasons to expect that the kindred enterprise of connecting Halifax and Montreal by Railway would be promptly and vigorously proceeded with.'[90]

Watkin clearly understood Newcastle's position and, as he carefully explained to Sir Thomas Baring, the railway to the East, the opening of the North-West, the Pacific telegraph and railway, and indeed the future of the Grand Trunk railway were inextricably bound together. 'Intercolonial is, in fine,' he succinctly summarized the situation, 'absolutely essential to Grand Trunk; and Intercolonial is, under present circ[umstance]s in Canada, dependent on this other movement [to the north-west].'[91]

Even though Watkin clearly understood the position of the Colonial Office, he persisted and, while on another visit to Canada in the summer of 1863, he drafted an ambitious yet practical scheme for western settlement. He suggested to Sir Edmund Head that the Hudson's Bay should cede the North-West to the imperial government, which could then establish a Crown colony. This move would free a commercial enterprise from the responsibility and expense of governing the North-West and allow it to concentrate on the business side of colonization – that is, trade and commerce, communications and transportation, banking and retailing. As the essential first step in opening the territories, Watkin argued, the state must subsidize the construction of a telegraph.[92] Here then, in rough outline, was a sketch for the settlement of the North-West that gave an active role to the Hudson's Bay Company and other investment opportunities for its shareholders. Incidentally, it would also prepare the way for the Grand Trunk to expand westward to the Pacific.

Edward Watkin laid these plans in the expectation that the new Hudson's Bay Company would abandon the fur trade as its primary objective. He was badly mistaken, however, as Sir Edmund Head, the company's new governor, proved extremely reluctant to make any significant changes in the company's purpose. The firm's new owner, the International Financial Society, was essentially a mutual investment association with global interests: its shareholders were interested initially in the security of their dividends and only secondarily in grand and expensive settlement plans. To Watkin's disappointment, the society did not permit the Hudson's Bay Company to alter its commitment to the fur trade. Clearly Governor Head wanted to consolidate the company's position and, while open to some administrative reforms, he was not committed to a dramatic reorientation of its historic mission. More important, the powerful fur lords in the western interior, who as a group were influential shareholders in the company, were not swayed by idealistic visions of settlement and civilization. Keeping his eyes clearly on the balance books, Head dared not alienate the most important factors in the company. 'Our intention is to keep fast hold on what we have got so long as we can and at the same time not lose sight of further chances of progress,' he reassured the company's worried governor in Rupert's Land, Alexander Grant Dallas. 'We have no intention of letting the Telegraph and other matters of the kind prejudice our officers.'[93] Head insisted that Watkin make no agreements until the full board had approved the project.[94]

Sir Edmund's instructions came too late, however, as Watkin had already dispatched a surveyor to the North-West and had ordered some telegraph material.[95] Extremely embarrassed by Sir Edmund's orders, Watkin rushed back to London, where he learned that the company's executive committee was not prepared to act quickly, if at all. After a stormy meeting, Watkin resigned from the company and abandoned the telegraph project. Still, characteristically, he remained interested in the project and offered free transportation on the Grand Trunk Railway for any telegraph equipment.

Even though the Hudson's Bay Company authorized a survey of the telegraph route and ordered one hundred tons of wire and supplies to be delivered at Victoria and Red River in time for the 1865 construction season, it never started the project. In part, the company may have abandoned the scheme because the Canadian government refused financial assistance. But the rebuff had come in February 1864, well before the company ordered the supplies.[96] Also damaging was the fact that in April 1865 Victoria was linked by telegraph to San Francisco. Although an argument could still be made for an all-British connection across the continent, the Hudson's Bay Company was no longer interested in assisting any scheme leading to the colonization of its fur preserve.

The failure to build the telegraph in 1864 was highly symbolic. Despite the lofty rhetoric, neither Canada nor Great Britain was ready politically to make the financial commitment to westward expansion. Moreover, British financiers were becoming increasingly cautious about further massive investments in British North America. Although the railway had survived the 1862 financial crisis, it was still far from profitable and its shareholders were no longer prepared to assume additional risks on visionary projects. One issue of London's *Railway Times*, for instance, published more than forty letters commenting negatively on the firm's management.[97] The arguments, informed by nearly a decade of dismal semi-annual reports, laid the blame on inept and corrupt Canadian managers. The editors of the *Railway Times* agreed. Although they correctly understood the competitive disadvantages the Grand Trunk faced, they still believed that the railway could be successful if management control were seized from the meddling grasp of corrupt Canadian politicians and placed exclusively under the London board. They also expressed the feeling that Baring and Glyn were in collusion with the colonists in order to manipulate the minor shareholders, who were being 'dealt with as figures on a chessboard.' It is not the pawns, the periodical charged, 'but the players who gain by the movement.[98]

For his part, Sir Thomas Baring refused to subscribe to the Pacific telegraph because he believed it premature. Moreover, he personally believed that the plans for the North-West were not crucial to the survival of the Grand Trunk; and he had come to the conclusion that the intercolonial railway should be built by the imperial government. For the time being, he wanted to concentrate on securing his precarious investment in the Grand Trunk Railway. For Baring, too, the realities of the semi-annual reports had gradually rubbed the gloss from the company's shiny first prospectus.

Although Edward Watkin continued to keep a close eye on colonial developments, events overtook him. In the summer of 1864, yet another political crisis in the Canadas resulted in a coalition government committed to the confederation of British North America. Early in the fall, conferences at Charlottetown and Québec subsequently established the framework for a transcontinental nation and renewed the impetus to build an intercolonial railway. After all the years of bickering, rationalizing, and political posturing, the Maritime premiers were in a position to demand an intercolonial railway.[99] Canadians, realizing they needed the Maritimers in order to break their political stalemate, had no choice but to accept the railway as part of the confederation bargain. And, finally, with all parties in favour of an intercolonial railway, the imperial government was ready with its promised guarantees.

In the end, then, the Grand Trunk neither built nor operated the intercolonial or the Pacific railway and Edward Watkin's ambitious plans to create the world's largest railway were not realized. His prescription for the financially troubled Grand Trunk Railway had consisted of cautious traditional tactics within a bold innovative strategy. On the one hand, his pragmatic business skills had called for conventional remedies for specific financial problems. The company's shareholders, who stood to lose millions of pounds should the company fail, were willing temporarily to accept reduced income in the expectation of long-term gains through revitalized profits or a government bailout; thus, they accepted Watkin's refinancing scheme. The visionary imperialism and civilizing mission, which had inspired his dreams of a transcontinental railway, were a different matter; Watkin's idealism ran afoul of a spirit of retrenchment that accentuated business principles and partisan, regional, and imperial divergencies. Painful financial losses and stalemated politics temporarily deflated the rhetoric that had created grand images of wealth, economic development, and the expansion of Canada from sea to sea. In the end, budgets and votes defeated the cooperation needed among the various governments. When the requisite subsidies did not materialize, the British shareholders balked; in this case, they discounted laissez-faire and laissez-passer as merely idealistic principles; without financial assistance from imperial and colonial governments, they no longer were willing to accept the risk of highly speculative ventures. While the expansionist creed and civilizing mission had impelled them to carry the Grand Trunk beyond normal limits, the company's chronic financial illness compelled investors by the mid-1860s to approve only established solutions to immediate problems. That cautious approach saved the company from instant bankruptcy, but it did not solve the company's fundamental problem – unsustainable competition from American railways and the St Lawrence River. Watkin's solution to that quandary – a transcontinental railway and the settlement of the North-West – was a risk his shareholders would not assume without massive state assistance. Consequently, the Grand Trunk never emerged fully from its financial difficulties, and when it finally participated in the construction of a transcontinental railway at the start of the twentieth century it was too late. At that time, expansion merely contributed to the final collapse of the company shortly after the First World War.[100]

The first decade of the Grand Trunk's history revealed that the new imperialism espoused by Great Britain was a complex web of competing and complimentary interests. No longer was the economic destiny of Canada to be guided by the Colonial Office and the designated governor. Instead, responsible government, free trade, and new informal techniques of imperialism assigned a much greater role to London investors and to colonial politicians and entrepreneurs. If, in the initial phases of the Grand Trunk's history, the colonists had eagerly curried British investment and expertise as well as imperial financial assistance, they always insisted on following their own agenda. To be sure, financial dependency limited their choices, but Canadians forced the Grand Trunk's owners to expand the initial relatively modest concept to one of international proportions; they insisted that the eastern section be built; they played a major role in the construction phase; and they resisted imperial pressure to commit still larger amounts of money for an intercolonial railway they did not need.[101] In the early 1850s, Canadian politicians, exuberantly charged by the optimism of their railway philosophy, eagerly committed huge sums to railway construction – much of which ended up in their own pockets – but by the 1860s the treasury was empty and the same politicians adopted a policy of retrenchment. While they enthusiastically applauded Edward Watkin's grand transcontinental vision, political and fiscal realities forced them to support only immediately profitable railway ventures.

By the end of 1863, Canada refused to be cowed by imperial pressures; it was not prepared to accept Britain's conditions for a guaranteed loan that would only ease but not assume the financial burden of constructing an intercolonial railway. Even when it became clear that the North would win the American Civil War, Canadians were not terribly concerned about the United States cutting off their winter access to the Atlantic. They refused to accept the most generous offer for assistance the imperial government could possibly grant. Although many issues divided them, most residents of Canada West and many of Canada East agreed that the risk of dependence on American thoroughfares was acceptable. After all, the primary objective of the Grand Trunk Railway, and for that matter the Great Western, was predicated on friendly commercial relations with the United States, an expectation embodied in the Reciprocity Treaty of 1854. Imperial concerns about limiting the influence of the United States in North America may have echoed in Canada's legislature and on its hustings, but it was not a compelling objective of its philosophy of railways until political stalemate forced Canadians to seek a federal union of British North America. The inescapable price for confederation was the intercolonial railway.

The British North American strain of railway imperialism, then, was intricate and subtle. Colonial secretaries needed the cooperation of British and Canadian businessmen and politicians to achieve their objectives on the continent. Similarly, the financial backers of colonial governments and railways could operate only within the agendas set by imperial and provincial administrations. Although powerful, the imperialists were not omnipotent and their plans were often upset by wily colonists who stubbornly pursued their own strategies. Meanwhile, Canadian ministers and capitalists, who were increasingly preoccupied with the economic environment of North America, depended on the London money market for virtually all their funds.

The first decade of the Grand Trunk Railway of Canada casts some light on this complex interplay among Colonial Office bureaucrats, Lombard Street bankers, London and Canadian board members, and Canadian politicians and entrepreneurs. For their part, the Grand Trunk crisis forced Canadians to assess their position within the empire, to look for commercial expansion not in the United Kingdom but westward to the United States and to Rupert's Land. Moreover, bearing the full cost of the philosophy of railways, Canadians needed to put in place the mechanisms of an interventionist state.

5

Saint John:
Fulcrum Metropôl

He shall have dominion also from sea to sea, and from the river unto the ends of the earth.

Psalm 72:8[1]

We see that these small kingdoms which we have guaranteed are marked out by the destinies of the world for destruction. Almost every successive generation sees the absorption of one or other of them into a larger empire. The great organizations and greater means of locomotion of the present day [1871] mark out the future to be one of great empires. The small Powers will have hard work to live at all.

Lord Salisbury[2]

Like her sister Maritime province, New Brunswick debated the confederation issue decades before its implementation and, similarly, its attitudes were intricately intermeshed with the philosophy of railways.[3] Unlike Nova Scotia's stance, however, New Brunswick's position on the proposed intercolonial railway was ambivalent. Inspired primarily by metropolitan concepts, the latter's doctrine of railways was informed first by economic rather than nationalistic or imperialistic considerations. From a commercial perspective, New Brunswick appeared to gain the most from a Halifax-Québec connection. The line would bisect the province and thus add to its commercial potential. On the other hand, it would derive maximum benefit from the intercolonial only if it ran directly through Saint John, its major urban centre. Should it bypass that city, the advantages of the road would fall primarily to Halifax, its chief rival. As long as the intercolonial routing remained undecided, therefore, the city would act as a fulcrum, deciding the success or failure of confederation.

As the province's largest urban centre, Saint John produced a tightly knit network of businessmen and politicians who defined and implemented New Brunswick's philosophy of railways. As in other colonial cities, this powerful group of individuals largely determined the province's stance on the interminable negotiations for the intercolonial railway. While they shared with their compatriots the unremitting sense of progress supposedly inherent in railway technology as well as a strong faith in a transcontinental, they never accepted the notion that such a railway needed to follow an all-British route. In their desire to create the largest possible trading area, the city's entrepreneurs naturally looked to the United States, a mere 107 kilometres away. While they welcomed a connection to Canada – if that meant Saint John was to be its winter port – they always insisted that the link to the United States must have priority. Saint John's powerful political lobby never shared the Colonial Office view that the intercolonial should be built essentially as a bulwark against the growing influence of, and possible attack from, the United States; it measured the railway in terms of economic benefit or liability to the city. That appraisal always included plans for a connection to the American railway system by way of Bangor and Portland, Maine.

Keenly aware that the American link was the most important objective for the city's merchants and manufacturers, the ideas of an articulate politician like Leonard Tilley, a Saint John native and provincial premier, would prevail if he could explain the benefits of the intercolonial and confederation and also promise an American rail connection. If he also wrapped his plans into the philosophy of railways and its civilizing theme, he might persuade his colleagues in the province's hinterlands and in the neighbouring colonies to support unification and integration.

By the early 1860s, Saint John had a population of about 38,000, making it the third-largest city in British North America. Founded in 1783 as a garrison town, Saint John was first ruled by an official élite quickly joined by a sympathetic merchant class that took advantage of the fine harbour and a preferential position in the imperial timber market to turn New Brunswick into a giant lumber yard. Located on the Saint John River near the mouth of the Bay of Fundy, the port established a commercial hegemony over the river valley and the bay. By 1825 it was the centre of the province's timber trade, sawmilling, and shipbuilding industries. Representing only 15 per cent of the provincial population, by mid-century, Saint John housed half of New Brunswick's merchants and half of its manufacturing capacity. As well as providing a major market for the province's agricultural production, it also handled half of all its exports and 80 per cent of all legal imports.[4]

With the introduction of free trade, the city became the stage for the interplay between the old and new economies. A modern and dynamic economic system, which emphasized the production of goods for a stable, integrated local market, gradually replaced an outmoded structure, built on the fluctuating, narrowly focused timber trade. As T.W. Acheson, the city's historian, has observed, 'A city that had only made the transition from mercantile dependency to artisans' shops in the early century was by 1860 home to interests that seemed capable of transforming the city into an industrial centre.'[5] This increasingly vibrant artisan/manufacturing class, which included wood and metal workers, shipbuilders, tanners, and saddlers, challenged the supremacy of a relatively large group of wealthy traders still pining for Britain's mercantilistic practices. Some of the masters, particularly in the foundry sector, managed to expand their operations into multiple partnerships and employed as many as seventy workers. Knit tightly through religious affiliation, ethnic origins, intermarriage, and the apprenticeship structure, the artisans developed a distinct self-consciousness and openly opposed the great merchants on some vital economic issues including tariff policy.[6]

Although the disagreement on tariffs began as early as the 1820s and cropped up sporadically, it came to a head at the beginning of the free-trade regime. The end of mercantilism opened the New Brunswick market to American products and Saint John's artisans asked the provincial government to direct some of its resources away from the timber trade to manufacturing and agriculture; they also requested a measure of protection from American and British competition. The merchants, incensed at the idea of a change in fiscal policies detrimental to the timber trade, strenuously objected and in the end defeated a full protectionist policy. The government compromised with a moderate shelter for all products manufactured in the city and not required in the timber trade. Despite the limited victory, the artisans had demonstrated their solidarity and strength on an important economic issue.[7]

The tariff question split the merchant ranks. Almost half of them, mainly lesser players not directly involved in the timber trade, were partially or totally committed to protectionism. In contrast to the great timber merchants, who had a transatlantic orientation, these minor traders saw Saint John as the locus of a more regional but also continental economy. Less affluent, they displayed a greater interest in local enterprises and were more willing to commit capital to community endeavours. They supported domestic industry and agriculture as well as provincial railways. In sum, after 1850, the more regionally focused wholesalers were aligning themselves more closely with the economic interests of the masters and artisans; together they were taking control of the city's development policies.

The economic turmoil of the 1840s provided an opportunity for this newly emerging and politically active group to move Saint John in a new direction. The members of this circle of men were relatively young and liberal- or reform-minded; most had only recently achieved affluence. Representing all the city's business activities and professional services, the majority associated themselves with the vigorous evangelical wings of the city's churches. They attributed their success to their individual diligence rather than social status, to their entrepreneurial skills rather than hoary institutions, and to their own energy rather than political privilege. Displaying a youthful confidence in the city, eager to exploit the new continental connections, they willingly challenged the traditional timber economy and channelled their restless energy into making Saint John a significant Atlantic entrepôt.[8]

A driving force among the Saint John boosters was New Brunswick's provincial secretary, Leonard Tilley. Born in 1818 in Gagetown, of Loyalist background, Tilley moved to Saint John and became a prosperous druggist. The key to his mentality was an active evangelical faith. Though a member of the Church of England, his energetic belief in individual salvation and social reform verged on Methodism. The driving force in his life was a dynamic commitment to stewardship over all of society. In consequence, he actively involved himself in municipal and educational reform, provincial politics, and economic development. Concerned about the moral, intellectual, and economic welfare of all members of the community, he taught Sunday School and frequently participated in the city's Mechanics' Institute. Similarly, his evangelicalism formed his strong views on temperance. A teetotaller, Tilley believed that legislated temperance was essential to solving serious social problems: his government briefly and unsuccessfully imposed prohibition on the rum-soaked province.[9]

By the 1850s, Tilley was a respected, prosperous businessman, an energetic participant in church, clubs, and Saint John society. Thorough, honest, and clever, he possessed a strong accountant's mind, able to remember and manipulate complex statistics. Politically, he was comfortable with mid-nineteenth-century liberalism and worked for the economic and moral progress of his community, committed to free trade wherever possible, but mildly and pragmatically protectionist when necessary. Conscious of his political duties, Tilley was part of the loosely connected clutch of Saint John businessmen who were exploring new directions for their city and province in the era of free trade.

In 1850, Tilley was elected to the legislative assembly on a platform based on the assumption that the current direction of imperial policies was likely to result in the full disintegration of the British Empire. In New Brunswick's chaotic politics, which comprised loose alliances of local and regional, social and economic interests, Tilley and his friends presented a political program that challenged traditional allegiances to the empire and the timber trade. They called for unlimited control over internal political affairs, the power to negotiate trade treaties, including reciprocity with the United States, and local political reform. In the legislature they sat in opposition to the government.[10]

In 1854 Tilley, named the provincial secretary in the Charles Fisher administration, became the most powerful and respected member of the cabinet with control over public works, finance, and education. In the 1855 session he introduced the province's first formal budget, which included a slight tariff increase to make up for revenues lost because of the Reciprocity Treaty and to pay for the province's proposed railway program. By strategically placing a higher tariff on those imported goods that were also manufactured in the province, Tilley set a modest protectionist policy with which he attempted to apply the 'principle of justice to all the industrial interests in the Province.'[11] He also took from individual assemblymen their right to initiate money bills and transferred that power to the cabinet, effectively centralizing budgeting and ending purely parochial expenditures. Lastly, he established a board to supervise the construction of roads and bridges. Along with electoral reform, which favoured the urban middle class, the Fisher-Tilley administration was a typical liberal government, in some ways several years ahead of its Canadian counterparts.[12]

Leonard Tilley found a soulmate and voice in George Fenety, the aggressive editor of the *Morning News*, one of the most influential newspapers in the province. Born in Halifax in 1812, Fenety received his apprenticeship under Joseph Howe, absorbing his mentor's zeal for political reform and economic progress. After a brief stint in the United States, where he immersed himself in the principles and practices of Jacksonian democracy, Fenety moved to Saint John in 1839 and founded the *Commercial News and General Advertiser*, 'the first penny paper in the Maritimes.'[13] Renamed the *Morning News* a year later, Fenety's paper adopted Howe's mission to educate readers in the evils of oligarchic rule and the virtues of liberal political principles and responsible government. An active, evangelical Anglican, Fenety supported the temperance movement, public education, and improved conditions for workers. Convinced that the timber trade was an outmoded enterprise, his *Morning News* became a tireless promoter of Saint John as a metropolitan centre with its own industries and growing hinterland. Much less enchanted with imperialism than Howe, Fenety believed that British North America would eventually be almost totally independent from England and that therefore the colonies must learn to rely on their own initiatives and develop modern technologies for themselves. As early as 1847, for example, he installed a telegraph line from Fredericton into his office to ensure that his readers had up-to-date news from the capital. By the early 1860s, the *Morning News* was the largest paper in the province and its editorial position was closely identified with the government of Leonard Tilley, a close personal friend.[14]

George Fenety shared with Tilley an earnest faith in railways as the prerequisite for future economic growth for Saint John and New Brunswick. Like his fellow colonists in Canada and Nova Scotia, Fenety saw railway technology as a panacea for economic stagnancy. In general terms, he argued that railways would stimulate the industrialization of Saint John and create a growing market for the province's agriculture and North Shore fisheries. Moreover, because the railway would open the country and settle the wilderness, it would create employment and thus stem the tide of New Brunswickers leaving the province. In time, new job opportunities would attract immigrants to the province's cities and interior lands and finally stop its stalled population growth.[15]

In keeping with the mid-nineteenth-century North American philosophy of railways, Fenety could not conceive of a more crucial means of stimulating the New Brunswick economy and breaking it out of its dependence on the export of unprocessed resources. 'It is universally allowed that Railroads are almost as essential to our future growth and prosperity, as pure air is to a sick chamber,' he laconically observed. 'Without them we must remain pigmies – be content with digging and delving, to obtain a subsistence for all time to come.'[16] The editor of the *Morning News* guaranteed his readers the dawning of a new age if they only seized the opportunity. 'No era of the world's history is more strongly marked than that of the introduction of the Railway. Other inventions, preceding this, show more marked influences upon the general tone of the world's civilization – that of printing, perhaps. But the Railway has and still promises to exert, a greater degree of influence upon trade and industry than any other known agent. It is a perpetual and indefatigable teacher of progress. The breath of the iron horse is the very soul of, and incentive, to energetic action.'[17]

Although Fenety, like his colonial counterparts, dealt in sweeping generalities, he also developed relatively detailed reasons for his boundless optimism. Beginning with the definition that commerce was the interchange of the products of industry among people, he asserted that the amount of trade was absolutely dependent upon the efficiency, that is, the cost and speed, of transportation. In a lengthy detailed argument he applied this principle to specific examples, demonstrating that without productive, inexpensive, and fast transportation, farmers, fishermen, and manufacturers could never expand beyond local markets. Then, in a novel twist, he stated that railways would have the greatest impact on passenger travel where speed was of the essence. 'But improvements which facilitate the transport of persons are paramount to all others; as travellers in general belong to the superior and more intelligent classes, their time is proportionally valuable; the time of their transport is represented by the value of their labour, and their expenses on the road,' he reasoned. 'When cheapness is combined with speed, then considerable advantage is gained by the operative classes; because labour can shift its place, and seek those markets where the demand is greatest.'[18]

Fenety also employed a spiral argument that touched upon one of the cardinal characteristics of technology. He explained that railway technology contained an inherent expansionist feature; once commenced, it continuously grew and incrementally produced wealth. After a main line has been completed, 'of course the branches must be undertaken,' he maintained, for 'it would be as unreasonable to expect our City to be finished in the next fifty years, as that Railroads once began, can be completed in our day and generation. One road begets another – one settlement arouses another – railroads lead to improvement – improvement to population – population to wealth.'[19]

Equally explicit in Fenety's economic-progress arguments were the assumptions about moral progress that had become an accepted tenet in North America's philosophy of railways. By encouraging the intermingling of people from different regions, nations, and continents, the barriers of mistrust and misunderstanding between various people would gradually disappear, he believed. The railway 'will prove the means of putting new life and activity in the people,' he wrote. 'It will ... create new ideas, a new soul, enterprize, aspirations, in the community. It will ... make the people more intimate, and fond of each other's company.'[20] Looking into the future, Fenety predicted that the great North American transcontinental railways would create a harmonious blending of human interests. 'These living tides of men, intersected by the thousand other streams will mingle together freely, each adding something to the other's knowledge, modifying and harmonizing in opinions, and gradually wearing off the prejudices of section and cast, until the whole continent will become but as one great family, identified in interest, thought and opinion upon all the great and really essential cardinal elements of human progress and happiness. The railway is thus, after all, the great leveller or equalizer of the age.'[21]

In addition to the economic and social-progress themes, Fenety echoed the prevailing civilizing-mission motif. Lamenting that so much of New Brunswick's interior was still a wilderness, he challenged his readers to turn the province into a garden. In one instance, he denounced the sterility of the ship and timber trade and called upon his readers 'to sharpen our tools for other purposes. Let us get into the woods and make havoc of the trees with a view of cultivating and bringing better fruit out of the soil upon which they grew.'[22] Clearly, in his view, agriculture was a more productive enterprise than lumbering, creating more prosperous citizens; at the same time, he implicitly pointed to the Victorian perception of the farmer as an industrious and morally superior being to the lumberjack, who supposedly was a migrant and a drunkard.[23] New Brunswick, Fenety insisted, must make the transformation from lumber yards to farm fields, and that metamorphosis could only be carried out 'through the agency of Railroads.'[24]

Despite the enthusiastic rhetoric, construction of railways in New Brunswick was relatively modest. As early as 1835, a number of businessmen in St Andrews held out the prospect of a railway to Québec, but the project was delayed for years initially by the long-standing boundary dispute with Maine and subsequently by the lack of capital. Although they commenced construction in 1847 on the basis of a promised land grant and loan guarantee to be paid once the road was completed to Woodstock, progress was intermittent for the next decade. Reorganized as the New Brunswick and Canada Railway and Land Company, it had completed less than 120 kilometres of road north of St Andrews by 1858. All construction activity stopped in 1862 a few kilometres short of Woodstock, and a year later the company defaulted on its debts and was taken over by receivers. Since the road did not terminate in Saint John, that city's promoters viewed it as a competitor to their schemes and they blocked the government from granting it significant assistance.[25]

The centrepiece of Saint John's railway strategy was the European and North American Railway. This grand scheme, first proposed by John A. Poor, the aggressive Portland lawyer, envisioned a railway eastward from Bangor, Maine, through New Brunswick and Nova Scotia, to Halifax.[26] This scheme most suited the metropolitan objectives of Saint John. In the first place, the eastern segment of the railway, also known as the Saint John–Shediac Railway, could open the province's North Shore and perhaps Prince Edward Island to the city's commercial ambitions. Second, as Fenety never tired of observing, the section to the American boundary, popularly labelled the Western Extension, strategically proposed to link Saint John to the American railway network and all its major Atlantic ports. Lastly, if the Shediac railway were tied to the Nova Scotia Railway, Saint John expected to tap into a significant portion of British traffic destined for Canada and the United States.

Although Saint John was not to be the terminal of the European and North American, the railway amply satisfied its metropolitan aspirations. 'Our position when the rail-road is completed, will be the focus of two great and powerful Nations,' Fenety noted, 'England on the one side and the United States on the other – and let it be remembered that thousands and millions of Europeans and Americans will necessarily have to pass over the ground of this small City of Saint John, on their passage East and West.'[27]

Despite the tenacious Saint John lobby, no construction took place until 1854, when the Peto, Brassey, Betts, and Jackson syndicate commenced construction of the Shediac portion of the railway. In the following spring, the British firm failed to resume work ostensibly because of financial difficulties, and for another year the Charles Fisher government reluctantly sought a new arrangement that would not significantly increase its financial obligations. By early 1856, unable to reactivate the private contractors, it yielded to pressure from the railway's advocates and determined to undertake the project itself. As in Nova Scotia, the decision to build the railway as a public work was an important change in direction for the province. Like its neighbour, New Brunswick initially favoured the Canadian model of state-assisted private enterprise, but when no company appeared willing to assume the task, it chose the public-work option.[28]

However dramatic the change in direction, the move was not out of line with similar provincial fiscal developments, a shift in policy that illustrated the comprehensiveness of the boosters' agenda and its liberal-evangelical grounding. In 1854, for example, after a devastating cholera epidemic in Saint John killed 1500 out of a population of 30,000, a shocked Common Council converted the city's privately owned, piecemeal water and sewer system into a fully integrated public utility, at an estimated cost of £137,000. Although the great merchant-dominated council rejected the principle of public ownership, the provincial government overrode its objections and established a public utility. It also authorized the city to raise the necessary funds (which exceeded the city's entire indebtedness) through debentures and to pay the interest through water and sewer assessments. The owners were compensated with debentures. By 1860, Saint John had virtually completed the water and sewer system.[29]

At the same time, the province finished the Saint John–Shediac Railway. Having determined that the 'future growth' of New Brunswick would be 'greatly accelerated' by the introduction of 'instruments of progress, and other appliances of civilization' like railways, the government argued that the state should undertake the financing and construction of public works.[30] Using the standard rhetoric of economic progress, Fisher persuaded the Barings to place a total of £800,000 of debentures over a four-year period to finance the project. In consideration of the fact that annual provincial revenues barely reached £200,000, the government undertook to secure the loans with an increase of the provincial general tariff by 2½ per cent.[31] Clearly, the government, which had used the railway-construction argument to capture executive financial responsibility, intended to use its new powers in decisively mobilizing a development agenda. Despite forceful opposition, construction of the Saint John–Shediac portion of the European and North American Railway recommenced in June 1856 and was completed in August 1860.[32]

The necessity of financing a relatively large public undertaking and the need to offer security to the province's foreign bondholders, thus, forced New Brunswick to centralize and formalize its fiscal administration. But the establishment of modern bureaucratic procedures and government involvement in economic development was also the product of a coherent political process that wedged itself between the traditional factions, sections, and divisions. An activist government, riding the crest of economic prosperity, was able to implement a comprehensive political program. It pacified doubts about the province's ability to repay its debts and satisfied popular expectations.[33]

Although the Saint John boosters had achieved a measure of success, they had by no means attained all their objectives. Their railway policy was hampered by the venality and factionalism of local and provincial politics. While opposition in the assembly from constituencies not traversed by the railway was obvious and clearly motivated, obduracy in Saint John often arose out of a complex mesh of personal, social, economic, and religious biases. The northern and western sections of the province resisted the expensive expansionist plans of Saint John because they promised little economic benefit in their regions; the city's old guard, however, resented the erosion of their traditional political and economic power. Together these factions vigorously objected to spiralling construction costs, labour difficulties, increased taxation, and the unprecedented role of the state in a business enterprise. When they failed to thwart the government's plans with roadblocks, votes, and amendments, they launched several public inquiries into the government's railway policy.[34]

Saint John's boosters, some of whom sat on the railway's board of directors and in the provincial legislature, discounted the critics and persisted. Supported by voters from along the Bay of Fundy and the North Shore along the Northumberland Strait – the regions of the province that stood to benefit the most from the government's policies – the group worked out its strategy. It ensured that railways dominated city and provincial politics and despite numerous changes in governments, it continued to impose its will on New Brunswick, attempting to have the state build the remainder of the European and North American. As far as this group was concerned, the Saint John–Shediac line was only the beginning of an elaborate railway program in which 'every town and village in the Province, as in other countries, may be interlaced with iron bands, and brought, in point of time, within a few hours distance of the commercial emporium.'[35]

While most city businessmen supported Tilley's administrative policies and appreciated the benefits of the Saint John–Shediac railway, their views on a Halifax-Québec connection were ambiguous and at times contradictory, an ambivalence that arose out of the geographic location of the province's chief commercial city. Faced with a decline in its traditional British market, Saint John most naturally looked to develop its immediate hinterland, which included most of the Bay of Fundy's watershed. In that context, closer relations with the other British North American colonies presented problems. Saint John was so much farther removed from the major Canadian centres than several major American seaports that an all-British railway simply could not compete with American lines for export and import traffic. In some respects too, Halifax was Saint John's competitor, particularly if the intercolonial railway used a northern route and avoided the Fundy port altogether. Evaluated purely on financial and commercial grounds, an intercolonial trunk line, consequently, posed only threats and few benefits for Saint John.

The vacillating position of Saint John's businessmen was reflected in George Fenety's *Morning News*. Immediately after Joseph Howe's 1850/1 initiative had collapsed, the *News* opposed any new overtures. In the first place, as far as the paper was concerned, the railway was purely an imperial measure forced on New Brunswick in order to prevent it from slipping into the orb of the United States.[36] A Halifax-Québec railway was irrational because there were 'few commercial advantages to be gained from such a railway.' Canadians could always ship goods to Saint John more cheaply by way of Portland than on the much longer proposed intercolonial; therefore, Fenety concluded, the railway 'is entirely unwarranted by any commercial want or necessity.'[37]

By the end of the decade, Fenety had altered his views slightly. By then, Saint John had achieved its primary transportation objective by completing the crucial Shediac portion of the European and North American Railway. The imminent prospect of civil war in the United States raised the spectre that a hostile army might cut winter communications between the colonies. Though an all-British intercolonial railway assumed some advantage in an 'imperial sense,' Fenety made it abundantly clear that such a 'Royal military highway' should be built by the 'English Government exclusively,' with New Brunswick providing only a land grant and the right-of-way.[38] All the advantages of the railway, he insisted, were imperial rather than colonial.

In the first place, Fenety believed that the matter of defence was solely a British concern. Although he admitted that, in case of war, wintertime communications between the colonies were vulnerable, he believed that the likelihood of an American invasion was extremely remote and would come only after months and possibly years of diplomatic negotiations, presumably providing ample time for positioning troops and storing supplies. Put bluntly, he believed that the colonies 'require no defence.' While simplistic at the time, subsequent events vindicated Fenety's equanimity. His views meanwhile echoed the sentiment of many North Americans – that a high state of defence against invasion from the United States was unnecessary. Since 'the "military defence" of the Colonies [was] all in the imagination,' Fenety naturally concluded that the bulk of its cost should be borne by Great Britain.[39]

In the second place, Fenety repeated his argument that a Halifax-Québec railway had no commercial significance. He pointed out that commerce among the colonies was slight and that the only prospects for greater volumes of trade involved British manufactured goods and West Indies sugar. Since Canada already imported these goods by way of American ports, railways, and canals, Fenety scornfully dismissed the arguments that Canada would use an intercolonial railway and the ports of Halifax and Saint John. Montréal, the centre of Canadian commerce, he pointed out, was 464 kilometres from Portland and 1280 km from Halifax. 'Is there any one mad enough to believe that West India produce and British goods would go three hundred miles out of the direct road for Canada, merely for the sake of passing over British Territory?' he asked rhetorically, and answered, 'Both expense and speed enter largely into the argument against any such supposition.'[40] The completion of the Halifax-Québec railway, he added, would not change the 'current of trade ... in favor of the Provinces. The only way to divert it would be by making the distance between Halifax and Quebec shorter than between Portland and Quebec.'

Having rejected the immediate economic benefits of an intercolonial, Fenety did concede that in the future some advantages might result. 'If also Canada were a manufacturing country, like the United States, and we had Colonial reciprocity of trade, the case would be altered,' he offered. '[T]hen, an inter-colonial Railroad would benefit these Provinces.'[41] As a local connector route, moreover, the New Brunswick portion of an inter-colonial could tie Saint John to the province's interior or North Shore and thus fit into its metropolitan aspirations. Meanwhile, 'there is no commercial sympathy in common [with the other British colonies]. Instead, he observed, 'Our trade lies with the United States, our importations being chiefly flour and manufactured articles. We send very little in return, chiefly shore fish. And we pay for what we get in hard cash, or Bills of Exchange derived from our staple exportations to England. Lower Canada does the same thing; and each would continue to do the same even if we had six inter-colonial Railroads.'

Without clearly obvious economic benefits, Saint John spurned an inter-colonial in favour of the European and North American Railway. Also known as the Western Extension, this plan envisioned expanding the Saint John–Shediac railway westward from the city to the United States border. A western extension, so its proponents argued, would feed traffic to the Shediac section, which was not generating sufficient revenue to pay its debt charges. Others added that the projected road would also give Saint John a connection with the St Andrews and Woodstock Railway and enable it to capture the trade of the upper Saint John River. In this scenario, a western extension, although predicated on an American connection, could also form part of an intercolonial railway. As A.H. Gillmor, the assemblyman for Charlotte County, which contained St Andrews, noted, a western-extension scheme would establish connections between New Brunswick, the United States, and Canada. 'In our railway operations two leading objects were desirable,' he observed. '[T]he first was to connect with the United States, the next with Canada, and surely no one would deny that a continuation of the line from St John, to intersect the St Andrew's [sic] and Woodstock line, following that line to Woodstock, and thence to the Canada line, would be the best route.'[42]

Gillmor's observation matched Leonard Tilley's views. Tilley hoped to find a private firm willing to complete the European and North American and extend the St Andrews and Woodstock and thus establish his government's case for routing an intercolonial through the Saint John River valley. 'If carried on to G[ran]d Falls there can be little doubt that in time the connection between the G[ran]d Trunk Railway & Gr[and] Falls will be completed,' he summarized in a letter to Joseph Howe and then added that 'the connection would add vastly to the value of both roads to make the connection then completed and place Halifax as the terminus for *passing from* Europe [to] Canada & the United States ... [T]he link between Truro & Shediac ... [must be] put in place.'[43] As he confided to Howe, his final objective was a cooperative venture with Nova Scotia to complete a connection between the Shediac railway and Truro. Here then was Tilley's preferred railway policy: a railway from Halifax to Saint John where it would split – one westward to the United States and the other northward to Canada. It was a comprehensive package that encompassed the metropolitan ambitions of his home city, where, in the words of his colleague A.H. Gillmor, 'the union jack and the star-spangled banner of the United States were entwined with each other, in anticipation of soon being linked by the iron rail.'[44] This scheme clearly indicated that neither Tilley nor many of his supporters saw any contradiction in building railway connections to the United States as well as to Canada. They, in fact, wanted improved communications with both neighbours.

In the early 1860s, however, the province was unlikely to undertake any railway construction without outside financial assistance. Even though the Saint John–Shediac line had been built comparatively cheaply, there was much public criticism about cost overruns and about the less-than-anticipated earnings. New Brunswick's bankers politely but firmly reminded provincial authorities that the province's credit was reaching its limit. 'You will we are sure not consider as impertinent any observations that we may take the liberty to make on matters concerning the Provincial credit,' Baring cautioned, '[but] we venture to inquire whether there is any legislative limit to the increase of the Provincial debt, or in the absence of that restriction whether any reliable estimate can be given of the future wants of the Province.'[45] However diplomatically phrased, the message was clear: New Brunswick would have difficulty floating new railway debentures. At the same time, the government lacked widespread political support for further large-scale public enterprises and it was unable to find private contractors willing to assume railway construction.[46]

Faced with reluctant bankers abroad and mounting criticism at home, Tilley became more and more committed to the Halifax-Québec scheme. The only way the province could afford a western extension was to make it part of an intercolonial. The overwhelming advantage of the latter, he thought, was that Great Britain would provide loan guarantees and the neighbouring provinces would fund a significant portion of construction within New Brunswick's borders. One could hardly conceive of any cheaper way to acquire more than 400 kilometres of railway. Moreover, the massive influx of foreign capital into the province would generate sufficient confidence for private developers to complete a western extension.

Meanwhile, in the summer of 1861, Tilley became premier of New Brunswick and within months was deeply embroiled in another protracted round of intercolonial-railway negotiations. Although the outbreak of the American Civil War and the Trent Affair highlighted British North America's vulnerability in wintertime, the talks collapsed early in 1863, primarily because no Canadian administration enjoyed the political strength to commit their province to massive spending on an intercolonial railway, particularly if its financial success was unlikely and its military value questionable. As in previous attempts, New Brunswick felt very much aggrieved, having accepted an agreement only to have one or another of the parties withdraw at the last moment. Nevertheless, Tilley, committed to the project, was doggedly determined to succeed no matter what obstacles stood in his way. He wrote numerous letters, briefs, and memoranda; he travelled extensively throughout the colonies; and he crossed the Atlantic on several occasions.

Through his journeys and extensive correspondence, Tilley established an intimate rapport with a large circle of colonial leaders committed to the union of British North America and to a transcontinental railway. On excellent terms with Nova Scotia's Joseph Howe, the Grand Trunk's Edward Watkin and C.J. Brydges, as well as Canada's opposition politicians, John A. Macdonald and Alexander Galt, Tilley tirelessly discussed the political details of implementing an intercolonial-railway scheme. Although supportive of the plans for a Pacific railway, Tilley focused his attention exclusively on the Halifax-Québec proposal as the essential prerequisite for further action. Zealously intent on achieving his objective, he kept himself totally informed about the nuances of Canadian and Nova Scotian politics.

Despite the disintegrating support in Britain and Canada for an intercolonial, Tilley prepared the foundation for eventual success. In 1863 he placed before the New Brunswick assembly a bill authorizing the construction of the railway. In doing so, Tilley hoped to settle the issue in his own province, place the onus for failure with Canada, and free his hand to negotiate a suitable route for an intercolonial.[47]

In support of his legislation, Tilley warned his fellow assemblymen that 'there can be no more advantageous terms upon which these extensions can be secured.' With an imperial guarantee, the province could finance their construction more easily and 'at a so much cheaper rate of interest than we get it in any other way.' He implored his listeners to consider that 'we can build a great deal more road for the same cost than we could if it were pro-cured on our own responsibility.'[48] Reeling off the statistics, he concluded that with imperial guarantees New Brunswick could finance its entire rail-way program at a cost of less than £35,000 per year in interest. Moreover, he promised the assembly, once the intercolonial was completed, construc-tion could start on a western extension.[49]

By 1863 the issue had been debated so often that the arguments on both sides were predictable. Despite their familiarity, however, the critics of the government had lost neither their intensity nor their force, particularly when they came from Saint John. A long-time associate, businessman, and politician, John Cudlip, warned Tilley that he was unable to 'support a measure calculated to lay a heavy additional debt upon the Country for a Road to be located by persons entirely beyond our control.'[50] He noted that the province's 'scanty revenues ... already heavily encumbered' should not be squandered on a railway 'proposed to be built over a route in the selection of which it appears we are to have so small a voice.' Pointing to the extravagant hopes expressed at the launching of the European and North American, he sarcastically observed that none of the high expecta-tions had materialized, that immigration, for example, had decreased instead of increased. He therefore heaped scorn on the government's sug-gestion that the railway would develop coal mining in the province, observing that Canada already had alternative and competitive sources for fuel.[51]

Similarly, C.H. Fairweather, a prominent Saint John businessman, cau-tioned Tilley that the northern route was dangerous to Saint John. 'After all – it is – to many people problematic whether a Railroad, striking the Shediac Line 50 or 70 miles east of St John will be a benefit to the commer-cial capital or other wise,' he observed, and with good reason wondered, 'Will it not carry trade *through & past* us to Halifax?'[52] Other opponents trotted out equally familiar but devastating arguments, most of which belittled the government's economic anticipations. Cudlip expressed his disappointment that immigration as well as shipbuilding had declined despite the opening of the railway. It would be better, he concluded, to expend the province's scarce funds on a commercially viable railway than on an undesirable route even if heavily subsidized.[53] In support of Cudlip, some members argued that an intercolonial would never carry sufficient freight to pay its expenses and so it would increase the province's debt. A.H. Gillmor, for one, noted that, even if the commercially viable Saint John River valley were chosen, an intercolonial would be 580 kilometres longer than the Montréal to Portland railway and so could never compete for through traffic.[54]

Although the arguments were conventional, they were stronger than ever. In the first place, the critics had the advantage of being able to refer to past experience, to the painful fact that railways were more expensive than expected and that they delivered less than promised. In the second place, they mercilessly exposed the government's greatest weakness, the failure to name a route. Albert Smith, the member for Westmorland and until recently a Tilley supporter, hammered away at that point, repeatedly insisting that the government must state its position on the routing before the legislature could approve any expenditures on the road.[55]

All the protests were to no avail, however, and Tilley refused to name a route; after a thirteen-day debate his backers approved the bill. Indicative of the deep regional divisions in the province, five government supporters voted against the legislation, while eight opposition members supported the administration. In most cases, the defections were directly related to belief in one or the other of the proposed routes.[56] In any case, Tilley was immensely relieved. 'We have just got through with one of the hardest fought contests that I have ever been engaged in,' he confided to Howe. '[W]ith the strong feelings in our Province about [the] Route we had a difficult game to play.'[57] Tilley was particularly pleased that his legislation had squeaked through the assembly without his revealing that he was coming to the conclusion that the central route was likely the compromise settlement.

Passage of the legislation did not end the opposition, and a flood of petitions, many containing the signatures of government supporters, swamped the legislature.[58] The general thrust of the appeals was that the intercolonial-railway bill prevented the early construction of a western extension. The Saint John *Daily Evening Globe* summarized the prevailing mood. 'It is possible that the Government as a whole may cling to the Inter-Colonial road,' it scoffed. 'There may be imaginary promises from visionary Grand Trunk adherents; or splendid schemes propounded by English capitalists of fabulous wealth; or there may be some *ignus* [sic] *fatuus* which our rulers will chase, either to gain time, or in the honest belief that they will at last succeed in getting that road; but we fear that all of these will turn out as have our previous speculations respecting a great Inter-Colonial highway.'[59]

The situation was awkward and dangerous for Tilley. He feared the issue was eroding his political support and splitting the province. 'The country will soon recognize but two parties,' Cudlip fretted, 'a Railway and anti-Railway party, and the most powerful must lead.'[60] Although the statement appeared to suggest that the province was polarizing between advocates of an intercolonial to Canada and a western extension to the United States, Tilley himself had not taken an either/or position, but continued to assert the possibility of both railways being built in the near future. He clearly realized that as a single project New Brunswick would have to build the western extension on its own credit. If it constructed the line as part of an intercolonial, however, it could benefit from imperial guarantees and the support of Canada and Nova Scotia. Only after all hope for an intercolonial was gone should New Brunswick undertake a western extension on its own.[61]

To stop the haemorrhage of support and to buy time in anticipation of a new Canadian administration more favourable to an intercolonial, Tilley employed a brilliant political tactic. In March 1864 he introduced a bill that he expected would please all railway factions in New Brunswick. The measure promised bonuses for the completion of the European and North American from Maine to Nova Scotia, and for branch lines to Fredericton, Woodstock, and Miramichi, as well as Albert Mines in south-east New Brunswick. The 1863 intercolonial-railway legislation was to remain in place for another year, at which time the government would offer an annual subsidy of £20,000 for a railway to Canada.[62] On the one hand, the act incorporated Tilley's policy of combining the intercolonial and western-extension railways; on the other hand, it followed New Brunswick's well-established tradition of silencing opponents with promises of railway construction.

Although the measure was greeted with considerable scepticism, it halted the erosion of Tilley's supporters. Astonished at the speed at which the government implemented its change of mind, A.H. Gillmor said the legislation made him think of 'a huge lobster lying in the centre of the Province with claws stretching east, west, north, and south.'[63] Blatantly designed to appease most regions of the province, the 'Lobster Bill,' as its critics quickly dubbed it, had the desired effect, however, and several defectors returned to the fold.[64] It also signalled a change in the fortunes of the intercolonial promoters. The imminent abrogation of the Reciprocity Treaty and the prospect that the United States might also end the bonding system bolstered the commercial rationale for an intercolonial. Although an end to the drawback laws was unlikely, the possibility that Canadians might have to pay customs duties on goods shipped through the United States revived interest in Canada for an alternate all-British route. In fact, C.J. Brydges eagerly informed Macdonald that George Brown 'looks on intercolonial in a totally new light ... [T]he road will now be more favorably considered.'[65] C.H. Fairweather, one of the organizers of a Saint John's petition, told Tilley that New Brunswick should not contribute to an intercolonial because once Canada lost its bonding privileges, it 'will find a road through [New Brunswick] a necessity – and will be absolutely driven to build it even if she has to bear all the cost.'[66]

Although it was unlikely that the Canadas would ever bear the total cost of an intercolonial, events were occurring quickly that eroded its diffidence. In February 1864 Canada ordered at its own expense a preliminary survey of the intercolonial routes. In the late spring, a quick succession of ministries resulted in the formation of a coalition government dedicated to a union of British North America. Early in the autumn, at the Charlottetown and Québec conferences, which laid the basis of the confederation agreement, the mainland provinces finally found the consensus on an intercolonial railway that had eluded them for so long. Although the Halifax-Québec railway was still a politically sensitive topic in Canada West, Leonard Tilley was adamant and bluntly told a Québec audience, 'We won't have this union unless you give us the railway.'[67] Since confederation without fulcrum New Brunswick was impractical, the delegates expressly included an intercolonial in the Québec accord of October 1864; resolution 68 specified that 'the General government shall secure, without delay, the completion of the Intercolonial Railway.'[68] Interestingly, the two British North American provinces without a developed philosophy of railways, Newfoundland and Prince Edward Island, refused to accept the confederation agreement.

Tilley's ready acceptance of the Québec confederation resolutions should have come as no surprise. For more than a decade he had referred positively to a union of British North America, and his close friend, George Fenety, had occasionally published editorials mildly favouring confederation. In 1857, when the question of a union of British North America surfaced in the Canadian legislature, Fenety reacted cautiously. While he appreciated that union would enlarge the colonies' credit base and permit them to undertake large public-works projects like an intercolonial railway, he worried that New Brunswick would be overwhelmed by the larger provinces. Though he believed federation would stimulate the colonial economies and increase immigration, he feared the plan was unworkable because of the immense distances between settled places and the diversity of cultures, traditions, and institutions. In essence, he believed that the scheme was premature.[69]

On one item, however, Fenety was adamant. A merger could only follow the completion of an intercolonial railway. 'A union, however, without an inter-colonial Railroad, would be like the hind and fore wheels of a coach without the connecting bar. The Provinces could not move along together unless they felt each other's presence. The readiest way now to get to Canada is to proceed by way of Portland. It would never do to say the united Provinces cannot make laws unless our Representatives first proceed over American territory to get to the seat of Government. We require a direct road; one altogether British; and the union, if brought about, would then seem like a reality, because we should be united physically as well as politically.'[70]

The intercolonial-railway theme also featured prominently in a series of six articles the *Morning News* published in August 1863 on the topic of British North American union.[71] These pieces, written more than a year before the Canadian delegates officially broached the confederation scheme at Charlottetown, likely mirrored Tilley's views. Moreover, because they were written before the heat of debate, they avoided the excessive rhetoric, partisanship, and name-calling associated with New Brunswick's subsequent confederation elections.

The central theme of the *News*'s position was that as long as the colonies were divided they would remain as economic and political backwaters. The paper argued that the lack of communications among the colonies had kept them divided and estranged from each other. Although they were 'in constant communication' with their 'Republican neighbors,' they were 'comparative strangers' to their British counterparts. Indeed, the colonies had built separate, competing economies, hedged by clashing tariff walls; consequently, they were inefficient and weak. For example, the paper argued, New Brunswick's railway history showed clearly that as long as she stood alone the province's future was bleak. Concerned primarily with economic issues, the *News* warned that for New Brunswick to survive in the new laissez-faire economic order, it had to unite with the other colonies into a large economic entity. Using all the familiar arguments and examples, the *News* illustrated how unification would stimulate immigration, increase population, and generate economic prosperity. In conclusion, the paper observed that, 'where a unity of purpose and interests is found, power and influence will certainly follow.'[72]

Ironically, at the very time that the negotiations for an intercolonial were reaching a nadir of despair, the *News* confidently asserted that the railway would be built. In fact, the editor made it emphatically clear, as he had done six years earlier, that the Halifax-Québec line was the essential prerequisite for successful confederation negotiations. 'It is we believe acknowledged by all parties that before a complete and satisfactory Union of the Colonies can exist an Intercolonial Railway must be built,' he insisted. 'Indeed, so strong is the connection ... in the popular mind that the general belief seems to be that if a railroad communication were made with Canada, Union would follow almost as a matter of course.'[73]

In the end, however, the editor returned to the theme of greatness. Divided, the colonies had no influence in imperial councils, for their foreign policy was determined in London, where they were disdained 'as the claimants of a spurious nationality.' Although union did not mean independence, British North Americans, he urged, must be ready 'to leap at once into national existence' or remain insignificant minions subject 'to the great Empire to which we owe allegiance.' United, then, the colonies would be elevated from obscure, divided provinces to 'one people, united in heart by the remembrance ... of a common destiny, fit either to add strength and lustre to the Empire by a Union with it, or to create a future for ourselves to which the world will pay homage.'[74]

The News commenced the last of its confederation serial with a rational assertion that a maritime union should precede a general federation. Soon, however, the editor lost himself in his own rush of rhetoric. After listing the continent's wealth of natural resources and lauding the industriousness of British North America's people, he lyrically penned an ode to the birth of a mighty nation certain to rise out of its magnificent forests and expansive plains, its cities straddling majestic rivers and shoring royal lakes. Departing momentarily from the usual slash-and-burn technological oratory, the News also created a portrait of harmony with nature rather than conquest, seeking nourishment from it rather than destruction. 'Let us read our destiny in the flow of the murmuring brook and the current of the mighty river,' he warbled, and continued: 'Thus may we, if we but be true to ourselves and mindful of the gifts which nature has bestowed upon us and our country, raise for ourselves a name which the world will respect and honor, and become a great and united people, with power enough to resist the attacks of our enemies and magnanimity enough to make our friendship worth regarding.'[75]

Although distorted by the inevitable lapses of frothy rhetoric, the editorials were remarkable because they so clearly encapsulated the mid-nineteenth-century British North American mind. By limiting the discussion to the broad principle of unification, the newspaper unwittingly uncovered the tenets that underlay colonial prescriptions for economic growth and material wealth. In essence they were following the general pattern enunciated by many nation builders in the United States. New Brunswick's new bourgeoisie, concentrated in Saint John, sought to rebuild their provincial economy as part of an industrial nation connected to a new set of trading partners by an intercolonial railway. In tying their economic aspirations to closer associations with the other British North American colonies, the businessmen of Saint John never intended to spurn the nurturing environment of the British Empire nor did they expect to lessen commercial ties with their business associates in the United States. Indeed they continued to actively pursue a western extension railway. In that sense, the *Morning News* demonstrated that New Brunswick was part of that powerful consensus that was driving British North Americans to a closer union, an association cemented by a deep faith in technological progress.

Although the Québec accord secured the construction of an intercolonial as well as a western extension, Tilley's constituents spurned confederation. Ultimately, the critics objected less to union with Canada than to the specific terms of the Québec resolutions. As in Nova Scotia, the philosophy of railways became a central issue: how was it to be applied to New Brunswick in general and Saint John in particular? In addition to these questions, the electorate was disenchanted with a disintegrating liberal administration that had been in power since the mid-1850s, and with its leader, Leonard Tilley. Lastly, for a time, Tilley had moved beyond the entrepreneurial horizons of many of the province's businessmen; even in Saint John he was losing the support of bankers, manufacturers, and merchants who were reluctant to follow him into an unfamiliar relationship with Canada.[76]

In addition to partisan and railway issues, Tilley faced the strong opposition of Irish and Acadian Catholics. He had badly neglected the latter and they, afraid of Canada and its strong Orange Lodge movement, were unlikely to support his confederation option. Similarly, Irish Catholics in Saint John worried about union with a province in which the strident anti-Catholic George Brown and his Clear Grits dominated the political scene. Without a strong representative in cabinet, the Irish Catholics felt vulnerable and they looked to Timothy Anglin, the editor of the Saint John *Freeman*, for guidance.

Personally, Timothy Anglin's objections to confederation were not sectarian but loyalist, constitutional, and economic. Although a typical liberal, Anglin sat in opposition to the government. His doctrinaire free-trade leanings, laissez-faire social policies, and opposition to protective tariffs prevented him from supporting Tilley's administration. While he advocated a measure of industrialization, he glorified the agricultural way of life and emphasized trade and transportation in his economic-development policies.[77] Confederation offered few benefits to Anglin. He perspicaciously believed that, unless the new country imposed very high tariffs, trade between New Brunswick and Canada would not increase significantly. He also thought union premature because the population was too scattered and geographically diverse. He objected to the small number of representatives (granted to New Brunswick) in the Commons, arguing that the province's distinct character would not be adequately voiced. He also considered that confederation would seriously compromise loyalty to the empire; the mighty-new-nation rhetoric, he theorized, implied independence. Lastly, Anglin held that the financial arrangements were inadequate and the defence argument contrived.[78]

All these grounds for objection appeared soft and changeable. Although he never favoured federation, apparently Anglin believed it unlikely that New Brunswick would be able to survive much longer as a relatively independent but small economy, and that in the distant future union with Canada or the United States was inevitable. 'Ultimately the destiny of these Provinces must be either to drift into annexation with the United States,' he claimed, 'or to form one great Union or Confederation of some sort.'[79] Of the two options, Anglin preferred the latter.

In essence, then, Timothy Anglin's opinion was remarkably similar to Leonard Tilley's. In keeping with the expansionist logic of the age, Anglin believed in the efficacy of large economic units in which the question of transportation loomed important. Throughout his career, he proved to be an unflagging supporter of railways. Like Tilley, he advocated the integration of a western extension and an intercolonial, that is, he believed in rail connections to the United States, Canada, and Nova Scotia, but he parsimoniously argued that New Brunswick could not afford to construct both a western extension and a northerly routed intercolonial railway. Since Britain, Canada, and Nova Scotia stood to derive the greatest benefit from the suggested northern line, they should bear the cost of construction.[80] Anglin repeatedly urged Tilley to officially reject both the northern and central routes and choose instead to extend the St Andrews and Québec line to the Canadian border. With his strong Saint John bias, Anglin passionately believed that any route but the southern was detrimental to the city's interests and therefore automatically harmful to the province. With the decision left to Britain, he correctly prophesied, the choice of a northern route, which had greater military significance but lesser economic potential, was inevitable.[81] According to Anglin, the best course of action was to complete the European and North American, the great and potentially profitable artery between Europe and the United States, without delay as a public work and make it part of the proposed intercolonial.[82] With editorial after editorial hammering home the point, Anglin ensured that railways became the dominant confederation issue.

Although Anglin was a strong voice, the leadership of the anti-confederate movement gravitated to Albert Smith, a dissident member from Westmorland. Born in 1824 in Shediac, Smith trained to be a lawyer and in 1852 was elected to the assembly as part of the Reform movement. Equipped with a quick temper, energetic spirit, and firm tenacity, Smith was ideally suited for New Brunswick's chaotic politics. An advocate of popular rights, he professed to be a liberal and favoured active development policies, including railway construction. But he was also a cautious man, loath to spend government funds. Even though the intercolonial would traverse his county no matter what the eventual route, he opposed it because he considered it too costly for the anticipated benefits. He resigned from the Tilley government in 1862 to protest its railway policy.[83]

By 1864, Albert Smith was a mature, self-confident forty-year-old, a respected leader who had begun to enjoy new ventures into shipping and commerce. Secure in New Brunswick's prosperity, he was confident it could survive in isolation. Of all the options available to the province and under discussion from time to time – British North American confederation, Maritime union, American annexation, and the status quo – this liberal politician and businessman preferred a relatively independent New Brunswick within a loose informal British Empire. Confederation appeared the least attractive choice, and shortly after Leonard Tilley awkwardly revealed the details of the Québec conference at a November assembly in Saint John, Albert Smith rallied the forces of opposition.[84]

In an angry letter to the *Daily Evening Globe*, Smith voiced his objections to union with Canada.[85] Like Joseph Howe in Nova Scotia, he strongly protested the lack of consultation about such a fundamental change in his province's constitution. He flatly rejected the argument that confederation would deliver a cheaper intercolonial railway than earlier agreements. In fact, he added, George Brown had agreed to an intercolonial only after wresting a concession for the enlargement and extension of the canal system in Upper Canada. Thus, Smith charged, New Brunswickers would be liable for their share of this costly program. Moreover, they could expect significant tax hikes as the cost of government, defence, and tariffs increased. Lastly, he warned his readers that as a small province New

Brunswick would be swamped in the proposed federal legislature and senate. In sum, while Smith did not reject the principle of unification, he clearly disliked the terms of the Québec agreement.

Smith's letter became the magnet that attracted a disparate and heterogeneous collection of protesters united only in opposition to the Québec resolutions. Comprising Liberals as well as Tories, this group disagreed on railway and defence policy as well as on the nature of confederation. While some preferred a stronger union with greater centralization, others – including Smith – favoured more powerful local legislatures. A third group wanted no union at all and advocated annexation to the United States. For the moment, however, they rallied behind Smith, who as one of New Brunswick's best speakers, received enthusiastic receptions everywhere. Well prepared, his trenchant and dispassionate speeches questioned the motives of the Canadians, particularly concerning an intercolonial railway, and intimated that New Brunswick was being asked to assume Canada's debts. In contrast, he offered the security of a western extension and the American market. Seemingly united, the anti-confederationists challenged Tilley to call an election and in March 1865 defeated him.[86]

On the surface, the election of 1865 appeared to have split the province into two camps – supporters of an intercolonial railway and union with Canada against advocates of a western extension and closer ties with the United States. To be sure, the anti-confederationists anchored their arguments on the charge that the province's commitment to an intercolonial had killed a western extension. 'Which would they prefer,' Smith asked an audience, 'Western Extension or the Intercolonial Railroad?' He heard 'they favoured Western Extension.'[87] He then accused the government of holding a western extension 'in subordination to the Intercolonial Road.' When he cloaked this argument with an anti-confederation stand, he implied that New Brunswickers must chose between an intercolonial and a western extension, between a connection to Canada or to the United States.[88]

This anti-Canadian strategy was popular in many regions of New Brunswick because it played to the province's fulcrum character. On the one hand, most people still distrusted Canadians. When John A. Macdonald was provoked to say that the intercolonial was not to be in the constitution but was only one of the agreed conditions, the opponents of confederation immediately retorted that construction of the railway was not guaranteed and Canada could again renege on a sealed deal. Although a hurried exchange of telegrams reaffirmed that an intercolonial would 'of course be inserted in the Imperial Act,' the damage was done and the critics used the incident to inflame the widespread belief that Canada was ready to wriggle out of the agreement.[89]

On the other hand, southern New Brunswick had established close commercial ties with the United States, particularly as a result of the Reciprocity Treaty and the Civil War. Since the introduction of free trade had broken the traditional reliance on the transatlantic timber trade, the province's businessmen had looked to Maine for new markets. During the war, New Brunswick vessels had taken over much of southern shipping and regularly carried cargoes of cotton, tobacco, tar, and turpentine to Britain and even to the northern United States.[90] By 1863 the province's second largest volume of trade was in fact with the United States, and a government report of that year also detected a substantial increase in American investment in the province.[91]

Not surprisingly, entrepreneurs on both sides of the international border worked to increase the volume of trade. John W. Cudlip, of the Saint John Chamber of Commerce, was one of many memorialists asking that the wartime trade restrictions, which greatly hampered commerce between New Brunswick and the United States, be removed in order to accommodate the province's rapidly increasing consumption of bread, flour, and salt meat. He received support from American firms such as A. Smithers and Company of New York, which had been shipping breadstuffs into New Brunswick and Nova Scotia for more than a decade. Pointing to the $800,000 value of business, Smithers argued that the restrictions threatened to move this commerce to Canada, especially if the Reciprocity Treaty were abrogated and the drawback acts repealed.[92] Meanwhile, some Maine railway promoters revived the European and North American Railway and suggested that, as soon as New Brunswick and Nova Scotia granted consent for its portions of the road, shares would be 'readily taken up by the large capitalists of the United States.'[93] In other words, despite jingoistic language on both sides of the border, American and New Brunswick businessmen were quietly trading goods, making international investments, and planning joint transportation ventures.

Obviously, then, the western extension was closely identified with stronger ties to the United States. When editorialists tied that association to the anti-confederation forces, the railway could be perceived as anti-Canadian. The Halifax *Citizen* was afraid that New Brunswick might become part of the United States. 'The New Brunswickers in laying down the rails to the boundaries,' it predicted, 'would be forging link after link of a chain which would bind them inevitably to the chariot wheels of the North, commercially and socially at first, and probably politically afterwards.'[94]

Observing a tinge of American democratic sentiment in the province, the paper believed that with the railway this 'would sweep in and overflow the ancient British land-marks.'

Concomitantly, the proponents of confederation contributed to the polarization of causes by identifying their crusade with an intercolonial railway. Charles Fisher introduced a resolution which proclaimed that the destiny of New Brunswick was with an intercolonial and Canada.[95] Many of his constituents favoured a western extension, he admitted, and so would he, were he not already committed to an intercolonial. Even Tilley's words encouraged the split:

The friends of Western Extension, who are mostly the enemies of Confederation, asserted that with the facilities then provided, no roads would be built, and were demanding that they should be undertaken as government works – seeing that this could not be done under Federation they would not only oppose that measure, but would have embarrassed the Government by submitting a proposition, calling upon them to assume these Railways as government works, knowing that the Members of the Government must oppose it and in doing so ... [we] would lose the confidence of our Constituencies ... The people of S[aint] John have been so wild about this Western Extension question, that any member showing indifference upon it, was almost certain of defeat – The opposition took advantage of this state of things, made many of the people believe that in Confederation there would be no Railway Westward.[96]

The correlation between support for one or the other of the railways and for federation was not as straightforward as contemporary politicians appeared to suggest. Proponents of a western extension, for example, did not necessarily advocate annexation to the United States in preference to union with Canada. According to Lieutenant-Governor Arthur Gordon, Smith was strongly anti-American. '[He] belongs to the radical section of politicians,' Gordon noted, 'but, at the same time, is very hostile towards the U.S.'[97] In fact, with a vicious civil war 'desolating the United States,' with bitter feelings rising there against Britain, and with loyalism still a formidable faction in New Brunswick, annexationism was a waning force in the province.[98] Nevertheless, trans-border economic ties were important and thus some New Brunswickers argued that it was in the province's best interest to preserve friendly relations with the British North American provinces and with the United States. 'A closer commercial connection by means of railroads might be the best means to excite friendly relations,' Fredericton's *Headquarters* diplomatically asserted. 'In these uncertain times, the duty of New Brunswick is to draw, if possible, into closer relations with the loyal Provinces of Canada, though it may be for her interest to connect herself commercially with the United States.'[99] In 1864, it appeared to the *Headquarters* that '[d]uty and interest beg two different ways.' But the newspaper had no doubt that New Brunswickers preferred duty to interest.

Setting the logic on its head, the *Headquarters* argued that a western extension could act as an antidote to Americanization. If Maine completed its portion of the European and North Atlantic, the paper worried, then it could draw commerce from the upper Saint John valley, and detach that region from the rest of New Brunswick to the detriment of Saint John.[100] The paper strongly recommended the extension of the Saint John–Shediac Railway to the American border so that Saint John rather than Portland would become the entrepôt for north-western New Brunswick. Clearly, election rhetoric could take the nationalistic implications of a western extension either way.

Similarly, regional differences destroyed any clear correlation between pro- and anti-confederation and intercolonial and western-extension sentiments. An assemblyman from Kent county on the Gulf of St Lawrence, elected as anti-confederation, differed with the Smith government because he believed that the North Shore line must have priority over a western extension.[101] In contrast, some pro-unionists opposed the northern route, while a few resisted the western extension.[102] Tilley always insisted that a choice was unnecessary because the Québec resolutions permitted the construction of both lines. In fact, he claimed that a western extension would be built whether or not confederation succeeded, but if it failed, the province would lose the intercolonial railway. The supporters of confederation, who had no intention of sacrificing economic ties with the United States for union with Canada, saw no inherent contradiction in supporting both the intercolonial and the western extension. Although they insisted that union with Canada made no sense without an intercolonial, they did not perceive a cultural or political threat in a western extension.[103] In other words, while they recognized the unifying and centralizing properties of technology, they did not equate the proposed intercolonial railway with technological nationalism.

Soon after it took power, it became evident that the Smith government was a weak administration. It could not fulfil its promise to proceed vigorously with a western extension. Even though Smith confidently asserted that a contract with a private developer would 'satisfy the public mind and I think materially prevent the growth of the feeling for Confederation,' nothing was accomplished.[104] London financiers, undoubtedly influenced by the pro-confederation views of Edward Watkin, the Grand Trunk, and the Colonial Office, were loath to lend money to a company that appeared to be working against the union of British North America and imperial interests.[105] Watkin, like Tilley, had no objection to a western extension, but he did think that the anti-confederation movement had hurt the Grand Trunk cause and made New Brunswick vulnerable to American annexation. 'I would have assisted [the contractor] in his Western Extension as energetically as I assisted for the Intercolonial,' he assured Tilley. '[W]e should have taken our Capitalist in good humour, and with open pockets, along with us in carrying out a Railway connection with the United States. As it is, all our people say, "What is the use of our paying money simply to aid the annexationist party?"'[106]

The failure to proceed immediately with a western extension greatly weakened the Smith government. The abrogation of the Reciprocity Treaty seemingly closed the opportunity for expanded trade with the United States and lessened the need for a western railway. With the Civil War reaching its conclusion, the threat of invasion from an unemployed northern army seemed a possibility. More significantly, the Smith administration failed to deal decisively with minor incursions by the Fenians, an association of fanatic Irish-American rowdies. In sum, the government looked weak and incompetent; it lost several influential members, including Timothy Anglin. Unable to deliver the western extension and save reciprocity, Albert Smith had little to offer.[107]

By contrast, Tilley was fully in control of the situation. Retained as a member of the executive council, he continued to advise Lieutenant-Governor Arthur Gordon. Always convinced that New Brunswickers would eventually accept confederation, he asked for time to explain its benefits.[108] Once in opposition, Tilley visited his cronies in temperance groups across the province and slowly but relentlessly gathered their support.[109] His political strategy was to make union a sectarian and loyalty issue, to rally the Protestant vote by associating the Irish Catholics with Fenianism. This tactic was immensely successful in a province where religious divisions ran deep and the Loyalist tradition was strong. In the end, Tilley isolated Timothy Anglin and his cause.[110] Meanwhile he received immeasurable assistance from the Colonial Office, which applied subtle pressures to the Smith government, and from the Canadian government, which sent generous amounts of cash to cover election expenses.[111]

Stretching his constitutional powers to the limit, Lieutenant-Governor Gordon, at a propitious moment, pressured Smith to resign and effectively forced an election for May 1866. Tilley offered the electorate lower taxes, an intercolonial and western extension, a fair voice in the new government, and a market for New Brunswick's raw and manufactured goods. He handily won the vote and put confederation back on track. One of his final acts as premier was to pass enabling legislation authorizing the government to take $300,000 in stock in the European and North American, to grant the railway a subsidy of $16,000 per kilometre, and thus to facilitate completion of the western extension by October 1871. In 1872, the Canadian government commenced construction of the Intercolonial Railway.[112]

In the end, New Brunswick's electoral reversal was neither dramatic nor profound. The opposition to federation had never been strong, united, or sustained. The May 1866 election was as much about loyalty and empire as about the connected issues of confederation and railways. The anti-confederationists, who like Tilley clearly understood the politics of their province, desperately tried to disassociate their cause from the concept of disloyalty but failed. Lestock Desbrisay, the member for the impoverished northern county of Kent, pleaded for a western extension that his people needed to ship lumber to the United States. Seeking more American sales, however, he insisted, did not mean he was in favour of annexation. 'It is said we must go into Confederation, or annexation,' he angrily asserted. 'It is a cowardly proposition to put forward against those who are opposed to the [federation]. I am not afraid of annexation to the United States; not that I think this country is able to cope with the United States in warfare; but I can say we are able, very materially to assist Great Britain.'[113] His anti-confederation colleague, William H. Needham, the assemblyman from York, strongly supported a western extension and vigorously defended his patriotism. 'Another thing, I am willing to go the whole hog to show the British Government that we are sincere, and that we do not want to sever the connection existing between us, or annex ourselves to the States, (for I do not believe this feeling resides in the breast of one man),' he affirmed, and went on: 'I want them to know that the reason we rejected the [federation] scheme was because we love the connection with our mother country, and that the very men who voted against, are willing, if necessary, to shed every drop of their blood in defence of her cause and institution.'[114]

By 1866 any attempt to link an anti-confederation stand with loyalty sounded lame and ineffective. Since the mid-1840s the vigorous young business élite of Saint John had worked energetically to establish a new economic orientation for its city and, incidentally, the province. Their metropolitan vision, with its industrial aim, added a alternate dimension to the port's traditional transatlantic direction. The new bearing called for North

American continental trade alignments. That strategy was predicated on a strong commitment to railway construction. To draw more commerce to the city, Saint John required railways first to Maine, then to Nova Scotia, and lastly to Canada. Whereas the European and North American presented no special problems to the city's merchants, the routing of the Halifax-Québec railway caused serious concerns. When the imperial and Nova Scotia governments refused to sanction a southern route through Saint John, and when Canada, which already had connections to the Atlantic seaboard, remained lukewarm, New Brunswick followed Nova Scotia's example and built a local road – a segment of the European and North American.

By the early 1860s, various interests moved the colonies towards continental integration and made an intercolonial railway a reality. For Canada, specific political problems were the primary and immediate impulse for confederation, but she also shared with the Maritimes pressing economic difficulties. All the mainland British North America colonies accepted the notion of a large economic unit as the best way to compete with the United States. New Brunswick shared with them the vision of a transcontinental nation linked together by a railway as the avenue to seemingly boundless opportunities. As the *Morning News* prophesied, the railway 'would throw down the barriers which impede our commercial progress. It would open up new channels of trade. It would afford our manufacturers a wide field for the sale of their wares. It would give to the grain-growing country of the far West a ready outlet to the ocean at all seasons, and bring it into close connection with the commerce of the world. It would in time form a grand, unrestricted, uninterrupted highway from the Atlantic to the Pacific oceans, over which traffic and travel from continent to continent would unceasingly roll.'[115] Thus, as Phillip Buckner has so forcefully argued, confederation was not a matter of central Canadians subjecting unwilling, unprogressive Maritimers to a confederation scheme in which they had little interest. The negotiations at Charlottetown and Québec were a joint enterprise among people of like mind, sharing a common heritage and a mutual vision.[116]

Confederation of 1867 was possible because a group of men, drawn largely from the urban business and professional communities, wrote a constitution based on traditional loyalties, particularly their British identity. A complex of interacting local factors impelled New Brunswickers to first reject and then accept confederation, but like the majority of Anglophone British North Americans they possessed 'a common sense of Britishness and a desire to continue to live within the admittedly loose framework provided by the second British Empire.'[117] Drawing on a common pool of myths and images, the architects of confederation, who had been meeting in boardrooms and wining and dining together in hotels and banquet halls for more than a decade, overcame the numerous regional and local diversities and fears that had plagued earlier attempts at cooperation. Their mutual belief in the philosophy of railways, too, did much to overcome geographical, cultural, and political differences.[118]

For New Brunswick, in 1867 confederation was an option for the future. The agreement, which envisioned an integrated British North American economy, satisfied the metropolitan ambitions of Saint John because it also opened opportunities for closer commercial ties with the United States. A.R. Wetmore, a Saint John lawyer destined to become the province's first post-confederation premier, campaigned against the merger in 1865, changed his mind the following year, and subsequently argued that union promised New Brunswick two new opportunities for enhanced trade – an intercolonial connection with Canada and a western extension to the even larger market of the United States. Converted wholly to the philosophy of railways, he believed strongly that in the post–Civil War era increased commerce would bring not only economic prosperity but also peace and harmony. 'If we connect ourselves by railroad with the people of the United States it will establish a bond of unity between us, which will tend to prevent any hostile demonstration on the part of the people living under the American Government.'[119] John W. Cudlip, a Saint John liquor merchant who had consistently supported a western extension rather than an intercolonial railway, similarly welcomed increased trade with the United States and American investments in New Brunswick's mineral resources. Although he preferred a government-built railway to prevent American financial control over the western extension, he succinctly summarized the cardinal issue. The railway must be built. 'Railways, from the luxury of the age, have become a necessity.'[120]

6

The Pacific Scandal: Nationalism and Business[1]

If [the Pacific railway contract] were given to Sir Hugh Allan's Company it would exclude many representative men from Ontario, Mr. Macpherson's Company being comprised principally, though not wholly, of Ontario men.

If the contract were given to the Inter-Oceanic Company it would have excluded representative men from the Province of Quebec.

Alexander Campbell[2]

The philosophy of railways played a prominent role in the confederation of mainland British North America in 1867. Its idealistic rhetoric of cooperation and social progress, mutual understanding, and economic advancement, its faith in steam technology and its evangelical civilizing mission had provided common ground for the discussion of the specific political, economic, and diplomatic concerns addressed in the Charlottetown and Québec conferences. Unrealistically optimistic, even utopian, the railway creed was expressed nevertheless specifically in clause 141 of the British North America Act, providing for the construction of the Intercolonial Railway.[3] Despite arguments about local routing and technical standards, contracts were let quickly and the eastern section of the transcontinental railway was completed on 6 July 1876, when the first through train from Halifax arrived at Québec. Less precise, yet still salient in the deliberations, was the western segment, the railway to the Pacific coast. Despite the centrality of western annexation and a Pacific railway implicit in the agreement, Canada's first prime minister, John A. Macdonald, found it difficult to translate the lofty and buoyant nation-building oratory of the confederation debates into practical reality. After six years of dithering, he asked a

Montréal rather than a Toronto firm to build the road and immediately found himself in the midst of a regional and partisan battle that ultimately led to the Pacific Scandal of 1872, Macdonald's resignation, and further delays. The scandal taught a chastened prime minister that, despite noble declarations and elevated mission statements, the primary purpose of railway companies was not nation building but profit earning. By confusing nationalist sentiments and corporate objectives, political considerations and entrepreneurial ambitions, high-minded idealism and cold pragmatism, Macdonald helped sink the first attempt to build the Pacific railway.

The 1872 Pacific Scandal has become the starting point for most histories of the Canadian Pacific Railway. Interest in the scandal arises from the mythical place the road has assumed in Canadian history. By dramatizing the CPR as an iron bond tying diverse colonies and territories into a mighty northern nation, the railway myth has profoundly influenced the interpretation of the first decades of the nation's history. It has created, for example, two assumptions covering most accounts of the CPR's past. The first portrays the railway primarily as a patriotic adventure, an essential part of the government's national policies. The second, likewise derived from the nation-building theme, embraces the idea that the Pacific railway was always intended as an all-Canadian project financed and built entirely by Canadians through Canadian territory. By accepting these two tenets, most historians of the railway see the Pacific Scandal as a perilous moment in Canadian history, a crisis when the fledgling nation was almost lost to aggressive American manifest-destiny businessmen and politicians.

The nation-building thesis also colours how historians characterize the various personalities in the early history of the CPR. Even while telling the embarrassing Pacific Scandal story, Donald Creighton, for example, viewed Sir John A. Macdonald as a visionary statesman, whose railway policy was but one aspect of a transcontinental nation-building strategy. Creighton insisted that Macdonald acted patriotically throughout the affair; his hero appeared as a shrewd politician, cleverly manipulating obstinate and mischievous businessmen to achieve a nationalistic goal. One of the devious schemers was Montréal's shipping magnate Sir Hugh Allan, a particularly selfish man who sold out to the Americans and then lied to Macdonald about his connections. More honourable was Toronto's shipper and railway contractor Sir David Macpherson, a shrewd but patriotic Conservative friend, who proposed an all-Canadian route under all-Canadian management. Lurking in the shadowy background was Jay Cooke, the American robber baron and annexationist villain, plotting to gain control of the Canadian North-West for the benefit of his Northern Pacific Railway. In this melodramatic manner, the nationalist interpretation categorizes the players in the Pacific Scandal according to their apparent loyalties.[4]

Undoubtedly, the CPR was a major factor in Sir John A. Macdonald's nation-building program. The railway would make the occupation of the North-West feasible and provide a practical access to British Columbia. But the Canadian government faltered when it came to choosing a private syndicate to build the road. In its first form, the Canada Pacific Railway was primarily a cooperative business enterprise between Canadian and American capitalists, an alliance that enjoyed the active support of the Canadian government but ostensibly contradicted its stated objectives. The opposition, which eventually scuttled the Canadian-American alliance, was inspired less by patriotic concerns than by partisan considerations. Clearly, when the philosophy of railways was rendered into a multimillion-dollar business proposition, it quickly degenerated into a messy political imbroglio. In this instance, Sir John A. Macdonald emerges not as the consummate diplomat and visionary statesman but as a corrupt politician who naively, clumsily, and belatedly imposed an unworkable political settlement on a completed business deal.

Viewed as a political ideal, the western, or Pacific, section of the transcontinental railway had as a major objective the settlement of the North-West. Since the 1840s, the annexation of the western prairies had been a component of confederation debates and gradually the common perception of the western interior had changed from that of an inhospitable barren wilderness to an accessible verdant landscape, fit for settlement. Even if only naively aware of its potential, Joseph Howe, for example, expressly included prairie settlement in his vision of the Pacific railway, and his colleagues in New Brunswick and the Canadas appeared to concur. In the 1850s, George Brown, editor of the Toronto *Globe*, began to educate his readers about the vast expanses of the North-West and the seemingly limitless opportunities its lands promised.[5] In 1858 Alexander Galt, primarily occupied with saving the Grand Trunk from financial disaster and the Canadas from political stalemate, recommended the annexation of the North-West to a federated British North America.[6] Although premature at the time, Galt's proposal survived; it reappeared in the early 1860s and finally became reality at mid-decade.

Railway communication was crucial to western settlement. Practically, the region needed fast and inexpensive transportation first for the many prospective immigrants and subsequently for their bulky farm products. In idealistic terms, the railway possessed a mystical and very persuasive purpose. In the nineteenth-century mentality, the railway was the prerequisite tool for transforming empty wildernesses into productive fields, industrious towns, and bustling cities. Across the eastern and central continent, powerful locomotives were already hauling long trains laden with produce to distant markets. Here were the visible demonstrations that the railway could tame the wild and seemingly empty landscape. Impressed by the vastness of the expansive plains, for example, James Dickinson, who accompanied the 1857 Hind expedition, perceived the prairies as vacant land. Standing on the top of the Qu'Appelle valley bluff, he looked 'down upon the glittering lake 300 feet below, and across the boundless plains, no living thing in view, no sound of life anywhere.' To his mind, the grand vista spread before him would be completed only in 'the time to come when will be seen passing swiftly along the distant horizon the white cloud of the locomotive on its way from the Atlantic to the Pacific.'[7]

By 1864, the political will to make Dickinson's vision a reality had solidified. George Brown, prodded by C.J. Brydges, the Grand Trunk Railway's general manager, reluctantly accepted the Maritimes' ultimatum that a union of British North America must include an intercolonial railway. Brown began to see some sense in the project since the Reciprocity Treaty was to be abrogated and bonding privileges through the United States might follow suit. More important, he realized that his endorsement of an intercolonial was the best way to achieve his long-term goal of western settlement and a Pacific railway. By the spring of the year, he was ready to embrace an 'omnibus arrangement' including a Halifax-Québec railway, a federal union of British North America with representation by population in the lower house, annexation of the North-West, and a Pacific railway.[8] As the most powerful political figure in Canada West, Brown's willingness to serve in a coalition cabinet with his political rival, John A. Macdonald, whose majority support lay in Canada East, opened the way for confederation and the construction of a transcontinental railway.

The celebrations that welcomed the birth of the Dominion of Canada on 1 July 1867 did not signal an immediate start to construction of the Pacific railway. In fact, the first attempt to build the road became embroiled in the complex international world of railway technology, economics, and business. By the time the dust settled late in 1874, Canada's philosophy of railways, which had featured so prominently in confederation, lay in ruins.

Traditional historiography lays much of the blame for the failure of Canada's first Pacific railway on Jay Cooke, an ambitious American financier with a strong interest in the Northern Pacific Railroad, potentially a competitor to the Canada Pacific Railway. In actual fact, Cooke, like most of his counterparts, saw railways as investment opportunities rather than nation-building tools. His initial interest in railway projects was inspired not by visions of a transcontinental empire spanning all of the American western interior but by calculated business speculations. In many ways, Cooke became an agent of railway technology's propensity to expand constantly in order to remain competitive and profitable.

Throughout his career, Jay Cooke displayed the aggressive nature of an ambitious and innovative promoter. Born on the Ohio frontier in 1821, he became a rich financier. During the American Civil War, his Philadelphia investment firm initiated the practice of selling war bonds through a national network of agents and by aggressive advertising in leading newspapers.[9] His interest in railways emerged after the war when government business declined and his investments in western land development grew. In 1868 he visited Duluth on Lake Superior and bought extensive properties in the area. Expansionist by nature, Cooke became preoccupied by railways as engines of growth and development. He believed they presented a means of developing the resources of the West and of creating unparalleled opportunities for investment and profit. More particularly, his extensive properties around Duluth could increase in value only if its harbour became a major shipping point for western grain and iron headed for the eastern states and Europe. To compete with Milwaukee and Chicago, the undeveloped port of Duluth needed a network of feeder railways from the continent's interior.[10] Consequently, Cooke acquired an interest in the Lake Superior and Mississippi Railroad, which intended to link Duluth with St Paul on the Mississippi River. In 1869 Cooke also accepted an invitation to head a public bond campaign for the Northern Pacific Railroad.

The Northern Pacific represented Boston's long struggle to capture the trade of the Great Lakes and the American West. The Pacific scheme was a crucial component of the Vermont Central and the Vermont and Canada railways, whose management and finances were closely integrated as a consequence of a long and complex history of mismanagement, bankruptcies, and court battles. Although the exact composition of the boards of directors of the Vermont railways changed repeatedly, they always embraced one family of promoters. Central to this clique was the largest stockholder, J. Gregory Smith, the president of the Vermont Central, and his brother, W.C. Smith, from time to time a director and president of the Vermont and Canada, as well as the treasurer and the vice-president of the Vermont Central.

Encouraged by the prosperity of the post–Civil War era, the Boston investors turned to the perennial task of capturing from New York a portion of trade from the midwestern states. As a first step, they consolidated

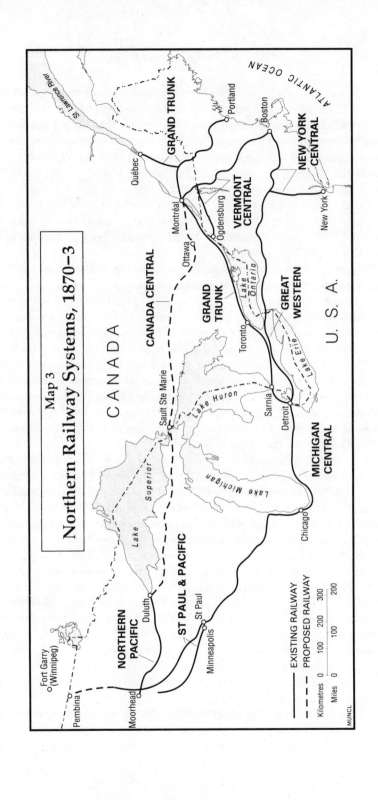

Map 3

Northern Railway Systems, 1870–3

CANADA

U. S. A.

ATLANTIC OCEAN

St Lawrence River

GRAND TRUNK

Portland

Boston

NEW YORK
CENTRAL

Québec

Montréal

VERMONT
CENTRAL

Ogdensburg

New York

CANADA CENTRAL

Ottawa

GRAND
TRUNK

Lake
Ontario

GREAT
WESTERN

Toronto

Lake Erie

Sault Ste Marie

Lake Huron

Sarnia

Detroit

MICHIGAN
CENTRAL

Lake
Superior

Lake Michigan

Chicago

NORTHERN
PACIFIC

Duluth

ST PAUL & PACIFIC

St Paul

Minneapolis

Fort Garry
(Winnipeg)

Pembina

Moorhead

——— EXISTING RAILWAY
– – – PROPOSED RAILWAY

Kilometres 0   100   200   300
Miles   0   100   200

MUNCL

the operations of seven northern New England railways that together made up a system running from Boston to Ogdensburg on the St Lawrence River. After prolonged negotiations and infighting, the six easternmost railways created a consolidated board of directors dominated by the Vermont Central and the Vermont and Canada. In 1870 the Vermont Central leased the Ogdensburg and Lake Champlain Railroad so that J. Gregory Smith and his friends controlled a main line from the Atlantic to Lake Ontario, as well as a fleet of steamers from Boston to New York. The New Englanders also planned to use the eastern end of Lake Ontario as a terminal for steamships from Chicago, but failed partly because such an operation was seasonal at best.[11]

Clearly, if Boston businessmen wanted to tap the trade of the Great Lakes and the West through Vermont, it required a Canadian rail connection. Forging one would have brought it into direct conflict with powerful Canadian business interests based primarily in Montréal. These entrepreneurs had hoped to capture the western trade with the construction of the Grand Trunk Railway and its subsidiaries to Portland, Maine. They built the Grand Trunk with a broad gauge of 5 feet 6 inches in order to hamper the interchange of goods and passengers with the Boston system and prevent the syphoning of traffic to the south. The Grand Trunk Railway, nevertheless, explored limited ways of cooperating with the Boston railway promoters and pieced together an uneasy alliance that did not work well, particularly for the Canadian railway.[12]

Both the Canadian and northern New England railways faced deadly competition from New York and more southerly Atlantic seaports. In 1869 both the Pennsylvania and New York Central consolidated their through routes from the seaboard to Chicago, placing the Grand Trunk and the Vermont Central with their circuitous routes at a great disadvantage. Neither railway could compete with the New York system, which had developed a shorter and more efficient transportation network to the Great Lakes, had better financial services, and a more extensive coastal trade. New York, moreover, could fatally injure any Boston railway by drawing traffic to its superior harbour. By the mid-1860s, a Boston railway, the Western, which connected Boston to a more southerly and direct route to the lakes, was virtually integrated into the New York Central system and became the Vermont Central's most damaging competitor.[13]

To meet the increasing rivalry from New York and to compensate for the weak link through Canada, Vermont Central's president, J. Gregory Smith, purchased the charter of the Northern Pacific. This visionary railway plan, incorporated in 1864, included among its founders Jay Cooke's brother, Henry. Although Smith and his associates intended to use the Northern Pacific in conjunction with the Grand Trunk to reach the far West, they never contemplated risking much of their own money. Instead, they planned to sell bonds to the public.[14] For that purpose, they sought the help of Jay Cooke, the accomplished pedlar of Civil War bonds.

Cooke had refused the Northern Pacific overtures before but in 1869 he relented. Goaded by his interests in western lands, particularly in the Duluth region, his speculative instincts overlooked the bleak history of previous Northern Pacific bond issues. The expectation of rising land values as a result of railway construction and the handsome commission on Northern Pacific bonds enticed him, and he accepted the company's offer.

Cooke's interest in the Northern Pacific and his plans for western investments sprang in part from the writings of James Wickes Taylor, an indefatigable publicist and advocate of the commercial potential of the American and British North-West. Taylor almost single-handedly created Minnesota's dream for the exploitation of Rupert's Land. A stream of pamphlets, editorials, and articles won him an appointment in 1859 as a special agent of the United States Treasury, commissioned to report on commercial relations and communications between Minnesota and the British North-West. Taylor exploited his official position to widen the audience for his notions of an overland transportation system, highlighting a northern Pacific railway route and including the St Lawrence River as an important conduit for Minnesota wheat. He corresponded frequently with his friend, the Grand Trunk's C.J. Brydges, and occasionally lobbied Washington on behalf of the Hudson's Bay Company. In 1860 he prepared a paper for Minnesota Senator Alexander Ramsey in which he stressed the geographical unity of the western plains and rivers and proposed a customs union for the region from the Red River to the Pacific. 'Free trade and navigation with British America would give to the United States, and especially to the Western States, all the commercial advantages, without the political embarrassments, of annexation, and would in the sure progress of events, relieve our extended Northern frontier from the horrors and injuries of war between fraternal communities.'[15] The abrogation of the Reciprocity Treaty in 1865, which appeared to kill his western free-trade block idea, caused Taylor to advocate peaceful annexation, a position that assumed fanatical proportions by the time of the Red River uprisings in 1869.[16]

Taylor's later annexationist views did not represent current mainstream thinking in the United States. By 1869, the militant rhetoric of the Civil War had subsided and a view of friendly neighbours sharing the continent prevailed. Although expansionism was still a potent force in the United

States, in the case of relations with Canada it had taken on a style similar to Britain's informal-empire strategy in that it was likely to take the shape of commercial advancement in preference to territorial expansion. Buoyed by prosperity, rising industrialization, and a diversifying economy, the post–Civil War United States was formulating a 'New American Empire' that included a search for markets for its manufactured goods and processed foods. Whereas they still viewed the Mississippi as a main artery of European commerce, many American merchants hoped to develop trade with the Far East and thus wanted to enlarge Pacific ports and build a transcontinental railway.[17] After years of regional infighting and enormous physical difficulties, the United States completed the first transcontinental railway in June 1869, when the Union and Central Pacific met at Promontory, Utah.[18]

Since most Americans believed that eventually the United States would dominate the commerce of the continent, that its high energy and drive, its republicanism and laissez-faire economy would in time overwhelm Canada, they saw no urgent need to annex it. The newly formed nation fitted comfortably into their business projections. Nearly a century of commerce had created a wide band of intermingled trade and transportation that in 1869 ran from the Bay of Fundy to Detroit. Within this borderland, bridges, canals, rivers, and railways facilitated the easy international movement of people, goods, and capital. Geographic proximity, historical and personal ties, as well as cultural similarities encouraged the development of common business methods and economic compatibility; all these factors contributed to the belief that some time in the future the two economies would be merged into one. In any case, at the end of the war, American entrepreneurs – and Canadians too – sought to normalize business relations as quickly as possible and extend the borderland to the Pacific. American businessmen no longer considered Canada a British enemy base but realized that two similar but distinct nations were to share the northern continent.[19] Before James W. Taylor's frustrated enthusiasm carried him to excesses, he paid tribute to North America's common heritage and civilizing mission; he applauded any developments in British territory as ultimately beneficial to his adopted Minnesota. 'Believing firmly that the prosperity and development of this State is intimately associated with the destiny of Northwest British America,' he confessed in 1860, 'I am gratified to record the rapid concurrence of events which indicate that the frontier, hitherto resting upon the sources of the Saint Lawrence and the Mississippi, is soon to be pushed far beyond the International frontier by the march of Anglo-Saxon civilization.'[20]

Although James W. Taylor and Jay Cooke flirted with the idea of annex-ation, their primary objective was to establish beneficial business associa-tions. The central issue for Cooke was to find sufficient traffic for his railway to support its massive capitalization. Sometimes that goal required ruthless competition; at other times it called for friendly cooperation with rival railways. At the turn of the decade, collaboration with the Canadian promoters of a Pacific railway appeared most advantageous to the North-ern Pacific's strategy. If that purpose required the annexation of Rupert's Land, Cooke was prepared to work to that end. If it did not, so much the better.

Early in May 1869, after Cooke announced his affiliation with the Northern Pacific, Taylor offered his services as an expert on western affairs. He prepared a detailed report that drew Cooke's attention to Pembina as the gateway to the Hudson's Bay Company territory. Even though he acknowledged that Canada planned to construct a Pacific railway as its claim to the North-West, Taylor assured Cooke that no one would build north of Lake Superior 'within the century.'[21] To prevent Chicago and Milwaukee from draining traffic away from the Northern Pacific and the Lake Superior and Mississippi railways, he suggested that Cooke construct a network of railways linking the Mississippi and Saskatchewan trading systems with the Great Lakes at Duluth.[22]

Circumstances forced Cooke to follow part of Taylor's advice. The money crisis of September 1869 caused severe losses for Cooke and seri-ously depressed bond sales of the Lake Superior and Mississippi Railroad. Hoping to divert lucrative grain trade from the Iowa plains to Duluth by way of the Lake Superior railway, Cooke bought shares in the St Paul & Sioux City Railroad.[23] He also purchased part of the St Paul & Pacific Rail-road, which intended to link Pembina, on the U.S. boundary, with St Paul, thus threatening to divert potential Northern Pacific traffic to Chicago. Afraid that the St Paul & Pacific might complete its line to Red River before the Northern Pacific could establish its own hegemony of feeder lines into Canadian territory, Cooke determined to buy the railway. 'As to [St Paul & Pacific president] Becker he must be whipped, of course,' he wrote his brother. 'It would never do for that road to have the line down the Red River to Pembina. It would injure Duluth.'[24] Cooke spread adverse publicity against the St Paul & Pacific in Europe, the home of most of its investors, and in December 1870 purchased into its franchise at a bar-gain price. He gained control over a vital railway link that could tap traffic from the Canadian prairies to Duluth by way of the Northern Pacific.[25] Once committed to the Lake Superior and Northern Pacific railways, the

Philadelphia financier had to find traffic for these roads by expanding into other railway ventures.

To create traffic and revenues for his expanding railway empire, Cooke developed an intensive advertising campaign to lure settlers to the American plains. He intended to employ the techniques that had made the Civil War bonds a household word in the United States. 'Our idea is to carry the lands to the very firesides of the people throughout all our Northern States,' he explained to an associate, and predicted a vast movement of people westward as soon as the Northern Pacific was completed 'as far as ... those splendid Red River Lands.'[26] He also expected to recruit immigrants from Europe and proposed several group settlements. It was a comprehensive scheme, designed to route the flow of immigrants and their future production through Duluth by way of the Northern Pacific and the Lake Superior and Mississippi.[27]

The advertising campaign failed to persuade investors to buy large amounts of Northern Pacific bonds. Discouraged and beset by disgruntled partners, Cooke tried to withdraw from the venture, but Gregory Smith reacted quickly: 'There is no use in considering the question of releasing you from our enterprise. You are now too fully identified with us and have so essentially become a part of us in the public mind that I could not for one entertain any proposition of that kind ... It is an enterprise worthy of your best energies.'[28] While Cooke recommitted himself to the Northern Pacific, he insisted that the company build no farther than the Red River before seeking more financial aid from the government. The limitation reassured his partners and they accepted the scaled-down plans.[29] On 1 January 1870 Cooke signed the final agreement with the Northern Pacific. Jay Cooke & Company became the sole agent for the railway's bonds and for all its financial transactions. Although his company assumed little risk and had only limited control in the boardroom, its future rested on the success of the Northern Pacific. If the railway succeeded, Jay Cooke & Co. stood to earn a good profit; if it failed, the investment company would lose vital prestige.[30] Cooke's future thus was irrevocably committed to the destiny of the Northern Pacific.

Jay Cooke's interest in the St Paul & Pacific kindled temporary annexationist ambitions. Goaded by Taylor, he launched a publicity campaign to win political support for the acquisition of Rupert's Land. He approached George Sheppard of the *New York Times*, gave him a $4000 stock option in the Northern Pacific and some Duluth lots, and asked him to write favourable articles. He explained his motives to an associate: 'Referring to my conversation with him [Sheppard] the other night about the Winnipeg business I should like to be one of a number to employ his services wholly in manipulating the annexation of British North America, Northwest of Duluth to our country. This could be done without any violation of treaties, and brought about as a result of quiet emigration over the border of trustworthy men with families, and with tacit, not legal understanding with Riley [Riel?] & others there. The country belongs to us naturally, and should be brought over without violence or bloodshed.'[31]

Although his annexation ploy appeared peaceful, Jay Cooke attempted to exploit the chaos in the Red River settlement. He instructed his brother, Henry, to persuade the American president to assist the Fenians in their move against British possessions. 'In your talks with the President & Secretary,' he wrote Henry, 'Tell them the shortest solution of this matter would be the Fenians, & and if they say so, I will send for some of the leaders, & have the matter attended to in quick time.'[32] In the spring of 1870 he met one of Riel's commissioners, and in the following winter he may have interviewed the Fenian leader, W.B. O'Donoghue.[33]

Cooke's attempts to stir up trouble in Red River came to nothing. On the one hand, the American administration simply did not want to alienate the British government; it refused to support Jay Cooke's political ambitions.[34] On the other hand, with the resolution of the Red River crisis early in 1870, Canada assumed undisputed control over the North-West. Cooke's political imperialist platform was dead and he quietly dropped the annexationist scheme.

Although political appropriation was foiled, American commercial ambitions for the Canadian North-West were still alive. With the help of Taylor, Cooke worked out a plan with the lieutenant-governor of Manitoba for the transportation of a large party of immigrants with horses and teams from central Canada to Manitoba. They planned to use lake steamers from Detroit to Duluth, the Northern Pacific to the end of track, and overland trails for the remainder of the journey. Taylor also negotiated a relaxation of the regulations for transporting the goods of Manitoba-bound immigrants through the United States, enabling them to execute individual bonds at ports of entry and to choose their own route and manner of transport. It was another move designed to increase traffic through the port of Duluth and, as a side-effect, to tempt at least half of these people 'to settle in Minnesota.'[35]

Through a succession of business decisions, then, Jay Cooke had gained a crucial interest in north-western American railways. His plans for the port of Duluth, the Northern Pacific, the St Paul & Pacific, and other western railways could succeed only if the territories created sufficient traffic to pay for the large interest payments on the railways' bonds. Only if the western plains were settled rapidly could the railways survive. Who exercised political jurisdiction over these vast fertile expanses was of little consequence to Cooke's profit margin. He would be content as long the ruling state colonized the lands quickly. Canada's plans for a railway across the northern prairies suited his goals perfectly; as projected, the line promised to fit naturally into his St Paul & Pacific scheme and to become an important feeder into the Northern Pacific Railroad and the port of Duluth. Little wonder that he took a keen interest in Canada's transcontinental railway, especially when prominent citizens pressed him to take an active part.

Jay Cooke received encouragement from Canadian politicians and businessmen because he presented the most feasible rail route to the North-West. In 1865 the Toronto *Globe*, the foremost advocate of the annexation of the western prairies to Canada, argued that the Canadian government should support the Northern Pacific Railroad because it was 'the best means of access to a large portion of [Rupert's Land].'[36] Implicit in the editorial was the belief that railways were business ventures that operated on the accepted technical principles of efficiency and profitability, that railways were a sophisticated technology that recognized no national boundaries in their capitalization or operation. In keeping with its philosophy of railways, the *Globe* did not fear the Northern Pacific as an ominous threat to future Canadian sovereignty in the North-West, but welcomed it as the most efficient means of transportation to a region of enormous economic opportunity. It was an opinion shared by many Canadian financiers, railway men, and politicians, including Sir John A. Macdonald.

Nationalist sentiment, in fact, did not rule out business cooperation across the border. L.S. Huntington, the author of a 1869 pamphlet, *The Independence of Canada*, which argued that Canada's diplomatic dependence upon Britain hurt her chances of renewing reciprocity with the United States, was an active advocate of an international railway spanning the continent.[37] A committed supporter of the Liberal party, Huntington was the owner of the Eastern Townships' *Advertiser* as well as a shareholder in a railway and a copper mine in that region, the latter ventures dependent almost entirely on American trade. In 1869 he suggested to Jay Cooke that the Northern Pacific should form an alliance with the proposed Canada Pacific Railway. He promised to 'bring [Cooke] into communication with influential parties here [in Canada] who share my view.'[38] Huntington arranged several meetings between his Canadian associates and the American businessman. The sessions revealed not only that some Canadians were anxious to associate with the Northern Pacific but that there were several competing parties seeking Cooke's backing.[39]

One Canadian whom Huntington introduced to Jay Cooke was William McDougall, minister of public works and soon to be the first governor of the North-West Territories. McDougall, who may have met Cooke once or twice during the fall of 1869, supported the concept of an international railway. He proposed using New Brunswick's European and North American Railway from Saint John, crossing Maine, following the Ottawa Valley towards the Straits of Mackinac, dipping through northern Michigan, and running westward by way of the Northern Pacific to the Canadian North-West. McDougall promised to launch a vigorous program of immigration as soon as he was installed as territorial governor, and pledged to route newcomers to the North-West by way of the Northern Pacific Railway.[40]

Macdonald approved of McDougall's position. Although his administration had commenced construction of a wagon and boat route from Thunder Bay to Fort Garry, Macdonald hoped that within a year or so a railway would be constructed 'from the Fort Southward to a union with the American System of Railways,' giving the colony two modes of access 'by which we confidently expect an immediate influx of emigrants both from Europe and the United States.'[41] The prime minister, however, did not trust the Americans completely. He continued to insist on the wagon road to Thunder Bay and placed an immigration agent, Thomas Mayne Daly, at St Paul to ensure that those settlers destined for the Canadian prairies were not waylaid by Yankee immigrant recruiters.[42]

Meanwhile, the Canadian government encouraged cooperation with American railways. In 1869 Joseph Howe, secretary of state for the provinces, urged Taylor to draft a bill that would allow Canada's Pacific railway to connect with an American railway at Sault Ste Marie. Howe also requested the officers of the St Paul & Pacific to present Ottawa with a proposition for an extension of their Pembina branch to Fort Garry. Taylor prepared draft legislation and Joseph Howe endorsed it, an unmistakable signal that the Canadian government would approve a southern connection through the United States.[43]

The plans for a western Canadian railway were briefly interrupted by the Metis uprising in the Red River settlement. Under the leadership of Louis Riel, the Metis reacted angrily against Canada's arbitrary takeover of Rupert's Land. They prevented Lieutenant-Governor McDougall from entering Red River, took control of the colony, and demanded concessions from the Canadian government. The uprising clearly exposed Red River's isolation from Canada. McDougall, for example, depended upon the American telegraph service to communicate with his government. More embarrassingly, the Canadian government could not move troops to Red

River until spring break-up on the Great Lakes. Meanwhile, Macdonald contemplated building a fleet of small boats at Collingwood on Georgian Bay to use in a spring offensive against the Metis. He also planned to subsidize a shipping company to establish a permanent steamboat service between Collingwood and Thunder Bay.[44] Significantly, he expressed no immediate plans for a direct rail link through Canadian territory.

Macdonald, always keen on saving money, appeared much more interested in an American bypass than a direct Canadian route. During the Metis uprising he asked J.J. Hill, a St Paul merchant and shipper who controlled all the forwarding business to Red River, to prepare a report on the subject of western transportation. Hill, an expatriate Canadian, argued that the St Paul route was the only economical access to Fort Garry. He claimed it was much cheaper than either the northern approach from York Factory on Hudson Bay or the eastern access from Thunder Bay, especially because the St Paul & Pacific Railroad was projected to complete its line between St Paul and Pembina within three years. He suggested that, in the meantime, stage coaches and steamships could handle all freight between the end-of-rail on the Red River and Fort Garry.[45] Taking his own advice, Hill operated a very successful steamboat fleet on the Red River until the late 1870s.

After the settlement of the Red River insurrection, Manitoba's first lieutenant-governor, Adams Archibald, actively promoted Canadian cooperation with the Northern Pacific. Assiduously courted by Taylor, Archibald pledged to do all in his power to aid the Northern Pacific. Meanwhile, he asked Taylor to provide information about the Northern Pacific that he could forward to Ottawa. He also persuaded the Canadian government to reduce its spending on the Red River–Thunder Bay route.[46]

While Macdonald had not yet made up his mind about the nature of the Pacific railway, he clearly favoured the economical American connection. He believed that a southern diversion through the United States was a real possibility and he paid very little attention to Alfred Waddington, a British Columbia railway promoter who was one of a few arguing for an all-Canadian Pacific railway line. Instead, Macdonald consulted American experts like Hill and Taylor.[47] A memorandum, likely composed by Macdonald himself, argued that the Pacific railway should consist of two sections, the eastern running from Lake Nipissing to Lake Superior and the western commencing at Pembina, both linked together by the proposed mid-western American railway system. The memorandist claimed that the advantage of using American railways was that their reputation in Europe would enhance the prospects of the Canadian enterprise.[48] At the same time, however, Macdonald advocated a summer route through Canada, and he promised D.L. Macpherson of Toronto a mail subsidy for a planned transportation company between Fort Garry and Toronto. Clearly, Macdonald saw the railway question as a matter of economics, separable from nationalistic considerations. He supported the American option because it provided an inexpensive, year-round transportation system to British Columbia. The annexationist fear, which he and other politicians expressed at times, appeared to be political rhetoric based not on reality but designed to strengthen Canada's sense of national purpose.[49]

At the same time that Canadian government officials were preparing the ground for a connecting link through the United States between central and western Canada, one of Canada's most influential businessmen, Hugh Allan of Montréal, was making a bid for the Canada Pacific charter. A shrewd and innovative entrepreneur, Allan was owner of the Montreal Ocean Steamship Company, a large fleet of steamers plying the St Lawrence River and Atlantic Ocean.[50] By 1870 he was chafing under the domination of the Grand Trunk Railway, the primary supplier of traffic for his steamers. Allan wanted more traffic from the railway, particularly from the American Midwest. To escape reliance on the Grand Trunk, Allan moved into railways. He established links with the Canada Central Railway, the Montreal Northern Colonization Railway, the North Shore Railway, and the Ontario and Quebec Railway. These companies, some of which were only in the planning stages, could become a powerful railway network reaching from Montréal northward to Québec City, westward down the Ottawa Valley to the Great Lakes, and southward to Peterborough and Toronto. The proposed system, which threatened the Grand Trunk hegemony, formed a solid base for a Pacific railway.

Allan's connection with the Montreal Northern Colonization and Canada Central railways, his desire to escape the domination of the Grand Trunk, and his need for more cargo from western America made a joint venture with the Northern Pacific virtually inevitable. The date of the initial contact between the Canadian shipper and the American banker is not certain. Perhaps their negotiations followed earlier meetings with Huntington and McDougall. Both D.G. Creighton and Pierre Berton contend, however, that the first contact was made by William McMullen, an obscure Ontario-born publisher living in Chicago. This point must be accepted cautiously, not because it may be wrong but because it leads to an erroneous conclusion. Both authors suggest that McMullen brought the Americans into Waddington's scheme and then, through the offices of Francis Hincks, the minister of finance, approached Allan in order to replace the rather insignificant Waddington with the powerful Montréal businessman.

In their subsequent accounts, both authors argue that the Americans usurped a Canadian project and, though rebuffed by the dominion government, infiltrated the Allan organization without Macdonald's knowledge. In other words, Allan and his associates deceived the prime minister of Canada. Consequently, the blame for the Pacific Scandal ultimately falls on Allan and the Americans.

Although tempting from a nationalist perspective, this interpretation needs some revision. First, the Vermont promoters reached an understanding with the Canada Central by the end of 1870. The Canada Central's projected route from its connection with the Montreal Northern Colonization Company at Ottawa up the valley to Sault Ste Marie provided the Vermont group with the most direct access from the St Lawrence to St Paul.[51] Jay Cooke and his associates, consequently, acquired shares in a railway in which Hugh Allan had a considerable interest. Second, early in 1871, Allan informed Sir John A. Macdonald that he was about to become involved in the transcontinental railway. Macdonald assured Allan that while it was premature for the government to award any charters, he saw 'no objection to the Capitalists of Canada or of England, (or of the United States for that matter), joining together & making proposals for the construction of the Road.'[52] Macdonald's rather cavalier reply suggests that as early as February 1871 he had an inkling of Allan's American intentions.

The first meeting between Sir Hugh Allan and Jay Cooke on Pacific railway matters probably came somewhat later. In April 1871 Allan met Henry Cooke to discuss his Montréal steamers calling at Baltimore. He told Henry Cooke that he was anxious that 'the Canadas should participate in the benefits of the N.P. by an extension of it from its eastern terminus eastward through Canada to Montreal and Quebec.'[53] Obviously interested, the Cookes had several meetings with Allan and his associates in May. A month later, the negotiators met at Jay Cooke's summer estate, 'Gibraltar,' and concluded a preliminary agreement.[54] In July 1871 a large delegation, including Gregory Smith, Alfred Waddington, and George McMullen, visited Macdonald in Ottawa and placed the scheme before him and Francis Hincks.[55]

Allan's understanding with the Americans, then, was clearly and openly explained to the prime minister and his advisers. Hincks, for one, believed that the agreement would give Canada a line to serve her needs for years. He admitted that while political considerations prevented the Canadian government from proposing the route itself, it would accept the deal. 'It seems to me,' he explained to Macdonald, 'to be most desirable to attract investors of the first status of the money market and the type of the American Rail Road men Allan is anxious to go into it.' Since Canada still did not really know the country north of Lake Superior, he added, 'It is good that they are willing to take the risk. Allan's name will be able to carry it.'[56]

By the summer of 1871, therefore, the American backers of the Northern Pacific had every reason to believe that there were no objections to their participation in Canada's Pacific railway scheme. Jay Cooke, who believed that a merger with the Canada Pacific would enhance the value and sales of Northern Pacific bonds, was pleased that the Canadian government approved the negotiations. After meeting Francis Hincks in New York, he concluded: 'The Canadian government is extremely friendly to the connection of our road at Sault Ste Marie, and they will do all they can to connect with us at Manitoba & other points. I have no doubt whatever that arrangements can be made by which the Hudson Bay [sic] people, headed by Sir Stafford Northcote, can have an interest in our road and in its direction.'[57] Cooke intended to use the Canadian agreement to persuade the Hudson's Bay Company to join several German firms in a syndicate to take $20 million in Northern Pacific bonds.

On 1 December 1871 Gregory Smith visited Ottawa and discussed the agreement with government officials. They reassured him that they had no objection to his association with the Canada Pacific because, ostensibly, all the charter incorporators of the company were Canadian, including Sir Hugh Allan as president and Adams Archibald as one of its directors. Actually, it was Smith's request for a subsidy of 50 million acres of land and $30 million in cash that most concerned the Canadian government.[58] Allan 'is connected with strong men in the United States,' Macdonald informed Rose, 'but my fear is that they will ask for a larger subsidy & more land, than Parliament will be likely to grant them.'[59] Several weeks after J. Gregory Smith visited Ottawa, the American railway promoters, comprising all the prominent members of the Northern Pacific, including Jay Cooke & Co., closed a formal agreement with Sir Hugh Allan, the only Canadian signatory. The American businessmen pledged to take over and build the Canada Pacific Railway Company and to form the Canada Land and Improvement Company to develop the expected land grant.[60] Afraid that Canadian competitors and public opinion might scuttle the deal, the incorporators kept the agreement secret.

Their secrecy was well advised. Although the scheme promised to provide Canada with a relatively inexpensive railway to the western prairies, the obvious advantages accrued to the Americans. In addition to receiving a large subsidy and extensive lands, their faltering Northern Pacific and Vermont Central railways could gain economic control over the vast Canadian

North-West. The Canada Pacific Railway would 'be made to swell the volume of commerce of the Great North West and the earnings and profits of the Northern Pacific R. to which it would seem legitimately to belong.'[61] Canadian politicians, including the prime minister, nevertheless encouraged Jay Cooke and his associates to conclude a bargain with Hugh Allan and become the dominant promoters of the Canada Pacific Railway.

Secrecy was also essential because the deal was extremely vulnerable to opposition attack. Indeed, the collusion, which soon became common knowledge, unleashed a storm of protest and unbridled opposition. Politics and business rivalry combined to scuttle the ambitions of the Boston promoters even before they were realized. Ironically, few of the supposedly patriotic opponents of Allan and his American associates objected to using the American rail network to reach the Canadian North-West. Most critics, making a fine distinction between American financial control of and American access to the Pacific railway, opposed only the domination of the Northern Pacific in a heavily subsidized Canadian railway.

Among the most powerful rivals to Allan's Vermont associates was the Grand Trunk Railway. The Allan-Cooke alliance created a much shorter link between the American West and the Atlantic seaboard than the Grand Trunk's circuitous route through Chicago, and thus threatened to erode the Grand Trunk's midwestern traffic flow and thwart its ambitions for western Canada. Early in 1870 C.J. Brydges, the general manager of the Grand Trunk, warned Macdonald that the Northern Pacific intended to build near Canada's western territories in order 'to defeat a purely British line by proposing a series of branches to tap the Saskatchewan valley at leading points.'[62] Brydges fretted that Jay Cooke, 'probably the boldest, shrewdest, and at the same time, cautious man, in the Railway fraternity,' planned to take advantage of Canada's problems in the Red River colony to persuade the American government to annex the region.

Brydges obviously wanted to forestall a Canadian-American alliance that could cripple the Grand Trunk.[63] A year earlier, he and several Grand Trunk friends had formed a group to build a Pacific line across the prairies. They planned to apply for financial aid from the Canadian government 'to take advantage of the political necessity in England just now of saving the NW from the Yankees, etc. etc.'[64] Despite his cynical patriotism, Brydges did not intend to use an all-Canadian route. 'I am quite clear,' he confided to a friend, 'that railways from Fort Garry around the north shore of Lake Superior and Lake Nipissing could not be built except at a frightful cost, when built could not be worked successfully in winter, and if it could be worked would have no traffic to carry upon it.'[65] Brydges planned to link his prairie section of the Pacific railway to the Grand Trunk by way of American railways south of the Great Lakes. To help finance the Canadian section, Brydges demanded a subsidy of $5000 to $7500 a mile in cash, and a government-assisted immigration program.[66] Brydges's opposition, then, was not based on nationalistic concerns. He did not fear routing Canada's Pacific Railway through American territory, but was afraid that an alliance of the Vermont Central, Montreal Northern Colonization, Canada Central, Northern Pacific, and Canada Pacific would squeeze the Grand Trunk out of the American and Canadian West.

To prevent the deadly alliance, the Grand Trunk Railway launched a vicious propaganda campaign in Canada and England against the Allan interests. Backed by powerful bankers, including the Barings and Glyn and Mills, the Grand Trunk, by discrediting Northern Pacific bonds, contributed in no small measure to their lacklustre performance and the eventual failure of that railway as well as the Canada Pacific and Montreal Northern Colonization Railway.[67] Meanwhile, Grand Trunk backers in Montréal vigorously opposed Allan's attempt to secure a municipal subsidy for the Montreal Northern Colonization Railway. Perhaps most damaging, the Grand Trunk placed political pressure on George-Etienne Cartier, the company's solicitor and, as Macdonald's lieutenant, the most powerful French Canadian in the cabinet.[68]

The Grand Trunk's anti-Allan campaign also gained important assistance from John Rose, a close and very influential friend of Macdonald and, from 1867 to 1869, Canada's minister of finance. In the summer of 1869 the Canadian government had appointed Rose as an informal agent in London with the duty of arranging the transfer of Rupert's Land to Canada, of promoting emigration to the prairies, and of conducting other government business.[69] Rose's diplomatic chores were but a sideline: his primary objective in London was personal business. He became a senior partner in the prestigious London banking firm of Morton, Rose & Company and a governor of the Hudson's Bay Company.

Rose's private interests formed his attitude towards the Northern Pacific and Jay Cooke. In 1870 Cooke had established a branch in London called Jay Cooke, McCulloch & Company. The new bank competed directly with the Barings for the fiscal business of the United States and won a lucrative naval account. Understandably, the Barings, who were major shareholders in the Grand Trunk Railway, fiscal agents for the government of Canada, and close associates of John Rose, were extremely annoyed.[70] Not surprisingly, in July 1870 Rose wrote Macdonald a strongly worded objection to the Northern Pacific. He carefully explained that while he may have supported the Northern Pacific in the past, he had learned that its financial position was no longer sound and the Canadian government's reputation would be damaged by any association with the enterprise.[71] Obviously, Jay Cooke had antagonized an important figure in Canada's financial and political élite.

In alienating John Rose, Cooke also lost the friendship of the Hudson's Bay Company. Initially, the company encouraged the Northern Pacific's interests in western Canada because the company wanted to see the fertile portions of the territories settled as quickly as possible. Governor Lampson advised Cooke to 'communicate with the Canadian government,' which he believed was eager to open the country and might assist a railway venture with land grants and possibly with bond guarantees. Lampson promised to help promote the sale of the Northern Pacific's bonds in Britain.[72] Under Rose's guidance, however, the company adopted a neutral stand and refused to endorse the American railway unless the Canadian government approved the scheme.[73] Added to the active opposition of the Grand Trunk in London's financial circles, the Hudson's Bay Company's neutrality was a serious blow to Allan's proposals.

Aggravating the business rivalry that threatened the Allan scheme were sectional jealousies within Canada. Perhaps the most serious obstacle to Allan and his friends was the growing political opposition in Ontario. The proposed railway only skirted the north-eastern boundaries of the province and promised very little north-western commerce to Toronto businessmen. This was a serious flaw because the Conservative party was rapidly losing support in Ontario. Facing an imminent election with a weak platform for the province, Macdonald knew that he needed several respected Ontario businessmen in the Pacific company in order to win parliamentary approval. He approached his friend David L. Macpherson, a leading Toronto shipper, but to his chagrin Macpherson refused to join the Allan group, ostensibly because of its American interests but more likely because the proposed road left his city and province on the fringes of north-western commerce. Instead of joining Allan's group, Macpherson formed the Inter-oceanic Railway, whose all-Canadian board of directors promised to construct the Pacific line entirely through Canada.[74] Macpherson's proposal was very strong, particularly because of his intimate ties with the Liberal-Conservative party, his prominent standing in Ontario, and his close connection with the Grand Trunk.

The growing, powerful opposition to Allan's Northern Pacific alliance eventually coalesced the cabinet into a strong and ostensibly nationalist position. By the time the 1872 session of Parliament ended, cabinet had rejected the American presence in the Canada Pacific. Unfortunately, its actions were neither purely nationalistic nor decisive. Once Macpherson incorporated the Inter-oceanic, the question became one of regional politics. As Alexander Campbell, minister of the interior, testified at the Pacific Scandal Commission, Allan's Canada Pacific alienated Ontario businessmen while Macpherson's Inter-oceanic excluded Quebec promoters. 'It was a matter affecting not only the interests of the railway,' Campbell confessed, 'but the political existence of the Government.'[75] As time passed, regional rivalries intensified and members of the cabinet grew increasingly apprehensive. To them, the only acceptable solution was a political settlement and Macdonald and his colleagues spent months in vain attempts to merge the Montréal and Toronto interests. Political interference merely intensified polarization and, by the time Macdonald called a general election late in the summer of 1872, he could no longer accept the cheapest or even the most Canadian of railway schemes. Political considerations had become the predominant issue and eventually killed the project.[76]

That nationalistic concerns were secondary to political considerations is clear from the action of government during the 1872 session. The House approved both the Canada Pacific and Inter-oceanic charters in the hope that the incorporators could be induced to accept an amalgamation. Notably, in two identical clauses, the routes of both railways were only described in extremely vague terms as running somewhere from Lake Nipissing to the Pacific coast in British Columbia. On the matter of branch lines, the charters were more precise. Both railways were allowed to drive branches southward at Sault Ste Marie and Fort Garry 'so as to connect with the railway system of the United States of America.'[77] Moreover, when Cartier, a fiery opponent of the Northern Pacific's designs on the Canada Pacific, introduced the subsidy resolutions to the House he carefully explained that the government would assist two branch lines from Fort Garry, one to the head of Lake Superior and the other to Pembina 'to unite with the American system.'[78] That Jay Cooke had a substantial interest in the proposed connector at Pembina – the St Paul & Pacific – could not have escaped Cartier's attention.

By the time the government called the general election of 1872, the Pacific railway issue had not been resolved. During and after the election, the prime minister continued to press for a merger and, when failure was certain, he created an entirely new board, its members chosen proportionally as regional representatives from all parts of the Dominion. Completed by February 1873, the board resembled a cabinet, selected entirely for political rather than business reasons. The amended charter was fairly specific on deadlines, calling for the completion of the Fort Garry to Pembina line by December 1874, the western as well as the eastern sections to their respective ends of Lake Superior by the end of 1876, and the prairie and mountain parts by 1881. Significantly, the charter assigned no deadline to the route north of Lake Superior.[79]

Macdonald's political machinations were all in vain and the Canada Pacific was never built. One of Jay Cooke's minor associates, George William McMullen, allegedly gave the Liberal party a packet of judiciously selected letters and telegrams, some of which were stolen and some carefully altered. The package clearly showed that John A. Macdonald pressed Hugh Allan into making unusually large contributions to the Conservative campaign and used the funds to garner votes in a close election. A royal commission inquiring into the Pacific Scandal confirmed the charges of corrupt electioneering but found no evidence of shady dealings with the Americans.[80] Clearly, the cause of the Pacific Scandal was not Allan's supposedly secretive and subversive connection with the Americans but the corrupt electioneering tactics of a politically weak prime minister. The opposition of the Grand Trunk and its supporters, as well as regional and local rivalries, effectively emasculated Allan's alliance with the Americans well before the election and killed it shortly afterwards.

The intricate details of the Pacific Scandal are discussed in detail in several CPR histories and need not be discussed within the limited confines of this chapter. The nationalist historians, however, in their attempt to explain the shabby conduct of the Canadian players, have emphasized the annexationist ambitions of the American imperialists and the danger to Canadian nationhood. In doing so, they have not taken into account the nature of the philosophy of railways and the impact of technological nationalism upon the national identity.

Viewed from the American perspective, it is evident that neither Jay Cooke nor his Vermont confederates had a well-formed plan to fulfil America's manifest destiny in western Canada. Their attempts to gain financial control over the Canada Pacific resulted from an evolution of business objectives. Jay Cooke, a banker by profession, moved into railways in the late 1860s as part of his western interests. Mesmerized by the seemingly limitless opportunities for profit in the West, he sought to develop his properties in Duluth with feeder railways. His imperialistic annexationist ambitions for the Canadian North-West were recent, naive, and quickly squashed by Washington. The Canada Pacific was primarily a business proposition forced on him by necessity and fully discussed at all stages with Canadian businessmen and politicians. His hopes of mobilizing popular demand for western railway bonds in the United States, Canada, Great Britain, and Europe were misplaced and he failed to finance this rapidly expanding empire adequately.

The collapse of Jay Cooke's empire was largely a product of fierce international competition, both in the realm of banking and of railways. For years the Vermont Central, caught as in a vise between the Grand Trunk and New York Central railways, fought for the prospective trade of the American and Canadian West. Striving to divert western traffic from these competitors, the Vermont group attempted to reach beyond the influence of its arch-rivals; it sought to control the Northern and the Canada Pacific as feeder lines to its existing but starving eastern network. It was a premature and unrealistic plan that collapsed when British and Continental European financiers lost confidence in the Northern Pacific. The resultant panic of 1873 torpedoed most North American railway projects, including the Canada Pacific. Ironically, adverse propaganda spread by Canada's Grand Trunk Railway and Canada's financial agents helped to discredit all Pacific railway securities.[81]

As for Hugh Allan, the Canadian scapegoat, he understood the international character of the world of railways and finance. A shrewd, cosmopolitan entrepreneur, with extensive business connections in Canada, Great Britain, and the United States, and with money invested in virtually every sector of the Canadian economy, Allan recognized the realities of liberal economics; he knew that railway technology required international financing and interregional traffic. Like many of his colonial counterparts, he enviously eyed America's prosperity, discounted the international boundary, and supported closer economic relations. Accustomed to buy what he wanted in a world driven by the ethic of survival of the fittest, he obviously believed he could purchase the Pacific charter and turn it to his advantage.[82] Creighton's claim that Allan was a poor negotiator seems silly in the light of the gigantic commercial empire he created. Yet his stubborn desire to head the Pacific company forced him to bow to Macdonald's political dictates. Surely Allan's biggest error in judgment was to have accepted the Canada Pacific's politically appointed board of directors and to have attempted to sell the concept to London's sophisticated bankers. Moreover, Hugh Allan, like Jay Cooke, was infatuated by the opportunities the North-West offered; he failed to assess the weakness of Cooke's ambitious plans and to see the flaws in the Vermont Central and Northern Pacific empires. Once he bound the Canada Pacific to the Northern Pacific, the destiny of the Canadian road was inextricably bound to the collapse of the American company.

Whether Macdonald understood the full international implications of railway technology is uncertain. It is crystal clear that initially his government promoted the use of American railways south of the Great Lakes and encouraged American financial participation in the Canada Pacific railway. Jay Cooke and the Northern Pacific represented a practical and economically feasible way to open the North-West to Canada at a cost the small country could afford. The prime minister's correspondence nowhere suggests that he feared the dealings of hostile foreigners furtively plotting to make the Canada Pacific Railway a servile appendage to the Northern Pacific. Macdonald, in fact, did not withdraw support from Allan's Montréal-based scheme until he realized that he could neutralize Grand Trunk and domestic opposition only by admitting David Macpherson and his Ontario friends into the Canada Pacific's boardroom. His tactics at this point, however, became, even for him, unusually indecisive and totally partisan; in the end, his attempts to impose an incongruent political-regional settlement on a completed business deal were naive and clumsy, leading to fatal delays and, eventually, failure.

Sir John A. Macdonald did not sell the Pacific charter to the Americans; his cabinet awarded the charter not to Allan's original company but to an entirely new firm, organized according to Canadian regional interests. As Governor-General Lord Dufferin cogently observed, the Pacific Scandal ultimately arose out of the inordinate contribution Macdonald required from Allan and the way he and Cartier spent it, 'to the treating and to the payment of canvassers; to the conveyance of voters if not to the absolute purchase of voters.'[83] Clearly, as long as the issue was unresolved, Macdonald was wrong to ask Allan for unusually large contributions and then to spend them on a corrupt election campaign.

Patriotism, while loudly trumpeted, played only a minor role on the battleground of the 1872 election and the subsequent Pacific Scandal. Macpherson's strident call for an all-Canadian railway is questionable. As William Cumberland, an Inter-oceanic director, testified, the amalgamation negotiations broke down not for nationalistic reasons; personalities played a much greater role, as did regional economic interests.[84] Even after all the directors of the Inter-oceanic accepted Macdonald's merger scheme, which guaranteed that no American capital would be allowed to control the Pacific railway, Macpherson steadfastly refused to serve under an Allan presidency. His charter, like the Canada Pacific's, moreover, expressly allowed the construction of branch lines to American railways.

Obviously, in the early 1870s, the sense of nationalism among Canadian politicians and businessmen was weak. Seth Huntington, for example, who exposed the scandal in parliament, was the author of a book on Canadian independence, but encouraged Jay Cooke's participation in the Canada Pacific. He did not unmask the corruption for patriotic but for partisan and possibly personal reasons. Similarly, Prime Minister Alexander Mackenzie, who came to power in 1873, had a naive sense of national sovereignty. Only a stern lecture from Lord Dufferin prevented him from permitting the United States army to pursue whisky traders into Canadian territory.[85] Perhaps, as New Brunswick demonstrated so clearly in the 1866 election, British North Americans had not yet developed a clear sense of a unique identity that could be destroyed by close intercommunications with the United States. Perhaps nineteenth-century Canadians, who still defined their nationalism in British imperial rather than in North American terms, were so confident of the superiority of their inherited institutions that they did not fear American cultural imperialism.[86]

Intellectually and emotionally, young Canada's political élite may have treasured Britain's liberal heritage, which encapsulated the philosophy of railways and its development mission. When faced with specific political and economic issues, however, they were likely to make judgments from narrow and purely personal business viewpoints. How else can historians explain that even while a western Canadian member of parliament, Donald A. Smith, pontifically denounced Macdonald in the House of Commons, his partner, James J. Hill of St Paul, Minnesota, was scheming to take over the St Paul & Pacific? That plot earned Smith and Hill a fortune and established the base from which they, with the assistance of at least one more American and several Montréalers, including banker George Stephen, won the contract for the successful Canadian Pacific Railway. How else can one understand the actions of Lucius Huntington, who first exposed the Pacific Scandal, but who, with George Stephen and several other prominent investors, subsequently proposed to build the Pacific railway?[87] There is more than a little irony in the fact that the CPR's first locomotive in Winnipeg, the *Countess of Dufferin*, arrived by barge from St Paul.[88]

By the early 1870s, connections with American railways were still an important component in Canada's philosophy of railways. More than twenty years earlier, the 1849 Guarantee Act had recognized the international character of railway technology by legitimizing state assistance to the construction of the Canadian section of an international railway – the St Lawrence and Atlantic. The act also provided funds for the Great Western, which primarily served as a portage railway between main lines in New York and Michigan. Similarly, New Brunswick promoted the construction of the European and North American, a railway specifically designed to increase New England's commerce with Europe. The purpose of the Canada Pacific was to give Canadian businessmen access to the western prairies and British Columbia. Its proposal to work with the Northern Pacific and initially use its trunk line south of the Great Lakes fitted into a well-established pattern.

From the 1840s to the mid-1870s, members of Canada's urban élite did not perceive railways primarily as vehicles to foster nationalistic aspirations. To be sure, its philosophy of railways often invoked the ability of railway technology to unify peoples and homogenize social differences; they, therefore, insisted that a transcontinental must be part of the confederation agreement; but they perceived no inherent cultural danger in a railway bridge across the Niagara River. While they fervently believed that increased trade and easier communications with the United States would enhance their common prosperity, they did not presume closer ties would in any way endanger their nationalistic goal of establishing a transcontinental nation. Despite all the rhetoric of friendship and goodwill, they still saw railways primarily as technological tools to enhance the prosperity of themselves and the nation.

By the end of 1873, the philosophy of railways, which had been instrumental in the creation of the new nation, had collapsed. Shearing the rhetoric from the doctrine, regional and political jealousies reduced it to bare economic competition. The abortive history of the Canada Pacific aptly demonstrates that, despite lofty discourse, railway building was big business, involving millions of dollars, and, as it had in the past, could arouse fierce struggles between rival railway networks, financial institutions, metropolitan centres, and political parties. The philosophy of railways, with its lavish promises of certain economic progress and prosperity, helped create the scramble for profit and wealth that ended in bankruptcy and scandal. Sir John A. Macdonald's resignation thus uncovered the seamy underside of the railway dogma. It also made it painfully obvious that North American businessmen, interested primarily in ledger books and dividends, promoted railways for pecuniary rather than nationalistic purposes. Always in search of traffic and the shortest route, railway promoters would not be stopped by international boundaries. Political, regional, and international business rivalries destroyed the first attempt to build a Canadian transcontinental railway. When he returned to power in 1878, Sir John A. Macdonald would not allow that to happen again.

7

The National Policy:
Defining a Nation

Let it, therefore, be kept before the people that the immediate construction of the Canada Pacific Railway, with the increase of national debt which it has made necessary, the alienation of the lands of the North-west from the people who are its real owners which is the consequence of its being built in a hurry and under pressure, and the increased taxation which is required by investing so large a sum of money in the work before it is really required, and all the other evil consequences which flow from the premature construction of this immense public undertaking, are due to the folly and the dishonesty of Sir John Macdonald in making that worst of bad bargains with British Columbia.[1]

Patriot (Charlottetown)

A great weight has been lifted off the minds of the people of this Dominion of ours. We have escaped a great peril. The principles of the Mackenzie party are such that they were, and are, willing to sacrifice Canadian interests and Imperial interests if these conflict with their Free Trade notions.'[2]

Evening Reporter (Halifax)

Late in 1878, Sir John A. Macdonald's Conservatives returned to office with a solid majority. The party had won the election on a platform of aggressive, nationalistic measures that included a high protective tariff, vigorous work on the Canadian Pacific Railway, and the colonization of western Canada. The Liberals lost on a record consisting, ironically, of a more conservative position of incidental protection and cautious progress on the railway but a similar settlement policy.[3] Considering the fact that both parties concurred on the need to settle the North-West and that they disagreed only on the speed of railway construction, their fundamental difference centred on fiscal policies. It was the tariff question, in fact, that defined the election and it was that issue that forced the parties to articulate their concept of the new Canadian nationality.

The two parties' contrasting views on the Pacific railway and the necessity of tariff protection arose out of their understanding of the meaning of Canadian nationhood. Although the Conservatives focused the tariff debate primarily on the need to industrialize Canada's economy, they also implicitly intended their National Policy, as they shrewdly called their scheme, to protect the proposed Pacific railway. After his humiliating defeat over the Pacific Scandal, Sir John A. Macdonald was no longer willing to accept a transcontinental railway running through United States territory south of the Great Lakes. Understanding the commercial value of controlling access to the North-West, he would insist on an all-Canadian route. As indicated by its name, Macdonald's party designed the National Policy, in part, to push rail traffic between western and central Canada north of the lakes. The Liberals, by contrast, were still willing to accept temporary use of American railways to reach the North-West. Ideologically more sympathetic to free trade and a rural culture, they were also less committed to a forced industrialization program. A protectionist tariff, therefore, suited neither their ideas on political economy nor their transcontinental railway program. Even though Liberals, like their Conservative rivals, supported the basic tenets of the philosophy of railways, they differed fundamentally on routing and speed of construction and, thus, disagreed profoundly on the need for high tariffs to help finance and protect the Pacific railway.

Most historians have not been kind to the Liberal party, which held power from 1873 to 1878. While Arthur Lower thought of them as rapids in the stream, D.G Creighton dismissed their lack of nationalist vision, and Pierre Berton likened the 1878 Conservative victory to a resurrection miracle.[4] These judgments are not surprising considering the authors' commitment to the CPR nation-building myth. The Conservatives' strong protectionist stand, their vigorous railway construction program, and their call for increased immigration still give them the appearance of being more patriotic and nationalistic than the Liberals, who looked for free trade with the United States and adopted a cautious railway policy. In actual fact, however, the Liberal administration, which had a strong historic attachment to the North-West and actively pursued the construction of a transcontinental railway, simply believed that the so-called National Policy was an inappropriate development strategy for a fledgling nation since, they believed, it would arrest the economic and political progress of Canada.

The policies the Liberals enacted in their brief regime were very much a product of Prime Minister Alexander Mackenzie, the epitome of nineteenth-century economic liberalism.[5] Born in Scotland in 1822, Mackenzie grew up in a working-class family and at age sixteen apprenticed as a stonemason, achieving journeyman status four years later. That year, he and his family immigrated to Canada and established themselves first in Kingston and subsequently in Sarnia. Apart from learning his trade, Mackenzie educated himself in contemporary British liberal thought. The drive and determination shown in that endeavour coincided with a staunch, pietistic, Baptist faith that gave him great strength and comfort. He practised literally its doctrines of probity and sobriety. His working man's background, his evangelicalism, and his liberal reading made Mackenzie thoroughly egalitarian, believing strongly in the separation of church and state, social and economic mobility, and the values of an agrarian society. Dogmatically utilitarian, he measured all activities according to rigid standards of practical usefulness. Lastly, although fiercely imperialist, Mackenzie also sought to advance the stature of Canada as an emerging nation.

Driven by a strong sense of justice and reform, Alexander Mackenzie immersed himself in community organizations and party politics. In 1861 he was elected for Lambton and quickly rose through the party ranks. A forceful extemporaneous speaker and clever parliamentary strategist, Mackenzie soon emerged as the leader of the disparate wings of the highly divided Reform movement. In 1873 he was elected leader of the Liberal party, and within months, after the fall of the Conservative government, was invited to be the country's second prime minister. He called an election early in 1874 and won an overwhelming majority. Presiding over a party consisting of regional reform coalitions, Mackenzie spent much of his time appeasing high-strung colleagues, finding a consensus among a wide spectrum of opinions. That he managed to forge a national political party was a tribute to his persuasive skills, outstanding honesty and forthrightness, as well as labourious attention to detail.

When he assumed office, Alexander Mackenzie had no difficulty continuing his predecessor's North-West development strategy. The Liberal party, always inspired by George Brown, the editor of the Toronto *Globe*, had a long attachment to the region. For decades, Brown had used his editorial pages to extol the virtues of the region and to praise the benefits its development would bring to Canada. Thus, when the Liberals assumed power, they easily continued the policies set in place by the Conservative government. Not only did the Mackenzie administration conclude the series of treaties with the aboriginal people of the prairies, it also began to settle them on reserves. The new government endorsed John A. Macdonald's concept of a prairie police force, and under its direction the North West Mounted Police commenced their long march to the far western fringe of the plains. In addition to establishing law and order, the Liberal government also passed the North West Territories Act of 1875, which for the first time provided the region with a full constitutional timetable for future representative institutions. Lastly, the Liberals continued the policy of surveying the plains on the American township model and sanctioned the Conservatives' homestead policy.[6]

Not only did the new Liberal administration follow the details of the Conservatives' colonization plan, it also adopted the spirit of its development program. Both governments envisioned the opening of the North-West as an additional investment opportunity for eastern Canadian financiers, an agricultural frontier for surplus domestic farmers, and an inducement for European and American immigrants. With the experience of the United States clearly before them, Canadian authorities easily accepted some aspects and rejected other features of the American model. While Canadian governments readily adopted the homestead prototype and survey system, they determined that Ottawa would maintain strict centralized control over resource development, policing establishments, and administrative institutions. Consequently, neither newly established Manitoba nor the North West Territories were permitted to control their Crown lands or their natural resources, a distinct departure from the original confederation agreement in which all other provinces retained that right. Moreover, as historian R.C. Macleod has demonstrated convincingly, John A. Macdonald established the NWMP as an essential aspect of the nation's western-development policy; the prime minister was convinced Canada could not compete with the United States for settlers without peace, law, and order. Although he could easily have done so, Alexander Mackenzie did not alter the policy.[7] In a similar vein, Mackenzie followed Macdonald's plans for a relatively weak territorial government, heavily dependent upon the central government for financial support and legislative approval. Though his North West Territories Act of 1875 did provide for the gradual introduction of elected representatives to the appointed legislative council, it did not provide for the eventual establishment of responsible government.[8] In sum, both the Conservative and Liberal administrations ensured that the central government would control the development of the vast interior plains and forests for the 'purposes of the Dominion.'[9]

If the Conservatives and Liberals had achieved consensus on the settlement of the North-West, they held radically divergent views on the fiscal policy of the new nation. Whereas the Conservatives adopted a strict protectionist policy, the Liberals were struggling to return to a free-trade ethic. Interestingly, while each party claimed that its platform was the best means of building a strong northern nation, the perception of nationhood that inspired their tariff strategies and their railway programs varied dramatically.

Dressed in the rhetorical language of a political campaign, the tariff debate between the two parties in the late 1870s reflected positions that had hardened over two decades of discussions. In the late 1850s, an administration of which Sir John A. Macdonald was a member had introduced a protective tariff designed to stimulate the industrialization of the Canadas while raising revenues to help retire the province's enormous railway debt. The Galt tariff, as it became known, also used the technique of *ad valorem* duties to channel import and export traffic through the St Lawrence canal and railway network.[10] Using fiscal policy to increase traffic through Canadian channels was a tacit admission that, under free-trade conditions, communication technologies were vulnerable to rival foreign systems. Since railway technology and commerce did not heed international boundaries, Canada's newly constructed railways obviously needed protection from American competitors.

Galt's innovative 1859 tariff was accompanied by an unsuccessful Canadian attempt to federate British North America and expand westward to the Pacific. Although politically premature, mid-century British North Americans agreed that territorial acquisition and railway construction were keys to future prosperity and the creation of a nation.[11] They also concurred that to some extent the state was to play an active role in this process with economic planning and direction. Although reform and liberal politicians expressed doubts, the Liberal-Conservative party committed itself to protective tariffs, a British North American *Zollverein*, an intercolonial railway, and western annexation. Economic elements, such as railways, tariffs, and factories, were to replace cultural factors, such as heritage, language, and patriotism, as national building blocks.

The idea of a transcontinental country, embodied in the 1859 tariff, was one of the key elements that made possible confederation in 1867. During the union debates in the Canadian legislature, Alexander Galt reiterated the economic vision of a new nation. He painted a vivid picture of a mercantilist economy with commerce and manufacturing centred in the St Lawrence region, its resource supply and markets lying on the periphery, interconnected by a transcontinental railway network, and the whole protected by a common tariff structure. These economic policies, planned and directed by a strong central government, were to be the foundation of the new Canada. Eloquently echoing the sentiments of the time, Galt noted that the most immediate benefit to be derived from the merger of British North

America 'will spring from the breaking down of [tariff] barriers and the opening up of the markets of all the provinces to the different industries of each. In this manner ... we may hope to obtain from Nova Scotia our supply of coal; and the manufacturing industry of Lower Canada may hope to find more extensive outlets in supplying many of those articles which are now purchased in foreign markets.'[12]

Galt's vision for confederation demonstrated that the industrial sector of the economy, even if not organized, was becoming strong. Indeed, the idea of industrialization was a prominent theme in the 1867 centralization drive and its proponents found that an appropriate tariff level was among the difficult questions they needed to resolve. Clearly, the Canadas had to lower their tariffs to accommodate lower Maritime duties, but neither Nova Scotia nor New Brunswick was free from protectionist sentiment. By the 1860s, in fact, the Maritimes were abandoning their excessive reliance on staple exports and were increasingly turning from Atlantic to continental opportunities. Nova Scotia's confederation initiative included a strong industrial incentive as well as protection for its coal mines.[13] As a manifesto of interested citizens put it, 'In view of the abrogation of the Reciprocity Treaty, we are of the opinion that every reasonable encouragement should be afforded for creating and sustaining a manufacturing interest in Nova Scotia, in order that the farmer and the fisherman may find a home market as far as possible, for their productions, and the manufacturer, in turn, a nation of consumers for the proceeds of his skill and labor. Otherwise we believe that a heavy drain for the precious metals in return for foreign manufactures, will speedily set in upon our people, and tend greatly to the impoverishment of the country, and the embarrassment of all classes.'[14] In March 1870 Charles Tupper led a delegation to Ottawa in search of a 'national policy,' which included a moderate increase in protectionist duties.[15] Similarly, Leonard Tilley, a veteran of New Brunswick's protectionist movement, had frequently expressed the hope that federation would lead to the industrial expansion of his province. Strongly supported by his province's North Shore constituents, Tilley viewed an intercolonial railway as an avenue to the Canadian market for New Brunswick's industries. Simultaneously, he and Tupper designed the European and North American Railway as a tap into the United States, thus representing the region's lively interest in reviving free trade in natural products and protection for manufactured goods.

The seemingly contradictory reciprocity and protectionist objectives continued to be part of Canada's post-confederation fiscal strategy. At various times the Canadian government used subtle pressure and at other times access to its fisheries to press the United States for freer trade

accords, but to no avail. An economic slump in 1870 forced Canada to inch
the tariff upward slightly to meet the need for increased revenues but also
in response to yet another American rebuff. The revised customs duties
contained a more sophisticated *ad valorem* approach in order to conserve
the traditional St Lawrence empire and its emphasis on staple production
and exports, which had been damaged by the abrogation of the Reciprocity
Treaty. Thus, partially retaliatory and protectionist in its objectives, the
modest adjustment restated the basic commercial and industrial objectives
of confederation, that is, the deliberate shift to the internal Canadian market described by Galt.[16]

The 1871 Treaty of Washington, which followed on the heels of the tariff
adjustment, represented a watershed in Canada's fiscal policy. The treaty
gave Americans access to Canada's fisheries for ten years, as well as free
navigation on the St Lawrence River and its canals. In exchange, Canada
gained entrance into the United States fish market, a twelve-year bonding
agreement, navigation rights on Alaska rivers and American canals, and
limited reciprocity on the Great Lakes. The contentious San Juan boundary dispute and the *Alabama* claims were to be settled by arbitration.[17] Sir
John A. Macdonald, officially a British rather than a Canadian delegate,
achieved none of his objectives. Especially galling was the sale of the Atlantic fisheries without the long-sought reciprocal trade agreement.[18] The failure to secure reciprocity was a stark reminder that Canadians had to rely
on their own resources to create wealth and prosperity. It focused Canada's attention more sharply on the Intercolonial and its plans for a Pacific
railway. Coupled to a rising tide of nationalism, a protectionist platform
appeared to offer greater opportunities than free trade. Consequently, in
the election of 1872, the Conservatives adopted a mixed approach: while
holding out the prospects, however dim, for reciprocity, they called for
increased protection for domestic industries.[19]

The relationship between the Conservatives' fiscal and Pacific-railway
policies also became clear. During the campaign, Macdonald explained that
the government needed to augment revenues in order to finance the expansion of the country's transportation infrastructure. 'Now our taking the
duties off tea and coffee, ought to be sufficient proof to the manufacturers
that the Government will adopt a principle of incidental protection,' Sir
John A. Macdonald reassured a concerned voter. 'With our increasing
engagements for the enlargement of the Canals, and the construction of the
Pacific Railway, the deficiency in the revenue caused by taking duties off
tea & coffee must be made up in some way, & that can only be done by a
duty on manufactured goods.'[20]

Although Macdonald's Conservatives narrowly won the election of 1872, the ensuing Pacific Scandal brought the Liberals under Alexander Mackenzie into office. The new Liberal administration's position on tariffs was not unanimous, however, and opinions ranged from moderate protectionism to ardent free trade. In practice, the government, beset by a rapidly deteriorating economy, badly needed revenues, and in 1874 Mackenzie – who favoured protection placed incidentally on products manufactured domestically – increased the tariff. Like the Conservatives before them, the Liberals also made an ineffective pilgrimage to Washington hoping for reciprocity and, like their predecessors, returned empty-handed.[21]

Though committed to the economic development of Canada, the Liberals refused to institute a high protective tariff in order to accelerate railway construction. Most Liberals feared that protectionism would betray the party's free-trade heritage. Their objections were manifold. Would it not make Canada a more expensive place in which to live? Would it not reduce imports and damage trade, shipping, railways, and canals? In short, they asked, would it not end in disaster? Answering themselves, they painted a gloomy scenario of conflict and disunity, damage to imperial relations, regional strife, and paternalism. They argued that protectionism was an effete policy certain to lead to economic ruin. It would transfer wealth from the workers and farmers to the privileged few.[22]

The Liberals' inherent dislike of doctrinaire protectionism sprang from several deeply held principles. In the first place, they were innately suspicious of manufacturers and big business. The Pacific Scandal, they believed, was a clear example of the dangers of concentrating wealth and power in the hands of a few.[23] Driven by a Jeffersonian rural bias, they preferred a small-town Canada supported by prosperous farmers whose labours were morally and economically superior to industrial enterprises.[24] 'No man can desire more than I do to see our Canadian towns grow and thrive,' Finance Minister Sir Richard Cartwright asserted. 'But ... I have for a long time become convinced that a system or a policy which tended to promote the unhealthy growth of towns at the expense of the rural districts is most disastrous to the true interests of any country ... The cities of Canada are not what make Canada.'[25]

This sentiment was not a simplistic, nostalgic yearning for a bygone era, as the Liberal newspaper, the *Globe*, made clear. 'The development of a healthy manufacturing system is essential to the material prosperity of any country, and ... without it, neither true greatness nor independence can be achieved; that, in opening new fields to industry, it promotes population for agriculture to feed; gives birth to invention, from whence follows intelligence; rewards labour, which begets progress, succeeded by wealth, and with wealth refinement and power.'[26] Erastus Wiman, Canadian-born manager at New York's R.G. Dun and Company and a tireless proponent of commercial union between Canada and the United States, told an audience of Brampton farmers that he had 'come to the conclusion that the result of Commercial Union [between Canada and the United States] would be to make Canada one of the greatest manufacturing countries in the world.'[27] Even though Liberals believed that farming was a noble independent occupation while urban labour was not, they willingly acknowledged the importance of industry.[28]

Along with their deeply rooted agricultural bias, Liberals shared an inherent antipathy to strong centralized government. Given the luxury of choice, Liberals appealed to the teachings of Adam Smith and preferred to let the business world unfold without state interference, regulation, or assistance. While conceding that governments should manage important services such as the mails and telegraphs, the Montréal *Herald*, for example, concluded that 'the fact remains that Governments do best when they confine themselves as much as possible to the business of governing ... leaving all other business to their citizens or subjects in their individual characters.'[29] Or as *La Patrie* summed up the Liberal argument, 'la prospérité ne se crée pas par des actes de législation.'[30] A free-trade approach to business, Liberals argued, would make Canada an inexpensive place in which to live and do business. 'It ought to be our end and aim to make Canada a cheap country in which to live, and a profitable country in which to work,' the *Globe* sanguinely put it; 'not profitable because of preserving a restricted market and high prices, but profitable in the cheapness with which labour is procured, with which raw materials are purchased, and in facilities for foreign trade.'[31]

The Liberal ideal of a vigorous, free-trade economy also recognized the regional character of the young nation. The Winnipeg *Free Press*, whose editorial position was strongly nationalistic and which was the only western paper to call itself unadornedly Canadian, exposed a regional objection to protectionism. In a perceptive editorial, the *Free Press* predicted that a higher tariff would force the shipment of goods north of the Great Lakes at the expense of western consumers who could more cheaply and efficiently purchase goods by way of the United States and existing American railways.[32] Similarly, the Toronto *Globe*, still in perennial competition with Montréal, realized that a northerly routed railway would favour its rival. Protectionism, the *Globe* argued, would severely restrict the expansion of manufacturing in the province of Ontario because it would have to pay dearly for the tariffs on iron and coal from the Maritimes.[33]

Adding to the regional theme, the Halifax *Morning Chronicle* viewed high protective tariffs as the fulfilment of the dire warnings it had made in the 1867 unification debates that Ontario would dominate federal economic policies. As predicted, the *Chronicle* claimed, tariffs were lowered temporarily to make confederation palatable, but the argument that Nova Scotia could act as a counterbalance to central Canadian infighting and prevent further increases was proved false. 'The protectionists of the West [Ontario] will control the policy of the new Government, and with that selfishness which characterizes protectionism everywhere, they will insist upon their "pound of flesh," regardless of how the Maritime Provinces may think or act in the matter,' the paper asserted. The balance of power rested in Ontario, 'which is now more than it ever was the controlling section of the Dominion.'[34] For the *Chronicle*, in other words, the National Policy was an Ontario policy.

If, on the one hand, Liberal objections arose out of regional concerns, on the other hand, they revealed a continentalist perspective. Instead of looking at the United States as a dark and dangerous competitor, the *Globe*, for example, preferred the image of an ally.

Providence has placed the United States and Canada side by side on this Continent. Each has a goodly heritage, and intends to occupy and make the most of it through all the future. Come what will, the two peoples are destined to be perpetual neighbors, and neighbors in closer relationship than any other two nations under the sun. The territories lie side by side for a longer extent than those of any other peoples, and throughout a large portion of that extent are separated only by an imaginary line. The two have also more in common than any other two neighboring nations. They are of a common stock. They are heirs of a common and a glorious history. They have the same civilization, the same literature, the same religion. At the bottom their institutions and modes of thought and of government are identical. Both are essentially self-governing. Both pride themselves on their liberty, intelligence and enterprise, and the essential equality which is the birthright of their citizenship.[35]

Facing the fact that, as neighbours, the destinies of the two countries were closely interwoven, the *Globe* maintained that secure commercial ties and mutual respect were necessities. Goldwin Smith, an expatriate British professor, residing in Toronto since 1871, who eventually became an ardent advocate for annexation to the United States, recommended a customs union between the two countries.[36] 'The only measure which can materially increase the commercial prosperity of Canada,' he gratuitously advised Sir John A., 'is one which will give her free access to the markets and other commercial advantages of her Continent.'[37]

Even though regional concerns and a continental orientation informed the Liberal tariff position, it received its decisive inspiration from a fundamental preference for free trade. In his 1876 budget speech, Sir Richard Cartwright, the minister of finance and the most articulate proponent of laissez-faire liberalism, refused to raise the tariff despite an increasing deficit. Admitting that internal factors – excessive speculation and loose lending practices had led to glutted inventories, oversupplied markets, and plummeting prices – were contributing factors in the current depression, Cartwright insisted that the primary cause of Canada's economic woes was external. A depression in the United States, replete with falling wages and prices, had resulted in critical overproduction and dumping of underpriced goods in Canada [the 'slaughter market' as Cartwright called it]. The current state of the economy, he added, would have occurred even if the government had implemented protectionist policies. It was not in 'the power of this Government,' he professed, 'to make a country prosperous by the mere stroke of a pen or the enactment of Acts of Parliament.'[38]

Continuing in this theoretical vein, Cartwright warned that protectionism was a dangerous doctrine. Reluctantly conceding that in a young country like Canada, which was too dependent upon foreign manufacturers, 'a revenue tariff may be advantageously imposed and may afford considerable benefit in overcoming certain temporary obstacles which are invariably in the way of infant manufactures,' he earnestly denied that 'any tariff can overcome natural obstacles except at a very undue cost.'[39] The price for 'the protectionist bog,' he argued, was the loss of freedom with no proven advantages. Specifically, Cartwright denied that higher tariffs would create significant employment, generate more immigration, or stop emigration. These phenomena, he argued, were affected by fertile soil and favourable climate rather than by legislation. Tariffs, he concluded, benefited only a wealthy urban minority at the expense of the rural majority. They could only lead to alienation within and outside Canada.

Cartwright's budget speech, which was much more free trade in its ideological references than in its actual fiscal measures, touched the heart of Liberal doctrine. His approach was progressive and patriotic and, like that of the Conservatives, nation-building in its objective. Painting a bold vision of progress and expansion achieved not by protection from foreign trading partners but by full international cooperation, he created the foundation for the party's Pacific railway program. A free-trade continental economy, with railways crossing the border where commerce and business principles dictated, could only lead to prosperity and a higher standard of living. Such conditions were more likely to attract immigrants, he thought, and make Canada competitive in an international world economy. Liberals, Cartwright summarized, favoured the free-wheeling laws of economics that, left to themselves, would create growth.

In the final analysis, however, the goals of the free traders, like those of the Conservatives, were materialistic. According to Erastus Wiman, a passionate promoter of commercial union, free trade would increase production enormously because 'a free market can be had among the greatest money-making, money-spending aggregation of humanity that the world has ever seen, and which in the goodness of Providence, is right at her doors.'[40]

Cartwright's doctrinaire free-trade position provided Sir John A. Macdonald with a golden opportunity. In the first two years of opposition, he had quietly bided his time. Like a hunter stalking his prey, he had watched the Liberal program unfold, jabbing at its weak points but never attacking with full force nor offering a comprehensive alternative policy. By the end of 1875, however, he began to formulate a full-fledged protectionist position. Discouraged by the humiliation he had suffered in the Washington Treaty and disheartened by the failure to gain reciprocity with the United States, Macdonald countered with a thorough economic nationalism embodied in a high protective tariff, to be called the National Policy.

In an extremely partisan speech delivered in Montréal in November 1875, Macdonald tentatively outlined what would become the Conservative platform for the next election. Despite its rampant political prejudice, the rambling speech was important because it marked the rebirth of Macdonald's political career and because it touched on all the points of the emerging Conservative agenda. Beginning with a vigorous defence of his government's record, Macdonald justified the Intercolonial Railway, the acquisition of the North-West, and the wooing of British Columbia. He also ridiculed the Liberal railway policy and assured his partisan listeners that had he been permitted to remain in office he would have found a private developer to complete the project. In addition to explaining his railway scheme, Macdonald also touched briefly on the need for an explicitly protectionist stand. Anxious to show that this was not a new initiative, Macdonald explained that the Conservatives 'have always since 1859, when Mr., now Sir Alexander Galt, was Finance Minister, announced our policy to be a protective policy in the interests of native industries, and acting upon that policy, we have held that the duties should be so imposed as to provide incidental protection, and not to be so excessive as to prohibit importations.'[41]

After only touching on the protectionist topic, Macdonald charged the Liberals with disloyalty. He noted that a last-minute amendment to a bill to create a Canadian supreme court appeared to end the possibility of appeal to British courts. This, he charged, was the first step to complete separation from the empire. This amendment, he went on, illustrated the cardinal difference between the two parties – the Conservatives: loyal, patriotic, and pro-union – the Liberals: separatist, unpatriotic, and anti-union. Suggesting that Liberal policies were destined to head the country to independence, Macdonald clearly expressed his horror of separation from the empire. Canada was a happy, prosperous, self-governing country that enjoyed full liberty in its alliance with Great Britain. Reliant on Britain for its defence, Canada could not be independent. Any other course would lead to annexation and the loss of Canada's British heritage, which to Macdonald meant the 'enjoyment of peace, liberty, happiness, comfort, family felicity, and improvement, intellectual, moral, material and physical.' Allowing for the excessive rhetoric of a political speech, Macdonald reaffirmed the traditional loyalty to the British Empire. 'I am a British subject and British born, and a British subject I hope to die,' he exclaimed to the intense applause of his audience. With these stirring words, Macdonald had laid the foundation for his re-election campaign: protectionism, the Pacific railway, and western settlement were to be wrapped in a patriotic Canadian nationalist-imperialist banner.

Several months later, during the 1876 budget debate, Macdonald elaborated on the protectionist aspect of the Conservative platform and firmly committed his party to protectionism.[42] He proposed an amendment to Cartwright's budget, calling for a 'readjustment of the tariff, which would not only aid in alleviating the stagnation of business ... but would also afford fitting encouragement and protection to the struggling manufactures and industries, as well as to the agricultural products of the country.'[43]

Rejecting Cartwright's non-interventionist approach, Macdonald wanted to clearly record his party's commitment to assist manufacturers. Although he refused to give specific percentages, he clearly stated his belief that Canadian industries must enjoy the same level of protection as those in the United States. Recounting the numerous fruitless reciprocity missions, Macdonald called for an expressly retaliatory tariff on manufactured goods and some agricultural products. 'If they do not grant us reciprocity in trade, we should give them reciprocity in tariff.' The state, he concluded, has a duty to protect its manufacturers from unfair competition, especially dumping practices. These, he claimed, were 'crushing our native manufactures,' leading the country into a depression, unemployment, and poverty.

By the summer of 1876 the Conservatives commenced their political comeback. In the dismal economic climate of increasing competition, falling prices, and rising unemployment, the party had found a platform. Throughout the summer, Macdonald criss-crossed Ontario preaching the nation-building philosophy of railways that invariably touched on the Pacific railway, immigration, and protectionist themes.[44] Intensifying its pitch the following year, the party gradually won over wavering voters, particularly industrialists and other prominent businessmen. Early in 1878, the Tories formally called for the 'adoption of a National Policy, which by a judicious readjustment of the Tariff will benefit and foster the agricultural, the mining, the manufacturing, and other interests of the Dominion.'[45] The party also promised that the National Policy would halt emigration to the United States and the dumping of foreign goods on the Canadian market, expand interprovincial trade, and force reciprocity on the United States. Thus appealing to a wide variety of interests and emotions, the party created a broad appeal. It offered an end to the depression and an avenue for nationalist and latent anti-American feelings. In short, it proposed a political direction.[46] As National Policy historian Ben Forster summarized, 'The creation of a larger market through Confederation, the expansion of industrial capacity in Canada, and a depression that sharply limited export prospects while leaving the home market vulnerable to foreign producers: these formed the historical context in which the potential of protectionism increased and was ultimately realized.'[47]

The Conservatives were ideologically better suited to take advantage of the growing protectionist mood in Canada. More in tune with business interests than the Liberals, protectionism had been part of their political thinking since the late 1850s. Though the relationship was complex and never complete, the Tories were more urban in orientation and more likely to seek the nation's wealth and progress in industrial than in agricultural pursuits. Sir John A. Macdonald, their leader, was comfortable in the presence of businessmen and strove to please and flatter them.[48] In sum, having failed in repeated attempts to secure a reciprocity treaty, the Conservative party was ready to meet American protectionists head-on.[49]

Not as strongly committed to economic liberalism as the Liberal party, Conservatives were also more receptive to government-inspired economic-development policies.[50] Arguing that private business sometimes needed state assistance to battle foreign competitors, Nova Scotians, for example, pleaded for tariff protection for the Halifax sugar trade and the Cape Breton coal mines as well as subsidies for the Intercolonial Railway and branch-line construction. Other interests argued for western development policies or steam-line subsidies. 'The end of Government is not merely to collect and spend taxes,' they argued, 'but rather to develop and protect industries, to increase the value of land, to encourage immigration, to diversify labor, and to be a chief factor in the national prosperity.'[51]

The Conservatives also used their proclivity for community rather than individual interests to rationalize the rising cost of living that was likely to accompany protectionism. They rejected the pleas for a cheap country on the grounds of national interest. Cheapness, they claimed, indicated a lack of natural resources, slow growth, social instability, and rivalry among the various classes in society. Turning the Liberals' exploitation argument on its head, the Toronto *Daily Mail* maintained that real prosperity benefited all of society, while free trade profited only the wealthy and caused unemployment among workers. 'Besides, it must be borne in mind,' the paper lectured, 'that mutual dependence, which means mutual assistance, is the great social law – the principle which effectively binds men together in organized bodies.'[52] The more prosperous the nation, it continued, the more its citizens rely on each other and their community. In this way, the *Mail* set the individualist laissez-faire principle over against a community ideal. The establishment of a nation was worth a higher cost of living.

The Conservatives also rejected the Liberals' pastoral vision. Though they recognized farming as a healthy, natural occupation, a form of 'employment originally assigned to man by his Creator,' city life was less subject to the vagaries of weather and climate, more remunerative and intellectually stimulating.[53] Similarly, Montréal's *Daily Star* condescendingly asserted that while rural communities made an important contribution to the national economy, urbanization was the 'potent factor in the progress of mankind.' Cities, it continued, embodied 'the best intellectual and material results of modern progress.'[54] Leonard Tilley concluded his 1879 National Policy budget speech by summoning Canadians to abandon their traditional endeavours on the ocean and in the fields and forests and to adopt a modern industrialization policy. 'The time has arrived,' he challenged the house, 'when we are to decide whether we will be simply hewers of wood and drawers of water; whether we will be simply agriculturalists raising wheat, and lumbermen producing more lumber than we can use, or Great Britain and the United States will take from us at remunerative prices; whether we will confine our attention to the fisheries and certain other small industries, and cease to be what we have been, and not rise to be what I believe we are destined to be under wise and judicious legislation.'[55] Continued reliance on resource extraction, Tilley argued, would make Canada a subservient economy with servile politics, a poor country destined to stay a colonial backwater. Did Canadians want to remain an 'unimportant and uninteresting portion of Her Majesty's Dominions,' Tilley asked, 'or will [they] rise to the position, which, I believe Providence has destined us to occupy, by means which ... are calculated to bring prosperity and happiness to the people, to give employment to the thousands who are unoccupied, and to make this a great and prosperous country?'[56] Only industry, he implied, could bring wealth and prosperity and above all material progress. Only manufacturing could create sufficient jobs and wealth to make Canada a vital, independent, and great nation.[57]

The Conservatives also met the disloyalty cry squarely. As they shrewdly understood, one of the strongest arguments against protectionism was that it would be used against British manufacturers. The Tories made certain, however, that they would remain the standard bearers for the empire. 'We have no fear that the Conservative party will do anything to weaken the ties that bind us to the mother country,' the Montréal *Gazette* opined. '[T]he Conservative Party will vindicate its title to be regarded as the upholder of a loyal allegiance to the great Empire of which this Dominion forms a part.'[58] The paper argued loudly that high tariffs would benefit the mother country. It asserted that British goods were being driven out of the Canadian market by unfair American trading practices. More to the point, it intoned, 'the development of our resources, the building up of our industries, the settlement thereby of our vast domain, are not only not inconsistent with, but are the paramount duties of our allegiance to Great Britain.'[59] Was a weak, depressed Canada not a liability to the empire, it asked? Surely the continued migration to the United States could not be considered a 'source of strength to the Empire?' In fact, if the Liberals persisted in their free-trade course, then Canada was in peril, the paper insisted. '[W]e will finally become practically commercially dependent upon the Americans.'

Thus, the intertwining themes of anti-Americanism, British loyalty, and nation building became a powerful incantation. Even if it were meant in part to deflect criticism that the Conservatives were lackeys of industrial interests, even if it were political rhetoric, the Conservative patriotic cry became a powerful refrain. Locked in vigorous debate with the Toronto *Globe*, the Ottawa *Citizen* argued that Canada's economic existence could only be maintained if she developed an independent economy by means of a protectionist policy. 'The National Policy of Canada is what is going to bring ... about [independence from the United States]. The *Globe* is right in its aim, but entirely wrong in its method. By establishing free trade it would render these provinces tributary for all time to the United States. Commercial dependence would breed political dependence ... What our tariff does do is to develop the material independence of Canada; and, if the Toronto *Globe* were thoroughly consistent, it would see in the protection of Canadian manufactures the best of all material guarantees of our political independence.'[60]

The ringing call for action against the United States and the stirring nation-building rhetoric, mixed with a strident imperialism, gave the Conservatives an enormous advantage. On the one hand, they could paint the Liberals as a party of the status quo while they were a party of action. 'Si nous restons, les bras croisés, si nous ne faisons aucune tentative pour adapter l'exploitation de nos diverses ressources industrielles, agricoles, manufacturières au tarif de la protection que nous allons mettre en vigueur, ce tarif ne pourra produire tous les resultats qu'il est destiné à assurer' *Le Canadien* challenged its readers. 'Le pays a reclamé, avec force, un changement, nous le faisons avec courage, et pour un, je n'en doute pas, le succès courronera nos efforts.'[61] On the other hand, the Conservatives could portray the Liberals as disloyal; they could denounce them for sabotaging the Canada Pacific, for rousing English capitalists against the railway, for advocating loosening imperial ties.

The anti-American rhetoric, which was a new motif in the Conservative chorus, was in harmony with the mood of many Canadians. In part it countered the perception that industrialists and Conservatives were conspiring together, but it also spoke to a Canadian theme that business was the vanguard of economic progress. It built on the concept that capitalists were nation builders, that powerful, enterprising men like Hugh Allan, Donald Smith, and George Stephen were agents of the public good, boosting the nation, promoting its economic and social welfare. The Conservative rhetoric also appealed to the young country's garrison mentality and emphasized the need to weld Canada's various regions into one prosperous trading block, a solid federation able to withstand foreign assaults.[62] As they did in 1859 and again in 1867, the Tories sensed a beleaguered feeling among Canadians and so they gave them a national mission.

Although historians have attributed the overwhelming Conservative victory in the 1878 election to the National Policy, it should be noted that the party only attracted 52.5 per cent of the popular vote. As the Liberal share was 46.3 per cent and other parties 1.2 per cent, the margin of the Tories' success was only 5 per cent. Not unexpectedly, the only province to vote overwhelmingly in favour of the Conservatives was British Columbia. Elsewhere the difference was always less than 10 per cent, while in New Brunswick and Manitoba the Liberals won the popular vote. Admittedly, the Conservatives achieved a clear majority government, but Canadians were almost evenly divided on the two options presented by the politicians.[63]

The refusal to include a high protective tariff as a prop to support the philosophy of railways may have cost the Liberal party the election. The pace of construction during its regime, however, was popular across the country, especially in central Canada and the Maritimes. Alexander Mackenzie never questioned the necessity of the Pacific railway; he persistently criticized the details of the Conservatives' policy. The terms Macdonald offered to British Columbia to entice it into the union were too generous. The proposed subsidies, he argued, were too lavish. But outweighing all these objections was the overriding concern that without precise surveys the government did not know the full cost of completing the massive project within the promised decade. Of course, in the end, the whole exercise had been academic, as the Pacific Scandal, the adverse publicity that the Grand Trunk generated in Britain, and the collapse of the Northern Pacific had effectively scuttled any hopes of rapid completion. Under the circumstances, no private entrepreneurs emerged to undertake the project.[64]

When he became prime minister, therefore, Mackenzie faced the unenviable task of fulfilling the railway obligation to British Columbia as a public work at a time of rapidly declining government revenues. Nevertheless, he pledged that his government would spend a minimum of one and a half million dollars annually to complete a railway from Pembina to Fort Garry, to speed surveys across the prairies and through the Rockies, to build connecting railways between navigable lakes west of Lake Superior, and to finish the transcontinental telegraph. As a sweetener to disappointed Vancouver Islanders, he promised a Nanaimo to Esquimalt railway, a dockyard, and a $700,000 grant for local projects.[65]

Under adverse circumstances, the deal was reasonable, but British Columbians were not impressed; they insisted on the original bargain and took their grievance to the Colonial Office. That angered Mackenzie because he considered imperial arbitration an affront to Canada's ability to handle its own affairs. In the end, however, the British government forced him to accept a compromise, but the Senate, dominated by Conservatives aided by two dissenting Liberals, vetoed the deal and Mackenzie reverted to his original offer. He fully realized that a significant speed-up of construction could only be accomplished by a massive increase in taxes and that such a move would be deeply resented everywhere in Canada except perhaps in British Columbia.[66]

As the Senate vote indicated, Alexander Mackenzie's policy was fully in touch with the contemporary calls for restraint. In fact, parsimony had always accompanied Canada's plans for the transcontinental. On several occasions, Canadians had rejected big public expenditures on the eastern, intercolonial portion of the transcontinental and looked to Britain for substantial financial assistance. Mired in the economic depression of the mid-1870s, they were not prepared to assume extra taxes in order to satisfy a relatively small number of people on the Pacific coast.

Despite his penurious demeanour and his hard-line approach, Alexander Mackenzie actually accomplished a fairly ambitious railway construction program. In 1875, for example, his government appropriated $6 million or one-fourth of its entire budget for railway construction. During its tenure, the Liberal administration constructed more than 4000 kilometres of railway, including the Intercolonial – that is, the eastern section of the transcontinental railway.[67] It virtually completed the Pembina to Winnipeg line so that, by the fall of 1878, trains were ready to roll. Elsewhere, government surveyors examined more than 91,000 kilometres of possible routes, surveyed 19,000 kilometres, and determined that the best track was through the Yellowhead Pass, via the Fraser Valley, to Burrard Inlet. Mackenzie agreed and, in a decision based on completed surveys, approved a tender call for the Yale to Kamloops section. His government also finished a telegraph from near Thunder Bay to the Rockies.[68] By the time Sir John A. Macdonald returned to office, therefore, much of the eastern Canadian portion of the transcontinental was finished and most of the preliminary work for the Pacific section was completed.

While in opposition, Macdonald had devised a strategy for accelerating construction. He had pondered the errors that resulted in the disastrous failure of Sir Hugh Allan's Canada Pacific Railway. Three things had become clear to him. In the first place, he must not again permit sectional and political considerations to delay and dictate railway policy; therefore, he planned to promote the Pacific railway as a great national undertaking. Second, he had learned that the railway was first and foremost a commercial enterprise; thus, he must attract strong and influential businessmen to the endeavour and make it an attractive, that is, a profitable, proposition. Lastly, he had accepted the conclusion that the new Pacific railway had to take an all-Canadian route, that is, it must go north of Lake Superior. By the late 1870s, Macdonald was absolutely certain that a Canadian Pacific railway, consisting of minor sections in a giant integrated North American railway system, was no longer politically acceptable.

To ensure that an all-Canadian railway would be profitable, Macdonald seized on the National Policy. Though the protective tariff would be popularized primarily as a infant-industry strategy, it would also serve an important transportation function. The tariff, designed chiefly to shield Canadian industries from foreign competition thus became an integral part of the Conservatives' transportation initiatives. Their National Policy would fulfil one of the missing elements in the 1872/3 Canada Pacific Railway fiasco. Though he never explicitly tied the new tariff policy to the Pacific railway, Macdonald seized the opportunity provided by a widespread demand for protectionist tariffs to create traffic for the railway. Fully aware that no company would build a railway north of Lake Superior unless it were protected from competition south of the lake and were guaranteed a minimal amount of northern traffic, the Conservatives, following the precedent set by the 1859 Galt tariff, expected that a high protective tariff would stimulate interprovincial trade and, therefore, east–west traffic, especially north of Lake Superior. With the National Policy in place, they believed, businessmen would be more likely to accept the specification of an all-Canadian railway. At the same time, the anticipated revenues from the National Policy would help the government pay the large subsidies the railway investors required in addition to the land grant.

To sell speedy construction as well as the protective tariff, Macdonald injected a potent technological nationalism theme into his arguments. In his 1875 speech in Montréal, he lambasted the Liberals' railway policy as 'the abortion,' and asserted his promise that a railway to British Columbia within a decade was essential to the survival of a continental Canada. Without a Pacific railway, he argued, 'we could have no real connection with British Columbia. It would have been merely a connection on paper, and no connection in fact; and she would still be alien, alien in connection, alien in interests, and alien in prospects.'[69] Conveniently forgetting how his own blunders had torpedoed the Canada Pacific, he blithely suggested that if his government had remained in power, a private company would have built the railway and western land values would have increased sufficiently to recoup the cost of the railway. He was deeply disappointed that the railway was not being constructed aggressively because, 'until that road is built to British Columbia and the Pacific, this Dominion is a mere geographical expression, and not one great Dominion; until bound by the iron link, as we have bound Nova Scotia and New Brunswick by the Intercolonial Railway, we are not a Dominion in fact.' Overlooking his government's flirtation with the Northern Pacific, Macdonald exculpated his involvement in the Pacific Scandal and supposedly recommitted his party to a railway entirely owned by British subjects and controlled completely by Canadians. 'While we were fighting the Canadian battle, and while we were attempting to construct that great railway through Canada with Canadian and British capital, and with Canadian and British influences and means,' he warned, 'the completion of the present [Liberal] scheme, so far as ascertained, is intended to divert Canadian trade into American channels, and to open up to American interests our great railway means of communication.' By binding the Conservative party to an all-Canadian transcontinental railway, Macdonald clearly and unambiguously added a potent nationalistic mythology to the philosophy of railways. In doing so, he implied that to the railway's civilizing mission was added the task of neutralizing the so-called manifest destiny of the United States.

The National Policy, western settlement, and the Pacific railway were elements of a complex, interrelated development strategy. It was a renovated mercantilism. An urbanized and industrialized central Canada, flanked by rural and resource-based regions, would form the superstructure of a great and prosperous northern nation. As Galt's 1859 budget had suggested, transcontinental east–west transportation networks, protected by a high tariff wall, would encourage the growth of Canada's infant industries and stimulate interprovincial trade.[70] After repeatedly making unsuccessful overtures to Great Britain and the United States for preferential trade agreements, the Conservative party followed the example set by the latter and many European countries and adopted an isolationist stand. This policy, widely discussed since the 1840s, partially realized in the 1859 tariff and the federation of 1867, matured fully with the National Policy.

Meanwhile, the Liberals could only carp at the details of the contract that the Macdonald administration signed with the Canadian Pacific Syndicate.[71] They attacked the railway contract as overly generous and the land grant and cash subsidies as excessive. The monopoly clause was unacceptable, they said, the tax exemptions were unconscionable, and the timetable for completing the work was unrealistic.[72] These criticisms were based on their strong conviction that Canada could not afford the extra tax burden to pay for an unwarranted accelerated railway construction program.[73]

The Liberal views, repeated often, stridently, and at great length, did not mean that the Liberals lacked a national vision. They believed that free trade, rather than protectionism, would strengthen the Canadian economy and make the nation more self-reliant; they argued that their slow-paced railway plans, especially their call for temporary connections to the railways of the United States, entailed no dangers to the country's autonomy, but would preserve its credit and retain its relatively low cost of living. That approach, in some respects cautious, in other respects bold, made the Liberals appear less patriotic and definitely less heroic than the Conservatives. When Mackenzie exclaimed that the National Policy was a narrow course, that in contrast he believed 'not only in having Canada for the Canadians, but the United States, South America, the West Indies, and our share of the European and Australasian trade,' his remarks could easily be interpreted as anti-patriotic and injurious to nation building.[74]

In actual fact, Mackenzie was an ardent nationalist whose fervent admiration of the British Empire prevented him from following some of his Liberal colleagues into an independence movement. Like his arch-rival, Sir John A. Macdonald, Alexander Mackenzie admired British culture and placed his party's economic-development plans into an imperial context. Echoing Joseph Howe, Mackenzie freely mixed Canadian nationalism, imperial sentiments, enthusiasm for economic progress, and promises of moral growth. Thus, he referred to both a Christian and a cultural task when he spoke about western settlement and railway construction; both were an aspect of a God-given duty to evangelize all nations. 'For, sir, it is the mission of the Anglo-Saxon race,' he charged, 'to carry the power of Anglo-Saxon civilization over every country in the world.'[75] The opening of the North-West and the construction of the Pacific railway – as the resources of the country permitted – were sacred responsibilities. As a pragmatist, however, Mackenzie cautioned his audience not to move too quickly. With obvious reference to both the National Policy and the Pacific railway, he asserted that 'it would be the height of madness to imperil our credit in the English market and increase the taxation of this country, and make it dear for the emigrant to come to or the workman to live in.'[76] Mackenzie's nation building was more likely to focus on small steps like establishing independent jurisprudence, as in a Canadian Supreme Court, democratic institutions, as in the secret ballot, and a stronger domestic defence policy, as in the establishment of a military college. His philosophy of railways appealed to the principles behind the Guarantee Act of 1849. In his view, railways were international communication tools designed to carry goods, people, and ideas among regions and nations. No artificial policies, he thought, should hamper the free movement of trains, ships, goods, and people. Ever proud of his country, Mackenzie believed that Canada had weaned itself from economic dependence upon Great Britain, was asserting its own position, and was able to compete commercially and culturally in an international world.

Despite their conflicting opinions on protectionism and free trade and their differing views on the pace of railway construction, both political parties were committed to the economic development of Canada. While Liberals stressed agriculture, resource extraction, and the countryside, and

Conservatives emphasized industrialization and cities, both held that Canada could only survive if she had a robust, dynamic transcontinental economy. The Liberals, ideologically committed to free trade, considered that the tariff, already high, was appropriate for protecting many of Canada's industries and raised sufficient revenues to complete the necessary infrastructure. The Conservatives, recently converted to full-blown protectionism, were prepared to increase taxation levels substantially in order to speed their economic-development program, particularly an all-Canadian transcontinental railway. Both parties featured the colonization of western Canada as the centrepiece of their enrichment strategies and both recognized the importance of transportation to that initiative. As they had in 1849, Liberal and Conservative politicians supported the basic premise of the philosophy of the Pacific railway – the civilization of the prairie wilderness. By 1978, however, they disagreed fundamentally on whether the United States threatened to undermine that process and would appropriate that mission for its own people. The contradicting opinions on that question dictated Liberal and Conservative views on Canada's Pacific railway-construction program and the need for a protective tariff to safeguard its route. By naming their agenda the National Policy, the Conservatives grabbed for themselves the nation-building theme and they injected that slogan into their political philosophy of railways. In doing so, they transformed a universalizing doctrine into an isolationist technological nationalism.

8

The Philosophy of Railways:
Conclusions and Conjectures

We have lost population; we have lost shipping; there has been a great depreciation in the value of our real estate; we have lost representation in parliament; we have not at all kept pace with ... [central Canada] in manufacturing.

Saint John *Telegraph*[1]

I say the interests of this country demand that the Canadian Pacific Railway should be made a success ... But somebody may ask what about the interests of Manitoba? Are the interests of Manitoba and the North-West to be sacrificed to the policy of Canada? I say, if it is necessary – yes.

Charles Tupper[2]

On 7 November 1885 at Craigellachie, British Columbia, Donald A. Smith, one of the Canadian Pacific Railway directors, hammered in the transcontinental's last spike. The scene symbolized the realization of the national dream, that is, the creation and consolidation of a northern transcontinental nation.[3] That vision, dominated by a desire for economic progress, always stressed the notion that the transcontinental railway was needed to build the nation of Canada. As the Toronto *Mail* noted succinctly: 'We desired to preserve our autonomy and national integrity; we desired, following the example of our bustling cousins to the south of us, to give impetus to the colonization of our vast and fertile Western territory by making the progress of the railway and settlement contemporaneous; we desired to connect the two oceans by the shortest line of railway which was possible; we desired to make the Dominion the great arterial highway between the

Asiatic and the European continents; we desired to cultivate, encourage and make strong a true national sentiment in the northern half of the American continent.'[4]

The *Mail*'s cogent expression of the nationalistic purpose of the CPR – the desire to colonize the western plains, to establish Canada's independence from the United States, and to create a national identity – masked the actual, complex, and sometimes negative results of the philosophy of railways. To be sure, the CPR assisted in establishing effective communications between central and western Canada, thus expediting western settlement; it facilitated the transcontinental movement of goods and people, thus strengthening the economic bonds between the young nation's separate regions; and it located Canada strategically between Europe and Asia, thus enhancing its position in the British Empire. But did it preserve Canadian autonomy and 'national integrity'? Did it cultivate 'a true national sentiment'? Could Canada build a firm national identity on a transportation technology, artificially induced and then supported by an isolationist economic policy?

As Harold A. Innis's studies of the fur trade, the CPR, and the character of communications have documented so thoroughly, transportation technologies were powerful factors in the national and cultural divisions of the American continent.[5] By its inherent integrative nature, Innis claimed, railway technology encouraged the rise of nationalism in Canada, inspired and facilitated its territorial expansion, and spurred its centralization and bureaucratic growth. The railway aided the development of metropolitan centres and their monopolies.[6] In sum, Innis believed that communications media were not marginal but strong influences on the institutions and the social characteristics of society.

Expanding on Innis's theme, J.M.S. Careless, in *Frontier and Metropolis*, has suggested that the interrelationship of the city and its hinterland profoundly affected national as well as regional identities.[7] According to Careless, metropolitan centres employed trade, transport, and finance to control their surrounding territories. These factors worked, to various degrees and through infinite combinations, in concert with political, social, and attitudinal elements to establish the city as the leading catalyst in the formation of nations and regions. Although a region may define its identity in terms of its own unique structures and attitudes, it is, according to Careless, part of a larger environment. The 'continued interactions across actual or envisioned space are copiously displayed in the exchanges between town and country, between city and region, between metropolis and hinterland,' Careless wrote. 'Their interplay builds historical experience which pervasively influences all sorts of communal identities, above all those of region and nation.'[8] Careless thus interpreted Canada's history in the context of the relationship between urban centres and their surrounding hinterlands. Each city controlled its hinterland economically, politically, and financially, but also culturally, because it sent settlers, labourers, businessmen, and professionals to the frontier where they shared their religious beliefs, their political ideas, and their ethical values. Set in a new place and time, these ambassadors helped create a unique regional identity.

Careless's 'metropolitan' thesis is useful because it draws attention to the role of transportation in the conveyance of concepts and goods between cities and hinterlands. Careless noted that 'major transport services, which tapped or filled hinterlands and fed urban places, were all but primary in Canadian metropolitan growth that had virtually to start from scratch. Moreover, transportation readily related to the needs of communication, to moving information and opinion as well as goods and people over wide distances.'[9] Transportation networks, by facilitating the transfer of ideas, goods, and people, aided in determining the personalities of cities and their hinterlands.

The observation that transportation or communication techniques bias what they transmit and therefore influence the identities of past and present cultures can be observed in western Canada during the last half of the nineteenth century. This period witnessed a revolutionary change in transportation modes from human- or animal-driven techniques to steam-powered river boats and railways.

The arrival of the steam locomotive to the Canadian prairies in 1878 was followed quickly by the completion of the CPR in 1885 and a decade and a half later by two competing transcontinental railways. By 1902, Toronto entrepreneurs Donald Mann and William Mackenzie had expanded several minor Manitoba railways to Port Arthur, providing a second access to the Great Lakes; by the end of the decade, their Canadian Northern operated a 4800-km network across the plains and was advancing westward through the Rockies and eastward across the Shield.[10] Meanwhile, the Canadian government encouraged the Grand Trunk Railway to expand into a third, 5600-km transcontinental system, a project completed just before the First World War.[11] By 1914 the North-West possessed a magnificent network of railways that established hundreds of communities across the prairies and opened them to the factories, newspapers, mail, and people of North America, Europe, and the Pacific rim. Within several decades, the technology of railways had cemented the western region to the central heartland.

The completion of the transcontinentals made the intensive agricultural settlement of the prairies and immediately adjacent boreal forests feasible.[12] While the sweeping vastness of the interior plain, with its harsh climate, short growing season, and intense cold, still tested the skills and endurance of the newcomers and shaped them into a stubborn, persisting people, it was steam technology – manifested in railways and in lake and ocean vessels – that permitted the export of a vast and bulky surplus crop to overseas markets and supplied farmers with their daily necessities – clothes, tools, fuel, food, and machinery. Railways and steamboats indirectly ameliorated severe geophysical conditions and encouraged thousands of grain growers from Ontario, the United States, Great Britain, and Continental Europe to establish farms on the prairies. Between 1881 and 1911, western Canada's population exploded from 62,260 to 461,394, occupied farms multiplied from 10,091 to 199,203, while national wheat exports soared from 2.3 million bushels in 1885 to 114.9 million in 1914.[13] The national dream, first articulated in the late 1840s, had come true.

The integration of prairie culture into that of eastern North America began several decades before the completion of the CPR and occurred so quickly that it caused serious hardship and alienation among local populations. Using a combination of American railways, river steamers, and carts, Chicago and St Paul merchants penetrated a region previously preserved for the Hudson's Bay Company.[14] By the winter of 1857, free traders operated across the North-West, leaving only the far northern York and Mackenzie districts for the London-based company. The corporate charter was 'almost a nullity,' the firm's governor complained, 'set at nought by the Americans and their Half-breed allies.'[15] Meanwhile, the Hudson's Bay Company itself began to use Canadian and American railways to ship goods to and from Fort Garry.[16] Within a decade, the railway had ended the splendid isolation of the British American North-West and eroded the strong bond to the British empire that the company and Canadian traders had built.

Hudson's Bay Company officials were keenly aware of the implications of shipping goods through a foreign country under the supervision of foreign agents. They also wondered how the new transport route might affect the traditional cultural link between London and Rupert's Land and how the encroaching eastern North American railway empire would have an impact upon their fur preserve. 'As regards the trade with the United States,' F.G. Johnson, governor of Assiniboia, confessed, 'I feel a very strong and sad conviction that relations are being irrevocably formed between the two countries which in the peculiar conditions of both frontiers will not be conducive to British interests, and under the circumstance are detrimental both to the company's local commerce and the interests of the settlers.'[17]

Johnson's concern that changing transportation modes might erode Britain's cultural influence on the North-West reflected his awareness that the railway would revolutionize western Canada's society and economy. It would, of course, be erroneous to assume that in the pre-railway era life was static. Indeed, the fur trade had increasingly diverted native people from traditional occupations to the search for fur and provisions. It also employed mixed bloods as packers, suppliers, Red River cart drivers, York boatmen, and general labourers.[18] But the railway changed north-western life more quickly and completely than any previous alteration in transportation. In the pre-railway era, most native people migrated seasonally, subsisting on the natural products of the country. Tribal boundaries were flexible and land was held in common, with access open to all who possessed the skills to use its resources.[19] Meanwhile, the mixed-blood Metis lived in small settlements in Red River, subsisting on agriculture and seasonal work with the Hudson's Bay Company. The introduction of steam transportation unlocked the resources of the North-West to numerous American entrepreneurs, along with their capital and goods. The buffalo robe was but one commodity that assumed great value and for a time provided employment to the Metis, who settled in villages across the plains.[20] But, within decades, the bison was wiped out, leaving the prairie people destitute. By the late 1870s, the country could no longer support them; private property had replaced the commons. And, as steamers and railways displaced York boats and Red River carts, unemployment among the Metis soared. There was little left for them but poverty. The era of the 'private adventurers' was ended and most of the mixed-blood entrepreneurs, who had created wealth through their own ambition, initiative, energy, and knowledge of the plains, surrendered control over its resources to strangers armed with new skills and abundant capital.[21]

The 1885 Indian and Metis rebellion, which occurred only two years after the completion of the prairie section of the Canadian Pacific Railway, can therefore be viewed as a desperate attempt to protect the commons against the encroachment of a technological, urban society. To be sure, the virtual extinction of the bison and the resultant near starvation utterly demoralized the natives, so that a few hot-blooded young men could overrule traditional elders and lead the natives into violent rebellion.[22] That revolt coincided with the disenchantment of many Metis whose attempts to find security in traditional river-lot properties rather than township landholding patterns were dismissed by paternalistic, often arbitrary, government officials. Alone, the Metis may have endured their deteriorating economic conditions, but widespread complaints from disillusioned white settlers, the messianic leadership of Louis Riel, and the coincidental native uprising spurred them into precipitous action.

In 1885, however, conditions were very different from 1869/70. This time, the Canadian government could act speedily and, using the nearly completed CPR, it rushed troops to Saskatchewan. Within a few months, the rebellions were crushed. Little wonder that to both the native and mixed-blood rebels, the CPR represented not the consummation of Canada's grand transcontinental vision but the extension of eastern metropolitan empires to their traditional hunting and farming grounds. The insurgence expressed the deep alienation of the original prairie people.[23]

The 1885 Metis and Indian rebellion clearly illustrated that the new metropolitan-hinterland relationship, enabled by the railway, represented not an equal partnership but, in most cases, a disparate association marked by dominance and dependence. At best, that affiliation satisfied complementary needs: the metropolis, lacking the resources and markets that the frontier provided, supplied the capital, technology, and labour that the hinterland required.[24] Nevertheless, as Innis has suggested, the city, which embodied such large corporations as the Hudson's Bay Company, the Canadian Pacific Railway, and the Bank of Montreal, used the nation-state to control the region in order to protect the massive investment in transportation needed before it could exploit the resources of the frontier.[25] Western Canada had little voice in these boardroom and cabinet decisions and thus it felt estranged, perceiving an inequality that profoundly affected its identity.

The CPR, on its part, faced the problem of earning sufficient revenues to pay for the expensive, money-losing section north of Lake Superior and encountered stiff competition in central Canada from the St Lawrence seaway as well as Canadian and American railways. Logically, the company sought and obtained monopoly status in western Canada and permission to charge higher-than-average freight rates west of Thunder Bay. The latter were designed to offset losses on its eastern lines. Ontario and Québec rationalized the high rates, euphemistically called 'fair discrimination,' as necessary for national unity; western Canada, however, resented them deeply because it believed they retarded regional development.[26] Railway historian T.D. Regehr concurs and has suggested that excessive freight rates and the monopoly clause were significant factors in the slow settlement of western Canada in the last decades of the nineteenth century.[27]

The railway, in fact, affected the pace of economic development in myriad ways. The promised construction of the CPR, for example, sparked an interest in western Canada's extensive coal deposits; but it was the railway and not the prospectors who dictated the timing and location of their development. When the CPR's directors relocated the projected main line to the southern prairies, all northern exploration ceased and attention focused on Kicking Horse Pass and the southern prairies. The richer northern deposits had to await the arrival of the Canadian Northern and the Grand Trunk Pacific some two decades later. Similarly, the enormous deposits in Crowsnest Pass were not utilized until the CPR was induced to complete the first segment of this southern bypass. More significantly, as the industry's chief consumer, the railway's fuel demands determined each colliery's production cycle, resulting in highly volatile, unpredictable operations with attendant labour unrest. To break out of their cyclonic economy, western mine operators repeatedly asked the railways to lower their rates on eastward coal shipments and asked the central government to either subsidize coal movements to industrial Ontario and Québec or increase the tariff on steam coal from the United States. Both the railways and the federal government refused to grant any combination of these options and thus the western Canadian coal-mining industry never escaped the railway market.[28] To westerners, the failure to achieve a transportation subsidy or protective tariffs for its coal mines illustrated once again that railway rates and customs duties were biased favourably towards the industrialized East and adversely against the agrarian West.

Westerners clearly understood the direct relationship between the railway's prejudicial freight rates and the National Policy. Primarily intended to encourage the industrial development of the young nation, the policy was also designed to provide business for the projected transcontinental railway and shield it from the competition of the northern railways of the United States. On the one hand, the legislation restricted American and British access to the resources and markets of the North-West; on the other, it encouraged all eastern businessmen to use the CPR rather than American railways to reach western markets. The National Policy, therefore, protected the CPR and permitted the railway to create a stronger link between central and western Canada than would have been the case had trade been entirely free.

The National Policy gave a decided advantage to central Canadian businessmen. It contained measures that encouraged American factories and wholesalers to sell to Canadian wholesalers rather than directly to the country's retailers or consumers.[29] Central Canadian businessmen, therefore, competed in the North-West on more favourable terms than their

American or British counterparts; they easily increased their share of the western Canadian market from virtually nothing in the early 1870s to two-thirds of the total by the mid-1880s.[30] While this increase coincided with the completion of the CPR, it owed its disproportionate growth largely to the National Policy, which in the case of farm machinery stood at 35 per cent. The tariff, coupled to personal contacts, national loyalties, and corporate purchasing policies, permitted central Canadians to capture the lion's share of the western Canadian market.

The National Policy, which the central government deemed necessary to support the CPR, therefore, became an important instrument in the dramatic shift in western Canada's suppliers, a transformation westerners resented deeply. Why, they asked, could they not purchase goods freely in the least expensive city, be that Canadian, American, or British? Why must they sell their production without any protection in a highly competitive international market, when eastern manufacturers were sheltered by tariffs?

Added to political frustrations, the tariff became a powerful symbol of central Canadian domination. Why, westerners questioned, did the Dominion government surrender political power so slowly and reluctantly to the territorial legislature? Why did it give the new provinces of Alberta and Saskatchewan what they did not want – sectarian schools – and withhold what they desired – control over resources and land? These questions, which betrayed the feeling that westerners were unable to control their own destiny, inspired several vigorous protest movements that eventually became a central part of their regional character. The territories and later the provinces shared 'a peripheral mentality' that viewed central Canada as indifferent, if not hostile, to western interests.[31]

Of all the issues that angered westerners, none was more aggravating than the indispensable railway. Unable to establish economically efficient river transportation, the North-West came to depend upon the railway as the only feasible means of transporting goods into and bulky grain out of the region. Consequently, the CPR and subsequent railways became the most obvious target for prairie discontent. Beginning with Manitoba's successful campaign against the CPR's monopoly clause, western Canadians fought numerous actions to gain rate concessions, one of which culminated in the highly favourable Crowsnest Pass rates.[32] But the West never escaped the power of the railway, and time and again its attempts to develop regional resources to their fullest were frustrated.

Not surprisingly, in 1910, western farmers constituted the largest group among the angry protesters who marched on Ottawa in an unprecedented statement against the tariff. Less than a year later, after the Liberal government lost the Reciprocity election, Westerners began to talk more earnestly about a third force to break the perceived alliance between the traditional political parties and powerful central Canadian corporations, particularly the CPR.[33] These developments represented their rebellion against the darker, imperialistic face of railway technology, a stark counterpoint to the nation-building mythology in the philosophy of railways. For western Canadians, central Canada's enthusiasm for the CPR as a nation builder appeared shallow.

Westerners' disenchantment with the CPR nation-building mythology was also caused by the rapidity with which the railway transported pioneers onto the plains. The CPR carried the majority of settlers directly from their homelands to the frontier. Moreover, as David Bercuson has explained, Canada had no continuous westward-moving frontier and the prairies absorbed the colonists raw and unassimilated.[34] Their only experience with Canada was the blur of lakes, trees, and occasional cities outside the westward-speeding train window. As a result, the newcomers' perception of Canada was an abstraction of an insecure identity buried in a fading British imperialism, a conception made real only by the commercial ties of the grain market, the bank, and the railway company. Formed by their regional rather than national environment, immigrants became westerners. The predominant influences on settlers' lives were close and near: assimilation took place in fields and barns, at the local general store or barbershop, at the elevator or co-op. In other words, regionalism was more than a political struggle over control of resources. It involved a firm sense of place and community: the bonds and allegiances formed during the assimilation process were essentially local and western.

Consequently, the new prairie dwellers were more likely to perceive the railway as a highly visible symbol of domination and imperialism rather than as the creator of a transcontinental nation. Moreover, this widespread dislike of the railway became an experience that created a feeling of solidarity, a sense of unity against a common opponent. In sum, while the technology of railways achieved its intended purpose of welding together the disparate regions of Canada, the philosophy that supported its construction – and subsequently its management – established state and corporate policies that in turn created alienation and anger among western Canadians.

The policies of government and railway, which relegated prairie Canada to being a resource-extracting economy, appeared to have a similar effect on the Pacific coast. In a convincing exploratory essay, economic historian John Lutz used the boiler and marine-engine industry to demonstrate that the arrival of the CPR in Vancouver led to the erosion of manufacturing in the province.[35] In 1890, British Columbia's per capita manufacturing output was higher than in any other province, Victoria ranked tenth in industrial output among Canadian cities, and its Albion Iron Works was the largest plant north of San Francisco. Twenty-five years later, the province's overall industrial output had declined and Ontario, American, and British factories had replaced local producers of ship boilers and marine engines. Even though British Columbia's high wages were a contributing factor to the loss of the industry's competitive advantage, the railway link and discriminatory rates – that is, significantly lower rates for westward- than for eastward-moving traffic – confined coastal factories to a relatively small market while they opened its territory to continental competition and capital. Also important was the CPR's practice, as a large consumer of boilers and marine engines, of purchasing machinery abroad and in central Canada and shipping it at virtually no cost to its western mines and Pacific fleet. Other large non-local industries also avoided British Columbia products. 'The physical location of the ownership of British Columbia's resource, transportation, and manufacturing industries,' Lutz concluded, 'directed where interindustry linkages would be located.'[36] At the same time, however, Lutz also observed that by 1900 American and Scottish factories were able to displace central Canadian plants, so that Ontario itself was integrated into a larger system. 'The deindustrialization of British Columbia was a regional manifestation of the process by which Canadian manufacturing production became *centralized* in southern Ontario, itself part of a global centralization of manufacturing in a few locations such as the northeastern United States and Britain.'[37]

The establishment of a new imperialistic-type relationship between central and western Canada, and the alienation that it produced, was not a unique experience. In the United States, sectional strife between East and West was common and railway politics had also assumed a prominent role in clashes in that country. In his study of American railway rhetoric, historian James Ward observed that in the United States railway promoters featured national unity as a central theme in their discourse, a concept they based on the notion that technology would spread the knowledge and ideas essential to the preservation of American civilization.[38] By the early 1850s, however, the American unity theme was faltering as some newspaper editors were beginning to realize that giant railway companies were creating extensive imperial systems that competed amongst themselves. Gigantic corporate structures, with no soul and a ruthless obsession with profit and survival, appeared to betray the earlier awestruck, idealist vision. The American public was awakening to the fact that these powerful railway enterprises were pitting region against region, city against city, people against people.

The themes of regional conflict and alienation, which arose out of the railway history of western Canada and of the United States also became part of eastern Canada's heritage. The advent of railways had stimulated an industrial revolution in central Canada and by the time confederation was completed in 1873, the region possessed a crucial advantage over the Maritimes. The Grand Trunk and Great Western railways were large, vertically integrated corporations with sizeable repair shops at Montréal, Hamilton, Stratford, and London. Able to build their own rolling stock, including locomotives, they were 'among the largest manufacturing firms in Canada in the period.'[39] The Great Western's expenditures on manufacturing, for example, rose from $250,000 in 1859 to $750,000 in 1874, while the Grand Trunk's disbursement grew from $600,000 per year in the 1860s to $1.5 million in the 1870s. By the mid-1850s, the Grand Trunk Railway was Canada's largest employer, with a $110,000 payroll for 2600 workers.[40] As Tom Traves and Paul Craven have argued, railways became 'Canada's first large-scale integrated industrial corporations,' and instigators of industrialization.[41] By 1867, Canada had entered the first stages of an industrial economy considerably larger in size than the economies of the Maritimes.

At the time of federation, moreover, the mainland Maritime provinces had not completed a network of railways that would allow its factories immediate access to central Canada and the United States. By the time the Intercolonial (the eastern section of the transcontinental) Railway was completed, it did not bring the rapid economic growth to the region that Charles Tupper and Leonard Tilley had envisioned. Economic historians, in their attempts to explain the problem, have focused their attention on a whole range of factors, including the region's isolation, its dearth of resources and population, government policies, and the lack of an entrepreneurial spirit.[42] Not featured prominently in this discussion is the absence of a modern and efficient inland transportation system, which was, in fact, a crucial factor in the area's subsequent marginalization. Both Tupper and Tilley had accepted the philosophy of railways as a catalyst for the economic development of their provinces, but both had failed to follow the advice of Joseph Howe, who always insisted that the intercolonial must be completed before confederation was implemented.[43] It can be argued that, as a consequence, neither Halifax nor Saint John was given adequate opportunity to exploit its advantageous position as an Atlantic terminus on the transcontinental railway, nor were they able to develop their own hinterlands before being integrated into the national political economy and relegated to peripheral status.

In a recent study, Rick Szostak compared the speed of industrialization in England and France and posited the idea that 'a modern system of transportation was necessary for the Industrial Revolution to occur [earlier] in England.'[44] Although he acknowledged that many complex factors spurred the Industrial Revolution, Szostak argued that modern transportation, which he defined as an 'extensive and reliable system which could move bulk goods at low cost or high-value goods at high speed,'[45] created the opportunity for industrial expansion based on continuous technological change. Although he admitted that no special type of transport was necessary, Szostak argued that England's efficient land-based transportation system, particularly its railway network, had a profoundly positive effect upon the country's economy. Especially useful to an understanding of Atlantic Canada's place in Canada is his contention that modern transportation increased market size and production, causing some regions to specialize in certain products and dominate the national market. This argument fits Atlantic Canada, which in the first half-century after confederation lost its economic primacy and became a peripheral and underdeveloped region in the Canadian federation.

In two useful articles, T.W. Acheson has established the point that under the terms of federation, the imperial ties that had bound the Maritimes to Britain switched to Canada.[46] In the first decades after the union, Acheson suggested, Maritime entrepreneurs created a diversified local manufacturing sector that competed successfully on the international market in cotton, glass, sugar, confectionaries, and secondary iron and steel. Unfortunately, Acheson observed, the Canadian market could not absorb the entire domestic production and in the 1880s central Canadian producers purchased controlling interests in Maritime industries and rationalized their production by consolidating operations in their region; they also gained political control over the Intercolonial and bought connecting railways. 'Aided greatly by the reorganization of the vehicles of regional commerce,' Acheson commented, 'the Intercolonial and [CPR] Short Line railroads firmly fastened the region to Montreal and gradually eroded the traditional seaborne import trade of the Maritimes.'[47] In fact, the region became a branch-plant economy.

In his conclusions, Acheson noted that railway technology played an important role in the Maritimes' deteriorating economic status in the Canadian economic union. 'The tragedy of the industrial experiment in the Maritimes was that the transportation lines which linked the region to its new metropolis altered the communal arrangement of the entire area; they did not merely establish a new external frame of reference, they re-cast the entire internal structure.'[48] When they entered the Canadian union, the Maritimes were not a coherent region, he wrote, but separate colonies on the fringe of an empire, each with its own lines of communication and several metropolitan centres. Its waterborne transportation system was flexible and dynamic. 'In this sense the railroad with its implications of organic unity, its inflexibility, and its assumption that there was a metropolitan point at which it could end, provided an experience entirely alien to the maritime tradition,' Acheson concluded, and asserts that there is no evidence to suggest that maritime businessmen were any less efficient than those in Ontario and Québec, 'nor, given advantageous freight rates, that they could not compete for most central Canadian markets.'[49]

New Brunswick historian E.R. Forbes seconded Acheson's thesis by noting that sharply increasing freight rates in the first decades of the twentieth century were a factor in the comparative economic decline of the mainland maritime provinces.[50] Though the Intercolonial was built as part of the confederation agreement of 1867 for the economic development of Nova Scotia and New Brunswick, its managers, under the direction of their political masters, established relatively low and flexible freight rates. Wishing to remain competitive within the region, the CPR responded with similar tariffs. At the turn of the century, the rise of western Canada and its regional protest movements caused a westward shift in political power. In 1913, a Nova Scotia–born prime minister, Robert Borden, held in office by a central and western Canadian–based party, appointed a new cost-conscious management for the Intercolonial, and freight rates shot up dramatically, rapidly eroding the critical advantage that maritime industrial centres had enjoyed. With the absorption of the Intercolonial into Canadian National Railways, the central government steeply increased freight rates, effectively ending the competitiveness of Maritime factories in Canadian markets. Having acquired the extensive Grand Trunk harbour properties in Portland when it nationalized the railway, Ottawa abandoned its policy of developing the ports of Halifax and Saint John.[51] Feeling shut out of central Canada's economic prosperity, Maritimers rallied for a while under the dissident Maritime Rights movement, but when that failed to achieve the desired result, their disillusionment was profound and lasting.[52] In the end, the Maritime provinces fell into the trap described by Daniel R. Headrick in *Tentacles of Progress*.[53] Having voluntarily accepted the transfer of an encompassing technology, they became part of its imperial embrace. Tupper and Tilley's visions of the Intercolonial as an artery moving manufactured goods from the region to central Canada had lost to Galt's call for a new Canadian mercantilism.

Another dramatic victim of the philosophy of railways was Prince Edward Island. Driven by a strong sense of community, that province had consciously and explicitly scorned confederation. The island's decades-long struggle to wrest its lands from absentee landlords, its strong attachment to the soil, its fight to retain an independent government, its rural conservatism, and especially its insular isolationist mentality had created a distinct communal identity that was fiercely independent, profoundly patriotic, and sublimely optimistic. Prince Edward Islanders adamantly refused to be absorbed into a larger nation.[54]

In 1871, however, the island caught railway fever and its politicians and editors displayed all the symptoms so common two decades earlier in mainland North America. Included in the exuberant promises of infinite progress and wealth was the expectation of the industrialization of the island economy; excluded was any regard for mounting costs and unsustainable debt charges. And, as elsewhere, the opposition tended to focus on the pace and place of construction rather than on its principle and value; the legislature thus committed the island to a publicly financed trunk line and several branches.

Begun in the fall of 1871, the project was immediately ensnared in patronage and corruption, causing a considerable expansion in length and cost and eventually forcing a general election. After a rancorous, divisive campaign, in which the railway issue was complicated by quarrels about sectarian schools, Robert Poore Haythorne's Liberal party won a resounding victory. Although they had roundly criticized the Conservatives' expensive railway program, patronage considerations forced them to expand the project still further into a full-fledged trans-island railway. The new government committed the island to spend $3.8 million or $41 per capita on railway construction, creating annual interest charges that amounted to half of its revenues, an impossible burden for a small population faced with an economic recession. Early in 1873, the anti-confederation Haythorne government sent a mission to Ottawa to discuss terms of union.[55]

The initial union package answered most of Prince Edward Island's needs. Canada promised to assume the island's debt, including that of the railway, to loan money to buy out the remaining absentee landlords, and to provide adequate representation in parliament. Late in May, the legislature accepted the conditions but called for an election. Although the Haythorne government was defeated – largely on the sectarian-schools issue – J.C. Pope's Conservative government was committed to a better-terms confederation and subsequently negotiated a financially more rewarding package.[56] The Canadian government justified the more generous treatment of Prince Edward Island on the grounds that the province needed special concessions because it had no Crown lands and because it would not profit from the construction of the Intercolonial or the CPR.[57] Although most islanders were disappointed in the loss of their independence, they took comfort in the favourable terms. By 1873, in fact, they had little choice: economic necessity forced their decision to join Canada. The impetuous adoption of the philosophy of railways, followed by hasty planning, contracting, and constructing, accompanied by bribery and patronage, had resulted in an unbearable financial burden that wore down the island's independent spirit. A deep sense of loss, exacerbated by a stagnating economy and fed by nostalgia for a lost golden age, demoralized generations of islanders. 'Thus,' lamented David Weale and Harry Baglole, the island's nationalist historians, 'although the eventual entry of the Island into Confederation was part of the unfolding of the great Canadian National Dream, it also in many ways represented the disintegration of the Island Dream.'[58]

Further to the east, in Newfoundland, the philosophy of railways had a lesser impact on the province's loss of sovereignty than in Prince Edward Island. Straddled on the far eastern fringe of Britain's North American empire, Newfoundland through most of the nineteenth century ignored the rhetoric of railways and its transcontinental dream. Although an isolated editor occasionally broached the subject, most newspapers and politicians did not embrace the expansionist boosterism of mainland railway promoters.[59] Instead, their economic and cultural inspiration remained steadfastly North Atlantic. Not surprisingly, the island spurned all union overtures from the other colonies and in 1869 an election formally ratified its oceanic orientation.[60]

Railway politics came to play an important role in the island's repeated refusals to join the continent but also in its final surrender to continentalist pressures. In the late 1860s and again in the mid-1870s, Newfoundlanders discussed the construction of a trans-island railway, but no action resulted until 1881 when William Whiteway's Conservative government signed an ambitious agreement with an American company. By then the island was fully immersed in railway mania, with proponents arguing that the technology was necessary to encourage economic development outside the traditional fishery – in mining, lumbering, and agriculture. It was time, they asserted, that Newfoundland entered the modern age and developed the full range of its natural resources. Meanwhile, their opponents, concentrated in St John's, countered that a Canadian economic policy could not be applied to Newfoundland, that the scheme constituted an unnecessary and unbearable tax burden, and that the road would expose the province's merchants to unfair external competition.[61] Despite their objections, the syndicate, incorporated as the Newfoundland Railway Company, sputtered along for the next three years and by 1884 completed a 64-kilometre rail line to Harbour Grace on Conception Bay. By then, the company was also bankrupt. Consequently, the government assumed control over construction, and four years later a Reform administration finished a branch to Argentia on Placentia Bay. Finally, in the 1890s, a Liberal government reorganized the company and chartered Robert G. Reid of Montréal to extend the line to Port aux Basques on the south-west corner of the island. Although Reid's company completed the formidable task by 1897, the cost of construction contributed to the province's massive public debt and the financial crisis of that year. At the same time, however, Reid's success had bolstered the province's independent spirit and his lobbying among Montréal financiers helped restore its fiscal health. Once again, the province rejected a Canadian bid for union.[62]

By the turn of the century, the Newfoundland railway had become a recurrent, hot political issue. It had realigned traditional alliances and aided the fall of several administrations. In 1901, for instance, when the Robert Bond government reduced the generous land and resource concessions that a previous cabinet had granted, the Reids became actively involved in the 1909 election and contributed to Bond's defeat. The succeeding government improved the deal again, but finally, in 1923, Newfoundland bought out the company. Although railway construction had created temporary employment, it did not stop the chronic emigration of the island's young people to the mainland. It did permit, however, the settlement of some parts of the interior, the establishment of a strong pulp-and-paper industry, and the consolidation of several trading centres along the coast. Meanwhile, despite their initial fears, the railway helped St John's merchants to expand their hold over the island's trade and commerce.[63] In the end, the trans-island railway had created a disproportionally large financial debt that contributed to the province's bankruptcy in the early 1930s, the establishment of commission government, and ultimately union with Canada in 1949.

While, in the 1860s, neither Newfoundland nor Prince Edward Island had shared with Canadians the transcontinental vision of technological nationalism and instead chose to retain a distinct local culture, eventually they were fully incorporated into the transcontinental economy. As underdeveloped fringe regions in the national economy, they boarded their surplus populations on trains that carried them westward to jobs in central Canada, the western prairies, and the Pacific coast. The bonds of common language and history, essential to defining a people's identity, assisted their fusion into the nation, while the railway and the mails it carried permitted them to keep in touch with their home provinces.

The two components, the English tongue and British heritage, that allowed anglophone Canadians to mix easily into a new culture, were not features of a large and populous region – French-speaking Québec. A unique historical tradition and distinct language prevented that province's full integration into the national psyche despite the transcontinental railway. Few French Canadians were exposed to or excited by the philosophy of railways and its western settlement and nation-building components.

Although the French language and the Québec heritage prevented the full assimilation of rural francophones into Canadian culture, their strong sense of place also militated against migration to the North-West. French Canadians identified the St Lawrence valley as their homeland – la patrie. Resident in that geographical region was a distinct people bound by their peculiar institutions of law, customs, social organizations, and church.[64] 'Notre religion, notre langue et nos lois,' *La Minerve* asserted. 'Ne craignons pas de répéter ce cri national, qui n'est pas plus banal qu'aucun autre motto, aucune autre devise, et aucun chant national. N'ayons pas honte de notre drapeau.'[65] To be sure, the Québécois developed a vision of economic development, a program that emphasized agriculture and forestry but also included industrialization and the construction of roads and railways.[66] They confined these schemes to their province, however, and clearly recognized that such objectives were only the materialistic aspect of several nation-building blocks. Significantly, they sought to reinforce their nationalism with cultural traits, especially their religious beliefs. 'Pour les canadiens, le catholicisme c'est la nationalité,' *La Minerve* concluded and implicitly explained why French Canada considered the right to preserve their distinct identity – rooted within the confines of their national homeland – as the necessary condition for confederation.[67]

Inspired by their patriotic love for Québec, French Canadians had little interest in the settlement of the North-West. In fact, frequent appeals from the pulpit for aid to starving Metis and destitute natives, as well as bleak accounts from returning fur traders about inhospitable expanses, had created among the Québécois an image of the plains as desolate wastelands, unfit for agriculture and habitation. 'Le territoire du Nord-Ouest, quoi qu'on en dise, est une région désolée, impracticable durant une grande partie de l'année, et où rien n'attirera l'émigrant,' *Le Pays* scoffed. 'Lorsque tout le continent américain sera peuplé, qu'il n'y aura plus un pouce carré de terre disponible, peut-être alors se dirigera-t-on vers la Baie d'Hudson. Jusqu'alors on ne peut espérer des émigrants.'[68] In contrast to their Ontario and Maritime compatriots, French Canadians found little appeal in the vast lands of the western prairies. They did not share the transcontinental nation-building dream and its myths – not its pioneering aura, its agrarian radicalism, or, for that matter, the CPR.

Nevertheless, it was a French Canadian who conducted the negotiations that transferred Rupert's Land from the Hudson's Bay Company to Canada and promised a railway to British Columbia. But that diplomat, George-Etienne Cartier, was not a rural seigneur but an urban lawyer, who, as solicitor for the Grand Trunk, was fully immersed in Montréal's business world and its expansionist ethic.[69] Cartier's view of the North-West was a commercial perspective. He was not particularly interested in the North-West as a place for French Canadians, but saw it as a region that would use his city, its river and its railways, as a channel to and from Europe. 'Nous exporterons les produits de la Colombie et de Manitobe [sic] sur les marchés européens et nous importerons pour elles les produits manufactures dont elles auront besoin,' Le Courrier noted. 'Notre marine et nos importateurs en auront tout le bénéfice.'[70] As the paper observed, colonization was profitable: it meant traffic for Québec's railways, business for its merchants, and land sales for its speculators. Western Canadian trade would create jobs in Québec and keep its people home.[71] In other words, the completion of the Pacific railway became an important objective to Québec merchants and other businessmen; it represented another phase in the empire of the St Lawrence.

For Québec, therefore, a transcontinental railway, routed through the Ottawa valley to Montréal and Québec City, was 'la seule politique provinciale, vraie et nationale dans les circonstances.'[72] To achieve that objective, the province sold to the CPR its rights to the Montréal-Ottawa portion of the Québec, Montréal, Ottawa et Occidental. In this way, the province ensured that the St Lawrence port would become a major terminal on the transcontinental. Subsequently, Québec politicians forced the federal government to coerce the Grand Trunk Railway to surrender its control over the eastern section of the Québec, Montréal, Ottawa et Occidental (also known as the North Shore Line) to the CPR. Provincial and federal politicians thus ensured that Québec's capital enjoyed the services of two competing rail lines, both of which fed into major American and Canadian rail systems.[73] For Québecers, however, the Grand Trunk and Canadian Pacific railways were vehicles for promoting the economic welfare of their province and for strengthening the French-Canadian national-ity, rather than tools for building a transcontinental country.[74]

Despite its inward vision, therefore, Québec participated in the estab-lishment of the mercantile relationship between central Canada and the outlying regions. Strengthened by the commercial spirit of anglophone Montréal, the province helped frame the national railway and tariff policies that at once consolidated the new northern empire and created its regional disparities and established major metropolitan centres and their hinter-lands.

The relationship between the large cities and the countryside, which the railway cemented into place, was a complex association duplicated in min-iature metropolitan empires within the nation's regions. These minor met-ropolitan structures, tied together by railway and telegraph communi-cations, helped to alleviate the sense of frustration and alienation that the feelings of regionalism produced.

On the prairies, for example, rapidly growing Winnipeg took advantage of its geographical location to establish itself as a subordinate metropolitan system. Already ensconced as the territory's most important warehouse and wholesale centre, Winnipeg had the experience and access to credit to take advantage of the transportation revolution; the construction of the CPR across the plains accelerated the growth of traffic through the city and the prosperity of its business community.[75] By 1886, Winnipeg had nine-teen major establishments that specialized in exploiting the commerce of the western hinterland. Its merchants formed a powerful group that per-suaded the CPR to build the main line south through Winnipeg rather than Selkirk, wrested control over the grain trade from Toronto, and later demolished the CPR monopoly. More significantly, its board of trade suc-cessfully lobbied the railway and government for a 15 per cent reduction of freight rates on goods shipped west of Winnipeg, including manufactured items. In 1890, it also pressured the CPR to lower rates on items hauled from central Canada to Winnipeg.[76]

The discriminatory rate policy contributed substantially to Winnipeg's dominant position as the gateway to the Canadian prairies. The CPR's pol-icy of charging higher rates on manufactured goods than on raw materials transported from central Canada to Winnipeg aided the city's manufactur-ing industry, while lower rates on westbound freight assisted its wholesale trade. Some city merchants founded subsidiaries in towns built along the main line: J.H. Ashdown, hardware wholesaler and retailer, for instance, established a hardware store in Calgary. His and other firms replenished their stock from Winnipeg suppliers, which in turn ordered from central

Canada, Great Britain, or the United States depending upon price and quality. Dixon Brothers of Medicine Hat bought almost half its supplies from Winnipeg wholesalers, and most of the remainder from Montréal and Toronto.[77] Winnipeg merchants, therefore, represented a dual consolidating force: they established strong ties with central Canada, the eastern United States, and the United Kingdom and at the same time planted tight connections with the cities, towns, and villages spread across the expansive plain. That middleman position created an equivocal attitude among Winnipegers to western Canada's position in confederation.

One individual who represented Winnipeg's ambiguous metropolitan-hinterland relationship was Manitoba's Clifford Sifton.[78] Young, energetic, and pragmatic, Ontario-born Sifton believed that the exploitation of the resources of the North-West was central to the economic development of Canada. As minister of the interior in Sir Wilfrid Laurier's administration, Sifton adopted a business-like approach to the settlement process, treating the vast unsettled lands as commodities on a glutted market, to be sold cheaply through extensive advertising among experienced farmers in Britain, the United States, and Continental Europe.[79] Although he defended the extensive cattle preserves of southern Alberta, he admired scientific and technological farming methods, and became the first minister to support large-scale irrigation projects in the North-West.[80] When Ottawa granted provincial status to Saskatchewan and Alberta in 1905, Sifton agreed that jurisdiction over their natural resources should remain with the federal government, but when Laurier appeared to set up independent Catholic school systems in the new provinces, he angrily resigned. At worst, Sifton's stand on the school question may be interpreted as a manifestation of Ontario's anti–Roman Catholic, anti–French Canadian bigotry: at best, it may be seen as an indication of the North-West's belief that all newcomers should be taught British democratic ideals in a common English language. In any case, he wanted to establish on the prairies the social structures of his native Ontario.

Instructive of Clifford Sifton's close association with central Canada is his position in the 1911 election. Although a Liberal, he did not share the enthusiasm of his colleagues when the American government suggested a reciprocal free-trade agreement. Sifton strongly opposed the trade pact and actively campaigned against his party, receiving the grateful support of Canada's manufacturing and railway interests. Central to his opposition was the belief that free trade would disrupt the east-west trade patterns that the transcontinental railway system and the National Policy had so painfully wrought. Although Sifton's stand definitely ran contrary to the views of many western Canadians, it must be noted that the Brandon constituency that had consistently returned him to office voted Tory in the 1911 election.

The defeat of free trade obviously angered many western Canadians, but their alienation did not turn into separatist feelings partly because of the dual role that Winnipeg and other western cities played in the metropolitan-hinterland relationship. On the one hand, Winnipeg was the transportation gateway into the region and the largest wholesale distribution centre in western Canada. Its vote in the 1911 election clearly exposed the political alliance that the city's business élite had made with Canada's railway interests.[81] With the city serving as the region's primary grain market, Winnipeg's merchants continuously blocked the efforts of western farm organizations to gain control over the grain trade. Western farmers, therefore, denounced the city as an ally of the nation-state and its corporate backers. On the other hand, Winnipeg provided the political power to destroy the CPR's monopoly and gain important rate differentials, popular actions that won the approval of western farmers. At times, then, the city joined common cause with the countryside in the battle against Montréal and Toronto. The city's newspapers, particularly the *Free Press*, identified and fortified the concerns of prairie farmers, opinions echoed in the towns and cities of the North-West.[82] In this love-hate relationship, Winnipeg and other emerging prairie cities were at once opponents and champions of western causes. In either case, the city strengthened the region's sense of communal uniqueness. By controlling the means of communication along with its imports and exports, the city became a regional voice for the prairies and helped to establish the region's identity.

As the example of Winnipeg has illustrated, the metropolitan-hinterland relationship was complex and intricate. The feelings of alienation, which that association so often generated, were tempered by the close common cultural ties shared among the regions. Despite western Canada's quickness to protest, the region retained a strong identification with eastern Canada because the railway, which had transported settlers and their belongings from Atlantic and St Lawrence harbours, from the Maritimes, Québec, and Ontario, and from the United States, permitted the newcomers to maintain ties with their homelands as well as with eastern cities and institutions. As a fast and efficient means of communication, the railway ensured that the western identity, which the newcomers eventually created, was derived in part from contemporary attitudes in the United States and Great Britain, as well as eastern Canada.

While the newcomers spoke of creating a new society in an empty land

and laced their rhetoric with pastoral ideals and agrarian myths, with egalitarian democratic concepts, and with talk of individualism and cooperation, virility and opportunity, they quietly put in place familiar customs.
Although westerners spoke of a clean slate, their community presented no
spontaneous new world but an obvious derivation from western Europe;
they welcomed the police, the church, legislative assemblies, national
schools – or, simply put, law, order, and good government. The prophets
of the new society were typically the editors of local newspapers, who
never strayed far from the telegraph office or train station, and copied
freely from eastern dailies. Like Patrick Gammie Laurie, the editor of the
Saskatchewan Herald, they either looked to Great Britain for inspiration
or, like J.W. Dafoe, editor of the Manitoba *Free Press*, they admired the
United States.[83] They eventually created a distinctive western regional
identity, but that character remained fully exposed to the latest metropolitan political, social, and economic debates. The West's radical agrarian tradition, for instance, owes an enormous debt to concepts tried on the Great
Plains of the United States, while its labour radicalism found inspiration in
the coal mines of Pennsylvania and the factories of Great Britain.[84]

Despite their loud claims of distinctiveness, therefore, westerners attempted to imitate many features of metropolitan life. A clear illustration
of this phenomenon was the ranching community in southern Alberta. The
completion of the prairie section of the CPR in 1883 made large-scale
ranching economically feasible, particularly after the Canadian government
awarded several large grazing leases to a number of prominent Canadian
and British investors. Even though the ranching industry borrowed many
of its techniques from previous frontiers, particularly those of the United
States, its cultural and political inspiration came from central Canada and
the United Kingdom.[85] The tennis courts and grand pianos that graced the
luxurious ranches provided more than recreation in an isolated community; they served as symbols of gracious living on a crude frontier. The
ranching élite, which was closely associated with the officers of the North
West Mounted Police, carefully maintained lines of communication with
the eastern establishment and attempted, with some success, to institute on
the south-western fringe of the prairies a Victorian way of life.[86]

The shopkeepers in the small towns along the railway were no different
from the ranchers; their social activities and political alliances expressed a
similar conservatism. Their votes at election time demonstrated that they
appreciated the strong centralization tendencies emanating from the eastern establishment, while their social activities reflected their desire to establish an orderly and peaceful society.[87] Supporting their local press and

social institutions, the town's businessmen and professionals profoundly influenced the character of western Canadian society.

Since the railway provided the link between the metropolis and the hinterland, the timing of its appearance was important. The prairies were settled when the primary characteristic of its founders, the Montréal-Toronto metropolitan axis, was a Victorian industrial expansionism. The age celebrated the triumph of a laissez-faire liberalism, whose priorities included confederation, western expansion, and the construction of a transcontinental railway. Whereas the region's link with the metropolis during the fur-trade era had been slow, inefficient, and circuitous, by 1900 it was fast, efficient, and immediate. Assisted by the telegraph and postal service, the railway placed the North-West in immediate touch with central Canada. Consequently, the values of the city were transmitted directly and quickly to the frontier.

In fact, the value of progress that dominated nineteenth-century Canadian thought was accentuated in western Canada. Technology, science, and the machine promised to subdue the rigour and capriciousness of nature. After it deliberately routed the main line through the semi-arid southern prairies, the CPR established model farms throughout the West to experiment with improved hybrids and dogmatically propagate dry-land farming techniques. Its large irrigation project in southern Alberta, with its impressive dam at Bassano and massive concrete aqueduct at Brooks, demonstrated to the world that modern scientific farmers could grow crops where they pleased.[88]

Bolstered by its buoyant optimism in science and technology and its ebullient belief in moral and social progress, the prairie West possessed a utopian streak. Despite their basic political conservatism, westerners believed they were building a new and improved society on the plains. They wanted to share their vision with a perceived effete eastern Canada. Western visionaries and prophets, often disguised as politicians, travelled by train to Ottawa to participate in the councils of the nation and lay before its people the idealism of a young and vigorous region.

Despite its strong regional identity, western Canada, therefore, participated in national institutions and joined in national debates; it fitted itself into the national identity. Despite vocal protests about its regional uniqueness, the West possessed a sense of nationalism expressed at federal elections and in national organizations. A regional transportation network knitted villages, towns, and cities into a vital and dynamic entity; simultaneously, the railway blunted the sharp division between region and nation. In this integration the railway played a major part.

The prairie provinces, therefore, linked by rail and telegraph to the East, in many ways shared central Canadian values, but because they also felt threatened by that largely urban, industrializing society, they formed a unique culture. The CPR had opened the region to farmers, shopkeepers, and investors from eastern Canada; it had fulfilled – even if imperfectly – one of the hopes expressed by the Toronto *Mail*, cited at the beginning of this chapter; it had assisted in settling western Canada and in attaching the region to the Montréal-Toronto axis.[89] When the *Mail* expressed the hope, however, that the CPR would 'make strong a true national sentiment,' it articulated a central Canadian economic vision, which the railway helped to spread across the land. That aspiration met with considerable resistance in some regions and with studied rebuffs in others. It was a simplistic wish that hid the multifaceted nature of the metropolitan-frontier connection.

Similarly, to what extent was the *Mail's* wish for an independent northern nation a naive assertion? Did the completion of the CPR 'preserve' the young nation's 'autonomy and national integrity'? Did it ensure that Canada would not be absorbed into the United States? Had the editor skimmed lightly over the intricate, constantly mutating relationships of Canada with Great Britain and the United States? Did he understand to what extent the railway was assisting the country's orientation from a transatlantic to a continental alignment?

The completion of the transcontinental at Craigellachie in November 1885 represented the culmination of a vision expressed nearly four decades earlier in the Guarantee Act of 1849. Set in a turbulent decade, that legislation embodied a scheme for a distinct northern economy, competitive with that of the United States but never completely independent from it. It incorporated an almost universal optimism in railway technology as a response to a new economic order. It implied that this revolutionary means of transportation would permit the province's businessmen to expand their commercial activities across the continent into American as well as British territory.

In 1849, when Canada's affiliation was still primarily with the United Kingdom, it used the Guarantee Act to lure British technical knowledge, financial resources, and managerial skills to the province in order to build the Grand Trunk and other railways. At mid-century, Britain was one of the few countries that possessed the vast resources of capital, equipment, labour, engineering, and management skills required to build and operate railways abroad. As Daniel R. Headrick has demonstrated so cogently, Great Britain was a mass exporter of railway technology, sending its engineers, equipment, and capital to all parts of the globe.[90] Canada, a major recipient of this technology transfer, was drawn ever more deeply into and influenced by British culture and economics.

Headrick's observation amplified Gallagher and Robinson's 'imperialism of free trade' thesis, which argued that Britain expanded its empire significantly during the mid-nineteenth century despite the predominant free-trade ideology. 'The exports of capital and manufactures, the migration of citizens, the dissemination of the English language, ideas and constitutional forms,' the authors wrote, 'were all of them radiations of the social energies of the British peoples.'[91] By defining imperialism as the 'process of integrating new regions into the expanding economy,' Gallagher and Robinson argued that the growth of British industry forced Britain to employ both formal and informal methods to link undeveloped areas into its orbit.[92] Many regions became satellite economies, providing raw materials for Great Britain, wider markets for its manufacturers, and investment opportunities for its capitalists. In Canada, the Grand Trunk Railway reinforced imperial connections and imperial objectives. Subsequently, the Canadian Pacific Railway incorporated imperial ends as an important part of its mission.[93]

In the case of British North America, however, provincial governments and businessmen used the philosophy of railways to enhance their political power and control. The growing but transformed imperial influence, represented by bankers like the Barings and the Glyns, must be considered in light of the fact that in the 1850s both Nova Scotia and New Brunswick rejected British contractors in favour of government-directed construction and that Canada insisted that domestic businessmen receive a large portion of Grand Trunk construction work. Canada's precarious financial situation throughout the 1850s, caused primarily by faltering railways, increased its political self-determination. Ruling relatively large territories and enjoying a fair measure of self-government, colonial legislatures insisted on setting their railway agendas and simultaneously developed their own fiscal policies and expanded bureaucracies. That growing self-awareness was reflected in the public-works programs in New Brunswick and Nova Scotia, in the expanded size of the Grand Trunk Railway and complex state financial-assistance techniques, in Canada's 1859 tariff, and eventually in confederation.

Although British North America's mid-century railway boom strengthened informal ties with Great Britain, it also increased the colonies' orientation to the United States. This was a logical consequence of the philosophy of railways because virtually all colonial railways were designed to provide access to American markets or ports. While some were to serve as portages between the continent's interior and New England railways, others were to syphon trade from the American West through British American harbours to the Atlantic Ocean.

The Guarantee Act, which authorized government subsidies to rival portage-railways across Canadian soil, clearly revealed that the philosophy of railways did not contain the technological nationalism that is a part of the CPR mythology. The harsh realities of economic practicality as well as the predominance of economic considerations lying beneath the idealistic rhetoric informed government policies. Throughout the pre-confederation years, Canadians sporadically considered proposals for an intercolonial railway from Québec through New Brunswick to the ice-free port of Halifax. Its circuitous route, however, lessened the practical economic value of the plan. As far as Montréal's merchants were concerned, the primary purpose of any railway was to retain for their city the trade of Upper Canada and capture that of the American Midwest; therefore, they wanted the most direct, economically efficient rail route to the Atlantic. They also intended to compete head-on with American railways that had similar objectives. In the same way, Saint John and Halifax businessmen hoped to see their cities become major seaports for both Canadian and American trade routes and they planned their railway policies accordingly.

Even though the visionary pre-confederation schemes for a transcontinental railway had British imperial goals, all proposed routing the line south of the Great Lakes through the United States. Edward Watkin's plan, which was similar to many other outlines, illustrated this international perspective. An ardent believer in free trade between Canada and the United States, Watkin clearly recognized that railway technology was not limited by political boundaries. On one level, his transcontinental railway scheme represented the extension of Britain's informal empire of finance and commerce into North America.[94] On a different level, his proposal meant the creation of a Canadian empire westward to the Pacific and the settlement of the prairies. On yet another plane, Watkin proposed to build south of the Great Lakes and thus envisioned closer integration with the United States and the creation of a continental economy.[95] At these several levels, therefore, his proposed railway symbolized the expansionist and universalizing features of technology. It embodied all the outlines of the schemes that remained in vogue until the Pacific Scandal.

British North America's railway champions certainly understood the principle that this new transportation technology fostered, extended, and strengthened the power of international commercial empires. Even though they promoted the railway as a means of building a distinct northern nation within the British Empire, they also saw it as a method for attaching themselves to the dynamic economy of the United States. Railways like the Grand Trunk, Great Western, and European and North American facilitated the union of British North America, but they could not survive if they isolated themselves from the United States. Thus, the railway builders linked their projects into the American network and increasingly adopted American principles and technologies. When their isolationist broad-gauge policy proved to be economically unsound, Canada's railway managers undertook an expensive conversion to the American standard gauge.[96] By 1873, American and Canadian rolling stock moved unhampered across the international border.[97] On the one hand, railway technology at first informally and subtly strengthened the financial and social influence exerted by the British Empire; on the other hand, subsequently it casually and inconspicuously intensified commercial and cultural relations with the United States.

The new international reality, articulated in the philosophy of railways, was ostensibly rejected during the Pacific Scandal. The political and regional rivalries that rose to the surface during the crisis accentuated Ottawa's impotence at the repeated American rejections of reciprocity overtures and the degradation during the Treaty of Washington negotiations. Prime Minister John A. Macdonald was determined that the new Pacific railway would be all-Canadian in routing and management. He resolved to use the railway as a tool of nationalism.

Despite Macdonald's intentions, the international, universalizing character of the technology of railways was still very evident in the Canadian Pacific Railway. The syndicate that eventually built the western portion of the transcontinental railway arose out of the defunct St Paul, Minneapolis and Manitoba Railway, revitalized by a partnership of Canadian and American promoters and financiers. Following the instructions of the federal government, the CPR constructed an all-Canadian railroad from central Canada along the north shore of Lake Superior and across the prairies to the Rocky Mountains, permitting Montréal merchants to reinstitute the trade route their ancestors had lost and to re-establish their city's dominance in the North-West. But the board of directors quickly set aside the government's explicit nationalist purpose and leased, bought, or constructed several branch lines in the United States, including the Short Line from Montréal through Maine to Saint John and the Soo Line westward from Sault Ste Marie through Minnesota to St Paul and Minneapolis. On 3 June 1889, a through train ran the exact route that Hugh Allan and Jay Cooke had planned but the Pacific Scandal had scuttled, while a year later, the CPR launched operations on a direct line from Québec through Montréal and Toronto to Windsor, where it ferried cars across the river to be forwarded on the Wabash Railroad to Chicago.[98] The CPR's corporate objectives, therefore, were not defined by an exclusivist technological nationalism but by the broad internationalism of the railway and its search for profits.

The international integrative character of railway technology is muted in Canadian historiography because writers prefer to adulate the Canadian Pacific Railway as the great unifier of the northern transcontinental nation. Almost forgotten is William J. Wilgus's *The Railway Interrelations of the United States and Canada*, which studied about fifty gateways at the international boundary and concluded that the railways of Canada and the United States must be seen as an integrated network. In practice, Wilgus observed, railways operated 'as if there were no border to separate them politically,'[99] an observation that many nineteenth-century Canadians could have made and, with some reservations, applauded.

In like manner, the National Policy was never intended to completely bar American and British businessmen from Canada. In western Canada, for example, T.C. Power and Company, a trading firm based in Fort Benton, Montana, with a long history of activities on the south-western prairies, neutralized the effect of Canada's highly protective tariff by shifting some of its purchasing to suppliers in Montréal and shipping them to the North-West on the CPR. If prices warranted, however, Power also bought goods in New York, Chicago, or St Paul and imported them by way of Winnipeg.[100] Similarly, the Hudson's Bay Company adopted a mixed policy of buying some goods in Canada and importing others from Great Britain. It also adapted its operations to the agricultural economy; it diversified its operations, expanded its selection of wares, and established sales shops wherever populations warranted.[101]

Despite the protectionism inherent in the National Policy, the CPR, as an effective means of communication, created opportunities for shrewd entrepreneurs from New York, Chicago, and London, as well as Montréal and Toronto, to conduct business in the North-West. The railway permitted hundreds of shopkeepers to establish small stores in towns along its main and branch lines and to fill their shelves with an array of products manufactured in central Canada, the United States, or Great Britain. Travelling salesmen alighted daily from inbound trains to take orders for Winnipeg and Montréal wholesalers. In fact, the CPR allowed factories, such as Harris and John Deere, to set up farm-implement dealerships in most sizeable towns on the prairies. Large flour millers, like A.W. Ogilvie, erected mills in the North-West or gathered wheat for central Canadian or European plants.

The Toronto *Mail*'s claim, therefore, that the CPR would establish the national integrity of Canada has validity to the extent that, undergirded by the National Policy, the railway permitted central Canada to lay claim to the North-West and to establish its economic hegemony in the Atlantic region. It also facilitated the establishment of intercontinental trade and commerce. The assertion that the CPR would make Canada independent from the United States proved excessively sanguine when the railway connected itself to North America's railway system. In other words, British North America's philosophy of railways, first enunciated in the 1840s, helped create the Dominion but unintentionally introduced regional disparities and discontents into its mercantilistic federal structure; at the same time, while it envisioned a relatively independent Canada, it increased the nation's dependence on the United States.

The national dream, born in the heady expansionism of the mid-nineteenth century, arose out of the conviction that the railway would permit mankind to conquer the environment. This vision was especially strong in British North America, whose citizens, surrounded by an immense and seemingly hostile wilderness, eagerly embraced the new transportation technique as a potent means of freeing men and women from the harsh bonds of nature. The railway, which smoothed rough geological obstacles and softened harsh winters, promised economic growth and provincial prosperity. More intangibly, it supposedly ennobled people and promoted moral as well as economic progress. The new transportation technology promised to liberate them from the bonds of the environment and the frailties of their humanity. Emboldened by such a great prospect, British North Americans ardently and totally embraced railway technology and thus set the stage for an unparalleled railway boom.

Although technology's 'moral imperative' assumed a prominent place in promotional literature, it was primarily the hope for economic growth that energized conservative and reform-minded colonists and drove them into powerful alliances. While conservatives rejected the political ideas of their liberal opponents because they feared a threat to established order, they readily accepted the formula for economic progress and colonial prosperity as the best means of preserving their favoured way of life. This consensus on economic development created the fertile ground for British North America's railway extravaganza. Despite disagreements on details, most urban British North Americans embraced the technological nationalist dream, a vision of a transcontinental country eventually realized in the completion of the Grand Trunk, the Great Western, the European and North American, the Nova Scotia, and finally the Intercolonial and the Canadian Pacific railways. Collectively, these railways revolutionized transportation in the colonies and radically altered their political, social, and economic cultures in ways their advocates never envisioned.

Few of the railway philosophers, for example, would have foreseen the interventionist role the state came to play in private business. As Peter Baskerville has observed, with colonies investing so heavily in the railways in the late 1850s, 'private and public finances were, if not indistinguishable, well on the way to being so.'[102] Confronted by massive railway debts, moreover, governments reformed, solidified, and centralized their administrative structures, placing them under expert civil servants. At the same time, they assumed considerable control over faltering railway companies and encouraged them to adopt modern, decentralized managerial strategies. The state also initiated systematic inspections and public inquiries into accidents; it demanded the publication of detailed rules and regulations; and it certified the training of supervisors.[103] This process of growing state intervention in the management of private enterprise, theoretically abhorred by both liberal and conservative politicians, continued into the post-confederation period with the establishment of regulatory bodies and, after the First World War, with the nationalization of several bankrupt railways into a giant Crown corporation – Canadian National Railways.[104]

Simultaneously, the state increasingly used fiscal policies to direct the national economy. Ministers of finance increased customs duties to underwrite state commitments to railway construction and to protect domestic industries. But they also raised them to shield internal railways from competing American lines. This strategy, first enuciated in the Galt tariffs and fully articulated in the National Policy, became an integral part of Canada's philosophy of railways.

In the 1840s, then, British North Americans developed a comprehensive philosophy of railways, based on the perception that science and technology could help them conquer the vast wilderness in which they found themselves. For half a century they put into place the various policies that would permit them to realize their dream of a transcontinental railway. Finally accomplished in 1885, the CPR, the western segment of the transcontinental, represented the culmination of a technological nationalist vision – that of a nation tied together by bonds of steel. That belief, enunciated most strongly in the burgeoning cities of the Maritimes and the Canadas, began with the colonists relying heavily on the technological and financial wealth of Great Britain, but over the years they increasingly turned to North American resources. They drafted policies to enable them to implement their new strategy, the dream of a northern transcontinental nation. While their program implied a continental orientation, including closer economic intercourse with the United States, it also embraced strong centralist designs such as confederation and the National Policy. As an integral part of the philosophy of railways, these centralizing, nationalist approaches bestowed advantages on central Canada to the detriment of the eastern and western peripheries. The latter did not share equally in the growing prosperity of Canada and consequently expressed their alienation in regional protest movements. These remonstrations, however, were not attacks on the technology that had tied their region to the nation's heartland but opposed the policies that supported the railway. They clearly recognized that it was not the Grand Trunk, or the Intercolonial, or the Canadian Pacific Railway that determined the nature of the Canadian federation but the philosophy of railways.

Notes

Chapter 1: Technological Nationalism

1 E.J. Pratt, 'Towards the Last Spike,' in *Complete Poems*, ed. Sandra Djwa and R.G. Moyles (Toronto 1989), 2: 201–2

2 R.G. MacBeth, *The Romance of the Canadian Pacific Railway* (Toronto 1924); John M. Gibbon, *Steel of Empire: The Romantic History of the Canadian Pacific, The Northwest Passage of Today* (New York 1937)

3 Harold A. Innis, *A History of the Canadian Pacific Railway*, foreword by Peter George (Toronto 1971), 128

4 Ibid., 287

5 Harold A. Innis, *The Fur Trade in Canada: An Introduction to Canadian Economic History* (Toronto 1962), 393. This work is the best-known source for the thesis that modes of transport are decisive. Two essays, 'Transportation as a Factor in Canadian Economic History' and 'Transportation in the Canadian Economy,' in Mary Q. Innis, ed., *Essays in Canadian Economic History* (Toronto 1956) present sharper and condensed versions of the role of transportation in Canada's economic development.

6 Innis, *Fur Trade*, 6

7 Innis, *Canadian Economic History*, 229

8 Leonard Bertram Irwin, *Pacific Railways and Nationalism in the Canadian-American Northwest, 1845–1873* (New York 1968)

9 D.G. Creighton, *The Commercial Empire of the St Lawrence, 1760–1850* (Toronto 1937)

10 Donald Creighton, *John A. Macdonald: The Old Chieftain* (Toronto 1955), 2: 301–2; *The Young Politician* (Toronto 1952)

11 Lorne McDougall, *Canadian Pacific: A Brief History* (Montréal 1968), 1

12 Ibid., 41

13 W. Kaye Lamb, *History of the Canadian Pacific Railway* (New York 1977). Three years earlier, Omer Lavallée's *Van Horne's Road*, an illustrated history, had similarly stressed the technical achievements of the CPR and implicitly reaffirmed the unity theme.

14 Ibid., 16

15 Pierre Berton, *The Great Railway*; 1, *The National Dream, 1871–1881* (Toronto 1970); 2, *The Last Spike, 1881–1885* (1971)

16 Ibid., 1: 389

17 Bill McKee and Georgeen Klassen, *Trail of Iron: The CPR and the Birth of the West* (Vancouver 1983), 185. One can only wonder why the authors use the word iron in their title when the CPR used steel rails.

18 Hugh A. Dempsey, ed., *The CPR West: The Iron Road and the Making of a Nation* (Vancouver 1984)

19 John A. Eagle, *The Canadian Pacific Railway and the Development of Western Canada, 1896-1914* (Kingston and Montréal 1989)

20 Robert Chodos, *The CPR: A Century of Corporate Welfare* (Toronto 1973). This and the works discussed above by no means exhaust the CPR bibliography. Some other secondary works devoted to the railway are Keith Morris, *The Story of the Canadian Pacific Railway* (London 1923); J.H.E. Secretan, *Canada's Great Highway: From the First Stake to the Last Spike* (London 1924); Norman Thompson and J.H. Edgar, *Canadian Railway Development from the Earliest Times* (Toronto 1933). In addition, there are several biographies detailing the lives of heroic characters such as John A. Macdonald, Donald Smith, George Stephen, and William Van Horne. None of the biographers strayed far from the heroic interpretation first enunciated by Oscar D. Skelton in *The Railway Builders: A Chronicle of Overland Highways*: 32, *Chronicles of Canada* (Toronto 1916)

21 Chodos, *The CPR*, 2

22 Maurice Charland, 'Technological Nationalism,' *Canadian Journal of Political and Social Theory* 10, 1-2 (1986), 196–220

23 Ibid., 197

24 William J. Wilgus, *The Railway Interrelations of the United States and Canada* (New Haven 1937)

25 George Grant, *Lament for a Nation: The Defeat of Canadian Nationalism* (Toronto 1965); *Technology and Empire: Perspectives on North America* (Toronto 1969)

26 Grant, *Technology and Empire*, 64

27 Harold A. Innis, *The Bias of Communication* (Toronto 1951); *Empire and Communications* (Toronto 1972). I am indebted for my summary of Innis's thought on the bias of communication techniques to the excellent commentaries

by Arthur Kroker, *Technology and the Canadian Mind: Innis/McLuhan/Grant* (Montréal 1984), and Carl Berger, *The Writing of Canadian History: Aspects of English-Canadian Historical Writing, 1900–1970* (Toronto 1976), 85–111.

28 Charland, 'Technological Nationalism,' 217

29 Ibid.

30 McDougall, *Canadian Pacific*, 20

31 Lamb, *Canadian Pacific Railway*, 17

32 Lewis Mumford, *Technics and Civilization* (New York 1934), 45–59

33 Anthony Arblaster, *The Rise and Decline of Western Liberalism* (Oxford 1984)

34 This study uses the relatively simple definitions for science and technology proposed by A. Rupert Hall in 'Science, Technology and Utopia in the Seventeenth Century' (in Peter Mathias, ed., *Science and Society, 1600–1900* [Cambridge 1972], 33, that is, 'science is ... knowledge of our natural environment, while technology is the exercise of a working control over it.' Peter Mathias, 'Who Unbound Prometheus? Science and Technical Change, 1600–1800' (ibid., 54–80), discusses the gradually increased integration between the two.

35 Bob Goudzwaard, *Capitalism and Progress: A Diagnosis of Western Society* (Toronto 1979), 21–7; Mumford, *Technics and Civilization*, 132

36 Grant, *Technology and Empire*, 20–4

37 Adam Smith, *An Inquiry into the Nature and Causes of the Wealth of Nations* (Oxford 1976), 25–30, 264–7, 456; ibid., R.H. Campbell and A.S. Skinner, 'General Introduction,' 1–66; Robert L. Heilbroner, *The Worldly Philosophers: The Lives, Times, and Ideas of the Great Economic Thinkers* (New York 1961), 34–69

38 Smith, *Wealth of Nations*, 344–6

39 Ibid., 947

40 W.H.B. Court, *A Concise History of Britain from 1750 to Recent Times* (Cambridge 1965), 105–21

41 Victor Ferkiss, *Nature, Technology, and Society: Cultural Roots of the Current Environmental Crisis* (New York 1993), 49–52

42 Modern scholarship suggests that the industrial revolution was a slow and uneven process primarily because of lingering traces of pre-industrial artisanal and craft occupations and the persistent influence of a non-manufacturing business élite. Among the latest works, Jan de Vries, in 'The Industrial Revolution and the Industrious Revolution' (*Journal of Economic History* 54 [June 1994], 249–87), proposes use of the term industrious revolution in a broader historical setting. In his view, the industrious revolution was a 'process of household-based resource reallocation that increased both the supply of marketed commodities and labor and the demand for market-supplied goods. The industrious revolution was a household-level change with important demand-side features that preceded the Industrial Revolution, a supply-side phenomenon.' For an

excellent overview see Pat Hudson, *The Industrial Revolution* (London 1992). For a Canadian perspective see Graham Taylor and Peter Baskerville, *A Concise History of Business in Canada* (Toronto 1994), 84–5.

43 Cited in Michael Adas, *Machines as the Measure of Men: Science, Technology, and Ideologies of Western Dominance* (London 1989), 194
44 Ibid., 199–270
45 Walter E. Houghton, *The Victorian Frame of Mind, 1830–1870* (New Haven 1957), 27–53
46 Richard D. Altick, *Victorian People and Ideas* (New York 1973), 110; Herbert L. Sussman, *Victorians and the Machine: The Literary Response to Technology* (Cambridge 1968), 13–40
47 Thomas Carlyle, 'Signs of the Times,' in *Critical and Miscellaneous Essays* (New York 1969), 2: 60
48 Robert A. Stafford, *Scientist of Empire: Sir Roderick Murchison, Scientific Exploration and Victorian Imperialism* (Cambridge 1989)
49 Cited in Adas, *Machines as Measure*, 218
50 Ibid., 220
51 Rick Szostak, *The Role of Transportation in the Industrial Revolution: A Comparison of England and France* (Montréal and Kingston 1991)
52 M.J. Freeman, 'Introduction,' in Michael J. Freeman and Derek H. Aldcroft, eds, *Transport in Victorian Britain* (Manchester 1988), 1–56
53 Gourvish, 'Railways 1830–70: The Formative Years,' in ibid., 57–91
54 Mumford, *Technics and Civilization*, 199
55 'The Progress of Mechanical Invention,' *Edinburgh Review* (1849), 71
56 Charles Dickens, 'Mr. Dombey Goes upon a Journey,' in *Dombey and Son* (New York, nd), 1: 339
57 Donald Worster, *Nature's Economy: A History of Ecological Ideas* (Cambridge 1994)
58 Douglas John Hall, 'Man and Nature in the Modern West: A Revolution of Images,' in Richard Allen, ed., *Man and Nature on the Prairies* (Regina 1976), 83–6
59 Grant, *Technology and Empire*, 28
60 Daniel Webster, 'Opening of the Northern Railroad to Grafton, NH,' in *The Writings and Speeches of Daniel Webster* (Boston 1903), 4: 107–17
61 Leo Marx, *The Machine in the Garden: Technology and the Pastoral Ideal in America* (London 1964); Clarence Mondale, 'Daniel Webster and Technology,' *American Quarterly* 14 (Spring 1962), 37–47
62 Marx, *Machine in the Garden*, 209–15
63 Ferkiss, *Nature, Technology, and Society*, 64–83
64 Cited in Marx, *Machine in the Garden*, 196

65 Ibid., 192–5
66 Ibid., 75
67 James A. Ward, *Railroads and the Character of America, 1820–1887* (Knoxville 1986), 14
68 Ibid., 22–7
69 *American Railroad Journal*, 28 June 1851, 403
70 The Railroad Jubilee, *Account of the Celebration Commemorative of the Opening of Railroad Communication Between Boston and Canada, Sept 17th, 18th, and 19th, 1851* (Boston 1852), 3
71 Ibid., 48
72 Ibid., 185
73 Ibid., 166
74 Ibid., 94
75 Ibid., 13
76 Goldwin French, 'The Evangelical Creed in Canada,' in W.L. Morton, ed., *The Shield of Achilles: Aspects of Canada in the Victorian Age* (Toronto 1968), 15–35; Michael Gauvreau, *The Evangelical Century: College and Creed in English Canada from the Great Revival to the Great Depression* (Montréal and Kingston 1991). Although many Anglicans, Presbyterians, and Roman Catholics may not have shared the asceticism of the evangelicals, according to S.F. Wise ('God's Peculiar Peoples,' in Morton, *Shield of Achilles*, 36–61) they felt the same sense of divine purpose in their personal and communal lives.
77 French, 'Evangelical Creed in Canada'
78 Carl Berger, *Science, God, and Nature in Victorian Canada* (Toronto 1983)
79 Ibid., 3–18; Suzanne Zeller, *Inventing Canada: Early Victorian Science and the Idea of a Transcontinental Nation* (Toronto 1987), 4–6
80 Zeller, *Inventing Canada.* Nancy Christie, 'Sir William Logan's Geological Empire and the "Humbug" of Economic Utility,' *CHR* 75 (June 1994), 161–204, argues strongly that the Scottish-educated Logan manipulated colonial politicians into thinking he was searching for minerals but that in fact he was doing pure science. She also challenges Zeller's contention that Victorian science helped to invent the idea of a transcontinental Canada. She does not, however, invalidate the utilitarian scientific objectives of colonial politicians and businessmen.
81 Marcia Kline, *Beyond the Land Itself: Views of Nature in Canada and the United States* (Cambridge, Mass., 1970); Gaile McGregor, *The Wacousta Syndrome: Explorations in the Canadian Langscape* (Toronto 1985)
82 Margaret Atwood's *Survival: A Thematic Guide to Canadian Literature* (Toronto 1972) surveys the survival theme in Canadian literature. In chapter 2, 45–67, she discusses Canadians' distrust of nature.
83 Laurence Fallis, 'The Idea of Progress in the Province of Canada: A Study in the

History of Ideas,' in Morton, *Shield of Achilles*, 169–84. The strong thread of pessimism that pervaded Victorian society, identified by Stuart Pierson in 'Miserable Herschel Diagnosed: or, the Mid–Victorian Fear of Stasis' (unpublished paper, Midwest Junto for the History of Science, Norman, Oklahoma, 1994), is entirely absent in nineteenth-century Canada.

84 Fallis, 'Idea of Progress,' 176
85 'Railroad to the Pacific,' *Harbinger* 4 (19 Dec. 1846), 30–1
86 Robert Kelley, *The Transatlantic Persuasion: The Liberal-Democratic Mind in the Age of Gladstone* (New York 1969). Although Kelley's definition of liberal-democratic is more narrowly partisan than the liberal ideology I have described, his views are very useful.

Chapter 2: The Guarantee Act

1 Canada, *Statutes*, 1849, 12 Vic c29. Although popularly known as the Guarantee Act, the legislation was in fact entitled 'An Act to Provide for Affording the Guarantee of the Province to the Bonds of Rail-way Companies on Certain Conditions, and for rendering Assistance in the Construction in the Halifax and Quebec Rail-way.'
2 Adam Smith, *An Inquiry into the Nature and Causes of the Wealth of Nations* (Oxford 1976), 267
3 Canada, *Debates of the Legislative Assembly of United Canada, 1841–1867*, ed. Elizabeth Gibbs (Montréal 1977), 8 (12 April 1849)
4 T.C. Keefer, *Philosophy of Railroads and other Essays*, intro. and ed. H.V. Nelles (Toronto 1972)
5 Ibid., 8
6 Ibid., 9
7 Keefer's naming of Sleepy Hollow is a serendipitous reference to Nathaniel Hawthorne's description of the small, idyllic grove whose Sabbath-like repose was shattered by 'the whistle of the locomotive – the long shriek, harsh, above all other harshness.' *The American Notebooks*, ed. Claude M. Simpson (Ohio State 1972), 27 July 1844
8 Keefer, *Philosophy of Railroads*, 10
9 Ibid., 5
10 Ibid., 35
11 Ibid., 37–8
12 Ibid., 13
13 Ibid., xiii–xv (H.V. Nelles)
14 *Gazette* (Montréal), 5 Feb. 1849
15 Ibid., 8 Jan. 1851

16 *Globe* (Toronto), 14 Sept 1850. See also *Spectator and Journal of Commerce* (Hamilton), 6 Feb. 1850, and *Morning Chronicle* (Québec), 3 Oct. 1850

17 *Morning Chronicle*, 6 Jan. 1851

18 Ibid., 4 June 1850

19 Ibid., 27 Sept. 1850

20 Paul Rutherford, *A Victorian Authority: The Daily Press in Late Nineteenth-Century Canada* (Toronto 1982)

21 W.L. Morton, 'The Conservative Principle in Confederation,' *Queen's Quarterly* 71 (Winter 1964–5), 528–46

22 Gerald M. Craig, *Upper Canada: The Formative Years, 1784–1841* (Toronto 1963), 103–11

23 Jane Errington, *The Lion, the Eagle, and Upper Canada: A Developing Colonial Ideology* (Kingston and Montreal 1987); see also Ian Stewart, 'New Myths for Old: The Loyalists and Maritime Culture,' *JCS* 25 (Summer 1990), 20–43

24 Francis Hincks, *Canada: Its Financial Position and Resources* (London 1849)

25 G.P. de T. Glazebrook, *A History of Transportation in Canada: Continental Strategy to 1867* (Toronto 1964), 1: 63–71

26 Gilbert N. Tucker, *The Canadian Commercial Revolution, 1845–1851* (Toronto 1964), 38–41

27 M.J. Daunton, '"Gentlemanly Capitalism" and British Industry 1820–1914,' *Past & Present* no. 122 (February 1989), 119–58

28 Chester New, *Lord Durham's Mission to Canada* (Toronto 1963); David R. Cameron, 'Lord Durham Then and Now,' *JCS* 25 (Spring 1990), 5–23

29 Lord Durham, *Lord Durham's Report on the Affairs of British North America*, intro. and ed. Sir Charles Lucas (New York 1970), 2: 212–3

30 Ibid., 27–34, 294–5

31 Ibid., 13

32 Ibid., 288

33 Ibid., 13

34 Ibid., 288–94

35 Ibid., 309

36 Ibid., 318

37 Ibid., 319

38 Ibid., 320

39 Ibid., 3: 115–16

40 Glazebrook, *Transportation in Canada*, 76–84

41 Tucker, *Commercial Revolution*, 30–2

42 D.G. Creighton, *The Commercial Empire of the St Lawrence, 1760–1850* (Toronto 1937), 341–8

43 Tucker, *Commercial Revolution*, 63–7

44 David Thompson, *England in the Nineteenth Century, 1815–1914* (Baltimore 1950), 79–81
45 *Gazette*, 6 April 1846
46 J.M.S. Careless, *The Union of the Canadas: The Growth of Canadian Institutions, 1841–1857* (Toronto 1967), 107
47 Canada, Legislative Assembly, *Journals*, 1849, 'Second Report of the Select Committee on the Lumber Trade,' app. PPPP
48 Careless, *Union of the Canadas*, 114–18
49 Jacques Monet, *The Last Cannon Shot: A Study of French-Canadian Nationalism, 1837–1850* (Toronto 1969), 334–53, emphasizes the anti-French feelings among the Tory rioters.
50 John Beverley Robinson, *Canada, and the Canada Bill* (London 1840)
51 Annexation Association of Montreal, *The Annexation Manifesto of 1849* (Montréal 1881)
52 British American League, *Minutes of Proceedings of a Convention of Delegates* (Kingston 1849), 8–12
53 Cephas D. Allin, 'The British North American League, 1849,' Ontario Historical Society *Papers and Records* 13 (1915), 111–15
54 See Gregory S. Kealey, *Toronto Workers Respond to Industrial Capitalism, 1867–1892* (Toronto 1980), 3–12, for a convincing discussion of the role the league played in the rising industrial consciousness of Canada.
55 Samuel Rezneck, 'The Rise and Early Development of Industrial Consciousness in the United States,' *Journal of Economic and Business History* 4 (August 1932), 784–7
56 Alexander Hamilton, 'Report on Manufactures,' 5 Dec. 1791 in *The Reports of Alexander Hamilton*, ed. Jacob E. Cooke (New York 1964), 115–205
57 Thomas C. Cochrane and William Miller, *The Age of Enterprise: A Social History of Industrial America* (New York 1961), 16–50
58 Friedrich List, *The National System of Political Economy*, trans. Sampson S. Lloyd (London 1885). The original German edition appeared in 1841.
59 John Rae, 'Sketches of the Origin and Progress of Manufacturers and of the Policy which has Regulated their Legislative Encouragement in Great Britain and in Other Countries,' *Canadian Review and Literary and Historical Journal* no. 3 (March 1825) in R. Warren James, *John Rae: Political Economist: An Account of His Life and a Compilation of His Main Writings: Life and Miscellaneous Writings* (Toronto 1965), 1: 195–206
60 Robert Gourlay, *Statistical Account of Upper Canada* (New York 1966), 2: 666–80
61 Orville John McDiarmid, *Commercial Policy in the Canadian Economy* (Cambridge 1946,) 53–66

62 NAC, Colonial Office Records, vol. 114 (G126), Grey to Elgin, 31 Dec. 1846; Ged Martin, *Britain and the Origins of Canadian Confederation, 1837–67* (Vancouver 1995), 84–94, 207–10

63 Grey to Elgin, 2 Feb. 1847, in *The Elgin-Grey Papers, 1846–1852*, ed. Arthur G. Doughty (Ottawa 1937), 1: 12

64 NAC, Colonial Office Records, vol. 118 (G130), Grey to Elgin, 11 Feb. 1848

65 R.B. Sullivan, *Lecture Delivered before the Mechanics' Institute of Hamilton on the Connection Between the Agriculture and the Manufactures of Canada* (Hamilton 1848), 16

66 *Globe* (Toronto), 10 June 1851

67 Elgin to Grey, 4 Jan. 1849, in *Elgin-Grey Papers*, 1: 278–80

68 Chepas D. Allin and George M. Jones, *Annexation, Preferential Trade and Reciprocity* (Westport, Conn., 1971)

69 G.R. Stevens, *Canadian National Railways: Sixty Years of Trial and Error, 1836–1896* (Toronto 1960), 44–52

70 W.M. Robinson, 'Report on the Halifax-Quebec Railway,' in Canada, Legislative Assembly, *Journals*, 1849, app. N

71 Grey to Elgin, 14 April 1848, in *Elgin-Grey Papers*, 1: 138

72 Grey to Elgin, 18 May 1848, in ibid., 1: 147

73 Grey to Elgin, 22 March 1848, in ibid., 1: 125–7

74 Grey to Elgin, 16 and 24 Nov. 1848, in ibid., 1: 251–5

75 Ronald Stewart Longley, *Sir Francis Hincks: A Study of Canadian Politics, Railways and Finance in the Nineteenth Century* (Toronto 1943), 188

76 Elgin to Grey, 27 May 1847, in *Elgin-Grey Papers*, 1: 47

77 Elgin to Grey, 9 Dec. 1847, in ibid., 1: 102

78 Elgin to Grey, 19 Dec. 1848, in ibid., 1: 275–6

79 Elgin to Grey, 20 Dec. 1848, in ibid., 1: 277

80 Nova Scotia, Legislative Assembly, *Journals*, 1847, 539

81 Richard Henry Bonnycastle, *Canada and the Canadians in 1846* (London 1846), 1: 138

82 Donald MacKay, *The Asian Dream: The Pacific Rim and Canada's National Railway* (Vancouver 1986) is a modern and nicely illustrated exposition of John Murray Gibbon, *Steel of Empire: The Romantic History of the Canadian Pacific: The North West Passage of Today* (New York 1937).

83 Edward Chase Kirkland, *Men, Cities and Transportation: A Study in New England History, 1820–1900* (New York 1948), 206–10

84 A.T. Galt, *A Letter to the Chairman and Deputy Chairman of the North American Colonial Association* (London 1847), 7

85 Gerald J.J. Tulchinsky, *The River Barons: Montreal Businessmen and the Growth of Industry and Transportation, 1837–1853* (Toronto 1977), 140–7

86 NAC, Executive Council Office Records, Book J, vol. 71, 'Memorandum on Immigration and on Public Works as Connected Therewith,' 20 Dec. 1848

87 Longley, *Francis Hincks*, 31–8; William G. Ormsby, 'Sir Francis Hincks,' *DCB* 11: 406–16

88 Careless, *Union of the Canadas*, 67–70

89 Francis Hincks, *Canada: Its Financial Position and Resources* (London 1849)

90 Michael J. Piva, 'Continuity and Crisis: Francis Hincks and Canadian Economic Policy' *CHR* 66 (June 1985), 185–210, argues strongly against interpreting Hincks's policies as being in any way a new departure.

91 NAC, Executive Council Office, Book J, vol. 71, 'Memorandum on Immigration'

92 The New York Central was formed in 1853 out of several small New England railways.

93 Canada, *Statutes*, 1849, 12 Vic c29

94 Canada, *Debates*, 11 April 1849

95 Donald R. Beer, *Sir Allan Napier MacNab* (Hamilton 1984); Peter Baskerville, 'Allan Napier MacNab,' *DCB* 9: 519–27

96 Russell D. Smith, 'The Early Years of the Great Western Railway, 1833–1857,' *Ontario History* 60 (December 1968), 205–28

97 *Globe*, 1 July 1851

98 Canada, *Debates*, 11 April 1849

99 Brian Young, *George-Etienne Cartier: Montreal Bourgeois* (Kingston and Montreal 1981), 48–56

100 Canada, *Debates*, 11 April 1849

101 Ibid.

102 NAC, Executive Council Office, Book J, vol. 71, 'Memorandum on Immigration'

103 Stevens, *Canadian National*, 59, ties the Guarantee Act too strongly to the Halifax-Québec scheme. While technically correct, Steven's position fails to note Hincks's negative views on the road and his belief that no British capitalist would invest in the scheme.

104 Canada, *Debates*, 12 April 1849

105 Tulchinsky, *River Barons*, 148–68

106 Stevens, *Canadian National*, 389–99

107 Smith, 'Great Western Railway,' 205–28

108 Robinson, 'Halifax-Quebec Railway'

Chapter 3: Nova Scotia

1 Joseph Andrew Chisholm, *The Speeches and Public Letters of Joseph Howe 2, 1849–1873* (Halifax 1909), 170

2 *Herald* (Yarmouth), 21 June 1851
3 A different view is presented by Kenneth G. Pryke (*Nova Scotia and Confederation 1864–74* [Toronto 1979], ix): 'Suddenly in the mid–1860s Nova Scotia had to respond to an entirely new set of challenges and priorities in which other groups had claimed the initiative, had formulated policies, and Nova Scotia, unprepared and apathetic, had no alternative but to enter the Canadian Confederation.' Much earlier, D.C. Harvey ('The Maritime Provinces and Confederation,' Canadian Historical Association *Annual Report 1927*, 43) concluded that 'the Maritimes were honest dupes of their own enthusiasm as much as of the promises of Canadian Delegates.' In a more recent work, James L. Sturgis ('The Opposition to Confederation in Nova Scotia, 1864–1868,' in Ged Martin, ed., *The Causes of Canadian Confederation* [Fredericton 1990], 114–29) argues that the opposition in Nova Scotia was animated by the spirit and soul of a people content with existing conditions. On the other hand, Phillip Buckner ('The Maritimes and Confederation: A Reassessment,' in Martin, *Causes of Confederation*) challenges the common perception that Atlantic Canada's lack of enthusiasm for union revealed its inherent conservatism, a 'series of parochial communities content with the status quo and trapped in intellectual lethargy' (86). According to Buckner, the argument that Maritimers were dragged kicking and screaming into confederation is misleading because it underestimates the degree of support for Confederation in the region, oversimplifies the nuances in the debate, and trivializes the substantive objections that Maritimers voiced against the kind of union they were forced to accept.
4 Graeme Wynn, 'Ideology, Society, and State in the Maritime Colonies of British North America, 1840–1860,' in Allan Greer and Ian Radforth, eds, *Colonial Leviathan: State Formation in Mid-Nineteenth-Century Canada* (Toronto 1992), 284–328
5 Marilyn Gerriets, 'The Impact of the General Mining Association on the Nova Scotia Coal Industry, 1826–1850,' *Acadiensis* 21 (Autumn 1991), 54–8
6 Eric W. Sager and Gerald E. Panting, *Maritime Capital: The Shipping Industry in Atlantic Canada, 1820–1914* (Montreal and Kingston 1990), 23–77
7 Although her study falls outside Nova Scotia, Rosemary E. Ommer, 'The Truck System in Gaspé, 1822–77,' *Acadiensis* 19 (Fall 1989), 91–114, provides a nicely detailed analysis of a typical large fishing firm. See also Ommer, *From Outpost to Outport: A Structural Analysis of the Jersey-Gaspé Cod Fishery* (Montreal and Kingston 1991) and James K. Hiller, 'The Newfoundland Credit System: An Interpretation,' in Ommer, ed., *Merchant Credit and Labour Strategies in Historical Perspective* (Fredericton, 1990).
8 Rusty Bittermann, 'The Hierarchy of the Soil: Land and Labour in a Nineteenth-Century Cape Breton Community,' *Acadiensis* 18 (Autumn 1988), 33–55; Rusty Bittermann, Robert A. Mackinnon, and Graeme Wynn, 'Of Inequal-

ity and Interdependence in the Nova Scotian Countryside,' *CHR* 74 (March 1993), 1–43.

9 Maritimes historiography is flourishing under an extremely lively debate that centres around the question of regional underdevelopment. One question concerns the problem of retarded industrialization, while another focuses on Nova Scotia's so-called Golden Age, that is, the decades bracketing confederation. Among the latest contributions to this voluminous literature, and useful in the preparation of the preceding paragraph, were Julian Gwyn and Fazley Siddiq, 'Wealth Distribution in Nova Scotia during the Confederation Era, 1851 and 1871,' *CHR* 73 (December 1992), 435–52; Kris Inwood and Phyllis Wagg, 'Wealth and Prosperity in Nova Scotian Agriculture, 1851–71,' *CHR* 75 (June 1994), 239–64. The debate is nicely summarized in Graham D. Taylor and Peter A. Baskerville, *A Concise History of Business in Canada* (Toronto 1994).

10 Wynn, 'Ideology, Society,' 321

11 Thomas Chandler Haliburton, *The Sam Slick Anthology* (Toronto 1969)

12 D.C. Harvey, 'The Spacious Days of Nova Scotia,'*Dalhousie Review* 19, no. 2 (July 1939), 133–42; Harvey, 'The Intellectual Awakening of Nova Scotia,' in G.A. Rawlyk, ed., *Historical Essays on the Atlantic Provinces* (Toronto 1967), 99–121

13 The following sketch of Joseph Howe is based on J. Murray Beck, 'Joseph Howe,' *DCB* 10: 362–70, and on three essays in Wayne A. Hunt, ed., *The Proceedings of the Joseph Howe Symposium* (Sackville 1984), namely, J. Murray Beck, 'Joseph Howe – A Liberal, but with Qualifications'; George A. Rawlyk, 'J.M. Beck's Joseph Howe'; and David A. Sutherland, 'Joseph Howe and the Boosting of Halifax.'

14 J. Murray Beck, *Joseph Howe: The Briton Becomes Canadian 1848–1873* (Montréal and Kingston 1983), 2: 10

15 Rosemarie Patricia Langhout, 'Public Enterprise: An Analysis of Public Finance in the Maritime Colonies during the Period of Responsible Government' (PhD dissertation, University of New Brunswick, 1989, 1–4) contains a superb discussion of the radical restructuring of traditional patterns of public finance as a result of responsible government.

16 Howe to Moffatt, 8 May 1849, in Chisholm, *Speeches of Howe*, 25

17 Nova Scotia, House of Assembly, *Journals*, 1850, app. 17, 56–7

18 Ibid., app. 83, 246–52

19 Chisholm, *Speeches of Howe*, 76

20 *Morning Chronicle*, 5 Feb. 1853, cited by Beck, *Joseph Howe*, 2: 32

21 PANS, RG28A, Railways, sect. 4, vol. 12, Intercolonial Railway, Minutes of meeting in Cumberland, 30 Jan. 1846

22 *Novascotian*, 21 May 1849
23 Chisholm, *Speeches of Howe*, 83
24 Ibid., 91
25 Ibid., 95–6
26 PANS, RG1A, vol. 199, Minutes of the Council, 28 Aug. 1850
27 Harvey, 'Intellectual Awakening,' 101–14
28 David Sutherland, 'Halifax Merchants and the Pursuit of Development 1783–1850,' *CHR* 59 (March 1978), 1–17; Taylor and Baskerville, *History of Business*, 111–13
29 Howe to Grey, 25 Nov. 1850, in Chisholm, *Speeches of Howe*, 105–40
30 Ibid., 112
31 Chisholm, *Speeches of Howe*, 175–6
32 Nova Scotia, *Journals*, 1852, 29 Nov. 1851, 47
33 Chisholm, *Speeches of Howe*, 168
34 Ibid., 137–9
35 Victor Ferkiss, *Nature, Technology, and Society: Cultural Roots of the Current Environmental Crisis* (New York 1993), 65–71
36 Roderick Nash, *Wilderness and the American Mind* (New Haven 1973), 35–8
37 Chisholm, *Speeches of Howe*, 170
38 Ibid., 181
39 As his title implies, Doug Owram, in *Promise of Eden: The Canadian Expansionist Movement and the Idea of the West, 1856–1900* (Toronto 1980), describes the evolution of the Canadian westward expansionist movement, but even after 1867 his expansionists do not include Nova Scotians.
40 Chisholm, *Speeches of Howe*, 184
41 Ibid., 142
42 Ibid., 168
43 Ibid., 169
44 Ibid., 108
45 Ibid., 113
46 Ibid., 196
47 Ibid., 189
48 Canada, Legislative Assembly, *Debates*, 1851, copy of Howe's Report to the Assembly, 11 Aug. 1851, 1311
49 Michael Adas, *Machines as the Measure of Men: Science, Technology, and Ideologies of Western Dominance* (Ithaca 1989), 223
50 Nova Scotia, *Journals*, 1852, app. 10, Grey to Harvey, 27 Nov. 1851, 37
51 Ibid., Grey to Harvey, 9 Jan. 1852, 47
52 Chisholm, *Speeches of Howe*, 230–1; Nova Scotia, *Journals*, 1852, app. 10, Howe to Harvey, 11 Dec. 1851, 38–41

53 Nova Scotia, *Journals*, 1852, app. 10, Hincks, Taché, Young, memo, 29 Jan. 1852, 53

54 Ibid., Chandler, 31 Jan. 1852, 56–7

55 *Morning Sun* (Halifax), 2 Sept. 1850

56 Chisholm, *Speeches of Howe*, 86. The Shubenacadie Canal, commenced in 1826 after decades of planning and studies, had a troubled history of inadequate financing, government subsidies, and periodic bankruptcies. It was still not fully operational at the time of Howe's speech. Not completed until 1861, it could not compete with the Nova Scotia Railway and was abandoned at the end of the decade. See Barbara Grantmyre, 'The Canal That Bisected Nova Scotia,' *Canadian Geographical Journal* 88 (January 1974), 20–7.

57 *British Colonist* (Halifax), 21 Feb. 1854. From 1851 to 1855 the paper was called *The British Colonist and North American Railway Journal*.

58 Ibid.

59 Ibid., 21, 25, and 28 Feb. 1854

60 Ibid., 21 Feb. 1854

61 Beck, *Joseph Howe*, 63

62 David Alexander and Gerry Panting, 'The Mercantile Fleet and Its Owners: Yarmouth, Nova Scotia, 1840–1889,' *Acadiensis* 7 (Spring 1978), 3–28

63 *Herald* (Yarmouth), 3 Oct. 1850

64 Ibid., 12 Sept. 1850

65 Ibid., 21 June 1851

66 *British Colonist*, 23 Sept. 1854

67 Alfred D. Chandler Jr, 'Patterns of American Railroad Finance, 1830–50,' *Business History Review* 28 (September 1954), 249

68 Sutherland, 'Halifax Merchants'; Sager and Panting, *Maritime Capital* partially blame the collapse of the post-confederation Maritime shipbuilding industry on the concentration of capital in land-based enterprises. While this is a highly satisfactory answer for their problem of why Maritime shipping failed to adapt to iron and steam technology, it does not take into account the seaward emphasis in the pre-confederation period. In fact, private capital's failure to invest in railways may help explain Nova Scotia's inability to industrialize its economy. See Rick Szostak, *The Role of Transportation in the Industrial Revolution: A Comparison of England and France* (Montreal and Kingston 1991).

69 Langhout, 'Public Enterprise,' 46–8. The doctrines of free trade did permit 'bounties' to unprofitable industries in order to attract investors. See Adam Smith, *An Inquiry into the Nature and Causes of the Wealth of Nations* (Oxford 1976), 1: 505–23.

70 David E. Stephens, *Iron Roads: Railways of Nova Scotia* (Windsor, NS, 1972), 23–7; Beck; *Joseph Howe*, 71–5, 96–9, 127

71 Nova Scotia, *Journals*, 1856, app. 4, Howe to Baring, 20 June 1855, 37–8; Howe to Wilkins, 19 July 1855, 39; Wilkins to Howe, 19 July 1855, 40

72 Langhout, 'Public Enterprise,' 143–7, 152, 223–5

73 PANS, RG31–101, vol. 18, Receiver General's Office, James McNab Letterbook, Brown to Baring Brothers, 21 May 1857

74 Nova Scotia, *Debates*, 9 April 1857

75 Donald Howard Tait, 'The Role of Charles Tupper in Nova Scotia Politics, 1855 to 1870,' MA thesis, Dalhousie University, 1962, 2–13

76 Nova Scotia, *Debates*, 4 Feb. 1856

77 Nova Scotia, *Journals*, 1858, Laurie's Railway Report, app. 35, 282; cited in Langhout, 'Public Enterprise,' 51

78 Tait, 'Charles Tupper,' 8–13, 49, 79–90, 123–4, 212–16

79 Charles Tupper, *Recollections of Sixty Years in Canada* (Toronto 1914), Speech, Mechanics Institute, Saint John, 1860

80 NAC, Baring papers, vol. 4, Tupper and Henry to Baring, 14 July 1865; Baring to Tupper, 2 Aug. 1865

81 PANS, RG1, vol. 456, no. 33, Fleming to Brydges, 10 Dec. 1864

82 Beck, *Joseph Howe*, 125

83 Nova Scotia, *Debates*, 8 March 1864

84 Ibid., 28 March 1864

85 Ibid., 10 April 1865

86 Ibid., 5 April 1866

87 Ibid., 11 March 1864

88 Ibid., 12 April 1865

89 Ibid., 14 March 1864

90 NAC, Howe Papers, vol. 8, Howe to Bruce, 1 Aug. 1865

91 Beck, *Joseph Howe*, 186

92 Langhout, 'Public Enterprise,' 92–3

93 Nova Scotia, *Debates*, 13 April 1865

94 Ibid., 5 April 1866

95 Ibid.

96 Ibid., 17 April 1865

97 Ibid.

98 Ibid.

99 Delphin A. Muise, 'The Federal Election of 1867 in Nova Scotia: An Economic Interpretation,' *Nova Scotia Historical Society Collections* 36 (1968), 327–51, described the economic dichotomy evident in the province's confederation debate, arguing that the 1867 election represented the first clash between the Atlantic and continental visions. Obviously, that clash was apparent in the legislature since the early 1850s. See also his 'Parties and Constituencies: Federal

Elections in Nova Scotia 1867–96,' *Canadian Historical Association Historical Papers*, 1971, 183–202

100 Langhout, 'Public Enterprise,' 127, 160–3
101 Szostak, *Role of Transportation*

Chapter 4: The Grand Trunk Railway

1 Cited in Walter E. Houghton, *The Victorian Frame of Mind 1830–1870* (New Haven 1957), 43–4
2 J.M. Trout and Edward Trout, *The Railways of Canada for 1870–1* (Toronto 1871), 81–2, 86
3 Ronald Hyam, *Britain's Imperial Century 1815–1914: A Study of Empire and Expansion* (New York 1976), 31–6
4 John Gallagher and Ronald Robinson, 'The Imperialism of Free Trade,' *Economic History Review*, 2nd ser., 6, no. 1 (1953), 1–15. This seminal article launched a furious debate among imperial historians. Two dated but still useful introductions to the discussion are P.J. Cain, *Economic Foundations of British Overseas Expansion 1815–1914* (London 1980) and Roger Louis, *Imperialism: The Robinson and Gallagher Controversy* (New York 1976). An angry Canadian assessment of the impact of the informal empire thesis is Philip Buckner, 'Presidential Address: Whatever Happened to the British Empire?' *Journal of the Canadian Historical Association* (1993), 3–32.
5 Daniel R. Headrick, *The Tentacles of Progress: Technology Transfer in the Age of Imperialism, 1850–1940* (New York 1988)
6 Ronald Robinson, 'Introduction: Railway Imperialism,' and 'Conclusion: Railways and Informal Empire,' in Clarence B. Davis and Kenneth E. Wilburn, eds, *Railway Imperialism* (New York 1991), 3. As a logical outgrowth of his informal-empire construct, Robinson's model of railway imperialism provides useful insights in the history of British North American railways. Unfortunately, it is overly empire-centred and conspiratorial.
7 Lance E. Davis and Robert A. Huttenbach (*Mammon and the Pursuit of Empire: The Political Economy of British Imperialism, 1860–1912* [Cambridge 1986], 42–60) demonstrate that, while North America was the major recipient of British overseas investment during the last half of the nineteenth century, Canada received only a minor portion. The United States was the favoured destination.
8 Hyam, *Imperial Century*, 166–80
9 D.C.M. Platt and Jeremy Adelman, 'London Merchant Bankers in the First Phase of Heavy Borrowing: The Grand Trunk Railway of Canada,' *Journal of Imperial and Commonwealth History* 18 (May 1990), 208–27. Platt is a well-

known critic of the informal-empire thesis. See his 'The Imperialism of Free Trade: Some Reservations,' *Economic History Review*, 2nd ser., 21, no. 2 (1968), 296–306; and 'Further Objections to an "Imperialism of Free Trade,"' *Economic History Review*, 2nd ser., 26 (February 1973), 77–91. In his article with Adelman, Platt argues that the Grand Trunk's British investors did not manipulate the colonists and that the latter were not victims of imperialism. For a contrary, but simplistic, view see Donald W. Roman, 'Railway Imperialism in Canada,' in Davis and Wilburn, eds, *Railway Imperialism*.

10 The standard history of the Grand Trunk Railway is A.W. Currie, *The Grand Trunk Railway of Canada* (Toronto 1957). A more critical, acerbic interpretation is G.R. Stevens, *Canadian National Railways: Sixty Years of Trial and Error (1836–1896)* (Toronto 1960).

11 Currie, *Grand Trunk*, 1–18

12 Canada, *Statutes*, 1851, Vic 14&15 c73

13 NAC, Baring Bros Records, Baring to Hincks, 31 Oct. 1850, 17 Dec. 1851

14 Ibid., Hincks to Baring, 17 April 1851

15 Canada, *Statutes*, 1852, Vic 16 c22

16 Canada, Legislative Assembly, *Journals*, 1857, app. 6, Committee on the Grand Trunk Railway; Currie, *Grand Trunk*, 22–3. For a very critical view, see Stevens, *Canadian National*, 1: 245.

17 Currie, *Grand Trunk*, 22–3; Platt and Adelman, 'London Bankers,' cite a Baring letter to Rose, 17 Dec. 1851, in which the former suggests Canadian negotiators conned him and Glyn to accept membership on the board of directors. Of course, both gentlemen had the power to resign from the board at any time.

18 Currie, *Grand Trunk*, 53–74

19 Canada, *Statutes*, 1855, Vic 18 c174

20 Canada, Legislative Assembly, *Journals*, 1857, Committee on the Grand Trunk Railway, 2 June 1857, app. 6, Holmes testimony; NAC, vol. 1000, Grand Trunk Railway, Minute Book, Canadian Board, 6 July 1857

21 NAC, vol. 1000, Grand Trunk Railway, Minute Book, Canadian Board, 7 May 1857; Canada, Legislative Assembly, *Debates*, 6 May 1857

22 *Globe* (Toronto), 13 May 1857

23 Canada, Legislative Assembly, *Journals*, 1857, Committee on the Grand Trunk Railway, 2 June 1857, app. 6, Holmes testimony

24 Ibid.; NAC, vol. 1000, Grand Trunk Railway, Minute Book, Canadian Board, 6 July 1857

25 NAC, Glyn Papers, Glyn to Galt, 8 Oct. 1857

26 *Canadian News* (London), 21 Nov. 1860

27 *Times* (London), 12 June 1861

28 Canada, Legislative Assembly, *Journals*, 1858, 7 July, 815

29 Ibid., *Debates*, 5 July 1858

30 A.T. Galt, *Canada: 1849 to 1859* (London 1860), 40–1. Galt hoped that the tariff would make up $5.2 million or 70 per cent of expected revenues and anticipated an actual gain of $0.5 million or an increase of 10 per cent in revenues. Canada, *Debates*, 11 March 1859

31 D.F. Barnett, 'The Galt Tariff: Incidental or Effective Protection?' *CJE* 9 (August 1976), 407. The 1859 Galt tariff has sparked a lively historical debate. On one side, most historians have claimed the Galt tariff was intended mainly to raise revenue; any 'protection' it might have provided was merely a by-product. On the other side, a small minority continues to argue for a deliberate protectionist interpretation of the Galt tariff. See Barnett's essay cited above and my own 'Alexander Galt, the 1859 Tariff, and Canadian Economic Nationalism,' *CHR* 63 (June 1982), 151–78. Michael J. Piva ('Government Finance and the Development of the Canadian State,' in Allan Greer and Ian Radforth, eds, *Colonial Leviathan: State Formation in Mid-Nineteenth-Century Canada* [Toronto 1992], 271–4) and Graham D. Taylor and Peter A. Baskerville (*A Concise History of Business in Canada* [Toronto 1994], 240–2) still prefer the revenue-and-incidental-protection argument. Kenneth Norrie and Douglas Owram (*A History of the Canadian Economy* [Toronto 1991], 242) chose a protectionist interpretation.

32 Canada, *Debates*, 11 March 1859

33 Galt, *Canada*, 25

34 J.H. Dales, *The Protective Tariff in Canada's Development* (Toronto 1966), 145–7, argues that not only was Galt's a revenue tariff but it was an inefficient means of paying for Canada's canals and railways; subsidies, he contends, would have been a better way. This statement overlooks the fact that the canals and railways had already been built and that the tariff was needed to pay for existing subsidies for these ventures. As Galt pointed out repeatedly, there were no other sources of revenue the government could tap.

35 Canada, *Debates*, 11 March 1859

36 Ibid. Few commentators have read Galt's budget speech and seem to have missed his 'national policy' theme and call for commercial protection.

37 Canada, *Debates*, 14, 15, and 16 March 1859

38 The Toronto Board of Trade, which consisted primarily of wholesale traders, for example, opposed the 1859 tariff. Yet as Douglas McCalla ('The Commercial Politics of the Toronto Board of Trade, 1850–1860,' *CHR* 50 [March 1969], 58–9) points out, its objections were less doctrinaire than on previous occasions because of the influence of strong protectionist interests.

39 *Globe* (Toronto), 11 March 1859

40 J.M.S. Careless, 'The Toronto *Globe* and Agrarian Radicalism, 1850–67,' *CHR* 29 (March 1948), 14–39; McCalla, 'Commercial Politics,' 51–67

41 Among his well-known criticisms of the National Policy, J.H. Dales ('"National Policy" Myths, Past and Present,' *JCS* 14 [Fall 1979], 92–4) makes the telling point that the policy exacerbated provincialism and regionalism in Canada's political life. Although Toronto does not spring to mind as one of the victims of the National Policy, Dales's comment is a valuable insight, as the Brown-Galt controversy attests.

42 H.C. Pentland, 'The Role of Capital in Canadian Economic Development before 1875,' *CJEPS* 16 (November 1950), 457–74

43 *Times*, 21 Dec. 1860

44 Ibid., 8 Nov. 1860

45 NAC, Grand Trunk Railway, Minute Book, London Board, 30 July 1861

46 Ibid., Canadian Board, 8 Dec. 1862; Canada, *Statutes*, 1862, 25 Vic c56; Currie, *Grand Trunk*, 81–2; Ann M. Carlos and Frank D. Lewis ('The Creative Financing of an Unprofitable Enterprise: The Grand Trunk Railway of Canada, 1853–1881,' *Explorations in Economic History* 32 [July 1995], 273–301) argue that London investors kept their confidence in the Grand Trunk because they believed that the Canadian government would bail out the company should it face bankruptcy. The continued devaluation of the status of government debentures seemed to lend credence to this argument.

47 Grand Trunk Railway, *Directors' Report*, 24 Dec. 1861

48 Currie, *Grand Trunk*, 99–102

49 NAC, Grand Trunk Railway, Minute Book, Canadian Board, 27 Sept. 1853

50 Ibid., 18 Oct. 1861; Minute Book, London Board, 21 Nov. 1861, 1 and 23 Jan. 1862

51 *Herepath's Railway Journal* (London), 25 Jan., 1 Feb. 1862; Grand Trunk Railway, *Directors' Report*, 31 Dec. 1862, 30 June 1864

52 E.W. Watkin, *Canada and the States: Recollections, 1851 to 1886* (London 1887), Watkin to Baring, 13 Nov. 1860, 12–13

53 Ibid., 14

54 Ibid., 62

55 G.S. Dunbar, 'Isotherms and Politics: Perception of the Northwest in the 1850's,' in Anthony W. Rasporich and Henry C. Klassen, eds, *Prairie Perspectives 2* (Toronto 1973), 80–101

56 Doug Owram, *Promise of Eden: The Canadian Expansionist Movement and the Idea of the West, 1856–1900* (Toronto 1980), 38–58

57 Henry Youle Hind, *Narrative of the Canadian Red River Exploring Expedition of 1857 and of the Assiniboine and Saskatchewan Exploring Expedition of 1858* (Edmonton 1971), 2: 233–6; Irene M. Spry, *The Palliser Expedition: An Account of John Palliser's British North American Exploring Expedition, 1857–1860* (Toronto 1973), 283–4

58 Canada, *Journals*, 12 Aug. 1858, 1024

59 For detailed accounts of the negotiations for the transfer of Rupert's Land, see John S. Galbraith, *The Hudson's Bay Company as an Imperial Factor, 1821–1869* (New York 1977) and W.L. Morton, *The Critical Years: The Union of British North America 1857–1873* (Toronto 1964).

60 Watkin, *Canada and the States*, x

61 Michael Adas, *Machines as the Measure of Men: Science, Technology, and Ideologies of Western Dominance* (Ithaca 1989)

62 Hyam, *Imperial Century*, 54–9

63 Watkin, *Canada and the States*, vii

64 Ibid., 2

65 Ibid., 57–8

66 *Railway Times* (London), 11 July 1863

67 Owram, *Promise of Eden*, 59–78

68 Ged Martin, *Britain and the Origins of Canadian Confederation, 1837–67* (Vancouver 1995) correctly points to the long history of British support for confederation. His criticisms of traditional interpretations of the union movement, especially his views on the role of the intercolonial, appear to create more problems than they resolve.

69 Watkin, *Canada and the States*, 16

70 NAC, Newcastle Papers, ICR miscellaneous file, Newcastle, 11 March 1862, Remarks on Memo on the Intercolonial Railway

71 Watkin, *Canada and the States*, 65

72 Ibid., 11

73 Gene Lawrence Allen, 'The Origins of the Intercolonial Railway, 1835–1869,' PhD dissertation, University of Toronto, 1991, 291–2

74 *Canadian News* (London), 6 Feb. 1862; Allen, 'Origins of the Intercolonial,' 297–9

75 *Globe* (Toronto), 1 Oct. 1861

76 *Le Pays* (Montréal), 19 Oct. 1861

77 Allen, 'Origins of the Intercolonial,' 280–333

78 *Le Pays*, 20 Sept. 1862

79 Piva, 'Government Finance,' 271–4

80 Morton, *Critical Years*, 111

81 Peter Baskerville, 'Imperial Agendas and "Disloyal" Collaborators: Decolonization and the John Sandfield Macdonald Ministries, 1862–1864,' in David Keane and Colin Read, eds, *Old Ontario: Essays in Honour of J.M.S. Careless* (Toronto 1990), 243

82 Morton, *Critical Years*, 118–36

83 Owram, *Promise of Eden*, 41–6; J.M.S. Careless, *Brown of the Globe: 1818–*

1859, The Voice of Upper Canada; 1860–1880, Statesman of Confederation
(Toronto 1959, 1963)
84 NAC, Howe Papers, vol. 3, Macdonald to Howe, 18 Oct. 1862, 521–4
85 NAC, Colonial Office, 42/635, Memo by the Executive Council on the Inter-colonial Railway, 22 Oct. 1862
86 NAC, Newcastle Papers, Letterbook B-4, Newcastle to Monck, 20 June 1863
87 Karen Anderson, 'The Organization of Capital for the Development of the Canadian West,' MA thesis, University of Regina, 1974, 36–74; Elaine A. Mitchell, 'Edward Watkin and the Buying-Out of the Hudson's Bay Company,' *CHR* 34 (September 1953), 219–44
88 NAC, Watkin Papers, Confidential Proof Prospectus, Atlantic and Pacific Transit and Telegraph Company Limited
89 Newcastle to Watkin, 6 Jan. 1863 in Watkin, *Canada and the States*, 104–5
90 NAC, Governor General Papers, vol. 157, Fortescue to Watkin, 1 May 1863, 270–9
91 NAC, Baring Papers, Watkin to Baring Bros, undated 1607–14
92 Ibid., Watkin to Head, 24 July 1863
93 NAC/HBC, Head to Dallas, Private Locked Letterbook, 22 Jan. 1864
94 Ibid., A7/4, Head to Watkin, 18 Aug. 1863, 6
95 NAC, Watkin Papers, Fraser to Watkin, 13 Aug. 1863
96 NAC/HBCA, A2/3, General Court Minutes, 21 June 1864; Canada, Report of the Executive Council, 18 Feb. 1864
97 *Railway Times* (London), 1 March 1862
98 Ibid., 21 June 1862
99 Edward Whelan, *The Union of the British Provinces* (Charlottetown 1865), 72–3
100 In an interesting and convincing econometrics exercise Ann M. Carlos and Frank Lewis ('The Profitability of Early Canadian Railroads: Evidence from the Grand Trunk and Great Western Railway Companies,' in Claudia Goldin and Hugh Rockoff, *Strategic Factors in Nineteenth Century American Economic History* [Chicago 1992]) conclude that government subsidies were not sufficient to make the Grand Trunk profitable. Whether the railway was socially profitable is questionable, they argue, but from a financial perspective, it certainly was built prematurely.
101 Hyam, *Imperial Century*, 63–7, notes that informal imperial governments require mediating friends or collaborators in the colonies to carry out their policies. As an offspring of the informal-empire thesis, the literature on railway imperialism scorns these collaborators. Ronald Robinson, 'Introduction: Railway Imperialism,' 4, concludes: 'The railroad, up to 1914, was thus a main generator of those insidious partnerships of imperial, financial, and commer-

cial interests that go into the making of "informal" empires.' Peter Baskerville, in 'Imperial Agendas,' appears to accept that disapproving interpretation. While his argument – that the J.S. Macdonald ministries had an active and comprehensive legislative and administrative program to counter undue imperial pressures – is skilful and convincing, his contention that the other crowd was made up of unscrupulous collaborators is less persuasive. Luther Holton, J.S. Macdonald's minister of finance and, according to Baskerville, the chief architect of the fiscal reforms, not only was Alexander Galt's successor but also his business partner in Gzowski & Company, a contracting firm that nearly bankrupted the newborn Grand Trunk Railway at considerable personal profit.

Chapter 5: Saint John

1 Cited by Leonard Tilley, New Brunswick's premier, at the 1866 constitutional conference in London when he suggested the name Dominion of Canada.
2 *Hansard's Debates*, Parliamentary Debates, 3rd ser., 204 (6 March 1871), 1366–7
3 My position, that Maritimers actively debated and sought confederation, varies from that of New Brunswick's historian W.S. MacNutt, who wrote, 'A few leaders of imagination and daring had made themselves the instruments of the grand idea that was British North America's response to the problem of the time, to the urge for mergers and the manufacturing of great states ... [New Brunswick] bowed to the will of those from without. [Leonard] Tilley, [Peter] Mitchell, [Charles] Fisher, were servants of a Canadian initiative.' W.S. MacNutt, *New Brunswick: A History, 1784–1867* (Toronto 1963), 454
4 T.W. Acheson, *Saint John: The Making of a Colonial Urban Community* (Toronto 1985), 3–26
5 Ibid., 26
6 Ibid., 48–91
7 Ibid., 63–6
8 C.M. Wallace, 'Saint John Boosters and the Railroads in Mid-Nineteenth Century,' *Acadiensis* 6 (Autumn 1976), 71–91
9 Carl Murray Wallace, 'Sir Leonard Tilley, A Political Biography,' PhD dissertation, University of Alberta, 1972, 1–14
10 Ibid., 15–39
11 New Brunswick, Legislative Assembly, *Debates*, 1855, 39
12 MacNutt, *New Brunswick*, 364–7
13 C.M. Wallace, 'George Edward Fenety,' *DCB* 12: 313
14 Ibid., 313–14
15 *Morning News* (Saint John), 9 March 1849; 5 April, 29 May 1850; 27 July 1855; 7 April 1856; 8 May, 29 June, 7 Sept. 1857

16 Ibid., 17 March 1856
17 Ibid., 27 Nov 1850
18 Ibid., 29 July 1850
19 Ibid., 8 May 1857
20 Ibid., 10 June 1857
21 Ibid., 27 Nov. 1850
22 Ibid., 27 June 1855
23 Graeme Wynn, 'Ideology, Society, and State in the Maritime Colonies of British North America, 1840–1860,' in Allan Greer and Ian Radforth, eds, *Colonial Leviathan: State Formation in Mid-Nineteenth-Century Canada* (Toronto 1992), 310
24 *Morning News*, 27 June 1855
25 Alan W. Bailey, 'Railways in New Brunswick, 1827–1867,' MA thesis, University of New Brunswick, 1955, 218–20; MacNutt, *New Brunswick*, 298–9, 381
26 *Plan for Shortening the Time of Passage Between New York and London, with Documents Relating Thereto* (Portland 1850). Initially the plan suggested a point on Cape Breton Island for the eastern terminal.
27 *Morning News*, 7 Aug. 1850. Although the articles advocating the European and North American are numerous, the most important are: 5, 19 Aug. 1857; 2, 9 July 1858; 28 Oct. 1859; 7 Sept. 1860.
28 Rosemarie Patricia Langhout ('Public Enterprise: An Analysis of Public Finance in the Maritime Colonies during the Period of Responsible Government,' PhD dissertation, University of New Brunswick, 1989, 29–38) argues forcefully that the decision to construct the railway as a public work was a deliberate and preferred policy rather than a forced reaction to the failure of private enterprise to do the job. In light of the initial contract with the British firm, her assertion is suspect. See Gene Lawrence Allen, 'The Origins of the Intercolonial Railway, 1835–1869,' PhD dissertation, University of Toronto, 1991, 215–20, on this point.
29 Acheson, *Saint John*, 205–13. As early as 1845 George Fenety had suggested that the city follow the example of New York and purchase the water company, close all municipal wells, and offer piped water to all regardless of ability to pay. *Morning News*, 6 Aug. 1845
30 New Brunswick, *Journals*, 1856, Fisher to Baring, 26 Dec. 1855
31 Ibid., 15 March 1856 citing Fisher to Tilley, 6 Feb. 1856; NAC, Baring Papers, vol. 2, Fisher to Baring, 26 Dec. 1855, 982–1001; Bailey, 'Railways in New Brunswick,' 129
32 Allen, 'Intercolonial Railway,' 223–6
33 MacNutt, *New Brunswick*, 364, argues that practical necessity rather than ideol-

ogy brought financial reform, a thesis that fits his description of the chaotic and parochial nature of provincial politics.

34 *Headquarters* (Fredericton), 12 Dec. 1855
35 *Morning News*, 4 Oct. 1852
36 Ibid., 20 June 1851, 5 July 1852, 3 Jan. 1853
37 Ibid., 19 Dec. 1853
38 Ibid., 7 July 1858, 24 Oct. 1860
39 Ibid., 24 Oct 1860
40 Ibid.
41 Ibid., 7 July 1858
42 *Debates*, 29 March 1860, 96
43 NAC, Howe Papers, vol. 4, Tilley to Howe, 17 Nov. 1860, 65–76
44 Gillmor, in *Debates*, 29 March 1860, 96
45 NBM, Tilley Papers, Baring to Tilley, 14 Dec. 1860
46 NAC, Tilley Papers, vol. 9, Jardine to Tilley, 26 Dec. 1860
47 NAC, Howe Papers, vol. 3, Tilley to Howe, 25 Feb. 1863, 717–24; New Brunswick, A Bill to Authorize a Loan and for the Construction and Management of an Inter-Colonial Railway, in Gordon to Newcastle, 27 April 1863, Great Britain, House of Commons, *Sessional Papers*, 1864, vol. 41, Correspondence relative to a loan for an Intercolonial Railway (North America)
48 *Daily Evening Globe* (Saint John), 27 March 1863
49 *Morning Freeman* (Saint John), 9 April 1863
50 UNB, Tilley Papers, vol. 13, Cudlip to Tilley, 31 Jan. 1863
51 *Daily Evening Globe*, 27 March 1863
52 NAC, Tilley Papers, Fairweather to Tilley, 12 March 1864
53 *Morning Freeman*, 2 April 1863
54 Ibid., 2, 11 April 1863
55 Ibid., 31 March 1863
56 Allen, 'Intercolonial Railway,' 318–22; Wallace, 'Leonard Tilley,' 161–4
57 NAC, Howe Papers, vol. 3, Tilley to Howe, 13 April 1863, 762–9. If pressed, Tilley would accept a route through the centre of the province provided it used a substantial section of the Saint John–Shediac railway and departed for Canada shortly east of, if not actually from, Saint John. He told Howe that he had obtained Newcastle's provisional consent to a central line, but that it would not be wise 'to have stated that in public.'
58 New Brunswick, Legislative Assembly, *Journals*, 1864, 1, 2, 9 March 1864
59 *Daily Evening Globe*, 13 Feb. 1864
60 Ibid.
61 Nova Scotia, Legislative Assembly, *Journals*, 1865, app. 7, Brydges to Tilley, 4 March 1864, 6

62 *Daily Evening Globe*, 18 March 1864

63 Ibid., 21 March 1864

64 NAC, Tilley Papers, vol. 16, Boyd to Tilley, 10 March 1864; Allen, 'Intercolonial Railway,' 349

65 NAC, Macdonald Papers, vol. 191, Brydges to Macdonald, 22 Feb. 1864, 79431–5; see also Tilley Papers, vol. 16, Brydges to Tilley, 24 Feb. 1864

66 NAC, Tilley Papers, vol. 16, Fairweather to Tilley, 12 March 1864

67 Edward Whelan, *The Union of the British Provinces: The Union of the Provinces* (Charlottetown 1865), 15 Oct. 1864, 72; *Debates*, 4 May 1864, 22 June 1864; Donald Creighton, *The Road to Confederation: The Emergence of Canada, 1863–1867* (Toronto 1964), 39–69

68 Québec Resolutions, October 1864, in G.P. Browne, *Documents on the Confederation of British North America* (Toronto 1969), 165; also Hewitt Bernard's notes, 11 Oct. 1864, 93–9

69 *Morning News*, 12 June, 18, 23 Sept. 1857; 12 March 1858; 17 Aug., 31 Oct., 5 Dec. 1860

70 Ibid., 10 Aug. 1857, 22 Oct 1858

71 In 1863 Tilley appointed Fenety as Queen's Printer. Fenety moved to Fredericton and turned over the daily editing of the *Morning News* to Edward Willis, who with two partners purchased the paper in 1865. Wallace, 'George Fenety,' 313

72 *Morning News*, 21 Aug. 1863

73 Ibid., 28 Aug. 1863

74 Ibid., 24 Aug. 1863

75 Ibid., 31 Aug. 1863

76 Wallace, 'Leonard Tilley,' 193–209

77 William M. Baker, *Timothy Warren Anglin, 1822–96, Irish Catholic Canadian* (Toronto 1977), 3–29

78 *Morning Freeman* (Saint John), 20 Sept. 1864

79 Ibid., 19 Nov. 1864

80 Ibid., 6, 13 Jan. 1863

81 Ibid., 17, 20, 22 Jan. 1863

82 Ibid., 25 Aug., 13 Dec. 1864; 21, 28 Jan. 1865

83 Carl Wallace, 'Albert Smith, Confederation, and Reaction in New Brunswick: 1852–1882,' *CHR* 44 (December 1963), 285–6

84 Ibid., 286

85 *Daily Evening Globe*, 29 Nov. 1864

86 Wallace, 'Leonard Tilley,' 191–209; MacNutt, *New Brunswick*, 423–9

87 *Daily Telegraph*, 2 Feb. 1865

88 Alfred G. Bailey ('Railways and the Confederation Issue in New Brunswick,

1863–65,' *CHR* 21 [Dec 1940], 367–83) follows the Smith analysis and paints a stark correlation between pro- and anti-confederationists and intercolonial and western-extension supporters.

89 NAC, Macdonald Papers, vol. 51, Tilley to Macdonald, 13 Feb. 1865; Macdonald to Tilley, 20 Feb. 1865

90 MacNutt, *New Brunswick*, 394–7

91 New Brunswick, *Journals*, 1864, app. 12, 'Annual Returns of Trade and Navigation for 1863' 17, 20. Trade to the United Kingdom amounted to $5.3 million, while to the United States it totalled $4.7 million (p. xcii).

92 Bailey, 'Railways and Confederation,' 376

93 New Brunswick, *Journals*, 1864, Poor to Tilley, 16 Nov. 1863, 124. See also Poor to Tilley, 26 Jan. 1864, Tilley to Poor, 13 Jan. 1863.

94 Cited in Bailey, 'Railways and Confederation,' 379.

95 New Brunswick, *Journals*, 9 April 1864

96 NAC, Macdonald Papers, vol. 51, Tilley to Galt, undated [March 1865], 19993–20012

97 UNBA, Stanmore Papers, Gordon to Cardwell, 10 April 1865

98 *Headquarters*, 27 Jan. 1864

99 Ibid.

100 Ibid., 27 Jan. 1864

101 William S. Caie in *Debates*, 6 June 1865. His fellow countyman Lestock P.W. Desbrisay intended to vote in favour of the western extension because it would benefit the North Shore more than an intercolonial.

102 Bailey, 'Railways and Confederation,' 367–83; Wallace, 'Leonard Tilley,' 137, 183

103 *Daily Telegraph*, 23 Nov. 1864, 8 Feb. 1865

104 Cited in Allen, 'Intercolonial Railway,' 390

105 NAC, Tilley Papers, vol. 18, Parks to Tilley, 1 April 1865

106 Ibid., Watkin to Tilley, 30 March 1865

107 Wallace, 'Albert Smith,' 292

108 *Morning News*, 10 March 1865

109 Wallace, 'Leonard Tilley,' 217–19

110 Baker, *Timothy Anglin*, 104–8

111 W.L. Morton, *The Critical Years: The Union of British North America, 1857–1873* (Toronto 1964), 188–92

112 Wallace, 'Saint John Boosters,' 90

113 *Debates*, 29 April 1865, 10

114 Ibid., 1 May 1865

115 *Morning News*, 21 Sept. 1864

116 Phillip Buckner, 'The Maritimes and Confederation: A Reassessment,' in

Ged Martin, ed., *The Causes of Canadian Confederation* (Fredericton 1990), 86–113

117 Phillip Buckner, 'Presidential Address: Whatever Happened to the British Empire?' *Journal of the Canadian Historical Association* (1993), 22

118 Nicholas Landry ('Transport et régionalisme en contexte pré-industriel: Le projet du canal de la baie Verte, 1820–1875,' *Acadiensis* 24 [Autumn 1994], 59–87) argues that canal projects played an important part in transportation planning in mid-nineteenth-century Maritimes. Though the Bay Verte Canal, designed to connect the Bay of Fundy with the Northumberland Strait, was off and on the planning boards from the 1820s to the 1870s, it was never built.

119 *Debates*, 6 June 1865

120 Ibid.

Chapter 6: The Pacific Scandal

1 This chapter is a revised and enlarged version of an article previously published in *CHR* 69 (September 1988), 315–39. The author thanks the editors of the review for granting permission to republish the essay in this volume.

2 Canada, House of Commons, *Journals*, 1873, app. 1, 95

3 'British North America Act 1867,' in G.P. Browne, *Documents on the Confederation of British North America* (Toronto 1969), 335–6; references to the Intercolonial Railway and western annexation are numerous in confederation documents cited by Browne. See, for example, pp. 96, 130, 145, 152–3, 165, 189, 203, 205, 213, 228, 262.

4 Donald Creighton, *John A. Macdonald: The Old Chieftain* (Toronto 1955). Creighton's view is accentuated by Pierre Berton, *The National Dream: The Great Railway, 1871–1881* (Toronto 1970). Berton emphasizes the nation-building theme even more strongly than Creighton. The Canadian Pacific Railway, according to Berton, was a heroic struggle against nature, geography, and the hostile United States.

5 Doug Owram, *Promise of Eden: The Canadian Expansionist Movement and the Idea of the West, 1856–1900* (Toronto 1980), 7–78

6 *Globe* (Toronto), 8 July 1858; Canada, Legislative Assembly, *Journals*, 1858, 815

7 James Dickinson in Henry Youle Hind, *Narrative of the Canadian Red River Expedition of 1857* (New York 1969), 1: 373

8 NAC, Macdonald Papers, Brydges to Macdonald, 1, 22, and 24 Feb. 1864

9 Henrietta M. Larson, *Jay Cooke: Private Banker* (New York 1968), 1–122; Ellis Paxson Oberholtzer, *Jay Cooke: Financier of the Civil War* (Philadelphia 1907)

10 John L. Harnsberger, 'Jay Cooke and Minnesota: The Formative Years of the Northern Pacific Railroad, 1868–1873,' PhD dissertation, University of Minnesota, 1956, 26
11 Edward Chase Kirkland, *Men, Cities, and Transportation: A Study in New England History*, 1820–1900 (New York 1948)
12 A.W. Currie, *The Grand Trunk Railway of Canada* (Toronto 1957), 118–23
13 Kirkland, *Men, Cities, and Transportation*, 1: 364–72
14 Leonard Bertram Irwin, *Pacific Railways and Nationalism in the Canadian-American Northwest, 1845–1873* (New York 1968), 101–6
15 James W. Taylor, *Northwest British America and Its Relations to the State of Minnesota* (St Paul 1860), 8
16 Alvin C. Gluek, *Minnesota and the Manifest Destiny of the Canadian Northwest: A Study in Canadian-American Relations* (Toronto 1965); Hartwell Bowsfield, *The James Wickes Taylor Correspondence, 1859–1870* (Altona 1968)
17 Reginald C. Stuart, *United States Expansionism and British North America, 1775–1871* (Chapel Hill 1988), 190–3, 230
18 Thomas Weber, *The Northern Railroads in the Civil War, 1861–1865* (New York 1952); John Debo Galloway, *The First Transcontinental Railroad: Central Pacific, Union Pacific* (New York 1989)
19 Stuart, *United States Expansionism*, 191, 255–61
20 Taylor, *British America*, 9
21 HSP, Cooke Papers, Taylor to Cooke, 8 May 1869
22 Ibid., Taylor to Cooke, 28 Nov. 1869
23 Larson, *Jay Cooke*, 271
24 HSP, Cooke Papers, Jay to Harry Cooke, 2 March 1870
25 Ibid., 14 April 1870; Smith to Cooke, 26 July 1870
26 Ibid., Cooke to Coffin, 8 April 1870
27 Ibid., Cooke to Banning, 17 June 1869; Larson, *Jay Cooke*, 282–4
28 HSP, Cooke Papers, Smith to Cooke, 23 Nov. 1869
29 Ibid., Moorhead to Cooke, 13 Dec. 1869
30 Larson, *Jay Cooke*, 278, 284–8
31 HSP, Cooke Papers, Cooke to Sargent, 25 Feb. 1870
32 Ibid., Cooke to Harry Cooke, 11 and 14 April 1870
33 Ibid., Cooke to Sheppard, 11 April 1870; Larson, *Jay Cooke*, 338
34 James G. Snell, 'American Neutrality and the Red River Resistance, 1869–1870,' *Prairie Forum* 4 (Fall 1979), 183–96
35 HSP, Cooke Papers, copy of Taylor to Nettleton, 5 Dec. 1870
36 *Globe*, 9 Oct. 1865
37 Lucius Seth Huntington, *The Independence of Canada: The Annual Address*

Delivered Before the Agricultural Society of the County of Missisquoi, at Bedford, Sept. 8, 1869 (Montréal 1869)

38 HSP, Cooke Papers, Huntington to Cooke, 22 June 1869

39 Ibid., Huntington to Cooke, 12 Oct. 1869; Harry Cooke to Cooke, 7 Aug. 1869; Huntington to Cooke, 10 and 18 Aug. 1869

40 Ibid., Huntington to Cooke, 31 July, 10 and 18 Aug. 1869; Lamborn to Cooke, 17 Oct. 1869

41 NAC, Macdonald Papers, Letterbook 13, Macdonald to Carrall, 29 Sept. 1869; vol. 123, Macdonald to McDougall, 4 Nov. 1869

42 Ibid., Letterbook 13, Macdonald to Daly, 30 Oct. 1869

43 HSP, Cooke Papers, copy of Taylor to Johnson, 23 May 1871; Taylor to Cooke, 27 March and 10 April 1871

44 NAC, Macdonald Papers, Letterbook 13, Macdonald to McDougall, 23 Nov. 1869

45 Ibid., vol. 103, memo, Hill to Macdonald, December 1869

46 HSP, Cooke Papers, Taylor to Cooke, 28 Dec. 1870

47 NAC, Macdonald Papers, Letterbook 14, Macdonald to Brydges, 6 May 1870; vol. 123, Waddington to Macdonald, 22 Aug. 1870; copy Knight to Brydges, 17 April 1870

48 Ibid., undated, unsigned memo, 50408

49 Snell, 'American Neutrality,' 183–96

50 Brian Young and Gerald Tulchinsky, 'Sir Hugh Allan,' *DCB* 11: 5–15

51 HSP, Cooke Papers, Jay to Harry Cooke, 8 Dec. 1870

52 NAC, Macdonald Papers, Letterbook 15, Macdonald to Allan, 3 Feb. 1871

53 HSP, Cooke Papers, Harry to Jay Cooke, 6 April 1871

54 Ibid., Harry to Jay Cooke, 11 April 1871; Hazard to Cook, 8 May 1871; Pitt to Jay Cooke, 16 June 1871

55 NAC, Macdonald Papers, vol. 123, Memo: Parties Present in Ottawa, 14 July 1871

56 Ibid., vol. 224, Hincks to Macdonald, 4 Aug. 1871

57 HSP, Cooke Papers, Letterbooks, Cooke to Puleston, 23 Sept. 1871

58 NAC, Macdonald Papers, vol. 123, memo, Canadian Pacific Railway, 6 Oct. 1871

59 Ibid., Letterbook 16, Macdonald to Rose, 30 Nov. 1871

60 Canada, House of Commons, *Journals*, 1873, app. 1, Report of the Royal Commission, 216–18

61 HSP, Cooke Papers, Ogden to Cooke, 17 June 1871

62 NAC, Macdonald Papers, vol. 191, Brydges to Macdonald, 15 Jan. 1870; see also 26 Jan. 1870

63 Brian Young, 'Railway Politics in Montreal, 1867–1878,' Canadian Historical Association *Historical Papers*, 1972, 89–108

64 NAC, Galt Papers, Brydges to Galt, 18 July 1869
65 Cited by G.P. de T. Glazebrook, *A History of Transportation in Canada* (Toronto 1964), 2: 50
66 NAC, Macdonald Papers, vol. 191, Brydges to Macdonald, 2 Feb. and 19 April 1870
67 Ibid., vol. 125, Allan to Macdonald, 17 April 1873
68 Young, 'Railway Politics'
69 NAC, Macdonald Papers, vol. 583, Committee of the Privy Council, 30 Sept. 1869
70 Larson, *Jay Cooke*, 302–12; Dolores Greenberg, *Financiers and Railroads, 1869–1889: A Study of Morton, Bliss & Company* (Newark 1980), 36–7
71 NAC, Macdonald Papers, vol. 258, Rose to Macdonald, 13 July 1870
72 HSP, Cooke Papers, copy of Lampson to Rice, 7 May 1870
73 NAC, Macdonald Papers, vol. 258, Rose to Macdonald, 20 Jan. 1871
74 Canada, *Journals*, 1873, app. 1, 32–40
75 Ibid., 96
76 The bulk of the letters in NAC, Macdonald Papers, vols. 123–5, document the political problem of reconciling Ontario and Québec interests. Citing only one or even two letters is pointless, as the entire collection must be read to gain an appreciation of the political importance of the problem. In any case, space does not permit a detailed account of how Macdonald's attempt to solve these regional rivalries in the railway question torpedoed his grand national ambitions.
77 *Statutes of Canada*, 1872, 35 Vic c72 and c73
78 Canada, House of Commons, *Debates*, 7 May 1872
79 NAC, Macdonald Papers, vol. 125, CPR Charter, February 1873
80 Canada, *Journals*, 1873, app. 1
81 Larson, *Jay Cooke*, 401–8
82 Young and Tulchinsky, 'Hugh Allan'
83 NAC, Dufferin Papers, Dufferin to Kimberley, 10 Oct. 1873
84 Canada, *Journals*, 1873, app. 1, 75
85 NAC, Dufferin Papers, Dufferin to Kimberley, 24 Dec. 1873
86 Carl Berger, *The Sense of Power: Studies in the Ideas of Canadian Imperialism, 1867–1914* (Toronto 1970)
87 Mackenzie Papers, 703ff, George Stephen to Huntington, 14 Dec. 1874, cited in Dale Thomson, *Alexander Mackenzie: Clear Grit* (Toronto 1960), 219
88 Berton, *National Dream*, 220–9, 302–10

Chapter 7: The National Policy

1 25 Nov. 1880

2   19 Sept. 1878

3   J. Murray Beck, *Pendulum of Power: Canada's Federal Elections* (Scarborough 1968), 30–7. In Québec, church and state relations as well as the dismissal of a Conservative ministry by the lieutenant-governor were issues. Nevertheless, J. Israel Tarte, the Conservative leader in the province, stressed economic concerns.

4   Donald Creighton, *John A. Macdonald: The Old Chieftain* (Toronto 1955), 180–242; Pierre Berton, *The National Dream: The Great Railway, 1871–1881* (Toronto 1970), 262

5   Dale C. Thomson, *Alexander Mackenzie: Clear Grit* (Toronto 1960); Ben Forster, 'Alexander Mackenzie,' *DCB* 12: 647–59

6   Gerald Friesen, *The Canadian Prairies: A History* (Toronto 1984); Lewis Herbert Thomas, *The Struggle for Responsible Government in the North-West Territories, 1870–97* (Toronto 1956), 3–60; R.C. Macleod, *The North West Mounted Police and Law Enforcement: 1873–1905* (Toronto 1976)

7   Macleod's views are nicely summarized in *The North West Mounted Police, 1873–1919*, Canadian Historical Association Booklet 31 (Ottawa 1978). In *NWMP and Law Enforcement* (16), Macleod speculates that the establishment of the police force barely a month before Macdonald's fall was fortunate, as Mackenzie might have axed the enabling legislation. That counterfactual argument, which fits well into the John A. Macdonald–nation-building theme, neglects to note that the cost-conscious Mackenzie could easily have scuttled the fledgling force in the winter of 1874. The law-enforcement problem would have remained, however.

8   Thomas, *Responsible Government*, 73–9

9   Chester Martin, *'Dominion Lands' Policy*, ed. and intro. Lewis H. Thomas (Ottawa 1973), 7–27

10   See discussion in chapter 4.

11   H.C. Pentland, 'The Role of Capital in Canadian Economic Development before 1875,' *CJEPS* 16 (November 1950), 457–74

12   Canada, Legislative Assembly, *Parliamentary Debates on the Subject of Confederation of the British North American Provinces*, 7 Feb. 1865 (Ottawa 1951), 64

13   Ben Forster, *A Conjunction of Interests: Business, Politics, and Tariffs, 1825–1879* (Toronto 1986), 60; Delphin A. Muise, 'The Federal Election of 1867 in Nova Scotia: An Economic Interpretation,' *Nova Scotia Historical Society Collections* 36 (1968), 327–51; and his 'Parties and Constituencies: Federal Elections in Nova Scotia 1867–96,' Canadian Historical Association *Historical Papers*, 1971, 183–202

14   PANS, A.G. Jones Papers, vol. 523, item 3. Over a thousand businessmen, professionals, and workers signed the petition.

15   Forster, *Conjunction of Interests*, 75

16 Ibid., 68–75
17 Reginald C. Stuart, *United States Expansionism and British North America, 1775–1871* (Chapel Hill 1988), 251–5. The *Alabama* was one of several British-built confederate raiders that caused considerable damage to American shipping. The United States won a favourable settlement of the San Juan boundary dispute and $15 million for the *Alabama* claims. Canada was awarded $5.5 million for opening its fisheries.
18 Creighton, *Old Chieftain*, 70–102
19 Forster, *Conjunction of Interests*, 76–82
20 NAC, Macdonald Papers, vol. 520, Macdonald to McInnis, 17 June 1872
21 Thomson, *Alexander Mackenzie*, 204–8
22 Forster, *Conjunction of Interests*, 125–55; P.F.W. Rutherford, 'The New Nationality, 1864–1897: A Study of National Aims and Ideas of English Canada in the Late Nineteenth Century,' PhD dissertation, University of Toronto, 1973, 235–50
23 Forster, *Conjunction of Interests*, 133
24 Rutherford, 'New Nationality,' 235–40
25 Cited in Forster, *Conjunction of Interests*, 152
26 *Globe*, 26 Sept. 1866
27 Cited by Gary Pennanen, 'Goldwin Smith, Wharton Barker, and Erastus Wiman: Architects of Commercial Union,' *JCS* 14 (Fall 1979), 55
28 *Globe*, 7 Dec. 1877
29 *Herald* (Montréal), 10 Feb. 1880
30 *La Patrie* (Montréal), 16 April 1879
31 *Globe*, 9 April 1870. Cited in Rutherford, 'New Nationality,' 251
32 *Free Press* (Winnipeg), 23 Sept., 21 Oct. 1878
33 *Globe*, 28 Sept. 1878
34 *Morning Chronicle* (Halifax), 1 Oct. 1878
35 *Globe*, 17 July 1889
36 Pennanen, 'Smith, Barker, and Wiman,' 50–1
37 Smith to Macdonald, 4 Oct. 1878, in Joseph Pope, ed., *Selections from the Correspondence of the Right Honourable Sir John Alexander Macdonald, GCB* (Toronto, nd), 246–7
38 Canada, *Debates*, 25 Feb. 1876
39 Ibid. See also 10 March 1876.
40 Erastus Wiman, *The Perfect Development of Canada: Is It Inconsistent with British Welfare?* (New York 1887), speech of Erastus Wiman, 3 Dec. 1887, 15
41 *Gazette* (Montréal), 26 Nov. 1875
42 Although he concedes that the two parties began to polarize around the ideas of protection and free trade, Forster (*Conjunction of Interests*, 147, 173) rejects the

idea that 1876 was a decisive year in the Conservatives' adoption of protectionism. He argues the decisive conversion did not come until the Conservative
convention of 1878.

43 *Debates*, 10 March 1876
44 For descriptions of some of the picnics and speeches, see *Daily Mail* (Toronto),
   3 July, 24 and 31 Aug., and 7 Sept. 1876.
45 *Debates*, 12 March 1878, 1071
46 Creighton, *Old Chieftain*, 180–242; Forster, *Conjunction of Interests* (Toronto
   1986), 86–109
47 Forster, *Conjunction of Interests*, 109
48 Ben Forster, 'Coming of the National Policy: Business, Government and the
   Tariff, 1876–1879,' *JCS* 14 (Fall 1979), 40
49 *Debates*, 14 March 1879. The theme of Tilley's budget speech was that Canada
   turned to protectionism only after it made numerous attempts to break the
   United States' protectionist wall.
50 Rutherford, 'New Nationality,' 204–5
51 *Morning Herald* (Halifax), 6 Feb. 1877
52 *Daily Mail* (Toronto), 29 April 1876
53 *Daily Witness* (Montréal), 5 Jan. 1878
54 *Daily Star* (Montréal), 30 Nov. 1880
55 *Debates*, 14 March 1879
56 Ibid.
57 Rutherford, 'New Nationality,' 214–34; Forster, *Conjunction of Interests*, 116–
   25
58 *Gazette* (Montréal), 21 Oct. 1878
59 Ibid., 9 Aug. 1875, 14 Oct. 1878; *Spectator* (Hamilton), 21 Aug., 21 Oct. 1878
60 *Citizen* (Ottawa), 17 Nov. 1880
61 *Le Canadien* (Montréal), 18 March 1879
62 Forster, *Conjunction of Interests*, 201–5
63 Beck, *Pendulum of Power*, 37
64 Thomson, *Alexander Mackenzie*, 182–4; Forster, 'Alexander Mackenzie,' 653
65 Thomson, *Alexander Mackenzie*, 196–8
66 Ibid., 208-13, 233–6
67 Ibid., 228
68 Ibid., 327, 336–7; Forster, 'Alexander Mackenzie,' 653; Berton, *National
   Dream*, 208–18, 220–60
69 *Gazette*, 26 Nov. 1875
70 Harold A. Innis, 'Transportation as a Factor in Canadian Economic History'
   and 'Transportation in the Canadian Economy,' in Mary Q. Innis, ed., *Essays in
   Canadian Economic History* (Toronto 1956)

71 Canada, *Statutes*, 1880–1, Vic 44 c1. The terms of the contract are well known: a $25 million cash subsidy and 25-million-acre land grant, all completed sections of the railway turned over to the syndicate, the company to import duty free all railway construction materials, a perpetual tax exemption for right-of-way and station lands and twenty years for the land grant, and, lastly, no other company permitted to construct any railway running in a south-easterly direction south of the CPR main line.

72 The debate on the contract lasted 33 days and covered 748 pages in Hansard.

73 The CPR has not been subjected to an exhaustive econometric study of the need for 'ahead of settlement construction' as carried out by Albert Fishlow (*American Railroads and the Transformation of the Ante-Bellum Economy* [Cambridge, Mass., 1965]) and Robert William Fogel (*The Union Pacific Railroad: A Case in Premature Enterprise* [Baltimore 1960] and *Railroads and American Economic Growth: Essays in Econometric History* [Baltimore 1964]. For a discussion of these studies and his own work see Peter George, foreword to Harold A. Innis, *A History of the Canadian Pacific Railway* (Toronto 1971). George concludes that many more studies are needed before scholars can determine if a go-slow or go-fast policy was more beneficial to Canada's social and economic development.

74 *Globe*, 1 June 1878

75 Alexander Mackenzie, *Speeches of the Hon. Alexander Mackenzie During His Visit to Scotland* (Toronto 1876), 21–2

76 Cited in Thomson, *Alexander Mackenzie*, 249–50

Chapter 8: Conclusions and Conjectures

1 *Telegraph* (Saint John), 9 Jan. 1893

2 Canada, House of Commons, *Debates*, 4 May 1883

3 Pierre Berton, *The Last Spike: The Great Railway, 1881–1885* (Toronto 1971), 410–16

4 *Mail* (Toronto), 12 Jan. 1874

5 Harold A. Innis, *A History of the Canadian Pacific Railway*, foreword by Peter George (Toronto 1971); *The Fur Trade in Canada: An Introduction to Canadian Economic History* (Toronto 1962); *Essays in Canadian Economic History*, ed. Mary Q. Innis (Toronto 1956)

6 H.A. Innis, *Empire and Communications* (Toronto 1950); *The Bias of Communication* (Toronto 1951); Arthur Kroker, *Technology and the Canadian Mind: Innis/McLuhan/Grant* (Montréal 1984)

7 J.M.S. Careless, *Frontier and Metropolis: Regions, Cities, and Identities in Canada before 1914* (Toronto 1989)

8 Ibid., 74

9 Ibid., 60

10 T.D. Regehr, *The Canadian Northern Railway: Pioneer Road of the Northern Prairies, 1895–1918* (Toronto 1976)

11 G.R. Stevens, *Canadian National Railways: Towards the Inevitable, 1896–1922* (Toronto 1962), 2: 121–228

12 As noted in the previous chapter, Albert Fishlow (*American Railroads and the Transformation of the Ante-Bellum Economy* [Cambridge, Mass., 1965]), Robert William Fogel (*The Union Pacific Railroad: A Case in Premature Enterprise* [Baltimore 1960] and *Railroads and American Economic Growth: Essays in Econometric History* [Baltimore 1964]), and Peter George (foreword to Innis, *Canadian Pacific*) have questioned whether railways were really needed at the time for western settlement.

13 M.C. Urquhart and K.A.H. Buckley, *Historical Statistics of Canada* (Toronto 1965), 14, 351, 363–4

14 Oscar Osburn Winther, *The Transportation Frontier: Trans-Mississippi West, 1865–1890* (New York 1964), 7–11; Arthur J. Larsen, 'Early Transportation,'. *Minnesota History* 14 (June 1933), 149–55

15 NAC/HBC A7/2, Simpson to Shepherd, 2 Aug. 1856

16 NAC/HBC A12/10, Simpson to Fraser, 29 June 1860; Alvin C. Gluek, *Minnesota and the Manifest Destiny of the Canadian Northwest: A Study in Canadian-American Relations* (Toronto 1965), 115–16; Theodore Barris, *Fire Canoe: Prairie Steamboat Days Revisited* (Toronto 1977), 25–30; Alvin C. Gluek, 'Minnesota Route,' *The Beaver*, Outfit 286 (Spring 1956), 44–50; A.A. den Otter, 'The Hudson's Bay Company's Transportation Problem, 1870–85,' in John E. Foster, ed., *The Developing West: Essays on Canadian History in Honor of Lewis H. Thomas* (Edmonton 1982), 25–47

17 NAC/HBC, A11/96, Johnson to Smith, 29 June 1857

18 Carol Judd, '"Mixt Bands of Many Nations": 1821–70,' in Carol M. Judd and Arthur J Ray, eds, *Old Trails and New Directions: Papers of the Third North American Fur Trade Conference* (Toronto 1980)

19 Irene Spry, 'The Great Transformation: The Disappearance of the Commons in Western Canada,' in Richard Allen, ed., *Man and Nature on the Prairies* (Regina 1976), 21–45

20 Gerhard Ens, 'Dispossession or Adaptation? Migration and Persistence of the Red River Metis, 1835–1890,' Canadian Historical Association *Historical Papers*, 1988, 122

21 Irene M. Spry, 'The "Private Adventurers" of Rupert's Land,' in John E. Foster, ed., *The Developing West: Essays on Canadian History in Honor of Lewis H. Thomas* (Edmonton 1983), 49–70

22 John L. Tobias, 'Canada's Subjection of the Plains Cree, 1879–1885' *CHR* (December 1983), 519–48

23 The historiography of the 1885 Saskatchewan rebellion is formidable and highly charged. The latest scholarly entry is the remarkably balanced but still pro-government booklet by Thomas Flanagan, *Louis Riel* (Ottawa 1992). Another excellent survey is contained in Gerald Friesen, *The Canadian Prairies: A History* (Toronto 1984), 149–56, 224–36. The classic study by George F.G. Stanley, *The Birth of Western Canada: A History of the Riel Rebellions* (Toronto 1963), still has great value because he observed that the two Metis uprisings represented a defence of a local against an invading culture. W.L. Morton's introduction to his edited version of *Alexander Begg's Red River Journal and Other Papers Relative to the Red River Resistance of 1869–1870* (Toronto 1956) provided a necessary corrective to Stanley's contention that the mixed bloods were a primitive, as opposed to a civilized, people. Bob Beal and Rod Macleod, *Prairie Fire: The 1885 North-West Rebellion* (Edmonton 1984) is still the best account of the Saskatchewan uprising.

24 Careless, *Frontier and Metropolis*, 131

25 Innis, *Fur Trade*, 397

26 T.D. Regehr, 'Western Canada and the Burden of National Transportation Policies,' in David Jay Bercuson, ed., *Canada and the Burden of Unity* (Toronto 1977), 115–17

27 Regehr, *Canadian Northern*, 20

28 A.A. den Otter, 'Bondage of Steam: The CPR and Western Canadian Coal,' in Hugh A. Dempsey, ed., *The CPR West: The Iron Road and the Making of a Nation* (Vancouver 1984), 191–208

29 Ben Forster, *A Conjunction of Interests: Business, Politics, and Tariffs, 1825–1879* (Toronto 1986), 196–7

30 Gerald Friesen, 'Imports and Exports in the Manitoba Economy, 1870–1890,' *Manitoba History* 16 (1988), 31–41

31 David Breen, 'A Peripheral Mentality: The Case of Alberta,' *Zeitschrift der Gesellschaft für Kanada-Stüdien* 9 (no. 1, vol. 15, 1989), 9–10

32 John A. Eagle, *The Canadian Pacific Railway and the Development of Western Canada, 1896–1914* (Kingston and Montréal 1989), 38–49; Regehr, *Canadian Northern*, 62–5

33 Robert Craig Brown and Ramsay Cook, *Canada 1896–1921: A Nation Transformed* (Toronto 1974), 158–63

34 David Jay Bercuson, 'Regionalism and "Unlimited Identity" in Western Canada,' *JCS* 15 (Summer 1980), 121–6

35 John Lutz, '*Losing Steam*: The Boiler and Engine Industry as an Index of British Columbia's Deindustrialization, 1880–1915,' Canadian Historical Association *Historical Papers*, 1988, 168–208

36 Ibid., 202

37 Ibid., 201

38 James A. Ward, *Railroads and the Character of America, 1820–1887* (Knoxville 1986)

39 Paul Craven and Tom Traves, 'Canadian Railways as Manufacturers, 1850–1880,' Canadian Historical Association *Historical Papers*, 1983, 264. For a detailed history of the Grand Trunk's Stratford shops, see Dean Robinson, *Railway Stratford* (Erin 1989).

40 Craven and Traves, 'Railways as Manufacturers,' 261; Paul Craven and Tom Traves, 'Dimensions of Paternalism: Discipline and Culture in Canadian Railway Operations in the 1850s,' in Craig Heron and Robert Storey, eds, *On the Job: Confronting the Labour Process in Canada* (Kingston and Montréal 1986), 47. Although labour played a crucial role in the construction and operation of the railway and thus contributed to its culture, workers had no voice in the creation of the philosophy of railways.

41 Craven and Traves, 'Railways as Manufacturers,' 254

42 See chapter 3, note 5, for a discussion of the historiography of underdevelopment in the Maritimes.

43 *Morning Chronicle* (Halifax), 14 Jan. 1865

44 Rick Szostak, *The Role of Transportation in the Industrial Revolution: A Comparison of England and France* (Montréal and Kingston 1991), 3

45 Ibid., 6

46 T.W. Acheson, 'The National Policy and the Industrialization of the Maritimes, 1880–1910,' *Acadiensis* 1 (Spring 1972), 3–28; 'The Maritimes and "Empire Canada,"' in Bercuson, *Burden of Unity*, 87–114

47 Acheson, 'Empire Canada,' 94

48 Acheson, 'National Policy,' 27

49 Ibid.; Acheson, 'Empire Canada,' 96

50 E.R. Forbes, 'The Intercolonial Railway and the Decline of the Maritime Provinces Revisited,' *Acadiensis* 24 (Autumn 1994), 2–26. Forbes's article is the last instalment in a running debate with Ken Cruikshank. In his latest rejoinder, Cruikshank ('With Apologies to James: A Response to E.R. Forbes,' *Acadiensis* 24 [Autumn 1994], 27–34) minimizes rate differentials and argues that traffic on the Intercolonial was relatively light and mainly local. In sum, Cruikshank asserts that there is insufficient data to prove that freight rates had an impact on sales of Maritime industrial goods west of Montréal.

51 Ernest R. Forbes, *Aspects of Maritime Regionalism, 1867–1927* (Ottawa 1983), 13

52 Ibid., 21–2. For an elaboration of this theme, see Ernest R. Forbes, *The Maritime Rights Movement, 1919–1927: A Study in Canadian Regionalism* (Montréal 1979).

53 Daniel R. Headrick, *The Tentacles of Progress: Technology Transfer in the Age of Imperialism, 1850–1940* (Oxford 1988)

54 David Weale and Harry Baglole, *The Island and Confederation: The End of an Era* (np 1973)

55 Francis W.P. Bolger, *Prince Edward Island and Confederation 1863–1873* (Charlottetown 1964), 216–31, 235–42

56 Ibid., 243–80

57 Ibid., 286–8

58 Weale and Baglole, *The Island and Confederation*, 144

59 In the late 1840s St John's *Morning Courier* ran a series of editorials that advocated that St John's be made an entrepôt between Europe and British North America. The suggestion included a trans-island railway. See 12 June, 14 and 21 July, 14 Aug., and 1, 4, and 8 Sept. 1847. My thanks to Sean Cadigan for bringing these items to my attention. An extensive survey of Newfoundland's press during the 1850s and 1860s discovered only scant attention paid to British North America's philosophy of railways.

60 H.B. Mayo, 'Newfoundland and Confederation in the Eighteen-Sixties,' *CHR* 29 (June 1948), 125–42

61 James K. Hiller, *The Newfoundland Railway, 1881–1949* (St John's 1981), 3–8

62 Ibid., 9–15; Harvey Mitchell, 'Canada's Negotiations with Newfoundland, 1887–1895,' *CHR* 40 (December 1959), 277–93

63 Hiller, *Newfoundland Railway*, 15–23

64 A.I. Silver, *The French-Canadian Idea of Confederation 1864–1900* (Toronto 1982), 14–34

65 *La Minerve* (Montréal), 3 July 1880

66 Silver, *French-Canadian Idea of Confederation*, 47–8

67 *La Minerve*, 2 July 1867, considered that French Canada had attained that objective. 'Comme nationalité distincte et séparée, nous formons un état dans l'état.'

68 *Le Pays* (Montréal), 1 June 1869

69 Brian Young, *George Etienne Cartier: Montreal Bourgeois* (Montréal and Kingston 1981)

70 *Le Courrier* (St-Hyacinthe), 14 March 1872. Copied from a *Négociant Canadien* article that forecast that the Pacific railway would unite the country.

71 Silver, *French-Canadian Idea of Confederation*, 114

72 Louis Georges Desjardins, *Discours ... sur la résolution relative à la vente de la partie ouest du chemin de fer Québec, Montréal, Ottawa et occidental* (Québec 1882), 28

73 W. Kaye Lamb, *History of the Canadian Pacific Railway* (New York 1977), 90, 101, 111, 133

74 Silver, *French-Canadian Idea of Confederation*, 115–16

75 Donald Kerr, 'Wholesale Trade on the Canadian Plains in the Late Nineteenth Century: Winnipeg and Its Competition,' in Howard Palmer, ed., *The Settlement of the West* (Calgary 1977), 130–5. Kerr estimated that before 1878, 70 per cent of goods unloaded in Winnipeg had their origin in the United States or Great Britain. See also Alan F.J. Artibise, *Winnipeg: A Social History of Urban Growth, 1874–1914* (Montréal 1975).

76 Ruben Bellan, *Winnipeg First Century: An Economic History* (Winnipeg 1978), 49–53; Eagle, *Canadian Pacific Railway*, 218–19

77 Kerr, 'Wholesale Trade,' 139–52. In 1880, Winnipeg merchants captured almost 75 per cent of the Indian department's regular treaty supplies for Treaty Four, more than 50 per cent in Treaty Six, and less than 10 per cent in Treaty Seven. Canada, Parliament, *Sessional Papers*, 1880, 4: 272–6

78 D.J. Hall, *Clifford Sifton: The Young Napoleon, 1861–1900* and *A Lonely Eminence, 1901–1929* (Vancouver 1981 and 1985), esp. 2: 221–35

79 D.J. Hall, 'Clifford Sifton: Immigration and Settlement Policy: 1896–1905,' in Palmer, *Settlement of the West*, 60–85

80 A.A. den Otter, *Irrigation in Southern Alberta, 1882–1901* (Lethbridge 1975)

81 J. Murray Beck, *Pendulum of Power: Canada's Federal Elections* (Scarborough 1968), 127–8

82 Careless, *Frontier and Metropolis*, 86–7

83 Gerald Friesen, 'The Western Canadian Identity,' Canadian Historical Association *Historical Papers*, 1973, 14

84 Paul F. Sharp, *The Agrarian Revolt in Western Canada: A Survey Showing American Parallels* (Minneapolis 1948)

85 Lewis G. Thomas, 'Associations and Communications,' Canadian Historical Association *Historical Papers*, 1973, 1–12. A more detailed explication of this theme is found in David H. Breen, *The Canadian Prairie West and the Ranching Frontier, 1874–1924* (Toronto 1983). See also Simon M. Evans, 'The Origins of Ranching in Western Canada: American Diffusion or Victorian Transplant?' in L.A. Rosenvall and S.M. Evans, eds, *Essays on the Historical Geography of the Canadian West: Regional Perspectives on the Settlement Process* (Calgary 1987), 70–94, and 'Spatial Aspects of the Cattle Kingdom: The First Decade, 1882–1892,' in Anthony W. Rasporich and Henry Klassen, eds, *Frontier Calgary, 1875–1914* (Calgary 1975), 41–56; and Sheilagh S. Jameson, 'Partners and Opponents: The CPR and the Ranching Industry of the West,' in Dempsey, *CPR West*, 71–86.

86 Macleod, *The NWMP and Law Enforcement*, 36–7, 74–88

87 A.A. den Otter, *Civilizing the West: The Galts and the Development of Western Canada* (Edmonton 1982), 161–96

88 W.A. Waiser, 'A Willing Scapegoat: John Macoun and the Route of the CPR,' *Prairie Forum* 10 (Spring 1985), 65–81; A.A. den Otter, 'Irrigation and Flood Control,' in Norman R. Ball, ed., *Building Canada: A History of Public Works* (Toronto 1988), 143–68. David C. Jones (*Empire of Dust: Settling and Abandoning the Prairie Dry Belt* [Edmonton 1987]) recounts the disastrous consequences of the attempts to settle the semi-arid southern prairies.

89 *Mail*, 12 Jan. 1874

90 Headrick, *Tentacles of Progress*

91 John Gallagher and Ronald Robinson, 'The Imperialism of Free Trade,' *Economic History Review*, 2nd ser., 6, no. 1 (1953), 5

92 Ibid.

93 With steamers on the Atlantic and Pacific, the CPR provided Britain with a fast route to the Far East.

94 Gallagher and Robinson, 'Imperialism of Free Trade,' 1–15

95 Edward William Watkin, *Canada and the States: Recollections, 1851 to 1886* (London 1887), 145, 196, 232; see also chapter 18 on the Reciprocity Treaty.

96 A.W. Currie, *The Grand Trunk Railway of Canada* (Toronto 1957); Bruce Sinclair, 'Canadian Technology: British Traditions and American Influences,' *Technology and Culture* 20 (1979), 108–23

97 Currie, *Grand Trunk*, 118–21

98 Lamb, *Canadian Pacific Railway*, 165–75

99 William J. Wilgus, *The Railway Interrelations of the United States and Canada* (New Haven 1937), 144. Pierre Berton's monumental *The Great Railway*, which is the most extreme nationalist interpretation, does not list Wilgus in its bibliography. Ken Cruikshank ('Managing a Fragile North American Industry: The Canadian Railway Problem Revisited,' paper, Second Business History Conference, Victoria, 1988) used Wilgus as a springboard to examine the operations of Canadian railways in their continental setting.

100 Montana Historical Society, Power Papers, vol. 13A, file 8, J. Rattray & Co. to Power, 26 Sept. 1879; vol. 4, file 2, invoices, 29 July, 3 Sept. 1880; vol. 155, file 73, invoice, 3 June 1882; vol. 120, file 6, Kavanagh Brothers to Power, 1 Feb., 11 April 1885

101 HBC/PAM, A12/27, Grahame to Wrigley, 2 May 1884, fol. 134, 22 July 1884, fol. 241; A12/27, Wrigley to Armit, 6 July 1884, fol. 376. A.A. den Otter, 'Transportation and Transformation: The Hudson's Bay Company, 1857–1885,' *Great Plains Quarterly* 3 (Summer 1983), 171–85; Arthur J. Ray, *The Canadian Fur Trade in the Industrial Age* (Toronto 1990)

102 Peter Baskerville, 'Railways in Upper Canada/Ontario: The State, Entrepreneurship and the Transition from a Commercial to an Industrial Economy,' *Zeitschrift der Gesellschaft für Kanada-Stüdien* 7 (1987), 25

103 Peter Baskerville, 'Transportation, Social Change, and State Formation, Upper Canada, 1841–1864,' in Allan Greer and Ian Radforth, eds, *Colonial Leviathan: State Formation in Mid-Nineteenth-Century Canada* (Toronto 1992), 230–56

104 Ken Cruikshank, *Close Ties: Railways, Government, and the Board of Railway Commissioners, 1851–1933* (Montréal and Kingston 1991); John A. Eagle, 'Sir Robert Borden, Union Government and Railway Nationalization,' *JCS* 10, no. 4 (1975), 59–66

Illustration Credits

MAPS

The maps in this volume were prepared by the Cartography Lab at Memorial University of Newfoundland.

PHOTOS

Canadian National Railways (CN): Edward Watkin, 27200-14; Victoria Bridge, 54772-9; dining car, X37904; St Lawrence and Atlantic Railway locomotive, X32441; European and North American Railway locomotive, 36957; Grand Trunk locomotive (1860s), 36068; Toronto's Grand Trunk station (1857), 38969; Montréal's Bonaventure Station (1870), 43550; Halifax station (1868), 45815

National Archives of Canada: Joseph Howe, C-7158; Charles Tupper, C-010113; Leonard Tilley, PA-025549; Francis Hincks, PA-025467; Alexander Mackenzie, PA-026522, clay cut near Trois-Pistoles on Intercolonial Railway, C-14113; cutting embankments near Higgins Brook, C-17698; snowstorm stopping locomotive (1869), PA-138698; Engine No. 209 ('Trevithnick'), C-5164; Grand Trunk erecting shop at Point Charles, PA-138678

Index